SECOND EDITION

Nicole Ferdinand & Paul J. Kitchin

EVENTS MANAGEMENT

An International Approach

Los Angeles | London | New Delhi
Singapore | Washington DC | Melbourne

Los Angeles | London | New Delhi
Singapore | Washington DC | Melbourne

SAGE Publications Ltd
1 Oliver's Yard
55 City Road
London EC1Y 1SP

SAGE Publications Inc.
2455 Teller Road
Thousand Oaks, California 91320

SAGE Publications India Pvt Ltd
B 1/I 1 Mohan Cooperative Industrial Area
Mathura Road
New Delhi 110 044

SAGE Publications Asia-Pacific Pte Ltd
3 Church Street
#10-04 Samsung Hub
Singapore 049483

Editor: Matthew Waters
Assistant editor: Lyndsay Aitkin
Production editor: Imogen Roome
Copyeditor: Kate Campbell
Marketing manager: Alison Borg
Cover design: Francis Kenney
Typeset by: C&M Digitals (P) Ltd, Chennai, India
Printed and bound by CPI Group (UK) Ltd,
Croydon, CR0 4YY

Preface and editorial arrangement © Nicole Ferdinand and Paul J. Kitchin 2017

Chapter 1 © Nicole Ferdinand, Stephen J. Shaw and Emelie Forsberg 2017
Chapter 2 © Nicole Ferdinand, Simone Wesner and Yi-Fang Wang 2017
Chapter 3 © Nazia Ali, Nicole Ferdinand and Michael Chidzey 2017
Chapter 4 © Nigel L. Williams 2017
Chapter 5 © Bruce Johnson 2017
Chapter 6 © Rumen Gechev 2017
Chapter 7 © Paul J. Kitchin 2017
Chapter 8 © Paul J. Kitchin and Rob Wilson 2017
Chapter 9 © Brent W. Ritchie and Sacha Reid 2017
Chapter 10 © Jo-anne Tull and Nigel L. Williams 2017
Chapter 11 © Alessandro Inversini and Nigel L. Williams 2017
Chapter 12 © Elena Cavagnaro, Albert Postma and Marisa P. de Brito 2017
Chapter 13 © Adrian Devine and Frances Devine 2017
Chapter 14 © Nicole Ferdinand, Albert Postma and Christian White 2017

First edition published 2012
Reprinted in 2012, 2015 (twice)
Second edition published 2017

Library of Congress Control Number: 2016934970

British Library Cataloguing in Publication data

A catalogue record for this book is available from the British Library

ISBN 978-1-4462-9651-6
ISBN 978-1-4462-9652-3 (pbk)

At SAGE we take sustainability seriously. Most of our products are printed in the UK using FSC papers and boards. When we print overseas we ensure sustainable papers are used as measured by the PREPS grading system. We undertake an annual audit to monitor our sustainability.

Table of Contents

About the Editors and Contributors

Nazia Ali is originally from London, United Kingdom. She holds a PhD in Tourism Studies from the University of Bedfordshire and she has published widely on the tourism mobilities of the Pakistani diaspora in the United Kingdom, especially in relation to characteristics of identity such as ethnicity, nationality, religion and race. She has extensive experience in course leadership of undergraduate and postgraduate tourism and events management programmes, and lecturing in tourism and events management. Nazia also currently serves as an external examiner for several UK Higher Education Institutions in the areas of international events management, events marketing management and tourism management.

Marisa P. de Brito is a Senior Lecturer/Researcher at NHTV, Breda University of Applied Sciences, in the Netherlands, currently coordinating the research group Events and Placemaking alongside Professor Greg Richards. She has a PhD in sustainable supply chain management and a master's in Urban Management from Erasmus University Rotterdam. Her current research and professional interests lie in the areas of sustainability of events and destinations. As member of the Dutch Expertise Center on Leisure, Hospitality and Tourism (CELTH), she is also the project leader for a research project on Sustainable Strategies for Events, which includes members of the Dutch Green Events platform as well as the Leeuwarden 2018 Cultural Capital.

Elena Cavagnaro is originally from Rome, Italy. She holds an MA from the University of Rome and a PhD from the Vrije Universiteit in Amsterdam. In 1997 she joined Stenden University of Applied Sciences (The Netherlands); in 2004 she became Stenden professor of service studies; and in 2014 Stenden professor of sustainability in hospitality and tourism. In both roles, she has consulted several organizations in sectors such as hospitality, retail and health care on sustainability strategy and implementation. She is visiting professor at the University of Derby (UK). In keeping with her philosophy of sustainability as a multi-dimensional and multi-layered concept, her research focuses on issues that run across and connect the social, organizational and individual layers of sustainability.

Michael Chidzey is Marketing Director of leading events agency Chillisauce, which organizes thousands of activities and experiences for groups and companies across

Europe every year. Over the past eight years he has seen the company grow from 20 people to more than a hundred – now sending 140,000 groups of friends on memorable weekends away and organizing over 700 corporate events a year. His role involves leading the company's marketing strategy, recruiting and managing the team, planning and executing campaigns across multiple channels and ensuring that Chillisauce maximizes all possible marketing opportunities. Alongside his work with Chillisauce, Michael also lectures in event marketing at a number of universities, writes for 'Event Manager Blog', and founded industry-focused website 'Eventjuice'.

Adrian Devine is a Lecturer in the Ulster Business School at Ulster University, Northern Ireland. He is the Course Director for the BSc (Hons) Leisure and Events Management. Adrian has received two Emerald Literati Network Awards for Excellence for his research into inter-organizational relationships within the sports tourism policy arena and managing cultural diversity within hospitality and tourism. His current research interests are the strategic development of event tourism, institutional arrangements for government-funded event agencies and the relationship between public sector agencies and event organisers.

Frances Devine is the Course Director for the MSc in International Event Management in the Department of Hospitality and Tourism Management, Ulster University, Belfast, Northern Ireland. Frances lectures on Human Resources, Organizational Studies and Tourism Issues. She is actively involved in researching new trends in human resource management in the hospitality and tourism sector, presently focusing on inter-organizational relationships. Frances has been in academia for 15 years, winning one of the Highly Commended Emerald Literati Network Awards for Excellence for her research on managing cultural diversity.

Nicole Ferdinand is originally from Trinidad and Tobago. She is currently a Senior Academic in Events in the Faculty of Management at Bournemouth University and regularly publishes in the areas of tourism, culture, events and project management. Her most recent research projects focused on festival management and development. She has also been a visiting lecturer for the Stenden University of Applied Sciences in Leeuwarden, the Netherlands, and the Haagaa University of Applied Sciences in Porvoo, Finland. She holds a PhD in Culture, Media and Creative Industries from King's College London, and an MSc in Marketing and a BA in English, both from the University of the West Indies, St. Augustine.

Emelie Forsberg is originally from Sweden. Currently she is an event professional working and living in London as an Events Executive at the British Private Equity and Venture Capital Association. She graduated from Bournemouth University in 2015 with a Distinction in her MSc Events Management. Her research focused on the experiences of CrossFit athletes at competitive events.

Rumen Gechev is a Full Professor in Economics at the University of National Economy in Sofia, Bulgaria, and Director of its Research Centre on Sustainable Development. Currently he is a member of the National Parliament and Vice-Chairman of its Budgetary and Finance Committee. Rumen is a former Deputy Prime Minister of Bulgaria (1995–97) and Chairman of the 4th Session of the UN Commission on Sustainable Development. Dr. Gechev was a visiting/guest professor at universities in the US, UK, France, Denmark, Kazakhstan, FRY Macedonia, Cyprus, Greece and Belize.

Alessandro Inversini is originally from Italy. He is Associate Professor of Marketing at Henley Business School (University of Reading). Before joining Henley Business School, Alessandro has been Senior Lecturer and member of the eTourism Lab at Bournemouth University, Executive Director of webatelier.net (the research and development eTourism Lab of Universitá della Svizzera italiana), and Managing Director of Ticinoinfo SA, the regional competence centre for digital technology and tourism of Ticino (Switzerland).

Bruce Johnson is an experienced senior manager, trainer and change agent, with a track record of success in diverse environments, both blue chip and public sector, specialising in effective HRM to support performance improvement. Servant leadership and effective diversity practices underpin his approach. His objective is always to help organizations achieve strategic success by ensuring that all staff can and do succeed in their jobs. Prior to becoming an independant consultant Bruce held the roles of Academic Dean and Prinicipal Lecturer at the London School of Business and Management, and Senior Lecturer in Human Resource Management at London Metropolitan Business School.

Paul Kitchin is originally from Tasmania, Australia. He is a lecturer in Sport Management in the School of Sport at Ulster University. He is also responsible for employability within the School of Sport, the coordination of undergraduate and postgraduate placement students as well as enhancing other aspects of the student experience. Paul is a graduate of the University of Tasmania and Deakin University in Australia and completed his PhD at Loughborough University, which investigated organizational change in disability sport. Paul's research is focused at the intersection of sport management and organizational theory and he has experience in successfully raising funds to support this endeavour.

Albert Postma is Professor of Scenario Planning at the European Tourism Futures Institute, Centre of Expertise of the School of Leisure and Tourism Management at Stenden University of Applied Sciences in the Netherlands. His core business is to develop, disseminate and apply knowledge in strategic foresight, i.e. futures studies and scenario planning. Strategic foresight offers a fascinating and inspiring approach for businesses to deal with uncertainty and to develop innovative strategies, concepts, or business models. He gives lectures and keynotes at academic and business conferences to share the findings of the studies he has conducted. Albert is also co-editor of the *Journal of Tourism Futures*. He holds an MSc and PhD degree in Spatial Sciences, awarded by the University of Groningen. His PhD thesis focused on critical encounters in the development of tourism through the eyes of residents.

Sacha Reid is a Senior Lecturer at the Griffith Business School, Griffith University and a member of the Griffith Institute for Tourism. Prior to this, Sacha was the founding Director of Research and established the research capacity of DTZ, a global property advisor firm. She was instrumental in working with clients to provide strategic decision-making to support investment decisions and development advice in planning for commercial and residential communities in Australia and New Zealand. Her research interests are in vertical communities and high-rise living, community development and planning, and the social consequences of rural tourism and events. This has resulted in a number of active research projects such as 'Community rising: Determinants of "sense of community" in vertical communities in suburban Brisbane' and 'Crime in High Rise Buildings: Planning for Vertical Community Safety'.

Brent Ritchie is a Professor in Tourism Management at the UQ Business School. His research interests are associated with tourism risk management. His research has focused on understanding risk from an individual and organizational perspective, and he examines the factors that influence the formation of risk attitudes and behaviour by using social and organizational psychology theory and concepts. He has given over 50 journal papers and is on eight editorial boards including the *Journal of Travel Research*. He has secured over $1 million of grant funding and supervised 15 PhD students to completion.

Stephen Shaw is originally from London, UK. He has been Emeritus Professor at London Metropolitan University and Associate of the Stockholm Environment Institute, University of York since 2015. He has over 25 years' experience in the field of urban studies. In recent years, his research has informed the development of more inclusive public spaces, especially for tourism and events in major cities.

Jo-anne Tull is originally from Barbados. She has extensive experience lecturing in the fields of creative industries development, festival management and cultural entrepreneurship. She has also worked for more than ten years as a creative industries consultant in the Caribbean, with particular focus on strategy development and festival impact analysis.

Yi-Fang Wang is originally from Taiwan. Her background is in the third sector and she is focused on helping vulnerable populations by combining social work with event activities. She currently works as a project planner for a charitable foundation in her native Taiwan. She holds an MSc in Events Management from Bournemouth

University and her research was focused on the motivations of young Taiwanese people to participate in road running events.

Simone Wesner is a Lecturer in Arts Management and the Programme Director for the MA Arts Policy and Management in the Department of Film, Media and Cultural Studies at Birkbeck, University of London. She worked as curator and cultural producer in her native Germany and Austria before joining the UK HE sector and she has continued to collaborate with artists and researchers in Europe and in South East Asia ever since.

Christian White is a BA Events and Marketing graduate from Bournemouth University. He has a diverse employment background and has worked on a number of B2C events in the motorsport and charity sectors. During his final year at university, his research investigated the potential of Twitter as an evaluation tool in the identification of the social impacts at music festivals.

Nigel Williams is a Senior Academic in Project Management at Bournemouth University. Nigel also holds the Project Management Professional (PMP) qualification from the Project Management Institute. He leads units at the undergraduate and postgraduate level as well as supervising PhD students in the area of Project Management. His research examines project management in a variety of contexts including NGOs, festivals and mega projects.

Rob Wilson is a Principal Lecturer in Sport Business Management at Sheffield Hallam University. He has been involved in the Sport Management Industry since 1998 and has taught at Sheffield Hallam University since 2002. His main research interests are in the finance and economics of sport and leisure and his MPhil was based on the economics of sport events. Rob is an active researcher with the Sport Industry Research Centre and has published three books: *Finance for Sport and Leisure Managers: An introduction* in 2008, *Managing Sport Finance* in 2011 and *Sport Management: The basics* in 2016; numerous chapters on finance and financial management in sport and a number of peer reviewed journal articles. Follow him on Twitter using the @financeinsport handle.

Preface

The field of events management has witnessed a period of exponential and largely uninterrupted growth in the past three decades. This growth is apparent in the increase in number and scale of events that are being organized worldwide, the significant rise in employment that the sector provides, and the development of theory and research that underpins the study of the field as an academic subject. As both students and researchers in the field of events management since the early 2000s, we have witnessed truly remarkable changes in the development of the subject. The very first qualification in events management was launched by George Washington University in 1994 as a Professional Certificate Program to meet the needs of professionals in an emergent field. Just over two decades later, there are a plethora of both general and specialized BA, BSc, MA, MSc and even PhD programmes, targeted at students who have chosen, for their future careers, events management or related specialist fields such as event sponsorship, sport and experiential marketing.

So what does this text offer to these students? Like the first edition, it takes an explicit international approach to the study of the subject. It seeks to prepare students for the realities of working in a sector that is becoming increasingly international. As is the case with businesses in other sectors of the economy, the increased mobility of workers, the breaking-down of trading barriers, and developments in information and communications technologies have meant that many event organizations are now competing in a global marketplace. The text therefore seeks to highlight key critical global issues affecting events, with a special emphasis being placed on international events, and demonstrate that local forces and cultural issues within event destinations must be addressed if an event is to be successful.

In this second edition of the text we also focus on some of the key drivers of change within the events industry and explore new theoretical advances that have occurred in the study of the subject. In lieu of the extended case studies, we have added four new chapters to the text. Social media and its impact on event consumption and production is now the focus of one of the new chapters of the text, as well as a key theme that is developed throughout. There is also a more deliberate focus on the strategic use of international events in tourism, which is achieved by introducing a new chapter on the subject in the contemporary issues section (Part 3) of the text, as well as by emphasizing this topic in chapters in previous sections. This second edition also closes with a chapter seeking to look ahead to the future of international events management.

We have once again been extremely fortunate in being able to assemble a high-profile international team of authors, which include distinguished professors, lecturers, professional trainers and industry professionals. They have made it possible for the text to have a truly international flavour by featuring cases from across North America, Europe, Africa, Asia and also Australia.

It is our pleasure to offer this second edition of *Events Management: An International Approach* to readers seeking an international perspective on events management, which addresses the challenges and opportunities of working in a global world. We hope that it can be a source of inspiration and guidance as you seek to meet the formidable challenges presented by international events management.

Nicole Ferdinand and Paul J. Kitchin
Editors

Companion Website

Visit **https://study.sagepub.com/ferdinand2e** to find a range of additional resources for both students and lecturers, to aid study and support teaching.

For Students

Online readings: access to a selection of free SAGE journal articles providing students with a deeper understanding of the topics covered in each chapter.

Video links: author-selected videos to give students further insight into select concepts.

Xerte interactive resources: learning objects for each chapter which can be used as self-test materials, for in-class interaction or teaching in flipped lecture mode.

For Lecturers

Instructor's manual: a range of teaching materials for each section of the book including:

- Section overviews
- Teaching notes
- Tasks
- Video links

Part 1

Introducing an International Approach to Events Management

There are numerous reasons for events to be organized, just as there is great diversity in *how* they are organized. Often this diversity is rooted in the socio-cultural milieus of host communities. The political, economic and technological situations of different countries will also account for variations in the form and function of events. At the same time global issues such as rising migration, ageing populations, terrorism concerns and climate change have led to a great deal of convergence in event management practices throughout the world. Many metropolitan cities, such as Sydney, London and New York, boast a host of ethnic festivals dedicated to celebrating the cultures of migrant populations, as well as music concerts and other types of entertainment which cater to older attendees, mirroring current population trends. Increasingly, high levels of security, the implementation of sustainable event management principles and the deployment of sophisticated interactive communication strategies are synonymous with hosting events which are described as being of 'international standard', regardless of the country in which they are staged.

We are now living in a digital age which has led to a state of hyper-connectivity, in which individuals, especially the current generation of young people, described as millennials, are always on and connected to an endless array of media generated from a 24/7 online community. For both attendees and event organizers this has created a number of opportunities and challenges. For individuals this has meant they have more choices than ever before about events and other happenings that they can attend. However, it also means that they are being bombarded with more images of events than would ever be possible for any one person to participate in.

The result has been the creation of feelings of jealously and anxiety about missing out, especially when individuals can see friends and other people they know having a great time at events without them in photos and videos posted on social media websites such as Facebook and Instagram. For event organizations, this new reality has provided a number of alternative platforms for them to stay in touch with and also understand the needs of their customers. At the same time, it means customers have become more demanding, and thanks to new media platforms such as those provided by review sites, hundreds or even thousands of people can be informed of a single customer's displeasure with an event or event organization with the click of a button.

This first Part of *Events Management: An International Approach* examines the dual tensions at work in international events management – an engagement with the global issues impacting the events industry and an understanding of the specific local factors, which account for the differences in how events are staged from country to country. The chapters in this section of the text seek to provide the background for the approach taken throughout the text, by introducing the issues and challenges that characterize the contemporary events landscape.

Chapter 1 by Ferdinand, Shaw and Forsberg examines the ways in which events have shaped the lives of individuals, communities, organizations, cities and also countries across the globe. It compares and contrasts the meanings and functions of events in countries such as the United States, the United Kingdom, South Africa, Brazil and Sweden, and explores the diverse reasons why cities and communities in these countries have undertaken the hosting of events. The authors highlight how events have been used to respond to global issues, including excessive consumerism, racial, ethnic and class divisions and an increasingly competitive trading environment. They also outline the unintended consequences of events, such as the redistribution of public funds away from local communities (in the case of large-scale events), the perpetuation of ethnic stereotypes (which can occur within ethnic festivals) and the displacement and dislocation of local populations who can lose their homes, jobs and leisure options in order for international event infrastructure to be built. Additionally, the chapter highlights that international events can have long-lasting social benefits for participants and attendees.

In Chapter 2, Ferdinand et al. shift from a broad macro perspective of the events industry to a focus on the specific factors which shape events management in host communities – political, economic, socio-cultural and technological conditions; stakeholder relationships; resource availability; competitions; and intercultural differences. By outlining a model of the international events environment theses authors demonstrate how global and local forces interact to shape the staging of events and create significant challenges for event organizations operating both at home and outside their countries of origin. The cases in the chapter highlight how global migration patterns, social trends and also local population dynamics are creating opportunities and also challenges for event organizers.

This first section introduces key concepts such as globalization and event/experiential marketing which are built upon in the succeeding sections. It also strives to provide a balanced view of international events, highlighting their benefits as well as drawbacks. In summary, Part 1 seeks to provide a foundation on which a deeper understanding can be established of international events management practice and the critical issues involved.

Understanding International Events   1

Nicole Ferdinand, Stephen J. Shaw
and Emelie Forsberg

Learning Objectives

By reading this chapter students should be able to:

- Define the nature and scope of international events
- Explain the broader societal trends that have led to the growth in international events
- Identify the ways in which international events have been examined by researchers
- List and evaluate the positive and negative impacts that international events have had on communities and the environment
- Critically discuss the potential of international events to achieve long-term, urban regeneration and renewal.

Introduction

Events have been a part of human civilizations since ancient times. They have marked changing seasons, heralded the appointment of new leaders, celebrated religious rites and rituals and also signified births and deaths. In today's societies they continue to serve these functions but they have become significantly more complex and elaborate and their audiences have grown exponentially. The 2009 inauguration of the 44th American President Barack Obama set records for being the most-viewed presidential inauguration by attracting a live viewing audience of over 2 million and an online audience of over 45.5 million viewers (Heussner, 2009). It was an elaborate production costing over US$170 million (£104 million) to stage (Mayerowitz, 2009). The 2008 Beijing Olympics was viewed by a record 4.7 billion television viewers (Neilsen, 2008) and cost over US$40 billion (£25 billion) to stage, making it the most expensive Olympic Games of all time (CBC News, 2008). As enormous as these budgets were, both these events will be dwarfed in expenditure by the Qatar World Cup in 2022, which professional services firm Deloitte estimated will cost US$220 billion to stage (Bobel, 2013). These examples demonstrate how drastically the roles of events in societies have changed. Each of them can be considered global events, captivating the attention of people far beyond their host cities or nations. The potential for events to capture the hearts and minds of viewers around the world continues to make international sporting events, exhibitions and celebrations of arts and culture increasingly sought after by governments across virtually every continent.

The popularity of international events can be in some part explained by the growing importance of events generally. Like other leisure/symbolic/experience goods, events now have an ever-increasing value for individuals (Lash and Urry, 2002; Nazreth, 2007; and Pine and Gilmore, 2011). Toffler's (1970: 226) prediction that in the future individuals would 'begin to collect experiences as consciously and passionately as they once collected things' seems to have come true. This shift has also not gone unnoticed by corporations which are increasingly using events to position and differentiate their brands. Globally, events are at the centre of experiential marketing strategies, which transform brands into memorable and inspirational experiences. To succeed, these events need to be authentic, with a clear link to the brand (Mintel, 2010). The Adidas Runbase store in Tokyo, for example, has turned itself into an urban running club hosting regular running events, complete with staff on hand to provide training tips (Beattie, 2012). In the US some drug stores and discount retailers are offering massages and facials to customers shopping for basic toiletries, turning a mundane shopping trip into a special event. By appealing to emotions, experiences can enhance the 'feel-good factor' for consumers in simple, non-intrusive ways that satisfy their desire for novelty without alienating them (Mintel, 2010).

For communities, events have taken on new meanings. Whereas once community events marked the details of local life, in contemporary migrant communities, which are often composed of immigrants from many different countries, events have become a way of reconnecting with homelands and heritage. Many communities also host what have been described as 'placeless festivals' (MacLeod, 2006) which are not associated with any particular community or country, but rather represent shared interests and ideals or are staged purely for commercial reasons and target an international audience. The last two decades have also been marked by the rise of 'Eventful Cities', as international events have become central to strategies for change in cities. They are now increasingly being recognised for their potential to achieve a broad range of economic, social, cultural and environmental benefits when they form part of urban development plans (Richards and Palmer, 2010).

This chapter seeks to provide students with an understanding of the nature and scope of international events. It will also highlight broader societal trends that have been instrumental in creating and sustaining their demand. Additionally, the chapter will also explore the potential for international events to be catalysts for positive change and transformation as well as sources of unintended negative consequences and outcomes. Upon completing this chapter students should be able to critically discuss the range of issues involved in harnessing international events to achieve long-term urban regeneration and renewal.

What Are International Events?

Although the term 'international event' is widely used to describe a variety of events, it is not part of many event typologies (see for example Falassi, 1987 and Getz, 2005). Within academic literature the terms 'major', 'mega' or 'hallmark event' are used to describe events which would commonly also be referred to as 'international events'. For instance, Bowdin et al. (2006: 16) describe major events as events that are capable of attracting 'significant visitor numbers, media coverage and economic benefits' – noting that many international sporting events fall into this category. Additionally, Jago and Shaw (1998: 29) define mega events as 'one-time major events' which are 'of an international scale', such as the New York World's Fair (1939) and the Festival of Britain (1951). Moreover, Ritchie (1984: 2) describes hallmark events as those which 'were developed primarily to enhance awareness, appeal and profitability of a tourism destination'. The Edinburgh International Festival is perhaps a classic example of a hallmark event.

In the absence of an exact definition, some key characteristics of international events are apparent. Perhaps first and foremost is their explicit focus on attracting international audiences. Second, they are large-scale events which have a significant impact on their host communities. Third, they attract international or global media attention. Finally, these events have specific economic imperatives such as increasing tourism visitors, job creation and providing new business opportunities. Thus, international events may be

Table 1.1 Key characteristics distinguishing local events from international events

Dimensions	Local or Community Event	International Event
Size	Small-scale	Large-scale
Audiences	Local	Local and international
Media attention	Local	International or global
Impacts	May be restricted to social or community-building, with less focus on income generation	Will have a range of impacts including: increasing tourism visitors, job creation and creating new business opportunities

described as large-scale events which attract international audiences and media attention and meet a variety of economic objectives for the destinations in which they are hosted. So how are they different from other events? Using their key characteristics it is possible to distinguish them from events which are described as local or community events. See Table 1.1.

The Origins of International Events

International events can be traced as far back as the beginnings of leisure and tourism, to Mesopotamia (situated approximately in modern-day Iraq), which is known as the 'Cradle of Civilization'. It was there for the first time in human history that the surplus production of food and the formation of wealth led to that the emergence of a small 'leisure-class' of priests, warriors and others that did not have to worry continually about its day-to-day survival. This elite class that inhabited the early cities found them 'over-crowded and uncomfortable' and tried to escape whenever possible (Weaver and Lawton, 2006: 57). They escaped to other countries to visit historic sites, buy artefacts and also attend events. For example, the ancient Olympic Games, held between 776 and 261 BC, provides one of the first examples of an event with an international character and it is described as one of the first recorded examples of sport event tourism (Weaver and Lawton, 2006).

Early modern events which attracted international audiences were visited by travellers undertaking the classical 'Grand Tours', which first became popular during the mid-sixteenth century (Withey, 1997). 'Grand Tour' was a term used to describe the extended travel of young men from the aristocratic classes of the United Kingdom and other parts of northern Europe to continental Europe for educational and cultural purposes (Towner, 1985). These tours were not regarded as strictly leisure pursuits as they were seen as educational and cultural experiences that were vital for anyone seeking to join the ranks of the elite. They eventually gave way to simple sight-seeing and began to include aspiring members of the middle classes as well as aristocrats (Weaver and Lawton, 2006). For these travellers, attending cultural events and religious festivals were important features of Grand Tours and accounted in some part for the seasonal variations of visits to certain city centres. Rome, for instance, was particularly popular during Christmas, Easter and Carnival celebrations (Towner, 1985). These events, although rooted within the communities in which they were staged, became international because of the presence of these travellers on Grand Tours. It should be noted however that at this point events attracting international audiences and tourism generally would not have been widespread. The cost of travel, along with the lack of tourism infrastructure, made travelling to other countries an expensive, difficult and often dangerous affair.

Thomas Cook, a former preacher turned tour operator, has been credited with revolutionizing tourism travel by pioneering packaged tours. In so doing he democratized and also dramatically expanded tourism opportunities by making it much easier and cheaper for those wishing to travel, by charging fixed prices for accommodation, travel and even food for a given route. He and later his company Thomas Cook and Sons (officially established in 1871) negotiated much cheaper rates in block than would be possible for individuals to do on their own. Thomas Cook was also responsible for taking British tourists to some of the early modern international events such as the Great Exhibition hosted in London's Hyde Park in 1851 (the first ever World's Fair or exhibition) and the International Exhibition hosted in 1855 in Paris (Thomas Cook Retail Limited, n.d.).

World's Fairs and international exhibitions were among the first examples of international events as they are contemporarily understood. Britain and France were the principal sponsors of these events which were established between the late nineteenth and early twentieth centuries as these countries were the dominant colonial powers at the time. These events served to display their colonies, or their internally colonized peoples, to their home population, to their rivals and to the world at large (Benedict, 1991). The United States also hosted some of these early fairs and exhibitions, such as Chicago's World Columbian Exhibition in 1893 (Trennert, 1993) and the Louisiana Purchase Exposition (also known as the Saint Louis World's Fair) in 1904 (Benedict, 1991). Other notable international events established during this early period include the modern Olympic Games held in Athens in 1896 and Test Cricket, which was first played in 1877 (ESPN Sport Media Limited, n.d.).

Why are International Events on the Rise?

The growing popularity of international events has been linked to globalization and the subsequent dramatic growth of the experience/cultural/creative industries (see for example Richards and Palmer, 2010). Globalization can be defined in a general sense as a process by which compression of the world in a holistic sense has taken place (Robertson, 2011). This process has been marked by a rapid increase in the linkages between people, places, communities, countries and markets, which have been facilitated mainly by technological developments in transport, telecommunications, internet technologies and social media. Globalization has given rise to intense price competition, especially among manufacturers and retailers because organizations are now subject to international competition from firms which may have lower local costs of production and more favourable market conditions. This competition has prompted firms to respond by developing alternative competitive strategies based on innovation rather than price competition. One of the consequences of these strategies has been that in developed countries price premiums are paid, in many cases, for services and experiences rather than tangible products. In the evolving global economy, products have been described as increasingly 'commoditized' (Pine and Gilmore, 2011) or depleted of value (Lash and Urry, 2002). Event organizers of both small, local and large, international events have benefited tremendously from these developments. Many organizations now see events as integral to selling their products, promoting their brands and carving out a competitive position for their firms.

Manufacturers of products and retailers now use the experiences produced by event organizers as a means of 'progressing the economic value' (Pine and Gilmore, 2011) of what they produce. Coca-Cola perhaps provides the classic example of a brand that has successfully used events to maintain the economic value of its product offerings. It has a long history of sponsoring international events around the world. The company has the distinction of being the oldest, continuous corporate partner of the Olympic Games as well as supporting a host of other international events, including: National Association for Stock Car Auto Racing (NASCAR) events, National Basketball Association (NBA) games, American Idol (a televised singing competition), the London Notting Hill Carnival and FIFA World Cup Championships (Coca-Cola, 2012). By engaging in these activities Coca-Cola is able to transform its products by associating them with experiences, thereby capturing some of the economic value associated with them.

Table 1.2   Destination development roles for international events

Destination Development Roles	Description
Tourist attraction	International events attract a range of tourists who may otherwise have never come to a destination. In the case of an annual event it may be the main reason why tourists return year after year.
Destination imaging/ branding	International events which are hallmark events (i.e. events that are synonymous with a particular place) can serve to define a destination's image. A newly developed international event or programme of international events can also become part of the rebranding of a destination.
Place marketing	International events, by generating excitement, attracting visitors and also by encouraging the development of new infrastructure and amenities, make the destinations in which they are staged better places to live, work and play.
Animator	The staging of international exhibitions, festivals, conferences and sporting competitions can provide the reasons for both locals and tourists to visit large venues which may otherwise go unused. They can also be a means for destinations to spread tourist demand throughout the year as they may provide a reason for tourists to come to a destination when the peak tourist season is over.
Development catalyst	International events bring about a range of impacts which can potentially lead to the total transformation of a destination. For example, an impact such as increased tourism can snowball into the development of new businesses to cater to increased tourist demand, which can attract new jobs, which in turn can attract new residents to an area. In the long-term this can lead to more substantial impacts such as urban renewal and community capacity building.

Source: Adapted from Getz and Page (2015)

Globalization has also affected the ways the destinations compete with each other. Richards and Wilson (2004), for example, suggest that increasing integration of the global economy has meant that the built environment, infrastructure and amenities in many cities have become similar. Infrastructure and amenities once built though are very expensive to change or update significantly. Thus, city planners, destination management organizations, local governments and agencies charged with the responsibility of promoting destinations have turned to events and international events in particular as means of adding value to what would otherwise be 'fixed cultural capital' (Richards and Wilson, 2004: 1932). Getz and Page (2015) have highlighted five key destination development roles for international events. See Table 1.2.

What Do We Know about International Events?

Much of the research on events that has been created or developed for international audiences focuses on event/festival tourism, a term, which as observed by O'Sullivan and Jackson (2002: 326), has been used as a 'catch-all' which includes 'special event tourism and festivals of any size or organisational persuasion'. As event/festival tourism has become an increasingly important feature of the tourism development strategies for countries, governments and communities, there has been a significant increase in research publications in this area. Themes that have emerged are summarized in Figure 1.1.

International Event Audiences

Research studies in this area focus on understanding and segmenting audiences, which has implications for how these events are promoted to tourists and local visitors. A significant number are about determining the range of motivations or the reasons why people attend international events, such as the Crompton and McKay (1997) seminal study. Other studies have also sought to link motivations to other types of attendee behaviour such as satisfaction (Lee, Lee and Wicks, 2004) and repeat visits (Schofield and Thompson, 2007). Understanding the differences in motivation among attendee segments is also an area that has attracted interest, for example, differences in motivations between attendees of different ethnic groups (Lee, 2000) and nationalities (Lee et al., 2004). In addition, specific attendee segments, such as repeat and first-time visitors, have been shown to exhibit distinct types of consumer behaviour. For example, repeat visitors have been found to spend more money and to stay longer at events than first-time visitors (Kruger et al., 2010). Researchers have also used statistical techniques, such as structural equation modelling, to examine links between attendee motivation and satisfaction and future behaviour (Lee and Hsu, 2013).

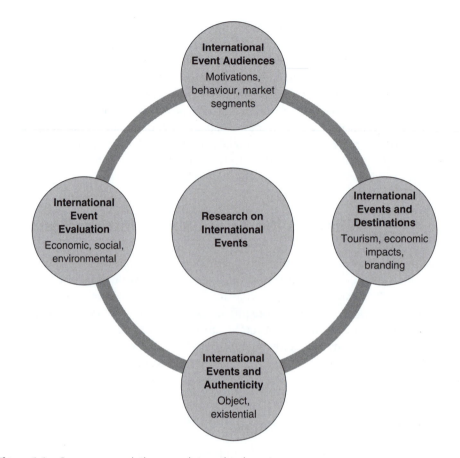

Figure 1.1 Common research themes on international events

International Events and Destinations

Destination studies examine the use of international events in marketing and developing a destination for tourist visitors. These tourists can be from overseas or from places just outside a particular destination. Tourism generated from international events has the potential to create new business, generate employment and increase the revenues of existing business due to the increase in expenditure tourists bring to a destination. Despite the many benefits of event tourism, in practice, accruing these benefits is far from straightforward and some may come with unintended consequences. Ferdinand and Williams (2012) highlight that while event tourism can breathe new life into heritage sites and create more economic and leisure options for locals, it must be approached carefully (particularly at religious monuments) so that these locations are not compromised by the substantial increase in visitors that tourism efforts can bring.

Furthermore, Prentice and Andersen (2003) explore the difficulty in changing ingrained images of a destination. In their research on the use of festivals in Scotland to market it as a 'creative destination', they conclude that festivals are, in fact, only a small part of a visitor's image of Scotland. Far more important to most visitors were their own imaginings of the destination, which tended to be centred on an idealised rural past. However, recent research continues to highlight the importance of international events within the economic restructuring and urban redevelopment strategies of cities (Richards, 2014 and Richards and Palmer, 2010).

International Events and Authenticity

Concerns about authenticity are especially prevalent when an event develops from a small, home-grown or community-based celebration to a major or mega event which is staged for the benefit of tourism audiences. Authenticity is cited as one of the key characteristics which give cultural events, especially, their 'specialness' (Getz, 2005: 17), and is related to their grounding in indigenous cultural values and attributes.

However, what exactly is meant by an authentic event is widely debated. Traditional notions of authenticity, as the term relates to cultural products such as festivals, seem to be linked to the concept of an 'object authenticity' which can normally be determined by objective criteria, such as scientific fact, or a known location or a historical figure (Wang, 2000). This would mean that an authentic event would be staged for its intended purpose and conform to a verifiable original format, such as in MacCannell's (1976: 160) concept of authenticity in tourism which he described as 'the pristine, the primitive, the natural, that which is as yet untouched by modernity'. Thus, many tourism researchers argue that when tourist attractions, such as events, are put on for the purpose of visitor display, their authenticity is compromised because they become distorted to suit the needs of both the guests and their hosts in the pursuit of tourism goals (Boorstin, 1991; Bruner, 1991; MacCannell, 1999). The often-cited Greenwood (1989) article 'Culture by the Pound' examines the Alarde, in Fuenterrabia in the Basque Country, Spain, and is perhaps the classic example of this phenomenon. It describes an event which depicts the ritual recreation of Fuenterrabia's victory over the French in 1638 that loses its authenticity when the ritual is exploited for tourism and economic gains.

However, there is also the concept of an 'existential authenticity'. As noted by Kim and Jamal (2007), event locations have the potential for individuals to experience this type of authenticity because they can be sites of self-making, meaning-making and belonging. This type of authenticity has nothing to do with an objective reality, as existential feelings are subjective and arise out of the particular meanings ascribed to events by individuals. Thus events, although invented, can still provide a feeling of specialness or authenticity because of the values that attendees ascribe to them. One such event is the WaterFire event hosted in Rhode Island in the United States. It was created in 1994 by Barnaby Evans as a commission to celebrate the tenth anniversary of First Night Providence, a major New Year's Eve festival in Providence that began in 1985 when the city sponsored First Night Providence to kick off the 350th anniversary of Rhode Island's founding (WaterFire Providence, 2015). WaterFire is further described in Case Study 1.1.

Case Study 1.1 – WaterFire

WaterFire began life as First Fire, a one-off commission by Barnaby Evans to celebrate the 10th anniversary of First Night Providence in Rhode Island. Two years later, in 1996, Evans created Second Fire for the International Sculpture Conference, which attracted thousands of participants from across the globe. Evans was then overwhelmed with requests from art enthusiasts to create an on-going fire installation and these enthusiasts also started a grass-roots effort to establish WaterFire as a non-profit arts organization (WaterFire Providence, 2015).

WaterFire is now considered one of Providence's signature events, which takes the form of an award-winning fire sculpture installation on the three rivers in downtown Providence. It features nearly 100 bonfires that blaze just

Figure 1.2   Image of WaterFire installation

Figure 1.3   Image of public performance at WaterFire

above the surface of the rivers. The fires form a continuous path which illu-
minates over 1km of public space. Music and artistic performances also
complement the display (Providence Warwick Convention & Visitors Bureau,
2011).

WaterFire happens just after sunset from May to November. The summer
time is an especially popular time to visit the installation. Dusk is when the
city begins to cool down, so it provides a perfect backdrop and atmosphere
for the event. When visitors approach the installation, they first experience
a very pleasant warmth which radiates from the bonfires. Next, they hear the
crackling of the wood and smell the blazing cedar and pine. There is also
evocative instrumental music played to accompany the process of the fires
being lit, which makes the experience of following the fires quite a moving
one for visitors. Some can become very emotional and contemplative as the
installation engulfs their senses. Visitors will also find their own meanings
within the burning fires which include peace and tranquillity, community,
beauty and inspiration (WaterFire, 2015).

The event is free and it is promoted as a must-see event for tourists. For
more on WaterFire go to: http://waterfire.org/

International Event Evaluation

Much of the funded research that is done on international events is done for the purpose of evaluation. Typically international event evaluations are undertaken in order to account to stakeholders, both public (for example, local councils, central government departments and funding agencies) and private (for example, sponsors, investors and donors), for the investments made in international events. It is hardly surprising that most of this type of research, whether undertaken by practitioners or academics, is focused on economic impacts. This sort of evaluation involves the calculation of tourism and other types of additional expenditure that is generated as a result of an event being staged.

The bias towards economic evaluation has been noted within academic literature, along with the urgent need to also take the social impacts of all types of events into account (Reid, 2007). Social impacts are somewhat less straightforward to evaluate as they involve more subjective types of data. Typically individuals are asked to make a judgement on the social impacts an event has for their communities or their lives generally. A number of tools have been developed which can be used to measure the social impacts of international events, including the Social Impact Attitude Scale (Delamere et al., 2001), Social Impact Perception (SIP) Scale (Fredline et al., 2003; Small, 2007), and Event Image Scale (Deng et al., 2015). See Table 1.3 for sample scale items which are used for this type of measurement.

The Finnish Event Evaluation Tool (FEET) is an evaluation tool which seeks to apply a more holistic approach to event evaluation and seeks to incorporate the measurement of both economic and social impacts of events. It includes questionnaires and interviews of event organizers; questionnaires of event attendees; questionnaires of local residents; questionnaires of local entrepreneurs; and questionnaires of local policy-makers (Pasanen et al., 2009); see Table 1.4. A more detailed discussion of the application of different types of economic and social event evaluation approaches, methods and tools can be found in Chapter 11 of this text.

Growing concerns about the environmental impacts that international events generate has prompted international event evaluators to look beyond economic and social impacts and also investigate their environmental impacts. A growing number of international events have now embraced the Triple Bottom Line (the measurement of social, economic and environmental impacts) in the evaluation of these types of events. Hede (2007) proposed an approach to applying the Triple Bottom Line to event evaluation which incorporates stakeholder theory so that it can be applied at the planning stages of events. This approach has also been applied by other researchers and specifically to international events such as the Kaohsiung World Games (Ma et al., 2011) and the Formula One Australian Grand Prix (Fairley et al., 2011).

Table 1.3 Sample social impact scale items

Sample Scales	Positive Items	Negative Items
Social Impact Attitude Scale – items adapted from Delamare et al. (2001)	• Discovering and developing cultural skills and talents • Feeling a sense of pride and recognition • Enhancing of community image • Learning new things • On-going positive cultural impact	• Pedestrian traffic increases too much • Vandalism increases • Delinquent activity increases • Over-crowding takes place • Uses too much community financial resources
Social Impact Perception Scale – items adapted from Fredline et al. (2003)	• Improvement in event area appearance • Maintenance of public facilities • Employment opportunities • Increased range of interesting things to do • Turnover for local businesses	• Noise levels • Rowdy and delinquent behaviour • Prices of some goods and services • Litter in the event vicinity • Excessive drinking and/or drug use
Social Impact Perception Scale – items adapted from Small (2007)	• Enhanced community identity • Increased pride in the town • Community ownership of the festival • Positive cultural impact • Togetherness within the community	• Difficulty finding parking • Road closures • Frustration with visitors • Disruption to normal routines • Under-age drinking
Event Image Scale – items adapted from Deng et al. (2015)	• Satisfies curiosity • Broadens horizons • Sufficient resting areas • Friendly and helpful volunteers • New and unique theme	*Not applicable*

Table 1.4 Finnish Event Evaluation Tool (FEET) components

Stakeholder	Questionnaire	Interview
Festival organizer	X	X
Festival attendees	X	
Local residents	X	
Local entrepreneurs	X	
Local policy-makers	X	

Source: Adapted from Pasenen et al. (2009)

Researchers have applied other evaluation approaches too which focus on the specific environmental impacts of events, such as Ecological Footprint Analysis (Collins et al., 2007). See Table 1.5. More on the growing importance of sustainability for international events can be found in Chapter 12.

Table 1.5   Ecological footprint components

Components	Estimated Using
Travel	• Visitor travel from home to event
Food and drink	• Quality and type of food and drink • Composition of food items
Infrastructure event venue	• Quantity and composition of materials • Transport of materials from manufacturer to venue • Number of visitors expected at venues
Waste	• Quantity and composition of waste generated that was land-filled and recycled

Source: Adapted from Collins et al. (2007)

The Impacts of International Events

The preceding section focused on the approaches, methods and tools used in the evaluation of international events. This section will examine the specific impacts that international events have for the destinations in which they are hosted. All international events will have significant economic, social and environmental impacts. The challenge for event organizers and other stakeholders involved in the staging of international events is to manage these impacts so that the positive impacts outweigh the negative consequences. They must also ensure that the benefits are seen to be distributed fairly throughout the community in which the event is hosted.

Economic Impacts

International events contribute specific economic outcomes that can be quantified, not only by visitors spending in the area concerned, but also through assessment of the number of business start-ups, as well as jobs created and retained through stimulation of a visitor economy. This is especially the case when international events have been used as a catalyst for urban regeneration. Urban regeneration can be described as a process by which a comprehensive and integrated vision and action brings about a lasting improvement in the economic, physical and environmental condition of an area which has gone through a significant change (Roberts, 2000).

Among the most visible, contemporary targets of event-led urban regeneration strategies are post-industrialized towns and cities which have become run-down and plagued by social problems, such as crime and unemployment, after the closure or decline of their major industries. One of the key roles of international events in urban regeneration plans in such cases is to assist in the re-imagination of localities that have not been regarded as safe or desirable destinations for leisure and tourism because of their associations with poverty and concerns that visitors have over personal security, especially after dark. The aim of such a re-imagination is to draw not only tourists but also new residents, in particular those who can be described as part of the 'creative class' – knowledge workers, intellectuals and various types of artists – believed to be a driving force for economic development in post-industrial cities (Florida, 2002). The creative class are associated with creation of businesses such as technology start-ups, small galleries, cafes and bistros, all of which cater to serve the needs of creative workers.

In practice, event-led urban regeneration, even when successful, is problematic because it is often difficult to strike an acceptable balance in organizing international events that simultaneously enthuse all sections of the resident population and appeal to external audiences, especially the highly mobile and elusive creative classes. International events are designed to re-imagine cities/localities in ways that attract the attention of footloose globe-trotters whose engagement with the place in question may be temporary and somewhat superficial, which is oftentimes at odds with the residents' views of their own communities. Frequent complaints are that urban regeneration strategies render cities/localities unrecognizable to local residents and that many of the benefits of regeneration accrue to newcomers, not long-time residents, who may not have the skills to benefit from the new jobs created or may be priced out of the market of new housing developments which become even more expensive as newcomers move in to an area.

Chang (2000) and Jayne (2006) draw attention to Singapore's events programme to support the city-state's Renaissance City branding that targeted international conventions, conferences and other business-related tourism. Criticism was levelled at its dual effect. Not only did it redistribute arts funding away from local cultural production, but the focus of the events programme on internationally oriented 'high culture' engaged only a very small minority of the host population.

Apart from the tensions that are created from event-led urban regeneration plans, there are also issues with the sheer costs of international events to consider. For example, mega sporting events such as the Olympics and Football World Cups are rarely profitable, especially in destinations which have no previous history of hosting these types of events. In preparation for such events, new sporting arenas and supporting infrastructure such as roads and transport systems would have to be built. South Africa spent a staggering US$3.5 billion to host the FIFA 2010 World Cup, building five new stadia, renovating airports, improving roads and creating the continent's first high-speed rail transport system. Years later, the event has come to be seen as a poisoned chalice for its host, with some of the stadia becoming little more than white elephants and most running at a loss (ENCA, 2014). In Brazil, where football is a national obsession, there were violent protests against the estimated US$11.5 billion bill for the FIFA 2014 World Cup hosted there (Watson, 2014). In both cases FIFA (the International Federation of Association Football) came under fire for making huge profits while the hosts – both developing countries facing an array of social and economic problems – absorbed the losses.

Social Impacts

For most people events are an integral part of daily life. They represent critical milestones and are among the most memorable experiences individuals can have. The persistence of wedding, birthday, graduation and farewell celebrations demonstrates the enduring relevance of events to human life. At the same time, as we as human beings have changed, so have the social meanings events have for us. For many in consumption-driven, Western societies, events are no longer a time of rest or recuperation from labour or times to reflect on religious values and beliefs, or even to mark the changing seasons and rhythms of life. They are instead sites in which individuals seek to connect with each other and find meaning, as opportunities for both are now in short supply.

Indeed, the emergence of modern-day music festivals and sporting events as forms of alternative spirituality has been observed by a number of commentators as a feature of post-modern life (Kommers, 2011; Parry, 2007; Partridge, 2006). One such event is the Burning Man Festival which has been staged annually since 1986. It is a celebration of self-expression, survival, sharing and radical self-reliance which features interactive art-making, gift-giving, performance and costuming. For regular attendees, known as 'burners', the festival site (the desert of Black Rock City, Nevada) is a place of pilgrimage where authentic, spontaneous expressions of spirituality can be experienced by all attendees regardless of faith. It also represents a stark contrast to the consumerism of modern life, as attendees are required to participate in a 'gift-economy', relying on gifts given to them by others to survive for the duration of the festival. Burning Man culminates in the burning of a 50-foot effigy of a man, which has various meanings for attendees. Sherry and Kozinets (2007) highlight some of these meanings in an ethnographic study of the festival. See Table 1.6.

In large cities that are gateways to immigration, events such as annual parades, festivals and carnivals (for example, St Patrick's Day, Chinese New Year, and Caribbean carnivals in Europe) bring together members of ethnic and cultural minorities, some of whom may be recent arrivals, while others may have settled several generations ago. As with food, music and other traditions, religious and secular festivals can play an important role in uniting those communities and reinforcing their shared identities.

Table 1.6 Symbolism of the 'Burn' at the Burning Man Festival

• Profound loss	• A stripping of the self
• Pure wonderment	• Purification
• A combustion of the id	• A loss of direction
• Release from restraint	• Crucifixion
• Sacrifice	• Adrenalized joy

Source: Adapted from Sherry and Kozinets (2007)

In some cases the event evolves over time and takes on new forms and meanings through fusion with other cultural influences. Thus, the bigger picture or mosaic of many festivals at different times in a city's annual events calendar may confer an image of diversity, inclusion and tolerance that can be promoted to external audiences as a positive feature. London's Notting Hill Carnival, Rotterdam's Zommer Carnival and Berlin's Karneval de Kulturen have become models of how international events can be used to engage residents of diverse cultural backgrounds and to provide recent immigrants with an opportunity to show their presence and affiliation. For the cultural organizations involved in these events, they are also occasions to feel proud of their culture, especially when it is displayed for an international audience.

As is the case with economic impacts, there are also negative social impacts that result from the staging of international events. Large crowds of people gathered together for an extended period, often under the influence of alcohol, can lead to the display of unsociable, dangerous or illegal behaviours. A common problem is crime and arrests among international event attendees. There is also the social dislocation experienced by the local population from the increased strain put on public services such as transportation, roads and even hospitals when large numbers of tourist visitors come to a destination to attend an international event. Some international events have particular social problems associated with them. Mega football championships have been observed to be linked to sex tourism (Bird and Donaldson, 2009; Richter et al., 2010), while celebrations which focus on the cultures of ethnic minorities can potentially lead to the reinforcement of cultural or ethnic stereotypes. Commercial sponsors may tend to promote such stereotypes in order to sell products such as ethnic food and drink and souvenirs. When this happens there is the real danger of culture and ethnicity becoming nothing more than commodities to be bought and sold.

Environmental Impacts

International events can have significant impacts for both the built and natural environments of destinations especially when they are linked to urban regeneration and urban renewal strategies. The former, as mentioned previously, involves lasting changes to the economic as well as physical and environmental conditions of an area, whereas the latter focuses specifically on land development. Urban renewal is thus defined as a process which involves both the re-planning and redevelopment of land, typically through demolition of existing structures, but it may also include the conservation of areas threatened by blight that are worthy of preservation because of their historical and cultural associations (Andrusz, 1984). Mega sporting events perhaps provide the most visible examples of international events which are staged for the purpose of urban renewal and the resulting positive impacts they can have on the built and natural environment. These include: the development of new and/or improved transport and communications infrastructure; showcasing of an area's natural environment; the creation of new accommodation and other facilities (for example events spaces, sporting arenas and hotels) for residents and visitors; and the promotion of best practices in sustainable international event management (Bowdin et al., 2011). The London 2012 Olympics aimed not only to inspire a generation to choose sport but also to regenerate East London, the destination in which it was staged. To this end there were a number of urban renewal projects incorporated within the building of the Olympic infrastructure:

- The Olympic Park, now renamed Queen Elizabeth Park, was earmarked to serve as a new attraction for the capital, offering world-class sporting facilities for athletes as well as the local community.
- The accommodation for athletes within the Olympic and Paralympic Village was to be developed with the long-term goal of providing thousands of new homes for sale and for rent (half of which was to be affordable housing).
- The Olympic and Paralympic Village, which would become known as East Village, was to be equipped with a new educational campus as well as a community health centre.

However, balancing the impacts of the urban structural and socio-spatial consequences of international events poses significant challenges. Critics point out that event-led urban renewal strategies can entail the evictions or displacement of existing poor and working-class populations and their replacement by the middle class (Hiller, 2000) when their homes and/or places of work are demolished to make way for new infrastructure. These displaced populations may also suffer dislocation from their work places and/or social networks. Additionally, resident populations which are spared eviction can still be subject to the deprivation and exclusion which results when an area's services and facilities are developed to cater to a different and more affluent social group (Whitson and Mcintosh, 1996). Moreover, traditionally, the global and future orientation of international events, like the 'placelessness' of the corporate architecture of shopping malls, theme parks and airports that are built as part of event-led urban renewal strategies, arguably destroy any sense of spatial and cultural identity that an area possesses (Relph, 1976). Ironically, city planners, by seeking to use international events to carve out a distinctive position for their cities in the eyes of the world, end up doing the exact opposite. Musing on the Ontario Place Exhibition complex in Toronto, Relph explained the underlying logic of events that are 'deliberately intended as points of innovation as trend-setters in design and style and taste: they are meant to be copied' (1976: 105).

Aside from the consequences of urban renewal, all events whether local or international have a number of negative impacts on the natural environment. These impacts can be divided into several categories: air quality, geological condition, water pollution, depletion of natural resources, and flora and fauna (David, 2009). The London 2012 Olympics, despite its lofty aims of regenerating East London and being the 'greenest games ever', was criticized for having a number of detrimental impacts

Table 1.7 Negative environmental impacts from the London 2012 Olympic Games

Environmental Impacts	Outcomes for the Community
Loss of biodiversity	• Permanent removal of nature reserve • Permanent loss of an estimated 42.47 hectares of sites of importance for nature conservation (SINCs)
Loss of allotments, common land and green space	• Loss of 100-year-old allotments by local gardening society • Loss of football pitches used by local footballers • Communities being pitted against each other for the limited remaining green spaces
Nuclear waste	• Risks of contamination from trains carrying nuclear waste travelling through the Olympic Park during the Games
Aviation	• Rise in the number of flights as well as noise, local air pollution and carbon emissions
Toxic waste	• Risks from exposure due to the 7,300 tonnes of contaminated soil being shifted in the run-up to construction

Source: Adapted from Corporate Watch (2014)

on the environment. One of the most reported in the news media was the permanent loss of allotments (shared land used by the community for growing food), common land and green space by the Manor Garden Society (MGS). The MGS was offered replacement grounds but it has been described as being of a much lower standard than the lands previously held (Corporate Watch, 2014). Corporate Watch (2014) also highlighted a number of other negative impacts that the London 2012 Olympics had for the environment (see Table 1.7).

However, it should be noted that the Olympics, as well as a number of other international events, have come a long way in minimizing the negative impacts they have on the environment. Chapter 12 of this text provides details on the strategies international event organizers have developed to manage negative environmental impacts.

Case Study 1.2 – The CrossFit Experience at the Swedish Open Fitness Tour's Gripen Grand Prix

CrossFit was initially conceived as a fitness programme but has grown to become an international competitive fitness sport. The most well-known of these events is Reebok's annual CrossFit Games, described as 'a gruelling (sic!) test for the world's toughest athletes' (CrossFit Inc., 2015a), in which participants compete for the title 'The fittest on Earth'. The rising participation

(Continued)

(Continued)

in 'the Open' (a series of qualifying events for the CrossFit Games) is testament to the exponential growth in both interest and participation levels in the sport. In 2011, its very first year, some 26,000 athletes competed in the Open. Just four years later in 2015, more than 270,000 people signed up. CrossFit is now unquestionably an international phenomenon (see Figure 1.4).

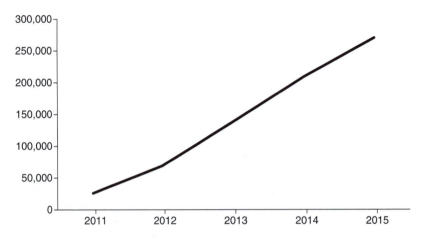

Figure 1.4   Participant rates in 'the Open' of the Reebok CrossFit Games 2011–2015

Source: Adapted from CrossFit Inc. (2015b)

This case study examines the experiences of ten CrossFit athletes at the Gripen Grand Prix, which is part of the Swedish Open Fitness Tour (SOFT). Like the CrossFit Games, it provides participants with the opportunity to test their fitness and compete for titles, either as individuals or in teams of two. It is one of the largest competitions for CrossFitters in Sweden. In 2015, 300 athletes, from Sweden as well other countries in Europe and North America, competed in the two-day main event. It was held at the Stadium Exhibition Centre in Malmo on 27–28 June (WODevents Europe, 2015). Over the two days of competition the event venue was converted into three arenas, with two grandstands (Gripen Grand Prix, n.d. *a*).

The Gripen Grand Prix required competitors to complete a series of fitness routines called 'workouts of the day' (WODs) with weights varying according to the competition class they have entered (see Table 1.8). One of the key elements of the competition (as is the case with other competitive CrossFit events)

Table 1.8 CrossFit competition classes

Class	Description
RX	Prescribed WODs are performed using prescribed weights, although different weights are used by males and females.
Master	Masters are males and females aged 35 and over. Their prescribed WODs are performed using weights scaled or 'adjusted' for their ages.
Team	Two women or two men performing prescribed workouts.

is the requirement that the WODs are issued only a few days prior to the event. This practice is part of the CrossFit philosophy of preparing athletes 'not just for the unknown, but for the unknowable' (CrossFit Inc., 2015c).

The Gripen Grand Prix organizers promote the event to local and tourist visitors as a fun and exciting weekend. Adult tickets are priced at 75 Swedish Krona for the day (just under US$10 or around €8) and children under 15 years of age pay just 30 Swedish Krona for the day (just under US$4 or around €3). There are also price discounts offered to attend the entire weekend (Gripen Grand Prix, n.d. *b*). Additionally, the event attracts sponsorship from a range of organizations. The Gripen Grand Prix includes, among its partners, equipment rental, sport nutrition, health and information technology companies (Gripen Grand Prix, n.d. *c*).

Figure 1.5 Image of visitors in the stands at the Gripen Grand Prix

(Continued)

(Continued)

For competing athletes there are a number of incentives offered for participation. These include: hotel rooms at the nearby Mecure Hotel at discounted rates; two free event tickets; access to an onsite chiropractor/massage therapist; and of course there is the prize money (Gripen Grand Prix, n.d. *b*). Across the three types of competitors, 40,000 Swedish Krona (about US$4,700 or around €4,250) is awarded in prizes (Gripen Grand Prix, n.d. *d*).

The ten CrossFit athletes that were interviewed for this case study were asked to reflect on the experience of participating in the Gripen Grand Prix at the SOFT and what larger meanings the event had for their lives. Interviewees comprised three RX competitors, three Master competitors and four Team competitors.

Among all interviewees a strong sense of belonging and community was apparent, making CrossFit as a sporting competition somewhat unique. Many sporting events can generate feelings of hostility and aggressive competitiveness (Atkinson, 2008). At the Gripen Grand Prix, competitors rather – than competing against each other – were more focused on improving their own fitness and performance. So while there was that spirit of competition found at all sporting events, individuals there competed against *themselves* rather

Figure 1.6   Image of CrossFit competitors in the 'box' at the Gripen Grand Prix

than each other. At the Gripen Grand Prix there was the same supportive, community spirit that is found at one's local CrossFit box (non-competitive spaces in which CrossFitters meet to exercise).

At the same time, competitors at the Gripen Grand Prix took the event quite seriously. All competitors were very focused on performing well and quite a few entered competitions with the objective of bettering their previous performances. Jon, one of the CrossFit athletes, explained that to do well, competitors must live 'the CrossFit way of life'. This involved following a strict diet, exercise and rest regime, which according to Jon's fellow CrossFit athlete Inga, leaves one with little time for much else. For example, she was no longer able to maintain social relations in ordinary life and her friendships were now limited to individuals within the CrossFit community. This supports research by Lalich and Langone (2006) who observed that among the key characteristics which identified CrossFitters were a gradual inability to relate to outsiders (individuals who do not participate in CrossFit) and a willingness to do whatever it takes to achieve the goal. These attributes, along with avid CrossFitters constantly talking about the virtues of CrossFit and the development of their own language describing the WODs, which is unrecognisable to outsiders, has also caused some researchers examining the sport as a phenomenon to compare it to a cult (Dawson, 2015). Anna, another competitor interviewed at the Gripen Grand Prix, also referred to the sport as a cult but it was not at all in a negative way. She described herself and other competitors as cult members sharing the religion of CrossFit, which has brought enjoyment to them all.

The significant sacrifices made by the CrossFit athletes in the name of what some would describe as a fitness cult are not without their benefits. Due to the absorptive nature of the CrossFit events, participants reported experiencing a profound sense of freedom from everyday life. Once competitors enter the arena they solely focus on performing the tasks required.

'This weekend you really live in CrossFit. There is nothing else that concerns you. You don't need to care about anything else. You can switch off everything else and just focus on what's at stake. That's why I think it's really great.' (Carl, CrossFit RX Competitor, Gripen Grand Prix)

(Continued)

(Continued)

'In the arena I only think go dammit! I don't know many people say they think a lot but I don't think at all, all I think is go, like all I got to do is do it until the clock stops. There's nothing else I need to do.' (Hanna, CrossFit Team Competitor, Gripen Grand Prix)

Additionally, the single-mindedness of competitors within the arena space brings a real sense of achievement and pride in their physical prowess. One competitor, Daniel, said competing at Gripen Grand Prix gave him the feeling of invincibility. Others described competing at the event as an 'adrenaline rush' or a 'euphoric sensation'.

It was quite striking that none of the competitors mentioned the possibility of winning the prize money as a reason for entering the Gripen Grand Prix. There was also no interest expressed in the fame or notoriety that would come from holding a championship title.

However, some of the positive impacts of the event for the competitors lasted after the Gripen Grand Prix weekend was over. By pushing themselves

Figure 1.7   Image of CrossFit competitor at the Gripen Grand Prix

through the gruelling tasks of the competition, they found they were also able to 'raise the bar in life'. They became more determined in pursuing their goals. As Ellinor explained after performing tasks that she never thought she would be able to do at the Gripen Grand Prix, she felt that 'nothing is impossible'.

Case Study Questions

1   Devise a comprehensive list of the social, economic and environmental impacts that are likely to come from the Gripen Grand Prix.
2   Compare and contrast the social impacts from sporting events like the Gripen Grand Prix to those arising from modern-day music festivals.
3   Suggest some changes that have taken place within modern societies which are driving the popularity of CrossFit events such as the Gripen Grand Prix.
4   Propose an evaluation tool that can be used by the organizers of the Gripen Grand Prix to evaluate the success of the event.

Chapter Summary

Events are a vital part of the human experience. They provide cherished memories, mark critical milestones and reinforce beliefs, values and cultures. In post-modern societies events have become a source of spirituality in and of themselves, as the fast-paced march of the modern world has left many individuals isolated and trapped by consumer-driven culture. The staging of cultural events for tourists is also a source of income and pride for the practitioners of indigenous cultural forms who may not have access to other resources.

The popularity of events can be traced to changes in the world's economies because of globalization. Increased global competition has been a key driver for organizations, communities and even cities to turn to international events to stand out in the minds of their customers, visitors and investors.

A great deal of the research done on international events centres on understanding them as tourism products. Common themes that have emerged are: understanding international event audiences; the role of international events in developing the image of destinations; the authenticity of international events; and the evaluation of international event impacts.

International events have great potential to be sources of positive long-term impacts in the destinations within which they are hosted when they are part of urban regeneration and urban renewal strategies. However, it can be quite a challenge to balance the positive impacts and negative consequences of such strategies. It is difficult to stage international events in such a way as to attract international tourists, inward investment and new residents while at the same time respecting the needs and desires of the local community.

Review Questions

1. How are international events used to transform the images of destinations?
2. Why might an international event such as WaterFire be described as inauthentic?
3. What are the arguments for and against staging ethnic festivals in communities?
4. Why is measuring the social impacts of international events more difficult than measuring their economic impacts?
5. What are the issues involved in using international events as part of urban regeneration and renewal strategies?

Additional Resources

Books / Book Chapters / Journal Articles

Getz, D. and Page, S. (2015). *Event Studies: Theory, Research and Policy for Planned Events*. Oxon: Routledge. This text explores the knowledge and theory behind planned events.

Richards, G., de Brito, M. and Wilks, L. (2013). *Exploring the Social Impacts of Events*. Oxon: Routledge. This text explores the variety of social impacts created by events in communities throughout the world, with case studies drawn from countries throughout Europe, Australia and South Africa.

Ritchie, J. R. B. (1990). Olympulse VI: A post-event assessment of resident reaction to the XV Winter Olympic Games. *Journal of Travel Research*, *28*(3): 14–23. This paper provides an example of how the social impacts of a mega sporting event can be measured.

Useful Websites

www.eventmagazine.co.uk/ – Provides free online access to feature articles, news and jobs from the printed *Event Magazine*, a guide to key trends and insights in the event industry.

www.event-solutions.com/ – Allows access to useful resources for corporate, association and independent event and meeting professionals.

www.worldofevents.net/ – Links users to relevant information for event industry professionals, educators, students and researchers.

References

Andrusz, G. (1984). *Housing and Urban Development in the USSR*. Albany: State University of New York Press.

Atkinson, M. (2008). Triathlon, suffering and exciting significance. *Leisure Studies*, *27*(2): 165–80.

Beattie, A.C. (2012, March 26). Adidas navigates Japanese market with creative flair. Ad age [online]. Retrieved from http://adage.com/article/cmo-interviews/adidas-navigates-japanese-market-creative-flair/233710/

Benedict, B. (1991). International exhibitions and national identity. *Anthropology Today, 7*(3): 5–9.

Bird, R. and Donaldson, R. (2009). 'Sex, Sun, Soccer': Stakeholder-opinions on the sex industry in Cape Town in anticipation of the 2010 FIFA Soccer World Cup. *Urban Forum, 20*(1): 33–46.

Bobel, R. (2013). Qatar will spend $200 billion on 2022 Fifa world cup — what else could you buy with that much money? Sportsgrid [online] Retrieved from www.sportsgrid.com/uncate gorized/qatar-will-spend-200-billion-on-2022-fifa-world-cup-what-else-could-you-buy-with-that-much-money/

Boorstin, D. (1991). *The Image: A Guide to Pseudo-Events in America.* New York: Vintage.

Bowdin, G., McDonnell, I., Allen, J. and O'Toole, W. (2006). *Events Management.* Oxford: Butterworth-Heinemann.

Bowdin, G., McDonnell, I., Allen, J. and O'Toole, W. (2011). *Events Management.* Oxford: Butterworth-Heinemann.

Bruner, E. M. (1991). Transformation of self in tourism. *Annals of Tourism Research, 18*(2): 238–50.

CBC News (2008). Beijing and the Olympics: By the numbers. CBC News [online]. Retrieved from www.cbc.ca /news/world/story/2008/08/08/f-beijing-by numbers.html

Chang, T. C. (2000). Renaissance revisited: Singapore as a 'Global City of the Arts'. *International Journal of Urban and Regional Research, 2*(4): 818–31.

Coca-Cola (2012). Coca-Cola sponsorships. Coca-Cola [online]. Retrieved from www.coca-cola company.com/stories/coca-cola-sponsorships/

Collins, A., Flynn, A., Munday, M. and Roberts, A. (2007). Assessing the environmental consequences of major sporting events: The 2003/04 FA Cup Final. *Urban Studies, 44*(3): 457–76.

Corporate Watch (2014, July 27). The real environmental impacts of holding the Olympics in East London. *Corporate Watch* [online]. Retrieved from https://corporatewatch.org/news/2012/jul/26/real-environmental-impacts-holding-olympics-east-london

Crompton, J. L. and McKay, S. L. (1997). Motives of visitors attending festival events. *Annals of Tourism Research, 24*(2): 425–39.

CrossFit Inc. (2015a). About the games. CrossFit Inc. [online]. Retrieved from http://games.cross fit.com/about-the-games

CrossFit Inc. (2015b). About the games – History. CrossFit Inc. [online]. Retrieved from http://games.crossfit.com/about-the-games/history

CrossFit Inc. (2015c). What is CrossFit? CrossFit Inc. [online]. Retrieved from www.crossfit.com/cf-info/what-is-crossfit.html

David, L. (2009). Environmental impacts of events. In R. Raj and J. Musgrave (eds) *Event Management and Sustainability* (pp. 66–75). Wallingford: CABI.

Dawson, M. C. (2015). CrossFit: Fitness cult or reinventive institution? *International Review for the Sociology of Sport.* Doi: 1012690215591793.

Delamere, T. A., Wankel, L. M. and Hinch, T. D. (2001). Development of a scale to measure resident attitudes toward the social impacts of community festivals, Part I: Item generation and purification of the measure. *Event Management, 7*(1): 11–24.

Deng, C. Q., Li, M. and Shen, H. (2015). Developing a measurement scale for event image. *Journal of Hospitality & Tourism Research, 39*(2): 245–70.

ENCA (2014, June 10) South Africa still counting cost of the 2010 World Cup. *ENCA* [online]. Retrieved from www.enca.com/south-africa-still-counting-cost-2010-world-cup

ESPN Sports Media Limited (n.d.) Origins and development: A brief history of cricket [online] Retrieved from http://www.espncricinfo.com/ci/content/story/239757.html#resource

Fairley, S., Tyler, B. D., Kellett, P. and D'Elia, K. (2011). The Formula One Australian Grand Prix: Exploring the triple bottom line. *Sport Management Review, 14*(2): 141–52.

Falassi, A. (1987). Festival: Definition and morphology. In A. Falassi (ed.), *Time out of Time: Essays on the Festival* (pp. 1–10). Albuquerque: University of New Mexico Press.

Ferdinand, N. and Williams, N. L. (2012). Event staging. In J. Connell and S. Page (eds), *The Routledge Handbook of Events* (pp. 234–47). Abingdon: Routledge.

Florida, R. (2002). The economic geography of talent. *Annals of the Association of American Geographers, 92*(4): 743–55.

Fredline, L., Jago, L. and Deery, M. (2003). The development of a generic scale to measure the social impacts of events. *Event Management, 8*(1): 23–37.

Getz, D. (2005). *Event Management and Event Tourism* (2nd edn). New York: Cognizant.

Getz, D. and Page, S. J. (2015). Progress and prospects for event tourism research, *Tourism Management, 52*: 593–631. Doi: 10.1016/j.tourman.2015.03.007

Greenwood, D. J. (1989). Culture by the pound: An anthropological perspective on tourism as cultural commoditization. In V. L. Smith (ed.) *Hosts and Guests: The Anthropology of Tourism* (2nd edn) (pp. 171–85). Philadelphia: University of Pennsylvania Press.

Gripen Grand Prix (n.d. *a*). Information about the competition. Gripen Grand Prix [online]. Retrieved from www.gripengrandprix.se/publikinfo/

Gripen Grand Prix (n.d. *b*). Information for all athletes. Gripen Grand Prix [online]. Retrieved from www.gripengrandprix.se/deltagarinfo/

Gripen Grand Prix (n.d. *c*). Partners. Gripen Grand Prix [online]. Retrieved from www.gripen grandprix.se/partners/

Gripen Grand Prix (n.d. *d*). Start. Gripen Grand Prix [online]. Retrieved from www.gripengrand prix.se/

Hede, A. M. (2007). Managing special events in the new era of the triple bottom line. *Event Management, 11*(1–2): 13–22.

Heussner, K. M. (2009). Obama makes internet history: Inauguration sets record for streaming online video. ABC News [online]. Retrieved from http://abcnews.go.com/Technology/president-obama-inauguration-sets-record-video-views-online/story?id=6699048

Hiller, H. H. (2000). Toward an urban sociology of mega-events. *Research in Urban Sociology, 5*: 181–205.

Jago, L. K. and Shaw, R. N. (1998). Special events: A conceptual and definitional framework. *Festival Management and Event Tourism, 5*(1–2): 21–32.

Jayne, M. (2006). *Cities and Consumption*. London: Routledge.

Kim, H. and Jamal, T. (2007). Touristic quest for existential authenticity. *Annals of Tourism Research, 34*(1): 181–201.

Kommers, H. (2011). Hidden in music: Religious experience and popular culture. *Journal of Religion and Popular Culture, 23*(1): 14–26.

Kruger, M., Saayman, M. and Ellis, S. (2010). Determinants of visitor expenditure at the Aardklop National Arts Festival. *Event Management, 14*(2): 137–48.

Lalich, J. and Langone, M. D. (2006). Characteristics associated with cultic groups. In J. Lalich and M. Tobias (eds), *Take Back Your Life: Recovering from Cults and Abusive Relationships* (pp. 327–8). Berkley, CA: Bay Tree Publishing

Lash, S. and Urry, J. (2002). *Economies of Signs and Space*. London: SAGE Publications.

Lee, C. K. (2000). A comparative study of Caucasian and Asian visitors to a Cultural Expo in an Asian setting. *Tourism Management, 21*(2): 169–76.

Lee, C. K., Lee, Y. K. and Wicks, B. E. (2004). Segmentation of festival motivation by nationality and satisfaction. *Tourism Management, 25*(1): 61–70.

Lee, T. H. and Hsu, F. Y. (2013). Examining how attending motivation and satisfaction affects the loyalty for attendees at aboriginal festivals. *International Journal of Tourism Research*, *15*(1): 18–34.

Ma, S. C., Egan, D., Rotherham, I. and Ma, S. M. (2011). A framework for monitoring during the planning stage for a sports mega-event. *Journal of Sustainable Tourism*, *19*(1): 79–96.

MacCannell, D. (1976). *The Tourist: A New Theory of the Leisure Class*. Los Angeles: University of California Press.

MacCannell, D. (1999). *The Tourist: A New Theory of the Leisure Class*. Los Angeles: University of California Press.

MacLeod, N. (2006). The placeless festival: Identity and place in the post-modern festival. In D. Picard and M. Robinson (eds), *Festivals, Tourism and Social Change: Remaking Worlds* (pp. 222–37). Clevedon: Chanel View Publications.

Mayerowitz, S. (2009). What recession? The $170 million inauguration. ABC News [online]. Retrieved from http://abcnews.go.com/Business/Inauguration/president-obama-inauguration-cost-170-million/story?id=6665946

Mintel (2010). *Empowered Consumer*. Mintel [online]. Retrieved from http://academic.mintel.com/display/479808/

Nazreth, L. (2007). *The Leisure Economy: How Changing Demographics, Economics, and Generational Attitudes Will Reshape Our Lives and Our Industries*. Ontario: John Wiley and Sons Canada.

Neilsen (2008). The final tally – 4.7 billion tune in to Beijing 2008 – more than two in three people worldwide: Nielsen. The Nielsen Company [online]. Retrieved from www.nielsen.com/us/en/insights/press-room/2008/the_final_tally_-.html

O'Sullivan, D. and Jackson, M. J. (2002). Festival tourism: A contributor to sustainable local economic development? *Journal of Sustainable Tourism*, *10*(4): 325–42.

Parry, J. (2007). *Sport and Spirituality: An Introduction*. Oxon: Routledge.

Partridge, C. (2006). The spiritual and the revolutionary: Alternative spirituality, British free festivals, and the emergence of rave culture. *Culture and Religion: An Interdisciplinary Journal*, *7*(1): 41–60.

Pasanen, K., Taskinen, H. and Mikkonen, J. (2009). Impacts of cultural events in Eastern Finland – development of a Finnish event evaluation tool. *Scandinavian Journal of Hospitality and Tourism*, *9*(2–3): 112–29.

Pine, B. J. and Gilmore, J. H. (2011). *The Experience Economy* (updated edition). Boston: Harvard Business School Publishing.

Prentice, R. and Andersen, V. (2003). Festival as creative destination. *Annals of Tourism Research*, *30*(1): 7–30.

Providence Warwick Convention & Visitors Bureau (2011). WaterFire Providence [online]. Retrieved from www.goprovidence.com/things-to-do/waterfire/

Reid, S. (2007). Identifying social consequences of rural events. *Event Management*, *11*(1–2): 89–98.

Relph, E. (1976). *Place and Placelessness*. London: Pion.

Richards, G. (2014). Creativity and tourism in the city. *Current Issues in Tourism*, *17*(2): 119–44.

Richards, G. and Palmer, R. (2010). *Eventful Cities: Cultural Management and Urban Revitalization*. Oxford: Butterworth-Heinemann.

Richards, G. and Wilson, J. (2004). The impact of cultural events on city image: Rotterdam, Cultural Capital of Europe 2001. *Urban Studies*, *41*(10): 1931–51.

Richter, M. L., Chersich, M. F., Scorgie, F., Luchters, S., Temmerman, M. and Steen, R. (2010). Sex work and the 2010 FIFA World Cup: Time for public health imperatives to prevail. *Globalization and Health*, *6*(1): 1–6.

Ritchie, J. R. B. (1984). Assessing the impact of hallmark events: Concepts and research issues. *Journal of Travel Research*, *23*(1): 2–11.

Roberts, P. (2000). The evolution, definition and purpose of urban regeneration. In P. Roberts and H. Sykes (eds), *Urban Renaissance: A Handbook* (pp. 9–36). London: Sage Publications.

Robertson, R. (2011). The 'Return' of religion and the conflicted condition of world order. *Journal of Globalization Studies*, *2*(1): 32–40.

Schofield, P. and Thompson, K. (2007). Visitor motivation, satisfaction and behavioural intention: The 2005 Naadam Festival, Ulaanbaatar. *International Journal of Tourism Research*, *9*(5): 329–44.

Sherry, J. F. and Kozinets, R. V. (2007). Nomadic spirituality and the Burning Man Festival. *Research in Consumer Behavior*, *11*: 119–47.

Small, K. (2007). Social dimensions of community festivals: An application of factor analysis in the development of the social impact perception (SIP) scale. *Event Management*, *11*(1–2): 45–55.

Smith, M. K. (2009). *Issues in Cultural Tourism Studies* (Second Edition). London: Routledge.

Thomas Cook Retail Limited (n.d.). Key dates. Thomas Cook Retail Limited [online] Retrieved from www.thomascook.com/about-us/thomas-cook-history/key-dates/

Toffler, A. (1970). *Future Shock*. New York: Random House.

Towner, J. (1985). The Grand Tour: A key phase in the history of tourism. *Annals of Tourism Research*, 12(3): 297–333.

Trennert, R. A. (1993). Selling Indian education at World's Fairs and Expositions, 1893–1904. *American Indian Quarterly, 11*(3): 203–20.

Wang, N. (2000). Authenticity. In J. Jafari (ed.), *Encyclopaedia of Tourism* (pp. 43–5). London: Routledge.

WaterFire Providence (2015). History. Retrieved from http://waterfire.org/about/history/

Watson, L. (2014, June 12). Brazilian protesters angry at the cost of the World Cup set fires in the streets and clash violently with riot police hours before opening match in Sao Paulo. *Mail Online*. Retrieved from www.dailymail.co.uk/news/article-2656102/Brazil-gets-ready-greatest-Earth-just-dont-mention-poor-pitches-subway-strikes-protests-hackers.html

Weaver, D. and Lawton, L. (2006). *Tourism Management* (3rd edn). Milton: John Wiley and Sons Australia.

Whitson, D. and Macintosh, D. (1996). The global circus: International sport, tourism, and the marketing of cities. *Journal of Sport & Social Issues*, *20*(3): 278–95.

Withey, L. (1997). *Grand Tours and Cook's Tours: A History of Leisure Travel 1750 to 1915*. London: Autumn Press.

WODEvents Europe (2015). Gripen Grand Prix. WODEvents Europe [online]. Retrieved from http://wodevents.eu/events/gripen-grand

The International Events Environment

2

Nicole Ferdinand, Simone Wesner and Yi-Fang Wang

Learning Objectives

By reading this chapter students should be able to:

- Describe what it means to take an international approach to events management
- Identify key changes in the global environment which are impacting events and event organizations
- Use strategic planning tools to identify and analyse the environment in which international events take place
- Understand how event organizations can formulate strategic responses to global changes
- Appreciate how culture and customs can dictate how event organizations operate.

Introduction

It is difficult to describe what it means precisely to take an international approach to events management. However, texts such as this one, which takes an international focus or approach to the subject, share a focus on international activities such as tourism and international sponsorship and are concerned with differences between cultures and countries (other examples include: Ali-Knight et al., 2009; Page and Connell, 2011; Yeoman et al., 2004). Additionally, they engage with a number of global issues affecting people and organizations, such as terrorism and sustainability. In essence they suggest that international events management or an international approach to events management requires an engagement with international activities, cultural differences and global issues. There is also a distinct focus on 'international events', which are becoming increasingly common in the events marketplace.

This chapter seeks to highlight the growing international dimensions of events management, whilst recognising the differences in events management practices that occur country to country. It starts by providing an understanding of the international events environment, which is divided into global, international and local/community factors. The chapter also highlights a number of frameworks and strategic planning tools that can be used to identify and analyse these factors. It then goes on to outline how these factors impact international events management practices.

The International Events Environment

In Chapter 1 of this text the impact of environmental factors on the development of modern-day international events was very evident. One of the most crucial factors affecting their development was the emergence of leisure, as without a leisure class there could not be an international event audience. The emergence of new tourism products, or tourism business process innovations such as those pioneered by Thomas Cook and Sons, were also very important because they facilitated the establishment of widespread event tourism, which continues to be a key driver of the international events market (Thomas Cook Retail, n.d.). Global politics greatly influenced the form and function of the first international events, such as international exhibitions, which were focused on demonstrating the political and economic dominance of their sponsors – the governments of the leading colonial powers at the time. Getz (2005) describes these types of factors as 'global forces' which impact the planning and management of events. He suggests that all events are part of a system of interacting elements which consist of organizational factors (human, physical and financial resources), the local or community context (key stakeholders, resource availability and competition) and global forces (forces impacting on events, event organizations and event tourism).

International events, in particular, are also heavily influenced by 'globalization' – a term which refers to a number of processes which have enabled companies, products, people, money and information to move more freely and quickly around the world (Morrison, 2006).

Event managers need to be aware of not only the global forces in the international events environment, but also the particular local situations in which they find themselves. They must recognize the specific requirements of international events management, whilst also paying due attention to the differences in event management practices that occur country to country and also amongst different cultures within

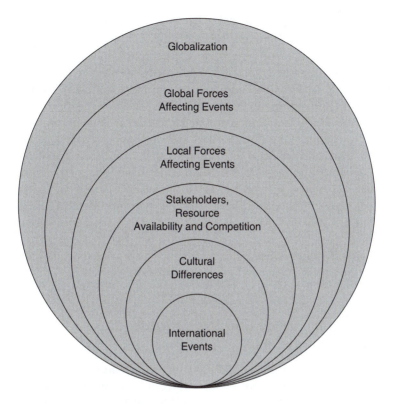

Figure 2.1 The international events environment

countries. International events management requires an understanding of the elements which constitute the international events environment and the formulation of appropriate responses.

By adapting Getz's (2005) events management system, it is possible to develop a model of the international events environment. Important additions to Getz's (2005) system are issues surrounding globalization and also cultural differences (see Figure 2.1).

Globalization

At the heart of globalization is a deeper level of integration amongst economies throughout the world, which has in large part been driven by formation of trading blocs and the increase in multi-national and trans-national corporations (MNCs and TNCs). MNCs are businesses which own divisions and offices in multiple countries whereas TNCs are companies which coordinate different aspects of their business activities across countries without necessarily taking ownership of the organizations performing these activities.

The proliferation of MNCs and TNCs has resulted in an unprecedented level of competition amongst manufacturers. This situation has been extremely beneficial for the growth of events and event organizations, as countries throughout the world, particularly the most developed societies, have been moving away from traditional production activities to focus on economic development strategies involving tourism, leisure and sport (Burbank et al., 2001).

Event and festival tourism, which was regarded as 'an emerging giant' (Getz and Frisby, 1988: 22) almost three decades ago, now occupies 'significant status' in both domestic and international mass tourism markets (Picard and Robinson, 2006: 2). Increasingly, festivals and special events are consciously being developed as tourist attractions (Getz, 1998) by festival and event organizers, local communities and governments. Throughout the world there have been unprecedented investments into event infrastructure, such as convention and performing arts centres, stadia and festival malls.

The following highlight some of the ways in which aspects of globalization have facilitated the growth of events and event organizations.

The increase in air travel and the cultural tourist market for events

Reductions in the cost of air travel and the convenience and ease of finding information about remote locales provided by the internet means that more and more people are travelling than ever before. The growth of the international tourism industry has been particularly striking in the last decade, and in the six years from 2010 to 2015 there was above-average growth in international tourist arrivals, with number of arrivals increasing 4% and above each year during this period. In 2015, tourism arrivals reached a record 1,184 million (UNWTO, 2016).

A significant number of these tourists would have been travellers going to a country for the specific purpose of attending cultural events. These tourists, also known as cultural tourists, are typically described as 'well-educated people with high status occupations and good incomes' who have travelled to a destination for the expressed purpose of experiencing culture (Richards, 2007: 18–19). In the last two decades cultural tourism has become a particularly important source of income for cultural facilities, festival and event organizers and also destinations.

In the past, cultural tourism was associated with 'high culture' and the relatively wealthy, as air travel and knowledge of foreign cultures was restricted to those who had the income and the education to acquire a lifestyle which included learning about rituals and practices of people in far-away places. Today cultural tourism is commonplace, so much so that it is beginning to lose all meaning as a distinct category of tourism (Richards, 2001). This dramatic shift was unthinkable just a few decades ago. In the UK for example, it is estimated that music tourism attracts some 9.5 million tourists who contribute £3.1 billion to the economy from the direct and indirect expenditure they generate (UK Music, 2015).

The increase in international organizations and the demand for international meetings, incentive travel, conferences and exhibitions (MICE)

The rise of MNCs and TNCs has also been accompanied by the internationalization of other organizations such as trade associations, charitable organizations and special interest groups. The increase in the numbers of international organizations throughout the world has led to a dramatic increase in the demand for events which provide opportunities for organizations to bring together colleagues scattered across the globe to meet and exchange ideas and information. The rapid expansion of the conference sector, in the latter half of the twentieth century in particular, can be directly linked to the proliferation of international organizations (Lawson, 2000). Today international meetings, incentive travel, conferences and exhibitions (MICE) have now become an established part of the events industry (Davidson and Rogers, 2006). It is estimated that annually 9,120 international conventions take place globally which generate US$13.8 billion in direct spending per year (ICCA, 2010, cited in UNWTO, 2012). Worldwide the MICE market as a whole has been estimated to be worth about US$650 million (Mintel, 2010).

The increase in market access facilitated by the formation of regional trading blocs and associations

The formation of trading blocs, which can be described as geographical areas or zones of cross-border trade cooperation, has opened a host of opportunities for event organizations. By eliminating barriers to movement of both people and capital, it has made it a great deal easier for event organizers to host events which target audiences across national borders. Europe, for example, is the undisputed leader of music festivals within contemporary music genres and is home to several of the largest festivals in the world, which draw hundreds of thousands of music tourists (Mintel, 2013). The growth of European music festivals has been greatly facilitated by formation of the European Union. It has an estimated population of over 500 million people and is now the biggest trading bloc in the world. The benefits of the union for festival organizers include passport-free travel of festival attendees within Europe, free movement of employees across European member states and a single customs check at all intra-EU boarders enabling goods and services to move freely across Europe (Single European Act, 1986, cited in Doole and Lowe, 2012). The European music festival market is also supported by the European Festival Association, Yourope. It boasts 65 members and facilitates close communication and information exchange between festivals, and hosts a range of seminars and workshops (Mintel, 2013).

Global Forces Impacting Events, Events Organizations and Tourism

Outside of globalization there are a number of other forces which affect the way in which events are staged across the world. These forces can be studied using strategic planning tools such as a PEST or PESTEL analysis. PEST includes **p**olitical and legal changes, **e**conomic conditions, **s**ocio-cultural trends, and innovations in **t**echnology. In a PESTEL analysis changes in **l**egislation are treated separately as are **e**nvironmental concerns, such as global warming and climate change. Event managers can use PEST or PESTEL analyses to continually scan the global environment and adjust their events and organizational plans to either avoid or minimize threats and capitalize on opportunities. These can be discovered by asking key questions, which can include:

- Have there been any recent changes in global politics that can impact events?
- What new international laws and regulations have recently been introduced that event managers should be aware of?
- What are current economic conditions like?
- Have there been any critical events affecting global financial markets?
- What are the key global socio-demographic trends impacting event audiences?
- Are there any other trends that event managers can take advantage of when designing event activities (for example, popular music trends and sporting activities)?
- What new technological developments can event managers take advantage of to improve the quality, efficiency and/or lower the costs of their events?

Figure 2.2 is an illustrative PEST analysis which demonstrates the implications that global forces have for the staging of events.

Local Forces Affecting Events, Events Organizations and Event Tourism

The local/community context in which events are staged impacts every aspect of an event organization's operations. Event organizations wishing to stage events outside of their country of origin need to research carefully the local/community context in which they are organizing events, as it has fundamental implications for strategy and planning decisions. For instance, the ease and the cost at which visas and work permits can be acquired will determine how much of the event organization's personnel travel to staff an event overseas and how many local temporary members of staff are hired. Similarly, wage levels and general living standards will affect the prices that can be charged for event tickets. Likewise, the ethnic mix of the population in a

Political	• **Terrorism** The 2013 Boston Marathon bombings and the terrorist attacks in Paris in November 2015 which took place outside the Stad de France and inside the music concert venue Bataclan are recent examples which highlight why terrorism threats are a continuing cause for concern for the organizers of events. The impact is perhaps most visible in sporting mega-events which are increasingly marked by security features such as enforced closure of public thoroughfares, the searching of individuals in and around stadiums and the constant monitoring of local residents and spectators by CCTV cameras (Giulianotti and Klauser, 2012).
Economic	• **Gradual growth in the world's key economies** Seven years on from the 2008 financial crisis, 3.3% average growth has been forecasted for the world's key economies. In the Eurozone growth will be supported by private sector confidence and credit markets but declining growth in China and other emerging markets also means reduced demands for European exports (Euromonitor International, 2015a). Uncertainty about the region's economic outlook has had a dual effect on some segments within the event industry. For example, in the MICE sector it has made organizations more cautious with their spending, whilst at the same time it has made Europe a more attractive conference destination because it has meant venues are offering competitive price packages (Mintel, 2012).
Social	• **The changing cultural, ethnic and religious mix within Western countries** Recent events such as the Syrian crisis, which caused more than 255,000 people to leave the country in a single year, coupled with other conflicts and the overall increasing mobility of individuals due to globalization, means that populations of many Western countries are becoming more diverse. This will create stronger demand for culturally appropriate weddings and other religious/cultural events, providing a host of opportunities for event organizers and related service providers (Euromonitor, 2015c).
Technological	• **The high usage of social media by event attendees** There are now estimated to be over 2 billion social media users worldwide (Euromonitor, 2015c). Not suprisingly, social media has emerged as a key channel for event-goers to get information and updates. Music tourists for example are especially active on social media channels and use them to find out about events, blog and use forums. Music concert and festival organizers have responded to this trend by developing their own social media channels to provide their customers with artist information, schedules and other information, much of which is delivered months in advance (Mintel, 2013).

Figure 2.2   Global forces impacting events

particular event location may mean that marketing materials, food and drink served and the event programme may have to be changed to suit local tastes. Moreover, political unrest and instability may result in some event organizations choosing not to bid to host some events as the costs to secure the company's property and staff in some countries may simply be too high. Event organizations in their enthusiasm to expand their operations overseas may not pay enough attention to the implications that local conditions will have on event operations, often with disastrous consequences. Underestimating the significance of these forces can ultimately be the source of event failure.

It is perhaps taken for granted that event organizations staging events in their own countries will be mindful of their local/community context. However, when local or community events are developed for tourism audiences, event organizers in anticipating tourist revenues can focus too much on international visitors, whilst neglecting the community that hosts the event. This situation can generate a great deal of local resentment towards visitors and the event itself, especially if the event receives public funds. International events management requires the careful balancing of the needs of local and international audiences.

PEST or PESTEL analyses should be done for the country/city/community in which an event takes place to reveal local conditions which can impact an event, event organizations and event tourism, especially those affecting local attendees or stakeholders. Table 2.1 provides a checklist of political, economic, social, technological, environmental and legal factors that are applicable in a local context. Environmental

Table 2.1   Local political, economic, social, technological, environmental and legal factors

Political conditions	• The presence of political unrest • Recent changes in political administrations
Economic circumstances	• Cost of Labour • Currency exchange rates • Wage levels • Interest rates • Reliability of the local banking systems • General living standards
Social trends	• Dominance of particular cultural practices or beliefs • Racial and ethnic make-up of local populations • Openness to outside influences
Technology levels	• Availability of telecommunications infrastructure • Availability of electricity and indoor plumbing • Level of internet penetration amongst local populations
Environmental issues	• Level of environmental consciousness amongst local population • General local weather patterns • Potential for extreme weather conditions due to seasonal fluctuations
Legal requirements	• Visa and work permit requirements • Health and safety laws • Labour laws • Insurance requirements • Regulations governing alcohol, cigarette and drug consumption at indoor and outdoor event venues • Licences and certification required by event staff

and legal factors are especially relevant within a local context, as there is such variation in these factors amongst different countries.

Case Study 2.1 – Chinese Winter Wonderland Comes to Dorset

Global/Local Context

By 2030, the population of China will reach 1.4 billion, making it the second-largest country in the word (Euromonitor International, 2016a). It is also a leading source of the world's tourists, international students and immigrants. China sends the largest number of students abroad for study and is ranked third in terms of numbers of asylum seekers. In 2011 China was ranked first as a source destination for immigrants from OECD countries (Euromonitor International, 2016b).

In the United Kingdom there are estimated to be 523,000 ethnic Chinese, and the number is predicted to rise to 720,000 by 2030 (Euromonitor International, 2016c). A key reason for this increase is the large number of international students that come to the United Kingdom to study. In the academic year 2014–2015, 89,540 Chinese students came to the UK to study – far exceeding the number of students of any other nationality (UK Council for International Student Affairs, 2016). Although the road to immigration and settlement has become increasingly difficult, there are significant numbers who do stay on after graduation to work and there are also other non-student Chinese nationals who settle in the UK. In 2012 the greatest numbers of immigrants to the UK came from China (Dominiczak, 2013). The centre of the Chinese population in the UK is London, which is home to about 30% of all the Chinese living in England and Wales (Office for National Statistics, 2012). However, there are ethnic Chinese resident in counties throughout the country.

Dorset, a county in the south of England, has a small but growing Chinese population. It is one of the least ethnically diverse counties in the United Kingdom, with 91.9% of the population being white and British. However, the last published census data for Dorset showed that residents from Black and minority ethnic groups were increasing – from 3.2% in 2001 to 4.4% in 2011. Chinese residents account for 0.5% of the population in Dorset (Dorset County Council, 2015). Although, as is the case elsewhere in

(Continued)

(Continued)

the UK, international students who typically speak English and are well-educated will account for a proportion of Chinese immigrants who settle in Dorset, many speak no English or speak it poorly. Those without English language skills struggle to participate in Dorset's wider community and access available services. A high proportion work in low-paid sectors. Notably 36% work in the hotel and restaurant industry and 18% in health and social work. These occupations are low paid and require employees to work long unsociable hours which further exacerbates the problems they face participating in their community and accessing vital services such as healthcare (Peters, 2012).

Event Rationale

The Chinese Winter Wonderland was developed as a non-profit project to support the efforts of three organizations – the Dorset Race Equity Council (DREC), the Dorset County Council (DCC) and the Bournemouth Chinese School (BCS). Together these organizations are working to improve the quality of life and counteract the effects of isolation, misunderstanding and discrimination that Chinese people in Dorset are facing. The money raised from the event was to be used to set up a telephone helpline and radio station to support less-able English speakers in Dorset (from Chinese as well as other ethnic minority groups). It was hoped that the helpline and radio station would help these individuals overcome language barriers and be able to better participate in their community and access the services that they needed. The idea for the Chinese Winter Wonderland was derived from a Chinese tradition of setting up markets the week prior to Chinese New Year. These markets feature products related to New Year's celebrations such as flowers, festive foods and decorations. The event was promoted as a traditional celebration of joy and happiness, which welcomed locals and visitors of all nationalities (ChineseWinterWonderland, 2016).

Event Organization

Communications on the event were found on the event website and in local newspapers. Flyers were also distributed in the areas immediately

Figure 2.3　Participants in fashion show at Chinese Winter Wonderland 2016

surrounding the event. Chinese Winter Wonderland also had its own Facebook page which provided those interested in the event with updates on the stalls, the entertainment planned and general information about Chinese New Year and its traditions.

Many of the volunteers that worked at the event were Chinese international students studying at institutions in Dorset but a few that participated were students that came in from London to join the event. Some of the international students participating were from other Asian nationalities. An interesting aspect of the Chinese Winter Wonderland was that, despite its name, it was a fusion event featuring aspects of other Asian cultures such as Thai and Korean. Asians as a group make up 2% of Dorset's population (Dorset County Council, 2015).

Future Outlook

Post-event, the Chinese Winter Wonderland was described in the local media as a first for the south of England and a celebration that attracted hundreds to the streets to experience Chinese culture (Howard, 2016). It seems likely that the Chinese Winter Wonderland will become an annual event, which will continue to showcase the cultures of Chinese and other Asian residents in Dorset.

(Continued)

(Continued)

Figure 2.4   Vietnamese student volunteer

Case Study 2.1 illustrates how migration trends are creating new challenges for host communities as well as opportunities for event managers working in third sector (voluntary and community) and public sector organizations. If current trends persist and Dorset continues to become increasingly diverse, there will be increased demand for events that serve the needs of ethnic minorities. For Dorset's third sector, and public sector organizations which typically lack funding, the availability of international students to serve as volunteers will be of great importance, as will low-cost promotional channels such as Facebook.

Stakeholders

Event stakeholders consist of a variety of individuals, groups and organizations which are impacted by or can influence the outcome of an event. Bowdin et al. (2011) for

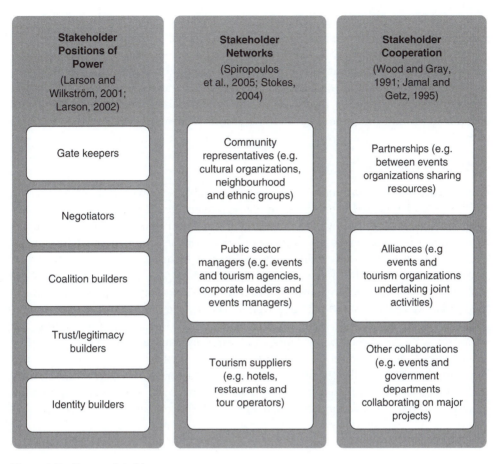

Figure 2.5 Event stakeholder types

example identify participants and spectators, host organizations, host communities, co-workers, media and sponsors as key event stakeholders. Getz (2007), citing a number of research studies, demonstrates how stakeholder theory can be used to analyse how different types of stakeholders can influence the outcome of events (see Figure 2.5).

For event organizers staging events outside of their home countries, understanding stakeholder power relationships, networks and the potential for collaboration amongst stakeholder groups in their events' host communities is particularly important. For example, identification and accessing of gate keepers (those who allow or deny entry to the local market) is an important first step for event organizations wishing to operate outside their country of origin. However, gate keepers can include a diverse group of individuals such as politicians, public sector workers, event managers and community group leaders, so identifying these individuals can be a difficult task. Working through local stakeholder networks and/or forming local collaborations are useful strategies that event organizations can adopt to enter new markets.

Stakeholder management is also important for event organizations staging international events in their own countries. The staging of large-scale events often involves entire communities, cities and also countries and requires the collaboration of stakeholders at multiple levels, especially when these events receive significant amounts of public sector funding (Ferdinand and Williams, 2011).

Resource availability

Events, like other organizations, need rare and valuable resources to build and sustain (in the case of repeated events) a competitive advantage. Signature venues, cutting-edge lighting systems, highly skilled crews and technical personnel are all examples of resources that can make an event stand out from its competitors. International events, in particular, require significant resources which are difficult to estimate in advance and the supply of these resources is subject to seasonal variations. Getz (2007) suggests that event organizations need to consider their positions in relation to the scarcity of resources and take appropriate action (see Figure 2.6).

Event managers staging events outside of their home countries, for example the organizers of international music tours, must carefully consider which resources they will carry with them from home and which they will trust overseas providers to supply. These decisions will be driven by a variety of factors which differ from country to country. A good tour manager will want to minimize costs, whilst ensuring that the quality of a tour across countries is maintained. Moreover, using local suppliers and

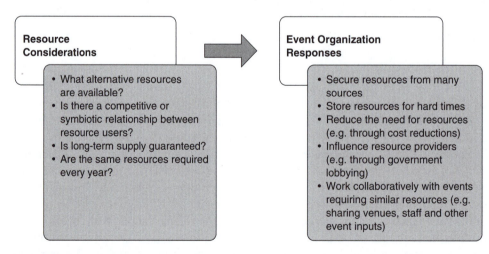

Figure 2.6   Resource considerations and event organization responses

Source: Adapted from Getz (2007)

Table 2.2 Considerations for using local resources

• Are all the resources required for the event available locally?	• Do the practices of local suppliers comply or conflict with the event's/ event organization's values? (For instance, do local suppliers share the event organization's sustainable or ethical values?)
• If there are resources that are not available locally, are there any alternatives?	
• What are the costs of local resources versus the costs of transporting resources from overseas?	• Will a failure to use local resources negatively impact the event? (For example, will local residents protest or boycott an event which does not hire local labour or businesses?)
• Are local resources (e.g. lighting, rigging and staging equipment) compatible with resources that will be brought in from the home country?	• Are there any financial incentives offered for using local resources?
• What is the quality of local resources?	• What has been the experience of the event managers from overseas who have used local resources?

contractors reduces the carbon footprint of an event and also contributes to the economy where the event is being staged, thus providing the event organization with the opportunity to not only save money but actually contribute to the wider society.

However, cost savings strategies need to be approached carefully as they are not appropriate in every instance. For example, in the United States, it is a vital requirement that event managers study union contracts carefully when dealing with unionized musicians and other entertainers. Failure to provide adequate compensation can result in severe penalties (Goldblatt, 2011).

Table 2.2 provides a list of local considerations for event managers working outside their home countries who are thinking about using local resources.

Competition

For event managers unfamiliar with a country, local competitors can be valuable sources of information – such as local trends, fee and pricing structures and the availability of materials and resources. However, event managers should by no means try to duplicate the efforts of local competitors but 'take their best ideas and make them better' (Nuntsu and Shukla, 2005: 183). Competing events within a destination also provide event managers with the opportunity to undertake cross-promotions and strengthen the offering of their individual events. For example, an international conference or exhibition organizer can publicize nearby arts and cultural events happening at the same time, thereby allowing attendees to combine a business trip with some interesting leisure opportunities. Event managers organizing similar or related events can also collaborate to target international audiences, as through collaboration they can offer attendees a package of complimentary events. This allows attendees to make the most of the money spent on travel.

At the same event too much competition or market saturation could signal that a particular type of event is approaching the end of its lifecycle and is in need of reinvention, or that the market is ready for something new and different.

Conversely, the absence of local competitors in the off-peak tourist season of a destination can also present several opportunities for events which target international event audiences. In off-peak tourist seasons the costs of many critical event inputs such as labour, catering and venues tends to be lower. Additionally, events may benefit from the support of local governments and communities for boosting tourism during these low periods. Likewise, hosting events in lesser-known towns or cities, which do not have many competing events, also provides the hosts of international events with many benefits. Lesser-known destinations can provide publicity and focus on an event which more popular ones cannot (Catherwood et al., 1992).

Cultural differences

In a world that is becoming increasingly interconnected, there is a need for event organizations to understand everyday cultural customs and practices which distinguish one country from another. Cultural sensitivity is increasingly relevant in a climate in which many event organizations are bidding for events overseas, and more and more event organizations are beginning to resemble MNCs and TNCs, which have operations which span countries across the globe. For example, event organizations which have employees of varying nationalities and ethnicities need to be aware of the potential pitfalls that can arise from language differences. They must also be mindful of languages spoken by event attendees and ensure that these are translated correctly and accurately. For example, in preparation for the Beijing Olympics there was a huge drive to stamp out 'Chinglish' on signs at public tourist attractions, which could potentially cause embarrassment. However, aside from the misunderstandings that can arise when language is translated, there can also be difficulties when individuals speak the same language but do not have the same communication style. Hall and Hall (1990) highlight four dimensions along which communication patterns amongst societies can be compared (see Table 2.3).

These differences have real implications for the planning and organization of events. For example, it is not uncommon in high-context cultures for agreements to be struck for the staging of events without contracts or with very simple contracts, where as in low-context cultures, contracts are likely to be highly detailed and descriptive. Likewise in monochronic cultures, clients are likely to be insistent on a timely start to a business meeting or conference and look unfavourably upon attendees who are late, whereas in polychronic cultures, a meeting scheduled for a 9:00am start may see attendees arriving up until 9:30am, expecting that others will be waiting for them. Event managers working with clients from cultural backgrounds different from their own need to be sensitive to these differences and be careful not to let personal value judgements affect the fulfilment of clients' requests. It is not up to the event manager to decide when an event should start and end and what its outcome should be.

In addition to language and communication differences, cultural values are becoming more important to event organizations. Perhaps the most influential study

Table 2.3 Dimensions of communication styles

Context	The amount of information that must be explicitly stated if a message or communication is to be successful. North Americans are perhaps the most famous examples of a cultural group which uses low context communication (very explicit in their communication) whereas Asian societies such as Japan and China are noted for high-context communication (much of their communication is implicit or unsaid).
Space	The personal space that must be maintained between individuals whilst communicating. South Americans are known for being particularly close to each other whilst communicating, as opposed to the British, who generally maintain a greater level of personal space.
Time	How time is interpreted – whether as monochronic or polychronic. In monochronic cultures, tasks tend to be tightly scheduled and sequenced one at a time. In polychronic cultures, time is more flexible and multiple tasks are performed at the same time. Germany is renowned for having a culture which is monochronic, as timeliness is highly valued by Germans, whereas their European neighbours from France are known for being polychronic; for French people human interaction and relationship-building are valued more highly than sticking to schedules.
Information flow	The structure and speed at which messages move between individuals and/or organizations, and how action chains work – whether they are geared more towards communication or task completion. The Spanish are known for the speed at which they share information, whereas in countries like the United States information is highly focused and compartmentalized; information flow is much slower.

Source: Adapted from Hall and Hall (1990)

of cultural values is Hofstede's (1991) study of IBM employees, in which he developed empirical profiles of different countries based on five dimensions of basic cultural values. These were power distance, uncertainty avoidance, individualism, masculinity/femininity and long-term/short-term orientation. In his later work, a sixth dimension – indulgence – was added (Hofstede et al., 2010). These are described briefly in Table 2.4.

Table 2.4 Dimensions of basic cultural values

Power distance	This is the degree to which a culture accepts a hierarchical or unequal distribution of power in organizations and society.
Uncertainty avoidance	This is the degree to which cultures accept or avoid risks in everyday life.
Individualism	This is the degree to which individuals see themselves as integrated or separated from social groups and free of or restricted by social pressure.
Masculinity/femininity	This is the degree to which masculine and feminine roles are separated and how un/favourably society looks upon aggressive and materialistic behaviour.
Long-term/short-term orientation	This is the degree to which a society is prepared to put off immediate gratification in favour of long-term goals.
Indulgence	This is the degree to which a society will seek to satisfy their desires as opposed to showing restraint. An indulgent society will seek to enjoy themselves and buy the things they want to make themselves happy.

Source: Adapted from Hofstede et al. (2010)

Table 2.5   Other cultural factors

• Religion	• Humour
• Early socialization and family structures	• Food and eating behaviour
• Small-group behaviour	• Work ethic
• Public behaviour	• Education system
• Leisure pursuits and interests	• Traditions
• Holidays and ceremonies	• History
	• Social class structure

As is the case with communication styles, an awareness of differences in cultural values is very important for event managers, especially when negotiating contracts. Event managers can run the risk of offending potential clients by failing to recognize and observe the protocol involved in very hierarchical organizations. In pitching concepts to clients, the degree of uncertainty avoidance will be an important cultural dimension to consider, as organization within cultures which are more prone to taking risks will be more open to or perhaps even expect concepts which are highly experimental and unusual. Table 2.5 provides a list of some other cultural factors to be considered by event managers.

Case Study 2.2 – Youth Participation in Road Running Events in Taiwan

Overview

This case study focuses on research which sought to explain the current popularity of road running events among young Taiwanese people. Young people between the ages of 18 and 35 were surveyed and asked what motivated them to participate in road running events. Respondents were asked to rate the importance of a number of items, adapted from the motivations of marathoners scale (MOMS) developed by Masters et al. (1993). Demographic information on the young people was also captured to determine whether factors such as age, sex or marital status had any impact on their motivations. It considers other factors too, such as the current push by sports apparel brands to make running sexy, and initiatives on the part the of Taiwanese government to make Taiwanese people more health conscious.

What are Road Running Events?

Road running describes the practice of running that takes place outside of a stadium on roads, pavements and other prepared surfaces (ARC, 2009).

Road running includes events such as half-marathons, marathons and ultra-marathons. A marathon can be defined as a road running event which requires competitors to cover a distance of 42.195km, whereas an ultra-marathon is any running event over 42.195km. An event which is under 42.195km is simply described as road running (Tseng, 2014).

Running in Taiwan

Running and jogging are activities that are becoming increasingly popular amongst Taiwanese youth. In fact, it is now something of a fashion amongst 20- and 30-something professionals in Taiwan, which is readily visible in the trendy sportswear worn by these young men and women. This trend is unique neither to Taiwan nor the current period because the fashion world has often collided with sport. However, globally, it has now reached an unprecedented level. There is a rising demand for running clothing which is both functional and stylish. The major players in the global sport apparel market have responded and they have focused their marketing efforts on making running look sexy, and it seems to have struck a chord.

Despite the current fashion for running and jogging amongst some young Taiwanese people, the country has a higher obesity rate than other Asian countries with a similar level of development, which has resulted in Taiwan having the dubious honour of being the 'fat Asian nation'. Amongst the reasons cited for Taiwan's obesity problems are the increasingly hectic lifestyles led by Taiwanese people and a resulting lack of exercise. Government education programmes are currently being run to educate the population about the importance of health and well-being, and public and private sector organizations have responded by organizing a range of exercise programmes, including running, for Taiwanese people of all ages.

Taiwan is particularly blessed in terms of its ability to provide attractive backdrops for road running. It has a year-round hospitable climate and a varied topography which includes forests, hills and mountains as well as stretches of beaches (Euromonitor International, 2014). In 2015 some 447 running events took place in Taiwan (Weng, 2015). One of the largest road running events in Taiwan is the Taipei International Marathon. Over 120,000 runners participate in this event, including significant numbers of international visitors (Hung, 2012).

(Continued)

(Continued)

The Profile of Taiwan's Youth Participating in Road Running Events

Table 2.6   Profile of survey respondents

Attribute	Percentage (total number of responses = 129)
Gender	
Male	48.1
Female	51.9
Age	
18–20	4.7
21–23	6.2
24–26	10.9
27–29	20.9
30–32	39.5
33–35	17.8
Education	
High school or equivalent	3.9
Undergraduate	73.6
Master's	22.5
Marital status	
Single	76.7
Married	23.3
Family status	
No children	89.9
One or more children	10.1

The survey revealed fairly equal participation between both sexes of Taiwanese youth in road running events – 48.1% of respondents were male whereas 51.9% were female. The most popular age range for respondents was 30–32 years of age, with some 39.5% of respondents belonging to this age group. The vast majority of the participants in road running events that were surveyed were university-level-educated – 96.1% were holders of at least an undergraduate degree. Most of the road runners surveyed were also single and/or had no children – 76.7% were unmarried and 89.9% had no children. These figures are not surprising since Taiwanese in 'middle youth' who are married with children find their lives dominated by home and the office with much of their leisure time being spent in simple television viewing (Euromonitor International, 2014).

Taiwanese Young People's Motivations for Participating in Road Running Events

Table 2.7 Motivations of young Taiwanese to participate in road running events

Motivations	Mean Scores (Answers ranged from 1 to 5, being least important and 5 being most important)
To push myself beyond current limits	4.87
To stay in good physical condition	4.83
To improve my health	4.82
To relieve stress	4.74
To improve my mood	4.66
To concentrate on my thoughts	4.64
To help my body perform better than before	4.62
To compete with myself	4.57
To enjoy an activity with family or friends	4.55
To add sense of meaning to life	4.55
To feel a sense of fulfilment	4.46
To have something in common with other people	4.35
To make my life more complete	4.35
To feel more confident in myself	4.34
To prevent illness	4.29
To feel proud of myself	4.24
To maintain my weight	4.2
To look slim	4.09
To stay physically attractive	3.98
To feel a sense of belonging with my environment	3.98
To improve my running speed	3.96
To socialize with other runners	3.86
To get recognition	3.67
To compete with others	3.63
To get compliments from others	3.28
To make my family and friends feel proud of me	3.23
To beat someone I have never beaten before	2.8

(Continued)

(Continued)

Despite running and jogging being somewhat of a fashion in Taiwan, having something in common with other runners or socializing with other runners were not amongst the top-rated reasons for Taiwanese young people to participate in road running events. The most highly rated motivation was the desire to push themselves beyond their current limits, closely followed by health-related reasons. Staying in good physical condition and improving health were the items which received the second- and third-highest ratings respectively among survey respondents. These findings are perhaps not surprising given that running does in fact offer significant health benefits, such as improving heart and lung capacity and even mental health (Hsieh, 2011), and 72% of Taiwanese who do exercise do so for health reasons (Sports Administration, 2013).

Among respondents there were some differences in terms of the ratings they gave to particular items. For example, men rated competition far more highly than women as a reason for participating in running events. Additionally housewives and the unemployed rated recognition more highly than working individuals and students.

Conclusion and Implications

Despite being described as 'Asia's fat nation' an increasing number of young Taiwanese are exercising and in particular enjoying road running and road running events. Among the possible reasons highlighted in the case study for the trend are global sporting apparel brands portraying a sexy image of running in their advertising and the Taiwanese government's education programmes, which promote the importance of health and well-being. However, the case study has highlighted that participants in road running events are strongly motivated by their own desires to push themselves to achieve something extraordinary, in addition to the various health benefits that running offers. Road running events appear to have specific benefits for individuals from particular demographic groups, such as providing a competitive outlet for young male participants and an opportunity for recognition for housewives and the unemployed. These differences highlight a number of opportunities for international event managers and other organizations involved in the marketing and management of running events.

Case Study Questions

1   What key global and local forces should an event manager pay attention to when taking a new road running event to Taiwan?
2   What opportunities and challenges does Taiwan as a destination pose for an international sponsor seeking brand exposure for a line of sport nutrition drinks and diet supplements?
3   If you were hired to devise a marketing campaign for locals and international visitors to compete in an international marathon in Taiwan, what would your key messages to these different market segments be?

Chapter Summary

This chapter highlighted the need for event managers to take an international approach to events management. The increase in air travel, the proliferation of multinational and trans-national organizations and the increase in market access facilitated by the formation of regional trading blocs and associations have created unprecedented opportunities for event organizations to expand their operations to meet new customer demands. These new opportunities come with the challenges of serving an increasingly international and diverse event audience. To make the most of these opportunities and to minimize any new threats, event managers need to be constantly scanning the environment for global forces that may impact their events, whilst at the same time being conscious of the local conditions within different countries. PEST and PESTEL analyses are valuable tools that can be used for this purpose.

Event managers taking a 'one size fits all' approach may find themselves hosting events which offend local communities and fail to meet client requirements, leading ultimately to event failure. The cultures and customs of societies can have a profound effect on the day-to-day business operations of event organizations with employees of different nationalities. During contract negotiation and event conceptualization, cultural traits such as those described by Hall and Hall (1990) and Hofstede et al. (2010) should be carefully considered by event organizations so that cultural misunderstandings are minimized.

Review Questions

1.   How has globalization expanded the market for international events?
2.   What are some key local conditions that event managers coming to your country should be aware of?

3. How does language differ from communication?
4. Using your own country as an example, highlight how communication styles impact the staging of events.

Additional Resources

Books / Book Chapters / Journal Articles

Meyer, E. (2014). *The Culture Map: Breaking through the Invisible Boundaries of Global Business*. New York: Public Affairs. This book explores how culture impacts the way business is done in different countries.

Rogers, T. and Davidson, R. (2015). *Marketing Destinations and Venues for Conferences, Conventions and Business Events* (2nd edn). Oxon: Routledge. This book provides excellent coverage of the current themes and developments involved in marketing destinations and venues to the MICE sector and includes case examples from across the globe which showcase innovative practices.

Sun, Y. (2015). Shaping Hong Kong cinema's new icon: Milkyway Image at international film festivals. *Transnational Cinemas*, 6(1): 67–83. This paper highlights how film festivals can be used as trans-national platforms for creating new international market opportunities.

Useful Websites

www.euromonitor.com/ – Euromonitor International is the world's leading independent provider of business intelligence on industries, countries and consumers.

www.ises.com/ – ISES is the International Special Event Society, which through its chapters throughout the world provides a range of resources for events managers.

http://oxygen.mintel.com/ – Mintel Oxygen hosts a wide range of market intelligence reports from across the globe including a wide spectrum of leisure activities such as spectator sports, the performing arts, the MICE industry and music concerts and festivals.

References

Ali-Knight, J., Robertson, M. and Fyall, A. (2009). *International Perspectives of Festivals and Events: Paradigms of Analysis*. London: Elsevier.

ARC. (2009). *Road, Cross-country and Trail Running Rules*. UK: ARC.

Bowdin, G., Allen, J., O'Toole, W., Harris, R. and McDonnell, I. (2011). *Events Management* (2nd edn). Oxford: Butterworth-Heinemann.

Burbank, M. J. Andranovich, G. D. and Heying, C. H. (2001). *Olympic Dreams: The Impact of Mega-Events on Local Politics*. Boulder: Reinner Publishers.

Catherwood, D. W., Ernst and Young, and Van Kirk, R. L. (1992). *The Complete Guide to Special Event Management: Business Insights, Financial Advice and Successful Strategies from Ernst and Young, Advisors to the Olympics, the Emmy Awards and the PGA Tour*. Hoboken: John Wiley and Sons.

ChineseWinterWonderland (2016). #About. ChineseWinterWonderland [online]. Retrieved from http://chinesewwonderland.wix.com/chinesewonderland#!-about/cjg9

Davidson, R. and Rogers, T. (2006). *Marketing Destinations and Venues for Conferences, Conventions and Business Events*. Oxford: Butterworth-Heinemann.

Dominiczak, P. (2013, November 28). Most immigrants to the UK now come from China. *The Telegraph* [online]. Retrieved from www.telegraph.co.uk/news/uknews/immigration/10480 785/Most-immigrants-to-the-UK-now-come-from-China-figures-show.html

Doole, I. and Lowe, R. (2012). *International Marketing Strategy: Analysis, Development and Implementation* (6th edn). London: Cengage Learning EMEA.

Dorset County Council (2015). Ethnicity. Dorset County Council [online]. Retrieved from www.dorsetforyou.com/article/325866/Ethnicity

Euromonitor International (2014). Consumer lifestyles in Taiwan. Euromonitor International [online]. Retrieved from www.portal.euromonitor.com/portal/analysis/tab

Euromonitor International (2015a). Global economic forecasts: Q4 2015. Euromonitor International [online]. Retrieved from file:///C:/Users/Nicole/Downloads/Global_Economic_ Forecasts_Q4_2015%20(1).pdf

Euromonitor International (2015b). Cultural diversity and its impacts on consumer markets. Euromonitor International [online]. Retrieved from www.portal.euromonitor.com/portal/ analysis/tab

Euromonitor International (2015c). Top 3 trends in social media for 2015: S-commerce, paid ads and smart social devices. Euromonitor International [online]. Retrieved from www.portal. euromonitor.com/portal/analysis/tab

Euromonitor International (2016a). Tops trends for the digital consumer in 2016. Euromonitor International [online]. Retrieved from: www.portal.euromonitor.com/portal/analysis/tab

Euromonitor International (2016b). China: Country profile. Euromonitor International [online]. Retrieved from www.portal.euromonitor.com/portal/analysis/contentlink

Euromonitor International (2016c). United Kingdom in 2030: The future demographic. Euromonitor International [online]. Retrieved from www.portal.euromonitor.com/portal/analysis/tab

Ferdinand, N. and Williams, N. (2011). Event staging. In S. Page and J. Connell (eds), *The Routledge Handbook of Events* (pp. 234–47). Abingdon: Routledge.

Getz, D. (1998). Event tourism and the authenticity dilemma. In W.F. Theobald (ed.), *Global Tourism* (2nd edn) (pp. 409–27). Oxford: Butterworth-Heinemann.

Getz, D. (2005). *Event Management and Event Tourism* (2nd edn). New York: Cognizant Communication Corporation.

Getz, D. (2007). *Event Studies: Theory, Research and Policy for Planned Events*. Oxford: Butterworth-Heinemann.

Getz, D. and Frisby, W. (1988). Evaluating management effectiveness in community-run festivals. *Journal of Travel Research*, 2: 22–9.

Giulianotti, R. and Klauser, F. (2012). Sport mega-events and 'terrorism': a critical analysis. *International Review for the Sociology of Sport*, 47(3): 307–23.

Goldblatt, J. (2011). *Special Events: A New Generation and the Next Frontier* (6th edn). Hoboken: John Wiley and Sons Inc.

Hall, E. and Hall, M. (1990) *Understanding Cultural Differences*. Yarmouth: Intercultural Press.

Hofstede, G. (1991). *Cultures and Organizations: Software of the Mind*. New York: McGraw-Hill.

Hofstede, G., Hofstede, G. J. and Minkov, M. (2010). *Cultures and Organizations: Software of the Mind* (3rd edn). New York: McGraw-Hill.

Howard, L. (2016, February 1). Pictures: Hundreds visit Chinese Winter Wonderland in Boscombe. *Daily Echo* [online]. Retrieved from www.bournemouthecho.co.uk/news/14242320.PICTURES__ Hundreds_visit_Chinese_Winter_Wonderland_in_Boscombe/

Hseih, L. (2011). *Jogging All Over Taiwan*. CommonWealth Magazine [online]. Retrieved from www.cw.com.tw/article/article.action?id=5004167

Hung, Z. C. (2012). Marathon: 120,000 participants ran! The number of new high in Fubon Marathon. ETtoday [online]. Retrieved from www.ettoday.net/news/20121216/140452.htm

Jamal, T. B. and Getz, D. (1995). Collaboration theory and community tourism planning. *Annals of Tourism Research*, 22(1): 186–204.

Larson, M. (2002). A political approach to relationship marketing: Case study of the Storsjöyran Festival. *International Journal of Tourism Research*, 4(2): 119–43.

Larson, M. and Wikström, E. (2001). Organizing events: Managing conflict and consensus in a political market square. *Event Management,* 7(1): 51–65.

Lawson, F. (2000). *Conference, Congress and Exhibition Facilities: Planning, Design and Management*. Oxford: Architectural Press.

Masters, K. S., Ogles, B. M. and Jolton, J. A. (1993). The development of an instrument to measure motivation for marathon running: The Motivations of Marathoners Scales (MOMS). *Research Quarterly for Exercise and Sport, 64*(2): 134–43.

Mintel (2010). Business travel world wide – International. Mintel [online]. Retrieved from http://0academic.mintel.com.emu.londonmet.ac.uk/sinatra/oxygen_academic/search_results/show-and/display/id=483944

Mintel (2012). The European MICE industry. Mintel [online]. Retrieved from http://academic.mintel.com/display/590632/

Mintel (2013). Music festival tourism – Worldwide. Mintel [online]. Retrieved from http://academic.mintel.com/display/643783/

Morrison, J. (2006). *The International Business Environment: Global and Local Market Places in a Changing World* (2nd edn). New York: Palgrave Macmillan.

Nuntsu, N. and Shukla, N. (2005). Sponsorship. In G. Damster, D. Tassipoulos, P. de Tolly, W. Dry, J. Gasche, D. Johnson and J. Knocker (eds) *Event Management: A Professional Development Approach* (pp. 173–204). Lansdowne: Juta Academic.

Office for National Statistics (2012). 2011 Census: Key statistics for Local Authorities in England and Wales. Office for National Statistics [online]. Retrieved from www.ons.gov.uk/ons/rel/census/2011-census/key-statistics-for-local-authorities-in-england-and-wales/rpt-ethnicity.html#tab-Differences-in-ethnicity-across-local-authorities-

Page, S. and Connell, J. (2011). *The Routledge Handbook of Events*. Abingdon: Routledge.

Peters, S. (2012). *Health Information for Chinese People Living in Dorset: Phase 1*. Dorset LINK [online]. Retrieved from www.healthwatchdorset.co.uk/sites/default/files/Final%2520Report%2520-%2520Chinese%2520Project%2520March%25202012%2520%25284%2529.doc.

Picard, D. and Robinson, M. (2006). Remaking worlds: Festivals, tourism and change. In D. Picard and M. Robinson (eds), *Festivals, Tourism and Social Change: Remaking Worlds* (pp. 1–31). Clevedon: Chanel View Publications.

Richards, G. (2001). *Cultural Attractions and European Tourism*. Oxon: CABI Publishing.

Richards, G. (2007). Introduction: Global trends in cultural tourism. In G. Richards (ed.), *Cultural Tourism: Global and Local Perspectives* (pp. 1–24). New York: Haworth Hospitality Press.

Spiropoulos, S., Gargalianos, D. and Sotiriadou, K. (2005). The 20th Greek festival of Sydney: A stakeholder analysis. *Event Management*, 9(4): 169–83.

Sports Administration (2013). *Report of Sports City*. Taiwan: Sports Administration.

Stokes, R. (2004). A Framework for the Analysis of Events-Tourism Knowledge Networks. *Journal of Hospitality and Tourism Management, 11*(2): 108–22.

Thomas Cook Retail Limited (n.d.). Key dates. Thomas Cook Retail Limited [online]. Retrieved from www.thomascook.com/about-us/thomas-cook-history/key-dates/

Tseng, S. W. (2014). A study of effect road runner endorser on consumers' participation intention (Master's thesis, National Taiwan University, Taiwan). Retrieved from http://ndltd.ncl.edu.tw/cgi-bin/gs32/gsweb.cgi/login?o=dnclcdr&s=id=%22102NTNU5727042%22.&searchmode=basic

UK Council for International Student Affairs (2016). International student statistics: UK Higher Education. UKCISA [online]. Retrieved from www.ukcisa.org.uk/Info-for-universities-colleges--schools/Policy-research--statistics/Research--statistics/International-students-in-UK-HE/#

UK Music (2015). Wish you were here: Music tourism's contribution to the UK economy. UK Music [online]. Retrieved from www.ukmusic.org/assets/general/WYWH_2015Report.pdf

UNWTO (2012). *MICE Industry – An Asia-Pacific Perspective*. UNWTO [online]. Retrieved from http://www.e-unwto.org/doi/pdf/10.18111/9789284414369

UNWTO (2016). *UNWTO World Tourism Barometer*. 14 (advanced release) [online]. Retrieved from http://dtxtq4w60xqpw.cloudfront.net/sites/all/files/pdf/unwto_barom16_01_january_excerpt.pdf

Weng, Y. L. (2015, May 10). Taipei city restricts road race events, steering outside the counties. Chinatimes [online]. Retrieved from http://www.chinatimes.com/newspapers/201505100002 79-260102

Wood, D. J. and Gray, B. (1991). Toward a comprehensive theory of collaboration. *Journal of Applied Behavioral Science*, 27(2): 139–62.

Yeoman, I., Robertson, M., Ali-Knight, J., Drummond, S. and McMahon-Beattie, U. (2004). *Festival and Events Management: An International Arts and Culture Perspective*. Oxford: Butterworth-Heinemann.

Part 2

International Events Management in Practice

In the first part of this text we have established the contextual factors that have facilitated the growth and expansion of international events. Although these events are not a recent phenomenon, a series of environmental factors have converged to create opportunities and challenges for event managers. If Part 1 focused on the environmental (macro) level of analysis, this section to follow will examine the practice of international events at the managerial (micro) level. Throughout this part it will become clear that the actions of individual event managers situated within their organizational settings can inform wider practice. Part 2 consists of eight chapters drawn from a range of international scholars in the field. Each chapter contains insights into practice, which are informed by a combination of contemporary research and event managers' perspectives along with case studies to demonstrate how these practices are implemented.

Ali, Ferdinand and Chidzey examine the key principles of event design in Chapter 3. Event design is managed by the development of an event theme that determines aspects such as creativity and ideas and is cognizant of cultural sensitivity – which, as expected, is particularly important for international events. Once this creative process is determined, event managers focus upon the theme's elements, which include venue choices, catering, entertainment and décor. Following this discussion the authors return to the topic of environmental trends, reinforcing the principles outlined in Part 1 of this text. From this discussion is it clear that event managers need to keep abreast of external environmental changes to ensure their event designs are relevant to the marketplace.

In Chapter 4, Williams outlines the importance of project management principles to successful international events. As such the key aspects of project management are succinctly applied to international events. In doing this Williams highlights the similarities between event management and project management – often separate areas of academic investigation. At the core of the chapter he outlines two models: the first is the event project management model, a five-step model for ensuring that objectives are met and that the event will be effective; the second is a five-phase event process used to ensure that events are managed effectively and in a timely manner, and that organizational learning can occur.

As a service experience, many events hinge upon the quality of their staffing resources. Managing these resources can be challenging particularly when events are relying on an often transient and footloose labour force. In Chapter 5, Johnson outlines the fundamental human resource management (HRM) principles that ensure staff are well sourced, adequately trained and properly motivated to offer an exceptional service. Johnson discusses how the principles of HRM can be challenged in event settings as a precursor to outlining key considerations that would ensure these are overcome through successful volunteer management.

The following two chapters focus on the application of marketing communications principles to international events. In Chapter 6, Gechev presents the peculiarities of event marketing before outlining a strategic approach to its development. Fundamental to this approach is the composition of the marketing mix that aims to successfully position the event in the marketplace. Related to this strategic approach to marketing communications, the following chapter sees Kitchin introduce event sponsorship (Chapter 7). Central to his chapter is the notion that sponsorship is both a resource and a competence. To this end, a five-stage model is presented that outlines various levels whereby event managers can add value to sponsorship management processes.

In Chapter 8, Kitchin and Wilson discuss the importance of financial management, in particular budgeting and financial reporting as it relates to effective and efficient event management. Not only is it critical for event managers to ensure that a sound financial position is maintained; it is also vital that they can communicate this information to a range of stakeholders. In addition to these regulatory principles Ritchie and Reid add a further layer of analysis to event management practice. In Chapter 9, they comprehensively examine the principles and processes of risk management. In particular their examination of risk treatment strategies makes a valuable contribution to how event managers mitigate risk through the implementation of numerous considerations, which if mismanaged could threaten an event's (and their consumers') survival. In seeking to evaluate the practices that have been introduced so far, Tull and Williams in Chapter 10 describe the identification, planning and implementation of evaluation processes for events in an international environment. It is through the successful implementation of an evaluation process that event managers can learn from their experiences and provide their various stakeholders with improved service.

Part 2, by focusing on the core competencies of events management and providing a range of examples from Africa, the Americas, Asia, Australia and Europe, concretizes international events management and its application in a variety of contexts.

It demonstrates the relevance of an international approach for not only event managers working on high-profile events such as the Olympic and Paralympic Games, the UEFA Champions League and the Calabar Festival, but also for those managing national, local and community events such as local exhibitions, religious festivals and weddings. In addition, this section introduces some of the emerging issues in international events management, such as the sustainability agenda and the increasing importance of corporate social responsibility (CSR) as well as the increased direct intervention of certain governments in supporting events, which are explored in greater detail in Part 3.

Event Design

3

Nazia Ali, Nicole Ferdinand and
Michael Chidzey

Learning Objectives

By reading this chapter students should be able to:

- Comprehend the various aspects of developing an event theme in view of the principles involved in theme design
- Recognize key theme elements associated with event design by focusing on venue, catering, entertainment and décor
- Identify international design trends and current trends in event design for consideration in the events management process
- Appreciate the importance of events design in the context of theming in the events management process.

Introduction

This chapter demonstrates the key principles of event design, which include theme development and creativity. The basic elements of theme development are described and the process by which these elements are integrated to build a unified event concept is analysed. The chapter also builds upon earlier chapters to illustrate how event managers should keep up with global social, technological, economic and political trends when considering event design. The chapter includes case studies that highlight the importance of selective event design for international events management.

Events Design and Events Management

Design features as a key activity component in the planning, development and management of events (Berridge, 2010a; Goldblatt and Nelson, 2001; O'Toole, 2011; Silvers, 2007a). In the event management process, Goldblatt and Nelson (2001) note design as a main activity, in addition to research, planning, coordinating and evaluating events. Silvers (2007a) conceptualizes design as a core 'domain' or function within events management, which consists of seven facets: (i) catering; (ii) content; (iii) entertainment; (iv) environment; (v) production; (vi) programme; and (vii) theme. These seven facets should not be considered as singular entities or in isolation, but rather interrelated and interdependent domains which drive events design. In terms of definition, event design according to Adema and Roehl (2010) is a two-fold concept which focuses on: (i) aesthetics of the look and feel of an event; and (ii) functional qualities associated with event success. O'Toole defines event design as 'a purposeful arrangement of elements of an event to maximize the positive impression on the attendees and other key stakeholders' (2011: 183).

Event design as a stimulus activates the five senses of hearing, sight, smell, touch and taste embedded in the event experience. The design of an event is both an experience-maker and experience-enhancer, which provides ample opportunity for the attendee to engage in sensory and emotional interaction with the event. As such, experiences are at the heart of event design. Thus, event design is not simply a matter of production but participation to create memorable and unique happenings. In today's experience economy, events design management should move beyond the ordinary to the extraordinary. Understanding the event's stakeholders is vital for designing an experience that both engages and excites them. According to Brown and James (2004: 53) the design of an event is 'the very heart and soul, the *raison d'être* of any truly great event'. However, despite the central role of design in events 'the job description for the typical event manager fails to include the "design" component' (Brown and James, 2004: 54). Thus it is imperative for international events teams to link theory (knowledge of design) with practice (professional conduct) to 'design management in events' (Berridge, 2010a) or 'theme design management' (Silvers, 2007b), the latter being of relevance to this chapter.

Developing an Event Theme

The emergence of themes in event design has added a dynamic and innovative dimension to events management. Today, theming is playing a critical role in the staging and marketing of events. Event management companies (EMCs) are involved in generating themes for their customers and specializing in theming for special occasions (for example, birthday, Christmas and wedding parties). Bowdin et al. (2011: 507) observe

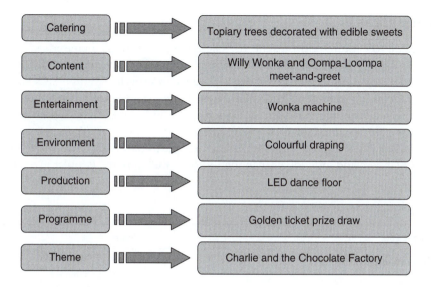

Figure 3.1 Seven facets of design applied to The Chocolate Factory theme

Source: Adapted from Silvers (2007a) and Office Christmas (2011)

that themed parties are a significant part of the event industry. In the United Kingdom, EMCs such as Office Christmas (2011) are involved in theming and event production for Christmas Parties. Office Christmas has hosted the themed event 'The Chocolate Factory' – a design inspired by the British children's author Roald Dahl's book *Charlie and the Chocolate Factory*. As Figure 3.1 illustrates, The Chocolate Factory theme is reflective of Silvers' (2007a) seven facets of design. On a more individual level, private or personal events are organized with themes reflected in, for example, colour, costumes, menu selection and music genres.

Principles

As theming is a characteristic of design, principles of design are applied to developing event themes. There is no consensus amongst event management practitioners about principles of theme design. Brown and James (2004) identify five principles which can be applied to event theme design management: (i) scale – size of event utilizing venue space; (ii) shape – layout of event; (iii) focus – directing attendee gaze to physical elements such as colour or movement; (iv) timing – the event programme/schedule/agenda; and (v) build – ebbs and peaks in an event. Principles of design according to Monroe (2006) 'should have a focus', 'must consider the use of space', and 'must consider and reflect the flow of movement' (cited in Berridge, 2007: 97; and Berridge, 2010a: 190).

Theme Ideas

It is difficult to capture and present the kaleidoscopic array of theme ideas. The aim here is to identify theme ideas that are an embodiment of international diversity and which are a reflection of globalized event product and service. Many EMCs specialize in event theme management, and their event themes, as presented in Table 3.1, are inspired by cultural/national identity, dance, food and drink, film, literature, music, nature, the past, sport, or travel, to mention but a few categories. There are also companies selling event 'theme kits', such as the American-based supplier Stumps selling to event planners and individuals wanting to host a theme party. Popular event themes

Table 3.1   Theme examples

Theme Areas	Ideas
Cultural/national identity	• African theme • Egyptian theme • Moroccan theme
Dance	• Line dance theme • Barn dance theme • Salsa theme
Food and drink	• British pub theme • Boston Tea Party theme • Cadillac diner theme
Film	• Film legends theme • Bollywood theme • James Bond theme
Literature	• Ali Baba theme • Narnia theme • Harry Potter theme
Music	• Jazz and blues theme • Rock 'n' roll theme • Boogie Nights theme
Nature	• Fire and ice theme • Fire theme • Tropical theme
The past	• Legends of the 20th century theme • Medieval theme • Titanic theme
Sport	• Cricket theme • Rugby theme • Sporting heroes theme
Travel	• Orient Express theme • Out of Africa theme • Around the World theme

Source: Adapted from Amazing Party (2011)

identified by Stumps are Arabian, Casino, City, Hollywood and Tropical (Stumps Party, 2011). Themes create what Bowdin et al. (2011: 493) refer to as 'unique and unforgettable events'. This is essential in terms of creating an experience, generating the 'wow' factor, and marketing an event to ensure it is successful in terms of the transition from the intangible to tangible.

Creativity

Developing an event theme is an act of creativity – a skill – and being creative is a prerequisite for a memorable and successful event. Moreover, event design and creativity are inseparable, in view of themes, because together they 'give something a visual identity and recognition' (Berridge, 2010b: 210). This visual communicative role of creativity is reinforced by another statement by Berridge: 'creativity is the one thing that really can make an event stand out from others of a similar kind' (2010a: 192). The act of creativity in event theme design management should, according to Silvers (2007b):

- Use a broad spectrum of stimuli
- Conduct brainstorming and other idea-generating exercises
- Remove restrictions of assumptions and traditions; and
- Combine ideas in new ways and make connections between unrelated ideas.

For creative inventions in event theme design it is vital that conceptions are unique, original and authentic. The uniqueness, originality and authenticity of a theme adds value to the 'wow' factor, but also presents a means of escapism to an imaginary or dream-like world. The notion of escapism is well developed in the context of travel and tourism, whereby tourism frees the tourist from her/his daily alienated life (Cohen, 1979; Cohen and Taylor; 1976; Wearing, 2002). Thus, event themes are articulated to represent a form of temporary escapism; they are beyond the reality of the everyday and produce a new experience from a previous or similar event. Therefore, event theme design requires the event planner and her/his team to adopt a 'blank canvas' approach to creativity. Berridge (2010a) advises against the use of past event design templates as these prohibit creative thinking. He urges event teams to forget about past events when crafting the next memorable experience. However, it may prove difficult to fully implement the 'blank canvas' technique as theme design may be constrained by attendees' desire to 're-live' or 're-visit' various elements of previous events. Therefore, to avoid compromising customer loyalty and retention, the 'blank canvas' approach can be applied to various operative areas of a themed event, rather than the entire theme. For example, with reference to Berridge's (2010a: 196–7) work, the following functional parts of a themed event, which can be creatively adjusted, are seen in Box 3.1.

Functional Parts of a Themed Event

- Sound
- Decorations
- Timeline
- Edible displays
- Interactive décor
- Parades and float design

Cultural Sensitivity in Theme Design

Events are international in form and content, which brings people and populations of different cultures together. As the global and local cultures meet it is important that cultural sensitivity is shown in terms of catering, content, entertainment, environment, production, programming and theming, because what is acceptable in one culture may not be the case in another culture. Despite culture being a significant theme in events design and considering the international reach of the events industry, cultural sensitivity is not well documented or researched in events management. Cultural sensitivity is defined as 'a matter of understanding the international customers, the context and how the international customers will respond to the context' (Clarke and Chen, 2007: 164).

Although event themes can be transferred from one place to another, the way they are staged will differ depending upon the international customers for whom the event is hosted and the country in which the event is taking place. Event planners should be aware of culturally sensitive matters such as attitudes and values within one society, use of body language, religious beliefs, and legal requirements relating to observance of cultural or religious laws. Krugman and Wright (2007), for example, highlight a number of considerations for event managers working in the Middle East:

- Key religious observances (for example, the month of Ramadan which involves fasting – an important pillar of Islam)
- The high value placed on reputation and personal connections – as opposed to contracts
- The need to have name badges which refrain from using nicknames and that don't make holes in the garments of female attendees (for example, by wearing them with a lanyard)
- Many parts of the Middle East use SECAM video systems, which are incompatible with the NTSC and PAL systems (used in the United States of America and Europe respectively).

Allen (2009) also draws attention to the problems that arise when a female event planner goes to an Islamic country, some which do not allow women on business to be unescorted.

Event planners should not shy away from cultural diversity and differences, but rather understand and address the cultural sensitivities they encounter. There are many benefits in accommodating, responding to and valuing cultural diversity and difference in view of theme design in the events management process. The advantage of having knowledge of international cultures gives an event theme a positive image and a competitive and creative edge in the global events market. As Reisinger states:

> The ability to utilize cultural differences and manage cultural diversity can provide the company with competitive advantage. Cultural diversity stimulates greater innovation, creativity, and responsiveness to customer demands and changing environments. (2009: 35)

Diary of an Event Manager – Anonymous, Event Manager, Brazil

This event manager works for an engineering-based firm which sells complex, customized equipment to the oil and gas sector in the Caribbean. Whilst the employees attend a lot of industry events, they do not host them very often. However, the company expanded to Brazil in 2010 and needed to find a way to introduce both the company and its products to Brazil.

The event manager remembers: 'While most multi-national companies are familiar with our products, the largest potential customers in Brazil are not. After examining existing marketing channels, we found that there were very few ways of reaching a geographically distributed audience in our industry. We decided on an event as a way of introducing the company and providing interaction with its products.'

It was crucial to find the right theme for the event. The event manager spoke to the local staff since she didn't want the company to be seen as foreign, noting that Brazilian culture is fiercely nationalistic. The staff suggested a 'home grown' idea in which the company was presented as a local company, using foreign technology and expertise. This theme was critical in selecting the location and it was decided to hold the event in the company's factory, so that customers could see its local staff. Since the venue was critical to making the theme work, the event manager had a big challenge, as production facilities are designed for technical workers and not for executives in suits.

(Continued)

(Continued)

The event manager also recalls: 'To make sure that visitors had a good experience, we stopped production for the day, but kept staff around to talk to visitors. This was a bit risky since our members of staff have differing educational levels, but we felt it was important to show that our products were made in Brazil, by Brazilians. We needed to train the staff to ensure that they would be able to answer questions or direct visitors to where the information could be found. In the middle of the factory we placed a locally made unit, painted in the colours of the Brazil national flag.'

Paying attention to Brazilian nationalism served this company very well and the event was very successful in introducing the company as a new local provider in the Brazilian market.

Theme Elements

Theme elements (for example, venue, catering, entertainment and décor) must be aligned with the event taking place (Bowdin et al., 2011). However, the importance of theme elements, in addition to creation of experiences, should consider the creation of emotional connections with an event (Nelson, 2009). After all, being 'wowed' and constantly reminded of the unforgettable is an emotional response to a significant occurrence in one's life. There are several ways that event theme design elements can be exploited to bridge experiences and emotions for both host and guests. It is achieved through drama, atmosphere and service delivery. Nelson (2009) – using Goffman's (1959) theory of dramaturgy, Kotler's (1973) conceptualizations of atmospherics, and Bitner's (1992) practices of servicescapes – presents a framework for studying theme elements as stimulants of experience and emotional connections in the context of design. Goffman's (1959) dramaturgy links to emotional connections formed through experiences with the event settings; Kotler's (1973) atmospherics draws upon emotions active through sensory experiences; and Bitner's (1992) servicescapes emotionally attach the attendee to a themed event through interactive experiences.

Venue

A venue is an essential ingredient in the management of planned event environments and is noted by Bowdin et al. (2011: 495) as an 'obvious part of the theme of the event'. Furthermore, O'Toole (2011: 193) states that venue location and layout are 'essential elements in event success'. When designing international events, agencies can assist with venue-sourcing arrangements. Organizations like the Hogg Robinson Group manage business travel and also venue arrangements for international brands such as Vodafone. The venue, selected provides the scaffolding around and within which to stage the themed event, consequently dictating the spatial layout. Venue layout has a bearing on the social interactions that take place between the hosts and guests (Nelson, 2009). The objective is to match the scale of the themed event to the venue, which subsequently influences the design principles by ordering the movement, experiences and emotions of audiences once they are encapsulated in the theme (Brown and James, 2004). There are many search techniques available to the event planners to ensure the right venue is selected, because location is core to event design and experience. Lindsey (2009) identifies five key avenues to explore during the pre-production stage when venue selection takes place:

- Trade books/CD-ROMs
- Tourist boards
- The internet
- Word of mouth
- Head/Sales offices.

Venues can be transformed or used in their original form to complement an event theme. The Ice Hotel (Quebec, Canada) is a venue which is built entirely from ice and is a perfect backdrop for a fairytale themed wedding. There is a wedding package put together by the Ice Hotel for potential customers wishing to stage a unique experience, such as a 'magical' fairytale wedding which consists of, for example, the use of the ice chapel and a stay in the Ice Hotel's theme suite with a fireplace (Hôtel de Glace, n.d.). Many EMCs plan Christmas parties for corporate clientele, requiring a link between venue and theme, which often requires considerable transformation. The Ultimate Experience event-organizers transform The Pavilion at the Tower of London to host the 'Bejewelled' theme (Ultimate Experience, 2007).

Catering

Bowdin et al. (2011: 507) recognize catering as a 'major element in staging, depending on the theme and nature of an event'. The choice of catering is as important as venue selection because the quality of food and beverages is a vital ingredient in visitor experience (Shone and Parry, 2010). Thus, as a sensory stimulator, the aromas and flavours of cuisine are critical in enhancing the thematic design and experience of an event. Catering design consists of such facets as menu selection, service style, alcohol management and catering operations (Silvers, 2007a). Food and drink provisions and functions in an event could be directed by a given theme, which interrelates with other aspects of design such as content, entertainment, environment, production and programme. The catering design may be unconsciously and/or consciously driven by whether the character of an event theme is the sacred or profane. A Bollywood-themed celebration could consist of servings of Asian-inspired gastronomy such as vegetable samosa for starters, curry and rice for main course and a selection of sweet-meats for dessert.

Catering design influenced by a certain event theme is evident in the following examples:

- Arabian-Nights/harem-themed party: filled vine leaves, Matbuha (Moroccan cooked salad with grilled peppers and tomatoes), couscous with chicken and vegetables, and sahlab for dessert (Harem Nights, n.d.).
- Retro-themed party: 'retro crisps' (Space Invaders, Wotsits and Monster Munch), pots of baked beans and toasted fingers, tea cups of prawn and salmon cocktail, mini iced fairy cakes, pots of candyfloss, and jelly and cream (Purple Grape Catering, 2011).
- Medieval-themed event: duck liver and wild mushroom pâté with spiced fruit chutney and Melba toast, luxury game pie (venison, pheasant, rabbit and pork), cabbage sautéed with apple and cider, steamed morello cherry pudding with fresh custard and hot mulled wine spiced with cinnamon, nutmeg, and cloves and ginger (Bonafide Food Company, n.d.).

Entertainment

Another prerequisite, in addition to venue and catering choice, is entertainment for a themed event. Many events, whether themed or not, would not be complete without some form of entertainment for attendees. When used, entertainment is a communicative device in an event which captivates the feelings and emotions of a guest, and cultivates the memories of the attendee (Matthews, 2008). The entertainment domain can be formal/informal, have appearances by celebrity look-a-likes or roving street entertainers, and performances by magicians or stand-up comedians (Berridge, 2010a). Entertainment in events, according to Matthews (2008), has evolved around four genres: (i) singing or music; (ii) storytelling/theatre; (iii) dance; and (iv) athletes or athletic pursuits. The reasons for entertainment in an event are wide and varied, but fall into eight distinct categories: (i) education; (ii) physically moving people; (iii) emotionally moving people; (iv) motivating and inspiring people; (v) decorations; (vi) announcing, introducing or advertising; (vii) creating ambience; and (viii) rewarding performance and for image purposes (Matthews, 2008). In the context of atmospherics and service-scapes, entertainment can be utilized to manipulate emotions and memories as a means of creating experiences at a themed event (Nelson, 2009). In Table 3.2 are presented some themed events where entertainment plays a central role.

Table 3.2 Themed events featuring entertainment

Theme	Entertainment
African event	Adungu (acoustic traditional African instrument), bass guitar, saxophone, African drums, tube fiddle, calabash, singers and dancers.
Bollywood event	Sitar and tabla players, and bands, dancers, karaoke, DJ and roadshows, props, Bhangra dancers and solo artists and duos of Bollywood style.
Medieval event	Jolly jesters and plague victims, medieval props, fire-eaters and performers, medieval-themed side stalls, caricaturists, medieval inflatable games, minstrels, medieval-themed stilt walkers, and DJ.
Las Vegas event	Las Vegas showgirls, Las Vegas casino tables with professional croupiers, Elvis and Rat Pack tributes and swing bands, Las Vegas props, 8-lane giant Scalextric, fireworks, DJ and disco.

Source: Adapted from Theme My Party (2010)

Décor

When staging a themed event, décor, as an act of creativity and ambience maker, has a bearing on the success of an event environment. Décor is reflective of theming because it involves transforming ordinary mundane spaces into innovatively 'wowing' settings. Types of décor available to an event planner are vast, and these can be utilized to construct an event theme. Some examples of décor are backdrops, themed sets, props, fabrics and soft goods, banners and signs, tension fabric structures, people or creatures, floral displays, inflatable materials, and elements of nature (Matthews, 2008). Matthews also draws attention to the 'escape' characteristic of décor in any event:

> People attend events to be transported into an environment that is different from their everyday life, whether it is a concert, a championship football game, or a formal dinner. (2008: 59)

The escapist or imaginary function of themed events in the context of décor requires both the host and guest to enter the world of make-believe. At a themed event, for example a Wild West setting, audiences may be requested to dress-up as cowboys or sheriffs to reflect the design of the event and to play an integral part of the entertainment (Bowdin et al., 2011).

Décor can be inspired by many thematic preferences, such as the traditional or modern, classic or chic styles, choice of flowers and floral arrangements, plain or patterned drapes and backdrops, special effects and sculptures. For an Asian wedding some main decorative areas are table centre-pieces, chair decorations, and table décor. Asian wedding planners Exclusive Events, based in the United Kingdom, Dubai, India and the United States of America, provide such decorations and props as stage sets, swings, sofas and stools; mandap backdrops and stage drapes; red carpet and aisle runners; LED and uplighting; mandap stage pillars and pedestals; aisle arches; pillars and pedestals; and aisle/foyer decoration and props (Exclusive Events, 2009/2010). The following images, in Figure 3.2, taken at an Asian wedding, are designed with the colour theme of pink, which is reflected in one of the table centre-pieces, chair decorations, table décor and stage drapes. Pink (according to Colour Wheel Pro, a colour scheme software tool) 'signifies romance, love and friendship' (cited in Matthews, 2008: 64).

Table centre-piece

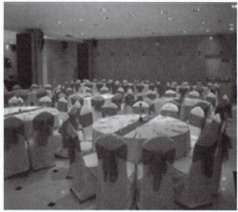

Chair décor

Table décor

Stage drapes

Figure 3.2   Theming with a pink colour scheme

Case Study 3.1 – When 'CEE' Spells 'Team': Meeting Nike Europe's Teambuilding Design Challenge by Chillisauce Limited

About Chillisauce Limited

Chillisauce Limited is an event production company that offers a variety of events which range from adventure weekends to corporate events. Established in 2002, Chillisauce aims to be more interesting, more creative, more resourceful and less predictable in everything it does. This dedication to continuous improvement has been rewarded, both in terms of customer growth and retention (Chillisauce boasts over 140,000 customers and organizes over 700 corporate events annually) and in terms of recognition by the UK events industry. In 2010 Chillisauce was the proud recipient of an Eventia Gold Award and the Event Management Grand Prix prize from the UK Event Awards. Well-known sports apparel brand Nike is one of many organizations that have approached Chillisauce with a request for a bespoke event which could achieve a variety of corporate as well as social objectives.

The Client Brief

Nike required an event to bring their European Head Quarters (EHQ) Central and Eastern Europe (CEE) team together in a relaxed, social environment, whilst promoting cross-department introductions and interaction. They also wanted to introduce the CEE leadership team in an informal setting and style whilst delivering a young, fun, interactive and artistic event. They required an afternoon event to take place in a unique urban venue located close to Hilversum in the Netherlands. The event would be for 100 Nike employees aged between 26 and 46 years of age.

Chillisauce's Response

Chillisauce recommended and provided the following:

- Venue and all facilities
- Team-building activity including all staff and equipment
- Catering

(Continued)

(Continued)

- DJ
- Creative introduction for leadership team
- Full event management (pre-, on-site and post-event)
- Evaluation and debrief.

Chillisauce suggested two creative solutions:

1   'Masterpiece Challenge', which required the whole group to create an oversized, replica of a bespoke design specifically for Nike. The group would be broken down into smaller teams and each team would work on their own segment of the design before the finale when all the pieces would be collated to create the final image.
2   '3D Letters', which would require the whole group to work together to design and craft 6ft 3D letters, spelling out CEE. The format would be similar to the Masterpiece Challenge, splitting the teams and collating each team's artwork into one for the finale. These letters would then be sealed with resin and displayed on the Nike campus.

Chillisauce suggested a venue in Westerpark, Amsterdam. This venue is also used for music gigs and has a very unique interior: industrial, urban décor,

Figure 3.3   Event venue in Westerpark, Amsterdam

graffiti art, tinted windows and the raw touch that Nike was looking for to echo their brand and image.

For an alternative way of introducing the leadership team, Chillisauce suggested that a DJ, comedian, rap artist or interactive screens could be used.

The Event

The 3D Letters option was chosen as the afternoon activity as it is unique, creative and incorporates a number of business benefits that tie in with Nike's requirements:

- Allowing staff to be aware of the bigger picture rather than focusing on individual tasks.
- Helping them to build trust between people that work together.
- Demonstrating issues related to team dynamics, problem solving, time management, organization, and leadership under time constraints.
- Creating a tangible statement that CEE (the smallest team on the Nike campus) are present and ready to grow.

Figure 3.4 Team members working together   **Figure 3.5** Completed giant CEE letters

The comedian was the selected means of presenting the leadership team, offering a comedic and entertaining edge. This enabled the CEE staff to get to know the leadership team in a relaxed and informal environment. A local comedian interviewed the seven members of the leadership team on stage, allowing guests to learn a little bit more about each individual. Once the interviews were completed, guests enjoyed food (including local favourites) and

(Continued)

(Continued)

drink, and were entertained by a local DJ. The event took place in Westerpark, Amsterdam, as suggested by Chillisauce and the venue was transformed specifically for the event.

Feedback on the Event

'The pre-event work you did was fantastic. The venue was perfect. Timelines and budget were clear. You were very responsive to many changes and requests regarding the creative. It was all very well-handled.'

'As for the event itself, I have heard it was a fantastic success. The letters look absolutely fantastic.'

Design Trends

The operations of the events industry stretch beyond the local to the global, and thus the sector is affected by international happenings and developments. As event theme design indicates, it does not matter where in the world an event is taking place: it can be created to reflect people, places and populations elsewhere. Thus, the events industry is a globalized product and service, which requires the events sector to keep up with international trends and current developments in event design in order to continue to create unforgettable and unique experiences (see also Ferdinand et al., Chapter 2 of this volume). The global trends examined in this section are based upon an external environmental scan, which consists of an analysis of political, economic, social and technological trends, as described in Chapter 2. The environmental scanning of future event design conducted by Adema and Roehl (2010) informs event design management with a view to keeping up with global trends. Current trends in event design focus upon issues of sustainability in the context of natural environments. As a consequence of climate change and the need to reduce the negative environmental impacts of events, it has been necessary, as part of the events management process, to respond to such environmental concerns.

Keeping Up with Global Trends

Events design will need to keep up with global trends in view of political, economic, social and technological changes. Moreover, these developments will have an impact upon the choice, design and management of future themed events. The environmental scan conducted by Adema and Roehl (2010) to study the future of event design offers an insight into the global trends that the events sector has to take note of. Adema and Roehl (2010) conducted interviews with eight event industry leaders who held influential positions in event production, event professional associations, and event education. Table 3.3 presents selected responses of these interviewees.

Table 3.3   Global trends in events design

Trend	Events Industry Perspective	Influence on Theming of Events
Social	'The actual world system will move so we're watching an evolution and I think events encapsulate that. They [events] are the opportunity where large groups of people come together to exchange emotions and feelings; that is, after all, what drives the world.'	To keep up with global happenings, which are of importance to different people and populations, and expose these in themed event settings. This will entail focusing on the 'non-business' element of the events industry as core in delivering the themed service encounter.
Technological	'I think you are going to see a huge integration of digital media online. You have already seen the capabilities of systems like Vivien design; the next step would be to take Vivien and if you could project it on the walls ... creating an event design backdrop in the room by either rear projection or front projection so that it creates a dimensional feel as well in the room but it is all produced by visual media.'	To keep up with the ever-evolving technological advancements at both national and international levels. Technology can be utilized to create virtual themed event settings inside (and outside) of venues and, with the power of 3D, transport attendees to different themed worlds. Also, theme elements such as décor can be easily created and adjusted to suit the needs of customers through the use of digital media.
Economic	'I think controlling costs and finding more value for less money is going to be the link to a lot of people's success.'	To keep up with design trends with limited budgets is a challenge. Cost can be controlled by sourcing local suppliers and forming EMC partnerships on both a national and international scale.
Political	'What I think we are seeing right now is that there is a change in government as there has been here [US] and a change in government in the UK; and I think we are moving into an area where there is going to be more caring in the world at a higher social agenda, and we are going to use all our resources and skills to try to make the world a better place than just turn a profit.'	To keep up with current political affairs, especially those promoting corporate socio-political responsibility. As national and international government agendas are driven by the concept of 'change', this needs to be embedded in the event theme design. Themed events could take on a political value and ask themselves – How, after this event, is the world a better or 'changed' place?

Source: Adapted from Adema and Roehl (2010: 202)

Current Trends in Event Design

The critical current trend identified to have an impact upon event design is environmental sustainability, which extends the analysis of external factors discussed in the previous section. Sustainable event management has emerged as a response to climate change and reducing the carbon footprint of global citizens. The BS 8901 – the British Standard for Sustainable Event Management – is used in Britain to ensure that planning, development and management of events do not compromise environmental resources (see also Cavagnaro et al., Chapter 12 this volume). Although no separate guidelines for 'greener' themed events can be found, the principles and checklists for events in general can be applied to ensure BS 8901 Sustainable Event Management is implemented. Many leading organizations and venues in the United Kingdom have sought to be compliant with BS 8901, for example Lords Cricket Ground, Seventeen Events, Live Nation, and London 2012 Olympics and Paralympic Games sites. Evidence suggests that the Olympic and Paralympic Games in 2012 prompted the creation of BS 8901:

> It's no secret that the creation of BS 8901 was promoted by the Olympic Games coming to London in 2012. Yet for every community, social, sporting or business event, the implications of using the standard reach far beyond a specific date in the calendar. At its heart, BS 8901 is a *whole new way of doing business*, building communities and managing enduring meaningful legacies. No matter how hard the present circumstances might seem, it offers a completely new way of planning a *practical* sustainable future by realising direct benefits in the present. (Sustainable Events Group, 2010, emphasis in original)

For event theme design management much can be learnt and put into practice in the theme elements of venue, catering, entertainment and décor. With reference to various guidelines and publications, event theme design can be sustainable, without compromising the uniqueness and 'wow' factor associated with experience, in the following ways:

- *Venue*: Use venues with environmental certification to a national or international standard, such as ISO 14001, ISO 201121, BS 8901 or BS 8555; or provide well-advertised and clearly-labelled recycling facilities (DEFRA, 2007).
- *Catering*: Serve Fairtrade products, such as coffee, tea and chocolate, or fresh food rather than prepared desserts (DEFRA, 2007).
- *Entertainment*: Supply sustainable lighting and audiovisual equipment (Seventeen Events, 2011); or use a venue which provides in-house audio equipment, as this reduces the need for transportation (DEFRA, 2007).
- *Décor*: Hire rather than purchase equipment or materials; or use reusable display materials and present materials in reusable format (Government Office for the South-West, 2010).

Case Study 3.2 – Turning Old into New York: The International Student Fusion Fashion Show

Overview

The Fusion Fashion Show hosted at Bournemouth University (BU) in the South of England was a concept developed by five of its MSc Events Management students. The group of students, who went by the name LATL Event Solutions, wanted to host an event which would interest BU's students and also members of the public who lived and worked within the vicinity of the university. They needed to attract not only attendees but also volunteers and stakeholders, such as sponsors to provide them with the required expertise and resources to make their event a success. None of the students possessed skills in fashion design; some had virtually no experience organizing events of any kind; and they had just eight weeks to take their Fusion Fashion Show from concept to reality. One of the key reasons that LATL was successful is the thought and attention the group members gave to the design elements of the fashion show.

Theme

LATL knew that they had to choose a theme that would translate well to BU's students and especially its master's students. In the academic year that the Fusion Fashion Show took place, there were 2,610 international students from 125 countries enrolled at BU, which was just under 15% of the university's total student population (Bournemouth University, 2015). However, on many of the university's master's courses the percentage of international students is close to 100%. For example, among the group of students which comprised LATL there was only one British student; the other four international students came from three different countries. There were also very few British students taking the course. The group settled on New York as their central theme because it is a city that is well known throughout the world and it is associated with fashion. The second aspect of their theme was turning old into new, which reflected LATL's collaboration with a charity clothing shop run by the People's Dispensary for Sick Animals (PDSA), which is the UK's leading veterinary charity (PDSA, n.d.). This charity supplied LATL with all the clothing that was shown at the fashion show. LATL in return donated all the proceeds from the fashion show to the charity. See Figures 3.6 and 3.7.

(Continued)

(Continued)

Figure 3.6   Stylist and model in front of New York-themed backdrop

Figure 3.7   PDSA charity shop

Catering

The catering for the fashion show was limited to providing non-alcoholic beverages to attendees.

Content

Much of the content of the fashion show was focused on communicating the event's theme, 'Turning Old into New York'. The fashion show was divided into five segments representing the five boroughs of New York – the Bronx, Manhattan, Brooklyn, Queens and Staten Island (Borangno, 2015). The models for the fashion show represented the diversity of not only New York's fashion scene but also the masters students at BU. There was a mix of ethnic groups, nationalities and body types represented in the fashion show. The fashions featured were styled with used clothing from the PDSA's charity shop but put together in a new way by students from BU's Fashion Network. There was also a photo booth for attendees with a backdrop featuring black and white images of New York. See Figure 3.6 above. Additionally, before and after the fashion show the PDSA ran a clothing stall and there was a raffle. These activities were to provide the PDSA with additional avenues for fund raising.

Entertainment

The focus of the entertainment was the fashion show. However, before and after the fashion show, attendees were treated to music played by the fashion show's DJ.

Environment

LATL had a considerable challenge in converting the venue they had chosen – the university's teaching restaurant – into a fashion show runway. This was achieved by rearranging the restaurant's seating into a U-shape and using red carpet as a runway. Lighting illuminated the ceiling above the runway. One of the restaurant's semi-enclosed areas was used as a clothing stall. Throughout the venue there were also black and white images of New York.

(Continued)

(Continued)

Production and Programme

The main production elements in the fashion show were the music and lighting, which was red, white and blue – colours found in the flag of the United States of America and also associated with New York (for example, red, white and blue are the team colours of the New York Yankees). See Figure 3.8. The programme was limited to two hours, running from 5:30pm to 7:30pm. The fashion show was just half-an-hour, leaving attendees with about an hour of shopping time in the PDSA's clothing stall. See Figure 3.9.

Figure 3.8   Red carpet runway illuminated with red, white and blue lighting

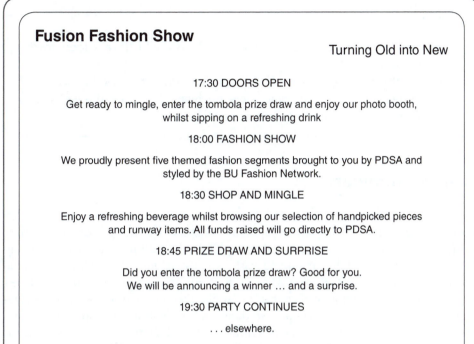

Fusion Fashion Show

Turning Old into New

17:30 DOORS OPEN

Get ready to mingle, enter the tombola prize draw and enjoy our photo booth, whilst sipping on a refreshing drink

18:00 FASHION SHOW

We proudly present five themed fashion segments brought to you by PDSA and styled by the BU Fashion Network.

18:30 SHOP AND MINGLE

Enjoy a refreshing beverage whilst browsing our selection of handpicked pieces and runway items. All funds raised will go directly to PDSA.

18:45 PRIZE DRAW AND SURPRISE

Did you enter the tombola prize draw? Good for you.
We will be announcing a winner … and a surprise.

19:30 PARTY CONTINUES

. . . elsewhere.

We really hope you will have a great time with us tonight.

Figure 3.9   Fusion Fashion programme

Event Results

BU students and also members of the public came out in their numbers to support a good cause. All 80 tickets for the fashion show were sold out and LATL raised a total of £322 for the PDSA (Chipperfield, 2015).

Case Study Questions

1   Which principles of design are evident in the case study? Describe how LATL executed these principles.
2   How did LATL address the cultural diversity of attendees at their event? What additional steps might they have taken?
3   LATL did not want to spend too much of their budget on décor because they wanted to make as large a donation as possible to charity. With this

(Continued)

(Continued)

in mind suggest some low-cost ideas which could have added to the event's décor.

4   Go to the Fusion Fashion Show website: http://t-r-a-v-e-l-e-r.wix.com/fusion-fashion-show. List some ways in which LATL used the website to communicate the event's theme.

Chapter Summary

This chapter on event design has considered matters relevant to theming of events in view of developing an event theme, theme elements and design trends. A variety of case examples have been included to highlight the international reach of event theme design management in staging various celebrations. Although much of the practice of theming events is skewed towards North America and Europe, the developmental and professional aspects can be applied to international events management. Event educators, planners and students should embrace global diversity and difference in their teaching, management and study of theming in events. There is an opportunity for intercultural dialogue through theming, which can contribute to alleviating cultural misunderstandings. This intercultural communication and recognition of culturally sensitive issues can enhance an event's design and experience, and continue to create unique, unforgettable and memorable encounters through theming. Theming compels the international events management educator, planner and student to consider the two worlds of events – the business (experience economy) and non-business (emotion-making) dimensions – when reaching out to event audiences.

Review Questions

1. What are the opportunities and challenges facing event managers in developing event themes for culturally diverse attendees?
2. Why do you think it is important to include the 'design' component in job descriptions for event managers?
3. How will global social, technological, economic, political and environmental changes affect event design in the future?
4. You have been asked to design a theme for an event entitled *Fast-Forward – Life in the Year 2112*. Consider the following theme elements: the venue, catering, entertainment and décor.

Acknowledgement

The authors wish to thank Mr William Bicknell, Director, Chillisauce, for giving permission for the reproduction of Case Study 3.1, which has been taken from www.add chillisauce.co.uk/work/nike

The authors also wish to thank LATL and Andrew Clements for the images used in Case Study 3.2. For more on the event, please go to the event's web page: http://t-r-a-v-e-l-e-r. wix.com/fusion-fashion-show

Additional Resources

Books / Book Chapters / Journal Articles

Berridge, G. (2010). Design management of events. In D. Tassiopoulos (ed.), *Events Management: A Developmental and Managerial Approach* (3rd edn) (pp. 185–206). Claremont, SA: Jutta. An informative chapter which demonstrates how a design-centric approach can be taken to events.

Bowdin, G., Allen, J., O'Toole, W., Harris, R. and McDonnell, I. (2011). *Events Management* (3rd edn). Oxford: Butterworth-Heinemann. This text includes chapters which focus on several of the key areas of event design, such as event conceptualization and staging.

Nelson, K. B. (2009). Enhancing the attendee's experience through creative design of the event environment: Applying Goffman's dramaturgical perspective. *Journal of Convention and Event Tourism*, *10*: 120–33. This article demonstrates that theatrical principles can be applied in event design.

Reisinger, Y. (2009). *International Tourism: Cultures and Behavior*. Oxford: Butterworth-Heinemann. Provides comprehensive coverage of cross-cultural issues and behavior in tourism including cultural events and festivals.

Shone, A. and Parry, B. (2010). *Successful Event Management* (3rd edn). Hampshire: Cengage Learning. A text which takes a practical approach to event design.

Useful Websites

www.aeme.org – A resource for event management educators which includes articles on the latest developments in the subject area.

www.juliasilvers.com – A website which features articles on the core areas of the EMBOK, including a specific focus on event design.

www.thesustainableeventsgroup.com – Features resources to help the public and private sector design, develop and implement sustainable event management systems.

References

Adema, K. L. and Roehl, W. S. (2010). Environmental scanning the future of event design. *International Journal of Hospitality Management*, *29*: 199–207.

Allen, J. (2009). *Event Planning Ethics and Etiquette: A Principled Approach to the Business of Special Event Planning*. Mississauga: John Wiley and Sons Canada.

Amazing Party (2011). Themed party, party themes and themed events. Amazing Party Themes [online]. Retrieved from www.amazingpartythemes.com/themes/THEMES.HTM

Berridge, G (2007). *Events Design and Experience*. Oxford: Butterworth-Heinemann.

Berridge, G. (2010a). Design management of events. In D. Tassiopoulous (ed.), *Events Management: A Developmental and Managerial Approach* (3rd edn) (pp. 185–206). Claremont, SA: Jutta.

Berridge, G. (2010b). Event pitching: The role of design and creativity. *International Journal of Hospitality Management, 29*: 208–15.

Bitner, M. J. (1992). Servicescapes: The impact of physical surroundings on customers and employees. *Journal of Marketing, 56*(2): 57–71.

The Bonafide Food Company (n.d.). Themed catering: Something a little different. Bonafide Food Company [online]. Retrieved from www.thebonafidefoodcompany.com/themed.htm

Borangno, L. (2015, March 7). Hands helping hands [blog post online]. Retrieved from http://t-r-a-v-e-l-e-r.wix.com/fusion-fashion-show?fb_ref=Default#!Hands-helping-hands/cmbz/54fad3530cf245859778df51

Bournemouth University (2015). Annual Review 2015. Bournemouth University [online]. Retrieved from www1.bournemouth.ac.uk/about/governance/annual-review-2015/bu-numbers

Bowdin, G., Allen, J., O'Toole, W., Harris, R. and McDonnell, I. (2011). *Events Management* (3rd edn). Oxford: Butterworth-Heinemann.

Brown, S. and James, J. (2004). Event design and management: Ritual or sacrifice? In I. Yeoman, M. Robertson, J. Ali-Knight, S. Drummond and U. McMahon-Beattie (eds), *Festival and Events Management: An International Arts and Culture Perspective* (pp. 53–64). Oxford: Elsevier Butterworth-Heinemann.

Chipperfield, H. (2015, March 27). The launch of the Fusion Fashion Show [blog post online]. Retrieved from http://t-r-a-v-e-l-e-r.wix.com/fusion-fashion-show?fb_ref=Default#!The-Launch-of-Fusion-Fashion-Show/cmbz/5514c7a50cf22035305c541e

Clarke, A. and Chen, W. (2007). *International Hospitality Management: Concepts and Cases*. Oxford: Butterworth-Heinemann.

Cohen, E. (1979). A phenomenology of tourist experiences. *Sociology, 13*: 179–201.

Cohen, E. and Taylor, L. (1976). *Escape Attempts: The Theory and Practice of Resistance of Everyday Life*. London: Allen Lane.

DEFRA (Department for Environment, Food and Rural Affairs) (2007). *Sustainable Events Guide*. London: DEFRA.

Exclusive Events (2009/2010). Asian weddings. Exclusive Events [online]. Retrieved from www.exclusiveevents.com/mandaps/asian-wedding-decorations.asp

Goffman, E. (1959). *The Presentation of Self in Everyday Life*. New York: Anchor Books.

Goldblatt, J. and Nelson, K. S. (2001). *The International Dictionary of Event Management*. New York: John Wiley and Sons.

Government Office for the South-West (2010). Greener events: A guide to reducing the environmental impacts of conferences and seminars. Our South West [online]. Retrieved from www.oursouthwest.com

Harem Nights (n.d.). Arabian night parties. Harem Nights [online]. Retrieved from www.haremnights.co.uk/party_themes.htm

Hôtel de Glace (n.d.) A magical wedding. Ice Hotel Canada [oinline]. Retrieved from www.icehotel-canada.com/hotel.php?action=mariage3

Kotler, P. (1973). Atmospherics as a marketing tool. *Journal of Retailing,49*(4): 48–64.

Krugman, C. and Wright, R. R. (2007). *Global Meetings and Exhibitions*. Hoboken, NJ: Wiley.

Lindsey, K. (2009). *Happiness is a Ticked-Off List! The Comprehensive Guide on How to Organise and Manage a Perfect Corporate Event*. Leicester: Matador.

Matthews, D. (2008). *Special Event Production: The Resources.* Oxford: Butterworth-Heinemann.

Nelson, K. B. (2009). Enhancing the attendee's experience through creative design of the event environment: Applying Goffman's dramaturgical perspective. *Journal of Convention and Event Tourism, 10*: 120–33.

Office Christmas (2011). Theming and event production. Office Christmas [online]. Retrieved from www.officechristmas.co.uk/theming-and-production

O'Toole, W. (2011). *Events Feasibility and Development: From Strategy to Operations.* Oxford: Butterworth-Heinemann.

PDSA (n.d.). About PDSA. PDSA [online]. Retrieved from www.pdsa.org.uk/

Purple Grape Catering (2011). Our menus. Purple Grape Catering [online]. Retrieved from www.purplegrapecatering.co.uk/site/menu.html

Reisinger, Y. (2009). *International Tourism: Cultures and Behavior.* Oxford: Butterworth-Heinemann.

Seventeen Events (2011). Our services. Seventeen Events [online]. Retrieved from www.seventeenevents.co.uk/about-seventeen/our-services/

Shone, A. and Parry, B. (2010). *Successful Event Management* (3rd edn). Hampshire: Cengage Learning.

Silvers, J. R. (2007a). EMBOK facets and applications. Julia Silvers [online]. Retrieved from www.juliasilvers.com/embok/Facets_Aps.htm

Silvers, J. R. (2007b). Design case study. Julia Silvers [online]. Retrieved from www.juliasilvers.com/embok/design_case_study.htm#Theme_Design_Overview

Stumps Party (2011). Event party themes. Stumps Party [online]. Retrieved from www.stumpsparty.com/catalog.cfm?cat=47431

The Sustainable Events Group (2010). Welcome to the future of events – make BS 8901 work for you. Sustainable Events Group [online]. Retrieved from www.thesustainableeventsgroup.com/

Theme My Party (2010). Theme my party [online]. Retrieved from www.thememyparty.co.uk/

The Ultimate Experience (2007). London Christmas parties 2011. Ultimate Experience Ltd. [online]. Retrieved from www.the-ultimate.co.uk/html/christmas-parties/

Wearing, S. (2002). Re-centring the self in volunteer tourism. In G. Dann (ed.), *The Tourist as Metaphor of the Social World* (pp. 237–62). Wallingford: CAB International.

Managing Event Projects 4

Nigel L. Williams

Learning Objectives

By reading this chapter students should be able to:

- Understand the benefits and limitations of applying project management concepts to events
- Understand the characteristics of a successful event from a project management perspective
- Evaluate project management techniques and issues, and recommend appropriate applications to event management
- Select and implement the most effective solution to manage an event project
- Review the management of past events to learn lessons for future work.

Introduction

The central task of event management is to create a unique experience for a target audience within resource constraints. Successful events therefore require a complex alignment of creative and commercial goals. In an international environment, this challenge is increased as stakeholders may be distributed geographically, making communication and coordination difficult. In order to meet the performance and accountability demands of the international environment, formal mechanisms are needed to support the event design and delivery process. These demands have been increased with the current levels of political and economic uncertainty (Devesa et al., 2015). Since events share some characteristics with projects, the discipline of project management may provide some useful tools. However, they need to be adapted to meet the unique characteristics of event management (Wåhlin et al., 2015). This chapter presents tools that can be utilized to support the entire event realization process from initiation to closure by:

- Presenting an overview of the similarities and differences between events and projects
- Highlighting the areas in which project management tools can assist event management
- Using a worked example, to develop and present a framework for event project management.

Events and Project Management

Events have been defined as 'a specific ritual, presentation, performance or celebration' (Allen, 2000). Events arise from a variety of circumstances and have been categorized using a number of methods. Researchers have used purpose (Goldblatt, 2002), scale (Bowdin et al., 2001) and circumstances (Shone and Parry, 2004) as means of categorizing event activities. Goldblatt (2002) has categorized four purposes of events: *celebration, education, marketing* and *reunion*. Celebration events are linked to particular occasions in a person's, organization's or institution's life, and commemorate times of historical significance. Formal education has grown in importance in the last century and linked to this growth are events that may be social or professional. Events are also used for marketing promotion, to encourage interest or grow sales. Marketers are faced with a high variety of media options and a similarly diverse customer base. Marketing events have been employed as a means of reaching and encouraging purchases. Finally, reunion events gather people to celebrate particular occasions.

Events also occur at a wide variety of scales (Bowdin et al., 2001). Small-scale local or community events serve audiences in the immediate area. Major events, by contrast, serve a greater audience and may even attract international visitors. Events known as hallmark events may emerge from local circumstances and become identified with a particular region. They may also grow to the point where they attract international attention. Entire countries or regions vie to host international-scale mega events such as the Olympics. Table 4.1 shows the diversity of events as conceptualized by previous research.

The demand for events has continued to grow as groups, organizations and institutions increasingly adopt them for a wide range of purposes, as seen in Table 4.1. At the same time, with experience, clients' expectations have increased, raising the level

Table 4.1 Events categorized by type

Getz, 1997	Bowdin et al., 2006	Shone and Parry, 2004	Goldblatt, 2002
Cultural	Cultural	Leisure (leisure, sport, recreation)	Civic events
Art	Sports	Personal (weddings, birthdays, anniversaries)	Exposition
Entertainment	Business	Cultural (ceremonial, sacred, art, heritage)	Fairs and festivals
Sport		Organizational (commercial, political, sales, charitable)	Hallmark events
Educational			Hospitality
Recreational			Meetings and conferences
Political			Retail
Personal			Social lifecycle
Celebration			

of complexity. Both of these trends have encouraged the adoption of formal mechanisms in order to properly manage events. Since they are both involved in the creation of intangible outcomes (Heineke and Davis, 2007), events share some similarities with services. However, traditional service-operations management techniques are unable to support event planning and delivery, as their goal is the optimization of an on-going process (Bitran and Lojo, 1993), not the management of a time-limited activity. Another discipline – project management – may offer more useful tools for event management. Emerging from a military and engineering background, project management tools have been applied in an increasing range of organizations. A project has been defined similarly to an event as 'a temporary endeavour undertaken to create a unique product or service' (PMI, 2013). Both events and projects have common characteristics:

- *Temporary* – Unlike other organizational processes, both projects and events are temporary in nature. They begin when authorization is granted and end once objectives are achieved.
- *Unique outputs* – Each project and event requires a particular combination of factors: location, date, resources and personnel. As such, the experience of planning and managing them will never be the same.
- *Executed by teams* – Both projects and events are executed by teams formed for that specific purpose (Matthews, 2008).
- *Outcome-based evaluation* – Since projects and events are unique, they are difficult to evaluate. As such, they are measured by their outcomes or the objectives to be achieved (Jugdev and Maœller, 2005).

While projects possess the above similarities, they also possess key differences that can influence planning and execution. A key difference between events and projects, is that part of an event's execution and consumption are simultaneous (Salem et al., 2004), while in projects they may be separate. Event experiences are co-created with participants, and adjustments during execution require processes that can operate quickly (Tum et al., 2006). The second factor is that dates for celebratory and reunion events generally cannot be adjusted, unlike projects where end dates may be negotiable. Where project management can contribute to event management is in helping to formalize processes such as planning, scheduling, resource allocation, communication and documentation. This can bring three important benefits to event managers operating in the current business environment.

Coordination and Communication

Events require the coordination of a group of stakeholders, each with distinct needs (Ali-Knight et al., 2009). As events grow in complexity, these stakeholders have progressively increased in number and diversity. Event professionals need to incorporate and manage these inputs to ensure successful execution (Turkulainen et al., 2015). Project management can provide a robust set of tools for integrating and disseminating event information, supporting coordination processes.

Improving Accountability and External Audit

Current trends of sustainability and corporate governance mean that event managers are increasingly called upon to account for their activities (Adema and Roehl, 2009). Increasingly, stakeholders are requesting that event managers minimize the impact of activities using guidelines provided by the sponsor or a standard such as BS 8901. The currently weak global economy following the financial market crisis has resulted in additional demands for monitoring of budgets, as organizations seek to shed non-essential spending. By adopting formal processes for event realization, documentation can be generated that records actions taken and their rationale. In this area, project management possesses an array of tools that can generate traceable documents, improving the transparency of the planning process and execution.

Build an Internal Event Knowledge Base

While events are unique, lessons learned from previous experience can be invaluable when designing future events. Since event teams are dynamic, much of this knowledge can be lost as individuals may leave the organization. The project management process can capture this information, supporting the development of an internal database of event management knowledge. Once compiled, this information forms a valuable input into planning and delivery of future events, enabling, for example, faster training of volunteers and selection of appropriate suppliers.

Recognizing the value that formal processes can bring to the event management field, a group of researchers and professionals have created the EMBOK or Event Management Body of Knowledge (Robson, 2009). While it is still being developed, even in its current form it can form a useful resource for managers seeking to implement formal management processes in their event organization (Silvers and Nelson, 2009).

Case Study 4.1 – Festival Management in Rural India

Introduction

West Bengal in East India has a rich heritage of folk music, dance, traditions and handicraft. In addition, there is natural beauty and ancient rock and terracotta temples. The art and cultural traditions of the rural and tribal communities are extremely colourful and attractive and offer tremendous tourism potential, and thus village festivals showcasing village art forms were started. The festivals converted these marginalized villages into cultural destinations. This has been achieved by showcasing the traditions, values and lifestyles of indigenous cultural communities to new audiences. The festivals have succeeded in strengthening locals' livelihoods, creating identity and establishing direct linkages between audience and cultural practitioners – establishing positive impacts for regional development.

From Trails to Events

The first step in this process is always identifying all of the natural beauty, forests, tribal villages, natural heritage sites, temple sites, crafts, museums and other interesting and diverse places around the art and craft village. Trails are drawn up so that tourists can enjoy tribal dance, drama and songs and also get an opportunity to live among tribal communities and participate in their festivals. In less than seven years, there are now 15 village festivals created by Banglanatak dot com, a social enterprise specializing in culture and development. Even tourism departments of the Federal and State governments in India now recognize these villages as possible cultural destinations.

'Art for Life' is the flagship initiative of Banglanatak dot com, where they build the community's capacity, directly link the community to tourist markets and promote exchange and collaboration. In about ten months' time, after some exposure of the communities to the outside world, a village festival is started in a village. Each village festival is on a weekend: three days and two nights, from 11am on Friday to 4pm on Sunday. Daytime is kept for the village visit, which includes, house-to-house visits, interacting with artists, and participating in workshops, learning about traditional village art and culture, and the first two evenings are kept for the folk festival. The media are also invited and they often write news stories about the preparation as well as the event itself.

Cleaning the village, painting the mud houses, straightening the roads, marking houses with artists' names, fixing workshop venues, fixing the folk festival venue, forming a local team to coordinate, drawing up a list of volunteers, fixing the menu of three meals for guests and visiting artists, arranging stay for guests, decorating the space, planning the light and sound, and the folk festival programming – all have been part of the mela process.

Planning starts at least two months before the festival, and the event team coordinates closely with local artists and communities in mobilizing them towards taking the lead role in organizing the festival. Since folk performances are an integral part of the festival, the team confirms artists' availability for the dates allotted. Necessary permissions from the designated authorities are obtained and partnerships with government departments, tourism organizations, travel agents and tour operators are arranged.

Site Preparation and Staging for a New Space

A month before the festival, a team of 4–5 people goes to the site, comprising the manager, two coordinators, a sound and light expert and a food expert. During this initial 3–4 days the team stays at the festival site, talks with local villagers in order to understand their expectations from the festival, and encourages them to take active participation. The team also checks the availability of supplies such as food and water at the event site. Since the festival is a 3-day event it is important to plan the programmes so that a tourist staying for 2 days can also have a glimpse of almost all folk forms. Promotion and publicity of the festival is important as it is imperative to generate interest among the potential visitors. The promotion material includes posters, invitation cards, letters, announcements and social media.

Sometimes, tourism departments support some publicity also. Both audio/visual and print media are used to promote this unique concept.

(Continued)

(Continued)

From the second year onwards, local teams start taking some responsibility and, from year 3, it evolves as a locally organized mela, with some financial and planning assistance from outside.

Holi – A Special Event Staging

Holi is known as Dol in Bengal – its festival of colours. One to two days of holidays are observed across the whole of India. This is not a weekend festival, but the date is as per the Indian calendar. In its eighth year of celebration, the festival is scheduled to take place on 22–24 March. Tourists start arriving in the morning. Our team provides cars at the station where a kiosk was set up. After the cars bring the tourists to the festival spot, they are registered at the festival venue and allocated their place of stay – tent/cottage, etc.

Over 500 persons stay overnight and local people gather around the festival site with their wares, carrying various food and snack items. In the morning of the day of Holi, all tourists congregate together, they shower colour on one another, and the folk artists sing and dance. The local liquor, Mahua, is enjoyed by all as they make merriment throughout the morning. The evening is folk music night, and then in the morning, workshops are provided for the tourists along with nearby site visits.

These initiatives have certainly created awareness, developed a new audience and thus a new market for local rural culture. Village festivals also have the added benefit of recognition for the rural artists, and the community as a whole is taking more pride in their own culture and heritage.

Many of the tourists who visited Purulia Dol in 2009 returned to enjoy the festival in 2015. Almost 30% of tourists in 2015 were repeat-visitors. The festival has even been able to attract international tourists, with visitors from Italy, Malaysia and Germany attending almost every year. As the festival ends on the third day, cars are provided to take the tourists back to the station.

Event Closure

The entire festival arena is packed up by the third day/night and the team leaves the next morning. The team then reviews the festival to determine the lessons for future events.

Event Project Management Model

Increasingly, stakeholders demand that event managers need to stage experiences of greater complexity within resource constraints and under external scrutiny. These requirements dictate not only that must the event experience meet expectations, but also that the delivery processes enable efficiency and transparency. For organizers in the current environment of increasing accountability, two areas are assessed to determine whether an event has been successful: the achievement of event objectives and the effectiveness of event management processes (Baccarini, 1999).

Event Objectives

Events are staged to attain a predetermined objective. These may range from building market awareness for a product, to celebrating an occasion, to regional economic development. As such, they shape all subsequent event activities (Allen et al., 2002; Bowdin et al., 2001) such as type, scale, location and audience. Refining these event objectives into actionable goals for managers generally requires the management of particular event characteristics. Usually, these are stated as cost, time and quality. However, for events, the second characteristic is frequently not negotiable. A more applicable framework will encompass four main elements:

Feasibility

The feasibility component describes all the components of the event to be delivered, their desired level of performance and the means of supply. Events managers need to

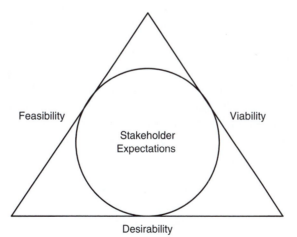

Figure 4.1 Event objectives

determine the tangible (stage equipment, décor) and intangible (licences, skills) inputs required to deliver event outcomes. Based on the demands that these inputs need to meet, managers also need to determine the appropriate level of performance or quality for these inputs. Finally, the event team needs to assess the source for these inputs, either internally or from suppliers.

Viability

Events need to achieve financial goals, and the viability component assesses the business case for a proposed event. Personal or hospitality events generally need to fit within organizational financial constraints or budgets. Other types of events may be required to generate an expected return or profit.

Desirability

Event concepts need to be desirable to both internal and external stakeholders and this criteria measures the attractiveness. A distinctive event theme provides several benefits to event organizers (Berridge, 2009). The first is that an exciting concept serves to interest planners and encourage active support. The second is that it differentiates the event from competing offerings, allowing event promoters to build anticipation of a unique or distinctive experience to a potential audience.

Stakeholder expectations

Planning and executing an event is a learning process for both event managers and stakeholders, defined as parties with an interest or affected by event outcomes. Early conceptualizations of project management sought to separate changes in stakeholder expectations from project deliverables, referring to them as an external factor known as 'scope creep' (Melton and Iles-Smith, 2009). This approach frequently resulted in outcomes that did not meet changing stakeholder demands. Recently, project management approaches, notably Agile, reflect the iterative, non-deterministic reality of formulating and delivering projects. Since event managers operate in an environment of high uncertainty, there is a need to incorporate these changing expectations, updating plans as necessary.

These components aid both the event planning and delivery process. At the planning level, they enable the conversion of objectives into actionable items. During delivery, event stakeholders also need to determine which criteria take precedence (see 'Managing Trade-Offs' box below).

Managing Trade-Offs (O'Toole and Mikolaitis, 2002: 71)

When problems inevitably arise in the event delivery process, the use of clear criteria, specified in advance, helps to make decisions in an objective manner. Key stakeholders need to agree in advance what the key constraint is: feasibility, viability or desirability. The event team's first task is to determine if any issue that arises is a real problem. If it is one that may affect the outcome of the event, the team needs to determine how resources will be allocated from areas other than the key constraint. This process needs to be properly documented, as event managers will be called upon to explain their decisions either at periodic planning meetings or during evaluation.

Event Processes

Once the initial objectives have been agreed and accepted by stakeholders, detailed planning of resources, time and services can then be initiated. Once resources are committed, the team needs to work to non-negotiable deadlines to execute and monitor event activities simultaneously. According to the EMBOK, these actions can be arranged in a sequence of stages including initiation, planning, implementing, event staging and closing (Silvers and Nelson, 2009) as seen in Figure 4.2. The following is a brief overview:

Phase 1: *Initiating* – The goal of this phase is to identify all potential ideas and determine which one is best suited to meeting event objectives.

Phase 2: *Planning* – This stage elaborates the selected idea and determines the resources required to deliver.

Phase 3: *Mobilizing* – In this phase, event set-up activities are performed.

Phase 4: *Staging* – The event is staged or performed.

Phase 5: *Closing* – Evaluation of entire process, and capture the learning from event activities.

Between phases 1 to 4 there are reviews which can influence the pattern of overall progress. At these points, the event team along with stakeholders can review progress against objectives and external conditions to decide if the project can progress as planned, if it needs to be modified significantly, if the previous stage needs to be repeated, or if the project should be cancelled. The outcome from the phase reviews

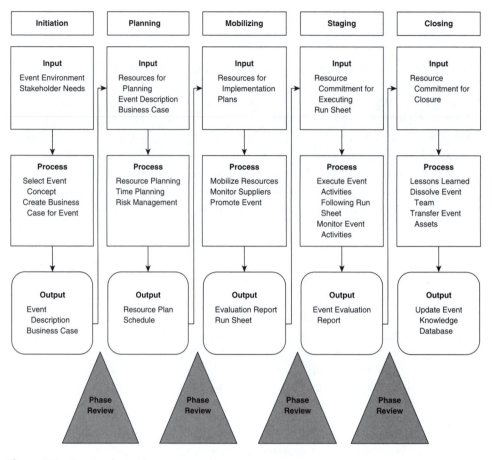

Figure 4.2   Event project cycle

can result in deterministic progress through the cycle (from phases 1 to 5) or iterative moving back-and-forth between previous phases (for example from 2 to 3 and
back to 2).

Phase 1: Initiating Process Phase

The initiating phase confirms the need for the event, examines alternative event concepts and decides on the concept that best meets the overall event objectives. While
the temptation exists for event managers to ignore this phase in order to focus on
planning and implementation, it is critical to devote sufficient time to initiation. At this
point, few resources are committed and event managers therefore have the greatest
opportunity to influence the outcome at the lowest possible cost (PMI, 2013).

Initiation inputs

As described in Part 1 of this text, external environmental forces influence the event industry as a whole. Event managers therefore need to examine the likely effect of these forces and ensure that they are able to manage potential threats and maximize possible opportunities. Once this macro analysis is complete, organizers then need to identify stakeholders and understand their particular interests. For most events, they will include the following (Getz et al., 2007): sponsors, media, audience, community and event team.

Sponsors provide resources to execute event activities in exchange for benefits such as building awareness with a particular audience, sales, or access to decision-makers (Tum et al., 2006) (and see Kitchin, Chapter 7 this volume). For public events, media is another key stakeholder. For a large-scale event such as the Olympics, television viewership is significantly larger than physical attendees, and is a key influence on staging and delivery. Even with smaller events, such as the religious festival described in Case Study 4.1, media helps to build anticipation and set expectations for the customer experience. The emergence of the interactive media facilitated by the internet may further shape how events are delivered in the near future (Adema and Roehl, 2009). Both public and private events are staged for the benefit a particular audience. Event managers need to anticipate, manage, meet and if possible exceed these stakeholder expectations in order for an event to be viewed as successful.

Events can impact the community in which they are staged (Robertson et al., 2009). As seen in the case example, event organizers need to consult these stakeholders in order to ensure that possible benefits are maximized and negative impacts minimized. Finally, the event team is responsible for the achievement of objectives by managing design and delivery and, as such, they are important stakeholders.

Initiation activities

For any given event objective, different types of events may be staged. The initiation process explores these options and selects the one that best provides the desired outcome. When developing event concepts, the '5 Ws' framework from Goldblatt (2005) is a useful structuring device:

1. Why? – The purpose of the event
2. Who? – The specific stakeholders that will be affected by the outcomes
3. When? – The date(s) on which the event is held
4. Where? – The location of the event
5. What? – The details of the event.

Within this framework, it is possible to brainstorm or generate a range of ideas that will meet event objectives. For small events, the event team may be sufficient. In the case of large public events, it is necessary to involve external stakeholders to contribute and evaluate ideas.

After options have been generated, they are assessed using the criteria of feasibility, viability and desirability to determine the best possible design that meets event objectives (Lawson, 2005).

Feasibility

The feasibility review assesses the resources along with the performance level required to deliver the event, and it determines if they can be provided directly from event team members, through volunteers or from suppliers. Event organizers will consider external requirements too, such as permits or licences. In the Holi festival described above, the event team not only needed to source sufficient accommodation (quantity) for tourists at the site; they would also need to ensure that tents were comfortable (performance level).

Viability

This screen establishes the business case for the event, determining if it meets cost or revenue generation criteria. Once the resource needs of a concept are determined, it is possible to generate a cost estimate. At this stage, an accurate estimate may not be possible; an acceptable range is +/−20% (Van der Wagen, 2007). The event team can then determine if proposed means of funding these options either internally or through ticket sales, donations, etc. are sufficient. For events that are required to earn revenue, expected profitability for each option can be forecasted in a similar manner and the results evaluated.

Desirability

Each event concept should be assessed and ranked on their desirability. While this is a subjective criterion, assessment of desirability can take the form of an internal and external scan. Internally, event concepts can be evaluated based on the attractiveness to the event team. Externally, the concepts should be compared to events that are planned during the same timeframe.

All ideas generated during brainstorming should be ranked according to the above criteria, using either a quantitative (1–5) or qualitative (high–medium–low) measurement. The highest-ranked proposal should be selected for development. For the case study, a weekend festival incorporating art, performances and food best fits the objective of encouraging cultural tourism in a rural Indian village.

Outputs

For the selected event, the team should convert the event description to a detailed description or scope of works to be used in the next phase, planning. At the same time, the team should also identify critical internal and external constraints in this scope that should be monitored as the event is developed. *Internal constraints* are related directly to the event and can be monitored using the feasibility, viability and desirability dimensions. Working with stakeholders, event managers need to identify which of these elements are non-negotiable and which can be adjusted. For example, Banglanatak dot com identified feasibility as the key constraint for their event. As such, the team was willing to acquire additional resources at additional costs if necessary, which would reduce viability. *External constraints* are factors imposed on the event such as legal requirements, suppliers and competitors.

Phase 2: Planning Process Phase

The planning phase converts the description to detailed working procedures that enable execution of event activities. These include:

- Work breakdown structure (WBS)
- Work schedules and deadlines
- Budgets and cash flow
- Areas of high risk, uncertainty and contingency plans
- Personnel plans and resource utilization plans
- Procurement plans
- Documentation management plans.

It is important to note that planning is an iterative process owing to the complexity of events and the need to incorporate stakeholder input. Individual documents also need to incorporate some element of flexibility in order to respond to changing circumstances. Before detailed planning can begin, the event team may consult with stakeholders to ensure that resources are still available, especially if time has passed between concept selection and detailed planning.

Define event deliverables

Event initiation activities produce a description of an event concept that best meets stakeholder requirements. In the planning stage, this concept is refined into actionable components. A tool that supports this process is a product breakdown structure (PBS), a diagram that represents the activities required to deliver the event as a hierarchical structure. Figure 4.3 shows an example based on the case study.

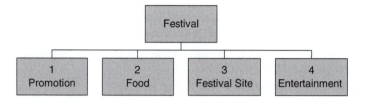

Figure 4.3   PBS overview for Holi Festival elements

As seen in Figure 4.3, the highest level of the PBS refers to the event. The second level generally refers to major event components such as venue, décor or entertainment. These major components are further decomposed into lower levels depending on the scale and complexity of the event. To support this process, each PBS element will have a unique code or identifier to enable resource assignment and tracking. The PBS is then converted to a work breakdown structure, or WBS, which identifies the activities required to deliver event components. The format is similar to the PBS and the numbering scheme will be maintained, but each element focuses on activity, not deliverables. Figure 4.4 shows an expanded branch of the promotion element of the WBS.

The lowest level of any WBS is known as the work package and is the point at which time and resources can be properly estimated by the event team (Lester, 2007). For any given event, an experienced team can adequately define the event with a few levels while a less-experienced team would need a WBS with more levels to ensure

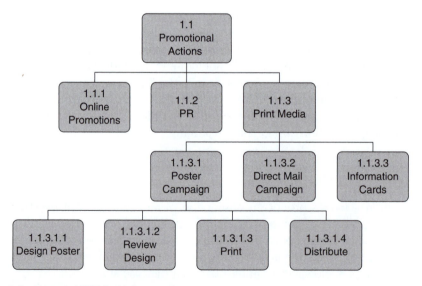

Figure 4.4   Expanded WBS for Holi promotion

that details are not missed. A WBS simplifies communication among various stake-holders by providing a standard representation of event components in a graphical form. It also aids the project team in refining these components to actionable items (work packages) that can be completed by team members or suppliers. Once a draft WBS has been created by team members, it should be reviewed by stakeholders to ensure that all event elements are accounted for. As the event progresses, the WBS will be further refined and updated to reflect any changes.

Determine resource requirements

Once an initial WBS has been completed, it is possible to determine the resources required to stage the event. The type and amount of resources can be obtained by compiling data from individual work packages. Once the event resource requirements have been collected, event managers can plan how to acquire them, either internally or from suppliers.

Estimate duration and effort for event

Once the requirements and sources of resources are known, it is possible to determine the duration of each activity. Using the WBS, the party responsible should provide an estimate for each work package based on available historical information or expert judgement. A good guideline is that estimates for work packages should be less than the reporting period for the event, in order to support later control activities. If they are, consider decomposing the work package into lower levels.

Sequencing of work packages

After the duration step is completed, the event team should work out the order or sequence of work packages. While some packages can be executed independently or in parallel, others are dependent on previous activities. The event team needs to iden-tify the sequence of dependent work packages in order to determine the overall time required.

Scheduling

Once the relationships, duration and responsibilities for work packages are deter-mined, it is possible to create a draft event schedule. This is commonly done in the form of a Gantt chart (see Figure 4.5), which displays activities using a vertical and horizontal axis (Wilson, 2003). On the horizontal axis, columns are used to display duration and person responsible for each work package. The bottom row shows the

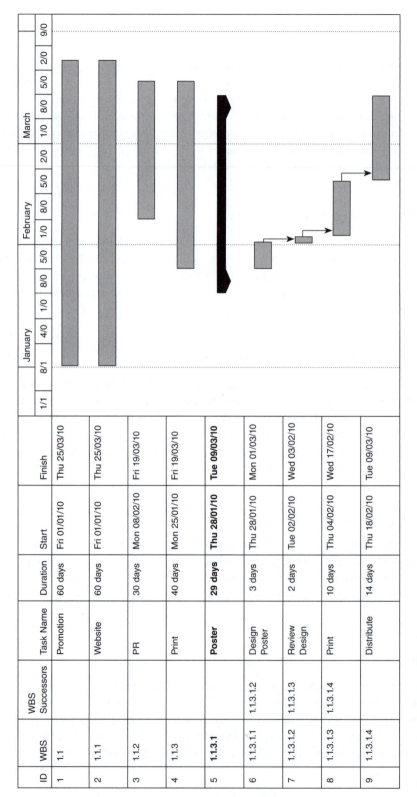

ID	WBS	WBS Successors	Task Name	Duration	Start	Finish
1	1.1		Promotion	60 days	Fri 01/01/10	Thu 25/03/10
2	1.1.1		Website	60 days	Fri 01/01/10	Thu 25/03/10
3	1.1.2		PR	30 days	Mon 08/02/10	Fri 19/03/10
4	1.1.3		Print	40 days	Mon 25/01/10	Fri 19/03/10
5	**1.1.3.1**		**Poster**	**29 days**	**Thu 28/01/10**	**Tue 09/03/10**
6	1.1.3.1.1	1.1.3.1.2	Design Poster	3 days	Thu 28/01/10	Mon 01/03/10
7	1.1.3.1.2	1.1.3.1.3	Review Design	2 days	Tue 02/02/10	Wed 03/02/10
8	1.1.3.1.3	1.1.3.1.4	Print	10 days	Thu 04/02/10	Wed 17/02/10
9	1.1.3.1.4		Distribute	14 days	Thu 18/02/10	Tue 09/03/10

Figure 4.5 Gantt chart example

duration of the event. Work packages are listed from top to bottom on the vertical axis in the order they will be executed. Work packages are displayed in graphical form as horizontal lines or columns, each line with the length showing the start and end dates. This process can be done manually, or using software. Once a draft schedule is created, it can be circulated for evaluation. After evaluation, the schedule can be finalized.

Function or run sheet

While Gantt charts are a useful tool in event planning, they are not sufficient to support event delivery. A function or run sheet (see Figure 4.6) should be used to show the sequence of activities during event staging (Tum et al., 2006). For small or less-complex events, managers may generate a chart showing the key elements of the event and their exact timing, along with any critical decisions to be made. Larger, more-complex events may incorporate a customer processing chart that anticipates how event attendees will enter and move during the event.

Holi Festival
March 30th, 2008
Purulia, West Bengal

TIME		ACTION / TASK	RESPONSIBLE	NOTES
Start Time	Duration			
9:00 am	8 hrs.	Greet guests at station and transport to site	Banglanatak dot com offsite team	
5:00 pm	2 hrs.	Register guests	Banglanatak dot com onsite team	
7:00 pm	3 hrs.	Inauguration	Chau, Jhumur and Baul artists	

Figure 4.6 Event run sheet for Holi event

Tips for Implementing Run Sheets

Goldblatt (2011) suggests circulating draft run sheets to stakeholders for approval. To ensure that the planner gets useful feedback, a memo should be included with specific instructions on how to review the run sheet, along with specific tasks for each reviewer based on their expertise. In this way, the team not only gets feedback on the entire document but also leverages the strengths of stakeholders.

Costing and budgeting

Once the resources and their source are finalized it is now possible to determine overall event cost by tabulating costs in the WBS. For large events that require extensive preparation such as the Olympics, an event cash flow determining financing requirements during preparation is also necessary. This can be generated compiling weekly or monthly work package costs using the event schedule. More detail on event costing is available in Chapter 8.

Risk management plan

Event managers also need to identify sources of risk, determine their possible effect and plan responses. Risks can be identified from the WBS and event flow chart, which provide a detailed overview of event activities and processes. Once identified, an analysis is performed to determine their possible effect. If these effects are significant, a response should be planned. The activities are required to mitigate risk and should be used to update the WBS, flowchart, schedule and budget. More detail on risk management is contained in Ritchie and Reid's chapter (Chapter 9).

For large-scale events, see Table 4.2 for additional plans may also be employed.

Phase 3: Mobilizing Process Phase

In this phase, the event team ensures that the event scope is delivered in a manner that meets stakeholder needs within cost requirements. The event team, along with

Table 4.2 Additional plans for large-scale events

Event Plan Element	Purpose
Change and configuration plan	Stakeholder demands are never static and they may request adjustments to the event plan over time. Successful event managers anticipate the need for change and design procedures in advance to incorporate the changing demands, in particular those that impact on function, feasibility or desirability.
Event documentation plan	Maintains central database of event documentation and controls who can access it.
Communication plan	Determines the information needs for each event stakeholder: frequency, level of detail and format. For large events, this task should be included in the WBS.
Team management	Evaluates the effectiveness of the event team, providing training or mentoring where necessary.
Procurement	Determines the need for external suppliers, sources a provider, manages delivery and evaluates performance.

suppliers, execute the actions described in work packages to deliver outcomes described in the WBS. While event plans guide this process, the event environment is dynamic and the team needs to monitor and control activities to prevent unwanted outcomes. As work packages are executed, managers also need to determine the appropriate response to risk events, generally using actions described in the risk plan.

Throughout implementation, the event team is required to evaluate performance against plans and communicate progress to stakeholders. If any variance occurs that can influence event outcomes, the team needs to decide on the necessary corrective action. The impact of these actions should be estimated and event plans updated, as necessary. Once work packages are complete, they may be formally evaluated to ensure that they meet performance requirements. In large events, this may take the form of testing by experts and the findings communicated to stakeholders. A pre-evaluation report may be completed at the end of implementation which can provide useful data for event staging such as expected attendance.

Phase 4: Staging Execution

Based on the findings of the pre-evaluation report, stakeholders will decide whether or not to approve resources for event execution. If approval is granted, event activities are performed and monitored. Data from the pre-event evaluation report is also used to update the run sheet, ensuring that the document reflects the site and supplier realities. As shown in the case example, coordinators manage the process, from pre- to post-event, ensuring that activities are executed in the planned sequence and to the desired level of quality. At the end of the process, an event evaluation report is produced using the guidelines in Chapter 10.

Phase 5: Event Closing

Like event initiation, the closing process is frequently overlooked by managers. However, it is a critical element in improving event planning and delivery. After resources are committed by stakeholders, the manager, in conjunction with the event team, organizes all documentation for archiving. During this process, the team reviews event documents to determine any lessons learned. Once the review is complete, the team compiles a lessons-learned report, which can be used to guide future planning. In the case example, attendance information was used to change performance times at the festival so that they were more suitable for attendees. The team ensures that all event-related financial issues are resolved, including supplier contracts. Depending on the scale of the event, any assets created specifically for it are transferred to the relevant operating authority.

Diary of an Event Manager – Tom Lunt, Former Event Manager for Christian Aid

I think the best lesson for managers to learn is 'Prepare for the unexpected, both good and bad' in event project management. While we can put everything in place, it's a good idea to have additional resources that can be drawn upon quickly. In 2008, my organization wanted to develop our fundraising event portfolio with under-represented groups of donors, in particular younger males aged 25–45. While our team looked at a lot of ideas, we wanted to embrace the idea of sustainability, so all concepts that included extensive travel were out. We decided on a sponsored bike ride through the rural UK.

The key to our event was finding potential riders who would make a commitment to fundraise and train for the event. This meant providing an efficient response to their initial enquiry that satisfied their query and then encouraged them to sign up. Once signed up, the key was to build a team ethos amongst a group of people who didn't know each other; this was done through social media and regular telephone calls. Social media took on a life of its own and the participants used it to capture their training and riding experience. We were particularly lucky as a *Guardian* blogger mentioned the event, helping to build our presence at no cost to us. It was not something that we planned, but it helped build camaraderie between the participants and, ultimately, this emergent action enhanced the event experience.

The surprises weren't all positive, however. With 20 people of different riding ability over a long ride, they completed the course at different rates, so we had staff at the lead, middle and back of the group. During the second day of the event, one of the riders at the back had a minor accident. While we were able to get assistance quickly, we would have appreciated a bit more support from our suppliers. Needless to say, we won't be using them again. Ultimately, what I've learned over time is that while formal processes are important, managers need to keep the spontaneous nature of events in mind. It's a difficult balancing act, to be flexible enough to take advantage of opportunities but structured enough to ensure that goals are met.

Case Study 4.2 – Calabar Festival

Cross River is an eastern state in Nigeria with a population estimated at 3.4 million (2011). In the year 2000, the Governor introduced the Calabar Festival, named after the capital, to attract visitors to the region. The first parade showcased the region's history and culture such as cocoa, local animals and ancient monuments. The festival has since grown and now spans 32 days with dozens of events, and attracts millions of visitors.

Planning for the event is conducted by the Events Management Unit and the Carnival Commission. Jointly, they form a programme organization called the Planning Committee, which enables delivery of events for the duration of the festival. The team then creates a programme infrastructure that incorporates management and technical elements to ensure a safe and successful festival. The management element incorporates all the personnel resources including volunteer recruitment and training. Technical elements include the systems, venues and procedures that facilitate festival delivery.

While planning for the festival is continuous, public activities begin in June when a theme is selected for the programme that reflects the culture of the region. In 2015, the theme was 'climate change'. Bands also select their themes at that time, with 2010's being Seagull Band, Bayside, Master Blaster, Passion Four, and Freedom.

The festival formally begins at the end of November with the Christmas tree lighting ceremony. Messages of goodwill are given and the tree is exhibited by dignitaries at the Calabar Millennium Park. A 'Christmas village' is set up at the Cultural Centre with shopping and food stands. The 32-day festival then begins and a number of events are staged that cater to different audiences. Over the period of the festival programme, visitors can attend fashion shows, food demonstrations, cultural exhibits, talent shows, music concerts, fun fairs, carol services, parades and picnics. The annual boat regatta is a colourful display of flamboyantly decorated boats pitting rival local teams against each other. A summary of the programme is provided in Table 4.3.

The largest event in the festival programme is the Calabar Carnival, which attracted an audience estimated at over 2 million and is known as 'Africa's biggest street party'. This event was introduced in 2004 and has been adapted from the Trinidad and Tobago Carnival, a festival of music and masquerade held on the Caribbean islands. With guidance from Trinidadian experts in 2005, costumes were introduced to the street parade. Participants form carnival bands based on themes, and five official carnival bands were created: Bayside, Freedom, Master Blaster, Passion Four and Seagull Band. These participants then demonstrate their routines and costumes in a parade that takes a 12km route through the city of Calabar. In 2007, His Excellency Governor Liyel Imoke made the Carnival a 2-day event, similar to

(Continued)

(Continued)

Table 4.3 The Calabar Festival programme

	Week 1	Week 2	Week 3	Week 4	Week 5
Monday		Theatre performance	Children's Carnival dry run	Sport event: Golf Tournament	Calabar Carnival
Tuesday	(November 30th) Tree Lighting Ceremony	Musical performance: Canaan Rhythms	Theatre performance	Water Carnival	Musical performance: Carnival Rocks
Wednesday	City Walk	Musical performance: Gyration Night	Final Carnival dry run	Youth Development Programme closes	Fashion Show
Thursday	Youth Development Programme	Theatre performance	Sport Event: Golf Clinic	Sport event: Golf Tournament	Musical performance: Naija's Most Wanted
Friday	Adult Carnival dry run	Sport event: Power Women	Theatre performance	Musical performance: Carol Night	Musical performance: Cross Over Night
Saturday	Musical performance: Mixed Festival	Musical performance: Roots Rock Reggae	Musical performance: Jazz in Paradise	Family Funfair	Interdenominational Thanksgiving Service
Sunday	Choral Competition	Sport event: Football Competition	Sport event: Football Competition Final	Children's Carnival	

Trinidad, by introducing a cultural parade and children's carnival. The street party has become a powerful tool for increasing tourism revenue. Before the Carnival, the local fashion industry are involved in making costumes, and local stores enjoy increased sales of related items. Hotels and guest houses are completely occupied during the time of the street parade. Finally, the carnival route, which is 12km long, generates income through sales of local food and handicraft along with advertising.

Over time, the festival has attracted international celebrities from the entertainment fields who perform at various events and act as ambassadors. The organizers have also upgraded the planning infrastructure, incorporating a website, www.calabarfestival.com. This site has been successful in promoting the festival worldwide, attracting tourists as well as sponsors.

Case Study Questions

1 Who were the key stakeholders in this case? How were their needs served by the event?
2 How would you evaluate this event?
3 In what way can project management processes contribute to the success of this event?

Chapter Summary

The forces of sustainability and austerity along with increasing customer expectations require event managers to adopt new methods in order to satisfy stakeholders. Successful event managers not only achieve their objectives but also manage the realization process effectively in order to provide accountability and capture learning for later work. The adoption of project management tools and techniques can enable the achievement of both goals by providing a structured approach to event delivery. The event realization process can be divided into five phases: initiation, planning, mobilizing, staging and closing. At the end of each phase, there is a formal review process that confirms stakeholder approval to proceed and resource commitment for the next stage. Once the event has been delivered, knowledge is captured in a database to aid in the design of future events.

Review Questions

1. For event success, why is it necessary to examine processes as well as outcomes?
2. Why is it important to engage stakeholders in the event delivery process?
3. How do event project management systems vary by event type?
4. For a given mega event, such as the Rio 2016 Olympics, how does project management support event delivery?
5. Using the case studies, discuss the limitations of applying project management tools to events.

Additional Resources

Books / Book Chapters / Journal Articles

Robson, L. M. (2009). Event Management Body Of Knowledge (EMBOK): The future of event industry research. *Event Management, 12*: 19–25.

Useful Websites

www.apm.org.uk/ – Website for the award-winning Association for Project Management, which is committed to developing and promoting project and programme management through its five Dimensions of Professionalism.

www.juliasilvers.com/embok.htm – Educational resource which presents the Events Management Body of Knowledge; it is maintained by Julia Rutherford Silvers.

www.PMI.org – Website for the Project Management Institute, the world's leading not-for-profit, professional association for project, programme and portfolio managers.

References

Adema, K. L. and Roehl, W. S. (2009). Environmental scanning the future of event design. *International Journal of Hospitality Management, 29*(2): 199–207.

Ali-Knight, J., Martin, R., Alan, F. and Adele, L. (2009). Part 4: Managing the event. *International Perspectives of Festivals and Events* (pp. 225–26). Oxford: Elsevier.

Allen, J. (2000). *Event Planning: The Ultimate Guide to Successful Meetings, Corporate Events, Fundraising Galas, Conferences, Conventions, Incentives, and Other Special Events*. Toronto, Ontario: Wiley.

Allen, J., O'Toole, W., Harris, R. and McDonnell, I. (2002). *Festival and Special Event Management* (2nd edn). Milton: John Wiley & Sons Australia.

Baccarini, D. (1999). The logical framework method for defining project success. *Project Management Journal, 30*(4): 25.

Berridge, G. (2009). Event pitching: The role of design and creativity. *International Journal of Hospitality Management, 29*(2): 208–15.

Bitran, G. R. and Lojo, M. (1993). A framework for analyzing service operations. *European Management Journal, 11*(3): 271–82.

Bowdin, G. A. J., McDonnell, I., Allen, J. and O'Toole, W. (2001). *Events Management*. Oxford: Butterworth-Heinemann.

Bowdin, G., McDonnell, I., Allen, J. and O'Toole, W. (2006). *Events Management*. Oxford: Butterworth-Heinemann.

Devesa, M., Báez, A., Figueroa, V. and Herrero, L. C. (2015). Factors determining attendance at a film festival. *Event Management, 19*(3): 317–30.

Getz, D., Andersson, T. and Larson, M. (2007). Festival stakeholder roles: Concepts and case studies. *Event Management, 10*: 103–22.

Goldblatt, J. (2002). *Special Events* (3rd edn). New York: John Wiley & Sons.

Goldblatt, J. (2005). *Special Events: Global Event Management in the 21st Century* (4th edn). Hoboken, NJ: Wiley.

Goldblatt, J. (2010). *Special Events: A New Generation and the Next Frontier* (6th edn). Hoboken, NJ: John Wiley & Sons.

Heineke, J. and Davis, M. M. (2007). The emergence of service operations management as an academic discipline. *Journal of Operations Management, 25*(2): 364–74.

Jugdev, K. and Maœller, R. (2005). A retrospective look at our evolving understanding of project success. *Project Management Journal, 36*(4): 19–31.

Lawson, B. (2005). *How Designers Think: The Design Process Demystified* (4th edn). Oxford: Architectural Press.

Lester, A. (2007). Work breakdown structures. *Project Management, Planning and Control* (5th edn) (pp. 40–45). Oxford: Butterworth-Heinemann.

Matthews, D. (2008). An introduction to special events and special event production. In: *Special Event Production* (pp. 1–18). Oxford: Butterworth-Heinemann.

Melton, D. T. and Iles-Smith, D. P. (2009). Set-up plan delivery. *Managing Project Delivery* (pp. 85–139). Oxford: Butterworth-Heinemann.

O'Toole, W. and Mikolaitis, P. (2002). *Corporate Event Project Management*. New York: Wiley.

PMI (2013). *A Guide to the Project Management Body of Knowledge (PMBOK Guide)*. (Vol. 5). Pittsburgh, PA: Project Management Institute.

Robertson, M., Rogers, P. and Leask, A. (2009). Progressing socio-cultural impact evaluation for festivals. *Journal of Policy Research in Tourism, Leisure and Events, 1*(2): 156–69.

Robson, L. M. (2009). Event Management Body Of Knowledge (EMBOK): The future of event industry research. *Event Management, 12*: 19–25.

Salem, G., Jones, E. and Morgan, N. (2004). An overview of events management. In I. Yeoman, M. Robertson, J. Ali-Knight, U. McMahon-Beattie (eds), *Festival and Events Management* (pp. 14–31). Oxford: Butterworth-Heinemann.

Shone, A. and Parry, B. (2004). *Successful Event Management* (2nd edn). London: Thompson Learning.

Silvers, J. R. and Nelson, K. B. (2009). An application illustration of the Event Management Body of Knowledge (EMBOK) as a framework for analysis using the design of the 2006 Winter Olympics opening ceremonies. *Event Management, 13*: 117–31.

Tum, J., Norton, P. and Wright, J. N. (2006). *Management of Event Operations*. Oxford: Butterworth-Heinemann.

Turkulainen, V., Aaltonen, K. and Lohikoski, P. (2015). Managing project stakeholder communication: The Qstock Festival case. *Project Management Journal, 46*(6): 74–91. Doi:10.1002/pmj.21547.

Van der Wagen, L. (2007). Event project planning. *Human Resource Management for Events*. Oxford: Butterworth-Heinemann.

Wåhlin, N., Blomquist, T., Malgorzata, J. and Beata, J. (2015). Unspread wings: Why cultural projects don't provide refreshing ideas for project management although they could? *International Journal of Managing Projects in Business, 8*(4): 626–48.

Wilson, J. M. (2003). Gantt charts: A centenary appreciation. *European Journal of Operational Research, 149*(2): 430–37.

Building an Events Team

5

Bruce Johnson

Learning Objectives

By reading this chapter students should be able to:

- Explain the importance of effective human resource management (HRM) in creating effective events
- Understand the fundamental principles of HRM in organizations and how they apply to building events teams
- Identify and apply the basic processes of HRM to building events teams
- Understand the particular characteristics of events that pose challenges for HRM
- Recognize the need for formal management of volunteers.

Introduction

Effective human resource management (HRM) leads to a positive impact on employee performance by enhancing the competence of staff, promoting motivation and commitment and designing work in such a way that staff are encouraged to make the fullest possible contribution (Guest, 2000). For the events industry, HRM can be particularly important. Boxall and Purcell (2011) give four reasons why good HRM is important in the service industry. First, labour can be a large proportion of total budgetary cost and, as such, a relatively small percentage saving in these costs can have a significant effect on financial performance. Second, the intangible elements of services such as the friendliness of staff rely heavily on 'the skills, personalities and moods of those who provide them' (2011: 147). This is particularly true in events teams, where there can be a lot of last-minute time pressure bringing the various elements of an event together; effective teamwork can do much to alleviate these pressures. Third, the need for services to be produced and consumed simultaneously requires a highly flexible workforce to cater for variations in demand. Lastly, customer service plays an extremely important part in overall customer satisfaction

We might also add to this list the fact that many events – whether they are flagship sporting events and a matter of national pride, smaller local events or corporate events vital to the promotion of companies and their products – depend heavily on effective teams of staff in order to achieve their basic marketing objectives.

All of these factors contribute to the need for a well-thought-through HRM strategy when building events teams. This strategy will involve making effective use of the principles and practices of HRM introduced in this chapter.

The Fundamental Principles of Human Resource Management in Events

For the events industry there is a particular need to energize one's staff so there is a positive atmosphere for both staff and customers (Van der Wagen, 2007). To achieve the objectives of building a committed, flexible, quality-orientated event team, organizations need to consider how they will plan their management, organizational and communication structures. When running an event staffed by volunteers, clear divisions of responsibility and authority will help all concerned contribute to its success.

HRM for events integrates with all aspects of event process management (see Williams, Chapter 4 this volume). Issues such as the need to have a clear design strategy and vision for the event, as well as effective project management to control costs and enable effective planning, and the need to understand the event environment in terms of culture and politics – all require effective event teams. Indeed, knowing how one wants staff to behave towards customers is a critical part of the event design and therefore integral to what one is trying to market. Equally, staff being clear about how they can contribute to the overall customer or audience experience can enhance their motivation and therefore their effectiveness.

Once the objectives of the event are agreed, HRM strategy is implemented using policies that are formulated to take into account stakeholder interests, as well as situational factors such as the availability of labour in the local market, business conditions, technology, workforce characteristics and legal and societal values (Beer et al., 1984). Ferdinand et al. outlined the stakeholder interests and situational factors for international events. The overriding aim of the HRM policies is to achieve the commitment, competence and cost effectiveness of the workforce. In events it is also particularly important to consider the security and safety of staff and public, with well-defined policy and practices covering access, safety inductions and procedures in the event of emergency.

Informed by the policy choices to do with staff influence, human resource flows, reward systems and work systems, specific procedures are created to support the delivery of HR objectives (Fombrun et al., 1984) in several ways. In general terms this covers the major areas of planning the work and selecting appropriate staff, who can then be trained and appraised in order to inform reward and further training decisions, both of which enhance performance, while also providing important feedback on the effectiveness of the selection process.

HRM Processes in Events
Planning and Organizational Structures

Once a well-defined design and a clear strategy are established, HRM planning can start to ask what staff will be required, in what quantity, from where, with what skills or competences and how they will be empowered or controlled.

Central to the planning of events staff is consideration of three different forms of flexibility: numerical, temporal and functional. Organizations would always like staff to be available in the perfect number to satisfy peaks and troughs of customer demand throughout the event (thus providing numerical flexibility), only when they are required (thus providing temporal flexibility), to do whatever is required (which is functional flexibility). But in practice of course this completely just-in-time approach to staffing is rarely totally achievable. A well-trained, highly motivated and totally reliable workforce who can be asked to deploy generic skills in a wide variety of contexts would take time to build, and the costs of this are a luxury that many events organizations, operating in increasingly internationalized and competitive markets, simply can't afford. Equally, this highly trained workforce is unlikely to put up with the insecurity and anti-social nature of unpredictable hours and therefore income. There is therefore a balance to be struck between securing the perfect workforce and the costs of doing so. Often a small core of staff is relied upon heavily to train and lead teams of casual or voluntary staff during an event; this can be seen at the centre of Figure 5.1. Additionally, teamwork may form an important part of the training, motivation and performance management of staff.

For a large event, subcontractors or the venue may provide many of the staff. Typically this might cover catering, cleaning, security, technicians, maintenance staff, car park attendants and even customer service staff. An organization may also be using volunteers, who will be discussed in more detail later in this chapter. It is also worth mentioning that even a small event, totally dependent on volunteers, is unlikely to turn away many people who offer their help. Therefore structures and plans may need to adapt around the skills that emerge from the volunteers, rather than seeking specific staff to fit into a narrowly defined set of plans and job roles, imposed from the top of the organization. Despite this, events will still benefit from a well-defined strategy, as a tool to unite the efforts of all staff towards the satisfaction of goals.

Typically, events organizations rely on a very small proportion of core staff, who might or might not be employed on either a full- or a part-time basis. This core staff is then responsible for expanding the organization substantially, often including large numbers of volunteers, to help run the event itself. This characteristic of events organizations has been described as 'pulsating' (Toffler, 1970) and is discussed further, later in this chapter. At the London 2012 Olympic and Paralympic Games the plan was for the 6,000 staff of the local organizing committee (London Organising Committee of the Olympic Games (LOCOG)) to work with 125,000 contractors from over 100 organizations, alongside 70,000 volunteers and more than 2,000 Young Games Makers, who were also volunteers.

A framework which can help organizations identify and differentiate between types of staff, identifying their different needs and therefore different approaches to managing varying groups or segments, is provided by the model of the flexible firm (Atkinson, 1984). This model suggests that staff can be divided into various groups. The core staff is most important to the organization, because of its unique knowledge and experience of the event's operations. The organization would like this core of staff to be as stable

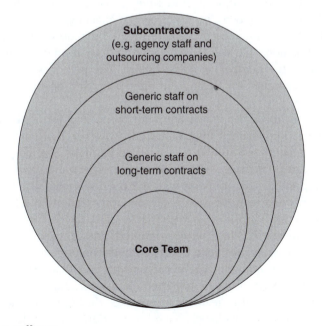

Figure 5.1 Event staff types

as possible, and should therefore reward them appropriately and provide development and career opportunities in order to help retain them to the event.

Outside this core there are two peripheral groups who are also employed, and then beyond them there are agency and subcontractor staff. The first peripheral group has generic skills that are relatively easy to replace from the job market, such as electricians or stage managers; they may be employed on regular contracts but would not attract the same level of development or training as the core group because they are relatively easily replaced and do not necessarily have knowledge unique to the organization. The second peripheral group is in a similar bracket in terms of skill availability in the job market but would be on temporary or short, fixed-term or casual contracts, still with the parent organization. Beyond the peripheral groups are subcontractors, agency staff or the staff of outsourced companies, and important in terms of events could be a large number of volunteers.

In reality, few events staff are engaged on full-time permanent contracts, and might therefore receive a significant amount of career development or long-term training from their employers. This core staff may be crucial to the longer-term survival of the organization, by providing an organizational memory of lessons learnt from previous experience, and they present a particular challenge in terms of retention (see below).

Job Analysis, Job Descriptions and Person Specifications

In terms of planning what people do and when, a combination of the HRM planning described earlier in this chapter and the project management processes described in the previous chapter would be used to create a work breakdown structure (WBS). This will identify the functions that staff have to perform both in preparation for and during events and indicate the number of staff required. The next steps in the process are concerned with techniques for finding the right people to do these jobs. This starts with job analysis.

Job analysis is a process by which the main purpose of jobs, the principal duties or tasks and the reporting lines are established. However, there are decisions to be made about which necessary tasks can be batched into jobs. The purpose of this is to design jobs that can be managed effectively by the organization and are manageable by the staff doing them. This connects with the need to create a flexible, committed and quality-driven event team as well as the previous section on HRM planning and organizational structure.

Kanter (2008) argues that in a service-oriented culture, clear standards achieved by standardized procedures facilitate effective employee performance. If one considers the complexity of running a large event, and the fact that large numbers of staff (including volunteers) are coming together for a short time with an immovable deadline, and that the need to learn from mistakes during the event must be minimized, the importance of well-established procedures, or at least well-defined objectives, becomes evident. In other words, all staff need to have a very good idea of what it is they are supposed to be doing and how they are supposed to be doing it. This could be through the use of procedural manuals, staff handbooks, job descriptions or simply through effective briefing. It is the purpose of job analysis to identify the tasks and responsibilities of all roles in order to inform the content of these documents or the briefing.

Before finalizing any job description it is worth considering if one has created jobs that staff, whether they are employed, subcontractors or volunteers, will enjoy doing. It may be easier to manage an organization in which all staff have single functions; however, if the single function in your job is always to spend an entire shift checking tickets at an entrance, one might reasonably succumb to a degree of boredom. Considering the variety of tasks (job enlargement or job rotation) and level of responsibility (job enrichment) that a job entails may pay dividends in terms of employee or volunteer satisfaction, which in turn could have big benefits for customer service and retention of staff. This could be expressed in terms of a mechanistic or motivational approach to job design (Bloisi, 2007), which focuses either on the processes or tasks to be performed, from a mechanistic perspective, or the human elements such as teamwork, and from a motivational perspective, empowerment and variety of tasks.

A major consideration in the design of jobs is the need to have a flexible workforce. This can be incorporated into a job description by ensuring there are clauses about following any reasonable management request or about the changing nature of requirements. Alternatively one might use deliberately generic descriptions of duties such as 'taking responsibility for all aspects of customer care and responding to information requests in a variety of contexts' rather than 'staffing the enquiries desk'.

An alternative approach might be to define the job in terms of the competencies required to carry it out successfully, rather than specify duties in a limiting or prescriptive way. Competencies describe what a job-holder should be able to do (see also Kitchin, Chapter 7 this volume). For instance, our customer service staff on the enquiries desk might need to be competent in terms of communication, problem-solving, customer focus and working under pressure. A competence-based approach can be particularly helpful when recruiting large numbers of staff against tight deadlines because the best way to establish the competence of staff is by questioning them about their previous experience. In an events environment in which there is very limited time to train staff, well-defined competencies, which can be inferred from applicants' previous relevant experience, will facilitate quick recruitment decisions.

In simple terms, the design of jobs is the result of job analysis, and the outputs of this process are a job description and person specification for the jobs that need to be filled. These two documents form the foundations of the recruitment and selection then training and performance management of staff. They do this by specifying what tasks need to be done and what knowledge, skills or competencies and abilities are required to do them.

The person who will be responsible for management of the relevant staff once they are in post normally carries out the job analysis. This person may gather information by interviewing staff who have done the job in the past or are currently doing it, from colleagues, from a human resources specialist if there is such a person in the organization, from group discussion amongst the design team and senior managers, or through analysis of critical incidents at previous events. A job description includes the following information:

- Job title
- Position (voluntary or paid) and grade
- Whether the job is full-time or part-time, permanent, temporary or casual
- Summary of job's main purpose
- Reporting lines, subordinates and managers
- List of main tasks
- Reference to any other relevant documents such as training manuals or procedures.

The job description then feeds into the person specification. This document identifies what skills, experience, knowledge, competencies or qualifications and personal attributes are required in order to carry out the duties in the job description, generally differentiating between which elements of the job are essential or only desirable.

Person specifications have various purposes. However, it is worth noting that the objectivity and accuracy of the specification is essential for recruiters to identify the best people for jobs and therefore for organizations to defend themselves against any allegations of unfair recruitment and selection practices. The need to provide equality of opportunity in employment is enshrined in the employment laws of many countries. The accuracy of the job description is crucial in creating an objective person specification, and therefore the job analysis process needs to be as accurate as possible. The objective and job-specific criteria in the person specification then allow selectors to compare candidates for selection as objectively as possible.

The preparation of the person specification for volunteers at the London 2012 Olympic and Paralympic Games identified the following personal characteristics that would then be assessed during the interview process:

1. Motivation, inspiration and passion
2. Honest and open
3. Teamwork and respect
4. Delivery
5. Distinction.

There were also questions about the functional areas that volunteers might be suitable for. The next section explains how these characteristics were explored during the interviews.

Recruitment and Selection

Having created the job description and person specification we now have the information with which to carry out the recruitment and selection processes. Recruitment is the process of attracting sufficient candidates for a job, and selection is the process by which the best of these candidates are selected. In order for these processes to be fair, they need to be based on the objective and relevant criteria that have been established in the job analysis and are now part of the job description and person specification.

The first process in recruitment is to advertise the job. Adverts have to be drafted that will give a clear idea of what the job entails and what the selection criteria are. There is a balance to be struck here, between making a job sound attractive so that there are sufficient applicants, and ensuring that there is enough information for inappropriate candidates to deselect themselves on the basis of the advert.

There is no single prescription on what should be included in a recruitment advert, although legislation on equal opportunities may well dictate what should not. Taylor (2008) suggests that issues to be considered should include how many candidates need to be attracted, how honest to be in terms of the challenges of a job and whether to focus on the organization or the job. De Witte (1989) found that clear information on job titles, workplace location and salary levels helped attract more candidates, and there is evidence that a clear statement of skills will likewise attract more suitable candidates.

Internet advertising is now used by 75% of employers in the UK for at least some of their jobs (CIPD, 2007), and increasingly sophisticated systems are being developed by which the recruitment and selection process is administered online and candidates can be taken through a series of exercises by which they either progress or are politely rejected as part of this process. Whichever media are used to advertise jobs, it is a good idea to monitor their effectiveness. This should help identify where suitable candidates are coming from, which media are attracting candidates from different ethnicities and backgrounds and which attract the highest number of suitable candidates. A quotation, often attributed to Lord Leverhulme, the creator of what is now Unilever, summed up one of the major issues in advertising: 'I know that half of my advertising isn't working, I just don't know which half.' Effective monitoring of how candidates hear about jobs and where the most suitable candidates are coming from is essential to identify the most cost effective systems of advertising.

Once a suitable pool of candidates has been attracted then selection of the best candidate for the job can commence. Traditionally, this would use what Cook (2004) describes as the classic trio: an application form, interview and the taking-up of references. In small organizations the use of application forms may be replaced by CVs; however, an advantage to having information on an application form is that it is easier to compare candidates when their data is always presented in the same format, as it would be on a form.

When it comes to interviewing, the requirement that candidates be objectively compared suggests using trained staff employing a structured interview, in which all candidates are asked the same or similar questions. This helps selectors, of whom there should normally be at least two, to make these comparisons. The questions should be structured around the essential criteria for the job listed in the person specification and be specific to the job or opportunity being offered by the organization. A written record of candidates' answers will help selectors compare candidates after the interview.

The interview process for the 70,000 volunteer Games Makers at the London 2012 Olympic and Paralympic Games was conducted by staff trained in equal opportunities and diversity, using an interview process that asked the same questions of all applicants and recording the responses before rating them on a scale of 1–4. All interviews started with a brief ice-breaking conversation, before progressing to the structured questions, using a script that explained the context of the questions as well as requiring interviewers to ask all candidates exactly the same questions. Here are the areas of interest and a description of the questions.

1. *Motivation, inspiration and passion*: Selectors were looking for people who knew a bit about the games and would be enthusiastic, motivated and inspired by taking part. Applicants were asked what their favourite Olympic and Paralympic event was and why. They were also asked what excited them about the chance to volunteer at the games.
2. *Honest and open*: Selectors were looking for volunteers who could communicate clearly, be really positive and, as the face of the games, would be friendly towards everyone they met. The questions in this section asked candidates to talk about when they had gone out of their way to be particularly helpful to a customer, colleague or member of the public.
3. *Teamwork and respect*: Teamwork is a vital skill for volunteers – to work with each other and the contractors and teams at the games. Questions explored interviewees' experience of working in teams.
4. *Delivery*: This section was about making the games as memorable as possible by staying motivated in busy and challenging circumstances. Questions explored experience with challenging tasks, the feelings involved, overcoming challenges and ensuring achievement of tasks.
5. *Distinction*: Distinctiveness explored Games Makers' pride in volunteering, ability to stand out from the crowd and levels of enthusiasm. Again this involved talking about how they had overcome challenges and felt proud of themselves.

This structured approach to the interviews ensured that candidates were being compared on similar grounds, by staff who were trained to both administer the interviews and interpret the answers they received, in order to ensure fairness and effectiveness in the process.

Induction and Training

Having defined the strategy, planning, structure and job designs for an event, then recruited the best people for the jobs, the overriding purpose of induction and training is to ensure that all staff understand how their efforts will enable the organization to get the event right on the day. Given the need to provide the best possible experience for customers, there may be little opportunity for learning on the job; therefore if only a little learning is needed to do a job it can be taught on the day with very little cost attached to that training. Staff who have learnt from experience of previous events will clearly need less training. If volunteers are involved the retention of previous staff will be helpful. These staff can then be used to train newcomers.

In terms of the need for an energized workforce, even where national pride was an important motivator for volunteers, as at the Olympic Games in Beijing, an enormous amount of training was also used (Ketter and Wang, 2008). In practice, for large events, contractors to whom functions such as security, cleaning or catering have been contracted will have done much of the training. Despite this, the parent organization should still be clear what standards of service they require their contractors to provide, and this will have formed part of the contract for that service. For mega events such as the Olympic Games or a football World Cup there would be some common orientation training for all staff that would have to include important health and safety issues such as major incident and evacuation procedures. This training provides a certificated pool of staff that have also cleared any necessary security checks in order to work at the event.

One way to potentially reduce the costs of induction is through the use of operational, staff or procedure manuals (Hanlon and Stewart, 2006). Available in hard copy or online, these documents can allow staff to understand as much of their job as possible before induction and training, which then becomes more a matter of testing what has already been learnt and filling any job-specific gaps in knowledge or understanding.

Performance Management

Performance management is an area in which the conventional practices of HRM need careful adaptation to the complex and varied staffing of events. If managing a cohort of volunteers, one might reasonably assume that motivation and the desire to get the job right can be taken for granted. Effective recruitment and selection should have supplied staff capable of doing the job, while appropriate induction and training should have made clear what would be expected in terms of job performance. These steps provide organizers, team leaders and the staff themselves with the understanding needed to tell good performance from bad in order to ensure event success and to provide job satisfaction for staff.

This need to communicate what constitutes effective performance on the day is a particularly important tool in the management of volunteers, for whom recognition of their efforts plays an important part in their reward. Equally, performance of contract staff should be evaluated on the day to ensure that jobs are being carried out correctly. The level of monitoring or control is dependent of the level of risk attached to the different activities. Risk management is looked at in more detail in Chapter 9 (Ritchie and Reid) of this book.

Performance management also provides feedback to core staff so their post-event evaluation can become one of the important tools of retention (Hanlon and Jago, 2004). Staff development for both paid and volunteer staff, creating the manuals for the following year, and providing staff with the satisfaction of knowing they did a good job – all spin off from the performance management system. Overall event evaluation can therefore be significantly enhanced by feedback from staff performance management systems, an important element of which would be analysis of customer feedback.

Reward and Retention

In any organization, the issues of reward and retention are closely linked. This is also the case in events organizations, even those that rely on a large proportion of their staff being volunteers. However, with both paid and voluntary staff it is important to appreciate that reward is not just about money.

The discussion of volunteers, later in this chapter, will consider the question of motivation for volunteers. However, it is also important to note that for staff who are employed, rewards may come in a host of forms. These could include career development within the organization, career development beyond the organization in terms of creating a strong CV with the necessary experience and training to progress, or the intrinsic satisfaction of both being involved in a particularly worthy enterprise and being part of a highly effective and highly motivated team.

Retention can be particularly problematic for event organizations that are running one event during the year, or even one mega event like the Olympics every four years. The problem relates to both volunteers and core staff and is caused by the highly energized, team orientation of the run-up to the event itself, followed by the relative vacuum immediately afterwards. For both employed and volunteer staff, a post-event evaluation provides important information about the success of the event that has just happened, capturing the knowledge acquired to improve future events and also providing recognition for staff of the often-incredible efforts they have just made to make the event a success.

As well as recognition, this evaluation is an opportunity for the organization to look at the future prospects for staff. For all staff, having a sense of what can be looked forward to at the next event, new or bigger roles, more challenge, or indeed less, may be the thing that will retain them with that organization. Additionally, there are some who suggest that making a proportion of pay dependent on completion of the event can help to encourage retention (Hanlon and Jago, 2004).

Cross-Cultural Factors, HRM and Events

As stated throughout this text, events are increasingly international in nature, either through use of foreign inputs or serving foreign audiences. Events teams are therefore required to work across countries and this demand raises additional personnel challenges for the event practitioner. Countries may vary in several dimensions that influence HRM practices, including legal regulations, the structure of employment markets (availability of workers) and national culture. While the first two factors are formal, and data will be available from secondary sources, national culture is a concept that has great influence on HR management, but is difficult to understand. Recently, models that have emerged that attempt to explain the effect of national culture on organizational performance include Hofstede (1991) (see also Ferdinand et al., Chapter 2 this volume) and GLOBE (see Chhokar et al., 2007). Hofstede (1991) identified five factors:

- *Power distance index (PDI)* – The extent to which hierarchical or unequal distribution of power is accepted by subordinates
- *Individualism (IDV)* – The extent to which individuals act alone or are integrated into groups
- *Masculinity/femininity (MAS)* – The extent to which roles are shared between genders and how un/favourably society looks upon aggressive and materialistic behaviour
- *Uncertainty avoidance index (UAI)* – The extent to which members of a culture can deal with unstructured environments, accepting or avoiding risks in everyday life
- *Long-term orientation (LTO)* – The extent to which members of a culture respect tradition and social obligations or are prepared to put off immediate gratification in favour of long-term goals.

The effect of these factors has significant implications for HRM policy design as they need to incorporate the communication preferences and views of authority of varying cultures. For example, in Western, individualist cultures with low power distance, staff may approach management directly with concerns or issues. Staff from other cultures may not, and critical problems may be hidden, resulting in excessive cost or even event failure.

The GLOBE studies build on Hofstede's work, evaluating both societal culture and leadership styles. The latter is of particular interest to events HRM as it is a team-driven activity. Six styles were identified (Chhokar et al., 2007):

1. Performance-focused leaders articulate a vision and attempt to motivate members to achieve it within parameters set by values and standards.
2. Team-focused leaders attempt to build a cohesive group that is focused on achieving a common goal through collaboration.
3. Participation-focused leaders attempt to minimize inequality within teams and delegate responsibility.

4. Humane leaders focus on the feelings of their team members and coach individuals to achieve performance.
5. Autonomous leaders emphasize the performance of individual team members to achieve team goals.
6. Protective leaders focus on the security of the team through procedures and risk-minimizing behaviours.

While incorporating these factors may be complex for events managers, they are critical for ensuring event success.

Table 5.1 Hofstede's leadership styles

Performance Oriented *Higher*	Team Oriented *Higher*	Participative *Higher*	Humane *Higher*	Autonomous *Higher*	Self- or Group-Protective *Higher*
Anglo	SE Asian	Germanic	SE Asian	Germanic	Middle Eastern
Germanic	Confucian	Anglo	Anglo	E. European	Confucian
Nordic	L. American	Nordic	African	Confucian	SE Asian
SE Asian	E. European		Confucian	Nordic	L. American
L. European	African			SE Asian	E. European
L. American	L. European			Anglo	
Confucian	Nordic			African	
African	Anglo			Middle Eastern	
E. European	Middle Eastern			L. European	
	Germanic			L. American	
Middle Eastern		L. European	Germanic		African
		L. American	Middle Eastern		L. European
		African	L. American		
			E. European		
		E. European	L. European		Anglo
		SE Asian	Nordic		Germanic
		Confucian			Nordic
		Middle Eastern			
Lower	*Lower*	*Lower*	*Lower*	*Lower*	*Lower*
Performance Oriented	Team Oriented	Participative	Humane	Autonomous	Self- or Group-Protective

Diary of an Event Manager – Sonja Werners, Event Organizer War Child, the Netherlands

Sonja is an event organizer at War Child. She does not organize an event every week, but she works with the organization regularly. In the week of 25 March to 1 April, 2011, War Child made a tour across the Netherlands with Radio 538 for the first time. As it was a new experience for the organization, it was a very hectic period.

Sonja relates: 'During the whole week we travelled across the Netherlands with two trucks in which a radio studio was built to collect as much money as possible for the war children. The team consisted of staff from Radio 538 and War Child and involved people for the contents of the radio programmes, for the fundraising, for the communication, for the organization of the events, and from the back office.'

While War Child is an international charity, an event of this type required a deep understanding of Dutch people. As a local Sonja provided the knowledge the charity needed to design appeals for Dutch people. While the language was not a major issue, understanding the local culture was critical to ensure participation and audience interest.

Sonja explains: 'Dutch people are very conscious of sustainability issues. Needless to say, that with events like these we always try to take environmental aspects into account. For instance, we print "timeless" promotion material, travel by carpool as much as possible and arrange things locally. Without this effort, I'm not sure if the event would have been well received.'

During the tour Sonja and her team visited 27 locations and was live on air 24 hours a day. The public could follow their activities on www.538forwarchild.nl. At all locations ordinary citizens and celebrities were challenged to do a stunt to attract attention and raise money. She recalls, 'For instance, we drove with a stretched limo through a car wash with celebrities on the roof: Marco Borsato, one of the most famous Dutch singers and also representative of War Child, presented the weather forecast at TV station RTL4; it was possible to abseil from the town hall in Apeldoorn, and much more. We also visited Leeuwarden. For each €300 they raised, the employees of City Marketing Leeuwarden ran on pumps and wooden shoes to the highest floor of a high office tower which was 115m, or 24 storeys.'

During the tour, War Child received many positive and enthusiastic reactions. In total it raised €650,000! With this money it can help more than

(Continued)

(Continued)

54,000 war children. Because of its success the organization also decided to make the tour an annual event.

Sonja says, 'What I've learned from my experience is that international teams can bring the best of both worlds – international best practices and local knowledge.'

HRM Issues Particular to Events

Building highly effective teams at work is a challenge for most organizations. However, when your organization can vary dramatically in size, when it relies on large numbers of volunteers or casual staff coming together for a short time on an occasional basis, and when it serves very large numbers of customers at high-profile events, the challenges increase. Add to this the likelihood that events could be happening in a number of different countries and in a variety of contexts and it becomes clear that building high-performing events teams brings with it a particular collection of challenges.

Pulsating Organizations

A pulsating organization is one that expands and contracts during the lifecycle of its regular activities (Toffler, 1970). In events management this is an inherent part of the business and can happen to an extreme level. Hanlon and Stewart (2006) give the example of the Australian Open Tennis Championships in which a staff of 20 expands to over 4,000 personnel and then back to its original size in a matter of weeks.

One issue for pulsating organizations is the challenge of creating structures that can grow rapidly, on a just-in-time basis, so staff are not paid to hang around waiting for an event to happen but are available to be properly briefed and trained for their tasks. In organizations involving a large proportion of staff who are volunteers, as in the case of the London 2012 Olympic and Paralympic Games, it is important for events organizations to achieve high levels of flexibility, in responding to the staffing needs of their events, while ensuring that all involved know what is required of them and how to achieve it.

This suggests another issue relating to the pulsating nature of organizations. This is the need to find ways of effectively inducting large numbers of staff, particularly in relation to issues of public safety, as efficiently as possible. Hanlon and Cuskelly (2002: 232) identify a generic four-step management induction process common in most organizations. These steps involve:

1. Providing a broad understanding of the organization and its goals
2. Establishing the working relationships which might also include some sort of team building
3. Providing resources such as policy and procedure manuals; and finally
4. Evaluating the induction process itself.

They go on to argue that this process needs adaptation to the event environment, to take into account the needs of different groups such as those who are outsourced or already have experience of the organization. An example of how this worked in relation to the volunteers at the London 2012 Olympic and Paralympic Games can be found in the case study at the end of this chapter.

The earlier section on HRM planning and organizational structures discussed ways to plan for pulsating events organizations, including out-sourcing and subcontracting, while the section on job analysis has discussed how jobs can be designed to help provide the flexibility and motivation required.

A common way of bringing large numbers of appropriately inducted staff together for events is for functions such as security, catering and customer service to be out-sourced. This would require a specialist supplier, who in turn will have a pool of suitably certified staff on whom they can call. It is worth noting that in the case of mega events, all staff who are likely to be used during the event, whether employed, subcontracted or volunteering, may need a common training programme covering basic knowledge such as venue orientation and health and safety, as well as some form of security screening (Van der Wagen, 2007).

Managing Volunteers

Volunteers form a vital resource for many event organizations. In the words of Sport England:

> Without the two million adult volunteers who contribute at least one hour a week to volunteering in sport, community sport would grind to a halt. Volunteers also play an incredible role in staging some of England's most prestigious sporting events. Without this volunteer workforce, the events simply wouldn't happen. (2015)

Van Der Wagen (2007) gives the following list of possible reasons for using volunteers at events.

- Establishing the event
- Expanding the workforce
- Expanding the level of customer service
- Contributing to the community
- Creating a social impact

- Contribution to diversity
- Expanding the event's social network
- Belief in the ethos of volunteering.

To this list one might add the use of volunteers as a source of advice and expertise, a sort of unpaid team of consultants upon which organizations may call, as well as being a way of expanding the event's network of professional supporters. In the case study of the London 2012 Olympic and Paralympic Games (see below), professional volunteers included staff from HRM departments of large organizations who were sponsoring the games, who in turn trained and supported the Trailblazers who were used to recruit the Games Makers.

A good example of two of the reasons Van Der Wagen lists for using volunteers – contributing to the community and creating a social impact – can be seen in the Volunteer Strategy of the London 2012 Olympic and Paralympic Games. One of the factors that contributed to the success of London's initial bid was the social impact the legacy of the games was predicted to have in terms of volunteering behaviour in the UK. An important contribution to this legacy, highlighted in the bid, was the pool of 70,000 volunteers who would be involved in the main games with 30,000 supporting the Paralympics. The bid committee hoped this large number of volunteers would contribute to an appetite for volunteering that the volunteers would continue to offer in the UK after the events.

The scale of this undertaking raises another important issue in the management of volunteers. In the run-up to the 2012 Games, LOCOG anticipated having to handle between 300,000 and one million expressions of interest from potential volunteers. Of these applicants 120,000 would be invited to selection events for the roles on offer. This then raises the potentially damaging problem of tens of thousands of people already being disappointed by the games before they even began. The solution to the problem was a carefully planned communications strategy, paying particular attention to managing the expectations of those who wanted but would not be able to take part in the volunteer programme.

Another important issue in the use of volunteers is the potential for friction between those staff who are being paid and those who are not. According to the National Council for Voluntary Organisations (NCVO), an important tool in the use of volunteers is a volunteer policy. Created in consultation with both paid and voluntary staff, this document should help create clarity on why and how an organization plans to use volunteers. This policy would cover important details such as how expenses can be met, how staff will be recruited and managed, the organization's approach to diversity and health and safety, its grievance and discipline procedures and what insurance is in place. The benefits of using an explicit and well-publicized policy are that it should contribute to a professional approach in many aspects of the management of volunteers and overcome any problems that might be caused by ill-defined lines of responsibility between paid and unpaid staff.

It is worth mentioning that the expenses issue is important, not only because potential volunteers could be put off if they do not know if or how they will be reimbursed for their expenses, but also because there needs to be complete clarity that reimbursement does not constitute payment and therefore bring volunteers within the scope of employee protection legislation such as minimum wage requirements.

Clearly, given the importance of volunteers to many events organizations, some understanding of the motivation of volunteers may prove useful. This is a field that has attracted considerable research. Monga (2006: 58) argues:

> Volunteers do not act due to any one particular motive but due to multiple reasons. Managers need to understand the reasons/motives and expectations people have for volunteering for an event. The responsibility lies with the management to provide for satisfaction of these needs and expectations for increased potential for retention of volunteers.

Case Study 5.1 –
The Use of Volunteers at a Mega Event

Introduction

As mentioned in previous sections of this chapter, the London 2012 Olympic and Paralympic Games made enormous use of volunteers. Their intended use played an important part in the initial success of the London bid, in which the benefit of using large numbers of volunteers to both the hosting community and the image of the Games as a whole was highlighted. It therefore became very important that the process by which the 70,000 volunteers were recruited, accredited, trained, motivated and managed was well thought through and effective.

First Steps

The first step in the recruitment of the majority of volunteers, to be called Games Makers, was to recruit the recruiters. The name of 'Games Makers' was designed to highlight to volunteers their importance in literally 'making' the games; however, before they could be recruited there needed to be a core of volunteers trained to carry out the recruitment process. These staff, known as Trailblazers, were led by HR specialists from sponsoring organizations, whose time and expertise were donated by their employers. The sponsors' specialist staff recruited and then led 60 Trailblazers, who were

(Continued)

(Continued)

engaged until one month before the start of the games, to recruit the 70,000 volunteers who were used for the Olympic and Paralympic games.

Recruitment Process

The recruitment process has been explained in some detail earlier in this chapter. The interviews were, whenever possible, carried out face-to-face but they could be done on the telephone if the applicant was unable to reach an interview centre. It was not unusual for the interviews to be telephonic because volunteers were attracted from overseas as well as from across Britain. It was also important for volunteers to be formally identified before they could be issued with the accreditation that would allow them access to restricted areas and venues, so if this did not happen in the recruitment process it had to be done at the training.

Induction and Training

All Games Makers should have attended at least three training events. First was the generic orientation and role session for all volunteers. Following this was specific training for any particular role they might have. Finally they would have training specific to the venues volunteers were working in. There was additional leadership training for volunteers with leadership responsibilities. Comprehensive workbooks and a supporting CD-ROM or Pocket Guide supported all training sessions.

Generic Orientation and Role Training

The generic orientation and role training workbook was planned, designed and delivered in association with some of the major corporate sponsors, thus making it extremely professional and well-structured. This workbook, introduced by Sebastian Coe, Chair of the LOCOG, included sections on Orientation and Roles, as well as one for volunteers to record their memories of the games. The introduction, designed to be motivational, emphasized the importance of the Games Makers to the games, drawing a parallel between the athletes' preparation and that of volunteers – another motivational tool. The purpose of the Orientation section was to equip Games Makers with knowledge on the history of the Olympic and Paralympic Games as well as introducing them to the London 2012 games.

The overriding purpose of the Common Role Training section was to provide volunteers with the operational knowledge that everybody would need to perform their role at Games time. This section focused on what was expected of volunteers and what they in turn could expect, as well as including pre-course work to prepare for the subsequent specific Role Training.

The Role Training section of the workbook therefore contained the following subsections:

- *Introduction to British Sign Language:* encouraging everyone at least to learn how to say their own name using sign language.
- *List and explanation of the nine client groups* that volunteers could be dealing with, from the athletes and team officials, to the general public.
- *Hosting actions:* this was explained using the acronym I DO ACT, in which each letter had the following meanings:

  I – be Inspirational

  D – be Distinctive

  O – be Open, approachable and honest

  A – be Alert, being aware of people's needs

  C – be Consistent, welcoming everyone as an individual

  T – be part of the Team.

  Examples were given of how each action might be used.
- *Diversity and inclusion:* covering responsibility in regard to disability, gender and gender identity, ethnicity and race, belief, age and sexual orientation. There was also considerable guidance on understanding and working with disability, ending in a pledge to uphold the values of inclusivity at the Games.
- *Communication:* emphasizing the need for, and providing guidance on, how to communicate effectively with both colleagues and public.
- *Delivering a safe Games:* covering basic health and safety responsibilities, manual handling, and safeguarding of children and vulnerable adults.
- *Delivering a secure Games:* covering security issues such as how to deal with suspicious items, suspicious activity, access control and information sharing about the Games.

(Continued)

(Continued)

- *Delivering a sustainable Games:* encouraging sustainable behaviour in use of resources, travel and waste management.
- *Incident reporting:* in case of damage, injury or near-misses.
- *Uniforms and their use:* emphasizing the pride volunteers ought to feel being part of the team and the fact they could keep the uniform afterwards.
- *Accreditation:* explaining the accreditation system for all staff (which was a vital part of security), how it controlled access to different areas, how it would be received and what to do if a volunteer's accreditation was lost.
- *A day in the life:* outlining how to prepare, travel to, arrive, be briefed and deliver a typical day as a volunteer at the Games.

Training Specific to Any Particular Role

One of the principles behind allocation of specific roles was that, where possible, it used the technical skills that volunteers brought with them. This meant that Games Makers could be deployed in technical specialisms such as drug testing, first aid, physiotherapy, building control, and health and safety, to name but a few. Equally, the large number of roles supporting customer services and administration provided opportunities for those without particular technical skills relevant to the Games to take part.

Training Specific to the Venues

The venue training was divided into Key Information, the Games-Time Workforce Code of Conduct, space for hand-outs and a general map of all Olympic venues. All this information was included in a Pocket Guide, which could be carried at all times during the games, to allow staff to refer to it as needs arose. The key information covered the following elements:

- A calendar for volunteers to record which shifts they were covering
- Information on security, including accreditation and how to deal with suspicious items
- List of prohibited items not allowed in any venues, with specific exclusions
- List of restricted items, which if found at a security screening would lead to their owners being advised that the item was restricted and could not be used in the venue
- Health and safety procedures, Incident Reporting Card and instruction on how to complete it

- A comprehensive schedule for all sports and where they would be happening
- Explanation of accessibility symbols
- Workforce and spectator FAQs.

The Games-Time Workforce Code of Conduct provided an A–Z of all the rules that Games Makers were expected to follow, from 'acceptable use of technology' through to 'your shift', taking in important issues such as 'gifts and tips', how to behave during the playing of national anthems and 'respect for people and our environment'.

Reward, Retention and Motivation

As important as the specific training needs of volunteers, was their motivation. As previously noted in this chapter, the public enjoyment of events is very much dependent on the enthusiasm and energy of staff. If visitors to an event are greeted by grumpy staff, this will colour their experience negatively, while a cheerful, smiling and helpful greeting will go a long way towards ensuring a positive experience. This is why considerable thought went into the motivation of volunteers.

In terms of reward, none of the volunteers received payment for their services. This is important because payment would have had to conform to minimum wage requirements and therefore would have made the Games much, much more expensive. The need to retain volunteers therefore rested on how effectively they were motivated to be reliable and enthused about their involvement. We have already noted that the role titles of Trailblazers and Games Makers were designed to enthuse staff at the outset of their involvement. This was supported by a system of badges, in bronze, silver or gold, that could be progressively earned, as well as additional stickers that were added to volunteers' accreditation, reflecting how many shifts they had completed.

Organizers maintained the initial momentum with daily email newsletters which included a quiz to help engage staff, social media groups connecting staff with each other and monthly events at which famous sports people would talk about their sport and Olympic experiences. Additionally there were parties at Christmas before the Games and once the Games were over. Volunteers were also used to help run test events at all the venues, many of which were built specifically for the Games, to check that they would function effectively.

(Continued)

(Continued)

During the Games, staff were provided with uniforms, so they could be very visibly connected to the Games when travelling to and from work as well as while there. They also received free travel and meals. Following the successful staging of the Games, and in addition to the post-Games party already mentioned, volunteers received certificates and had the memory section of their training workbook completed.

Conclusion

From the details listed above, it is clear that the Games Makers were expected to play an important part in shaping the event, and much thought went into the detailed training provided. Although this case study cannot provide a fully comprehensive account of all that went into the volunteer programme at London 2012, it does provide some insight into the detailed preparation that led to a Games widely recognized as a triumph for the Olympic movement, the communities around the various venues and the country as a whole. Ferrand and Skirstad (2015) attributed this success to the effectiveness of the volunteer programme.

Case Study Questions

1   How did the LOCOG manage their 'pulsating' organization?
2   How did they attract, motivate and retain their volunteers?
3   What did LOCOG do to ensure that international spectators were made to feel as welcome as possible?

Chapter Summary

High-profile events undoubtedly attract support from many people interested in their content, and wanting to be connected to the event can become a major motivator in its own right. Effectively, all of the HRM processes and practices discussed in this chapter are important when creating an effective events team. A clear strategy, with structures, policies and procedures designed to create a committed, flexible, quality-orientated staff; well thought-out jobs, aligning the efforts of staff with the strategy and goals of the organization; effective recruitment, reward and retention strategies ensuring appropriate staff with a clear understanding of how their own performance contributes to the event along with well-defined performance management and event evaluation – all of these elements support the delivery of successful events.

Review Questions

1. What are the primary functions of HR events management?
2. How can an HR manager ensure that volunteers perform effectively at an event?
3. Using an example of a conference, design an HR structure to manage a multi-cultural team.
4. What are the implications of 'pulsating organizations'?
5. Discuss this statement using HR theory: 'We've got a good plan. Once people follow it, the event will be fine.'

Additional Resources

Books / Book Chapters / Journal Articles

Hanlon, C. and Cuskelly, G. (2002). Pulsating major sport event organisations: A framework for inducting managerial personnel. *Event Management, 7*(4): 231–43. This article highlights the need to ensure staff are inducted as efficiently and effectively as possible in pulsating organizations.

Hanlon, C. and Stewart, B. (2006) Managing personnel in major sport event organizations: What strategies are required? *Event Management, 10*(1): 77–88. This article focuses on strategies developed specifically for events management.

Huczynski, A. and Buchanan, D. (2008) *Organisational Behaviour: An Introductory Text* (6th edn). London: Prentice-Hall. This book provides a comprehensive introduction to organizational behaviour. Using theory and examples, it examines the dynamics of human behaviour in a range of working environments.

Rayner, C. and Adam Smith, D. (2009). *Managing and Leading People* (2nd edn). London: Chartered Institute of Personnel and Development. This text takes an evidence-based approach to evaluate the tools, techniques and processes of leadership in public, private and voluntary organizations. It provides a wealth of practical evidence in the form of case studies drawn from small, medium and large organizations.

Watson, G. and Gallagher, K. (2005). *Managing for Results* (2nd edn). London: Chartered Institute of Personnel and Development. This book presents a strategic approach to management, with critical perspectives on the human resource area. Using cases and examples along with discussion questions and exercises, it integrates HR and general management theory.

Useful Websites

www.businesslink.gov.uk – Business Link provides support, information and advice on compliance for start-up businesses. Their website contains easy-to-use tools to help businesses start up, improve and grow.

www.CIPD.co.uk – The official website of the Chartered Institute of Personnel and Development (CIPD), Europe's largest HR and development professional body. It works to support and develop those responsible for the management and development of people within organizations.

www.HR.com – Contains templates, tips and ideas for human resource management.

www.SHRM.org – The official website for the Society for Human Resources Management, a comprehensive resource for HR and personnel theory and practice.

References

Atkinson, J. (1984). Manpower strategies for flexible organisations. *Personnel Management, 16*: 28–31.

Beer, M., Spector, B., Lawrence, P.R., Quinn Mills, D. and Walton, R.E. (1984). *Managing Human Assets*. New York: The Free Press.

Bloisi, W. (2007). *Introduction to Human Resource Management*. London: McGraw-Hill.

Boxall, P. and Purcell, J. (2011). *Strategy and Human Resource Management* (3rd edn). New York: Palgrave Macmillan.

Chhokar, J.S., Brodbeck, F.C. and House, R.J. (2007). *Culture and Leadership, Across the World: The GLOBE Book of In-Depth Studies of 25 Societies*. New York: Lawrence Erlbaum Associates.

CIPD (2007). *Annual Survey Report 2007: Recruitment, Retention and Turnover*. London: CIPD.

Cook, M. (2004). *Personnel Selection: Adding Value through People*. Chichester: John Wiley and Sons.

De Witte, K. (1989). Recruiting and advertising. In P. Herriot (ed.), *Assessment and Selection in Organisations* (pp. 205–17). Chichester: John Wiley and Sons.

Ferrand, A. and Skirstad, B. (2015). The volunteers' perspective. In M.M. Parent and J.-L. Chappelet (eds), *Routledge Handbook of Sports Event Management* (pp. 65–88). Routledge: Oxon.

Fombrun, C., Tichy, N.M. and Devanna, M.A. (1984). *Strategic Human Resource Management*. New York. John Wiley and Sons.

Guest, D. E. (2000). *Human Resource Management: Employee Well-Being and Organisational Performance*. Warwick: CIPD.

Hanlon, C. and Cuskelly, G. (2002). Pulsating major sport event organisations: A framework for inducting managerial personnel. *Event Management, 7*(4): 231–43.

Hanlon, C. and Jago, L. (2004). The challenge of retaining personnel in major sport event organisations. *Event Management, 9*(1–2): 39–49.

Hanlon, C. and Stewart, B. (2006). Managing personnel in major sport event organizations: What strategies are required? *Event Management, 10*(1): 77–88.

Hofstede, G. (1991). *Cultures and Organizations: Software of the Mind*. New York: McGraw-Hill.

Kanter, R.M. (2008). Transforming giants. *Harvard Business Review, 86*(1): 43–52.

Ketter, P. and Wang, W. (2008). Sprinting toward the finish line. CBS Interactive [online]. Retrieved from: www.google.com/search?sourceid=ie7&q=sprinting+toward+the+finish+line&rls=com. microsoft:en-gb:IE-Address&ie=UTF-8&oe=UTF-8&rlz=1I7SMSN_enGB341

Monga, J. (2006). Measuring motivation to volunteer for special events. *Event Management, 10*: 47–61.

Sport England (2015). Volunteers [online]. Retrieved from: http://archive.sportengland.org/support__advice/volunteers.aspx

Taylor, S. (2008). *People Resourcing*. London: CIPD.

Toffler, A. (1970). *Future Shock*. New York: Bantam Books.

Van der Wagen, L. (2007). *Human Resource Management for Events: Managing the Event Workforce*. Oxford: Butterworth-Heinemann.

Event Marketing 6

Rumen Gechev

Learning Objectives

By reading this chapter students should be able to:

- Identify the peculiarities of event marketing
- Develop appropriate event communication strategies aimed at event participants and attendees
- Use the event marketing mix to develop an event marketing strategy
- Appreciate the need to alter the marketing mix for event audiences in different countries
- Understand trends in the development of event marketing globally.

Introduction

Over recent years, the organization of events has become an almost ubiquitous phenomenon. Organizations, communities and countries throughout the world have embraced events and they are now an integral part of organizational growth and development strategies. This is because of the many benefits that are attributed to the hosting of events, which include:

- A high rate of investment return
- The positive thoughts and feelings that events generate for attendees

- The potential for organizations that stage events to carve out distinct market positions
- The opportunities events provide for meaningful interactions amongst those that attend.

On the one hand, events are subject to market forces much like any other product or service. Consequently, they obey basic market laws and principles, as well as the major requirements and mechanisms of marketing itself. On the other hand, they possess a number of peculiar characteristics, differentiating them from traditional goods and services. This implies the need for adapting existing marketing mechanisms specifically for events. This chapter begins by examining the differences between event marketing and the marketing of other goods and services. It then outlines how successful event marketing strategies can be developed by manipulating the event marketing mix. We highlight that the event marketing mix may need to be altered for event audiences in different countries. Following this, the chapter explores two current trends in event marketing. Particular attention is paid to how technological developments are impacting upon the practice of event marketing. The chapter concludes by bringing together many of these elements into a case study examining 'Made in Bulgaria'.

Is Event Marketing Different from Marketing?

The Dual Meaning of Event Marketing

Today event marketing is an increasingly important part of modern business practice. It has opened new opportunities for cost-effective and very beneficial communication to market segments. As Hall and Sharples (2008: 30) note, this type of marketing:

> can keep in touch with the event's participants and consumers (including visitors), read their needs and motivations, develop products that meet these needs, and build a communication programme which expresses the event's purpose and associated products' purpose and objectives.

However, this statement fails to encompass all the levels of interaction and dependencies of event marketing because it only focuses on the relations between the organizer of a given event and the respective participating companies on the one hand, and between the organizer and the visitors, on the other. Developing a space for the relationship between the various stakeholders of an event is also of great importance, as this is a key outcome of event marketing (see also Ferdinand et al., Chapter 2 this volume). Companies seek to participate in another organization's events as a means of building relationships with the event attendees. This could occur for a variety of reasons, such as their seeking to introduce themselves, build their brand awareness or encourage brand trial or switching.

Thus event marketing can involve the marketing of an organization's event to attendees and/or the marketing of the participating organizations' brands/goods/ services to event attendees. In one sense it follows the traditional understanding of marketing, as in the marketing of a particular product – in this case an event – and in another sense it describes a particular type of marketing that organizations participating in events undertake, to promote their brands, goods and/or services. It is a type of marketing which seeks to build relationships with event attendees even though the organization may not be responsible for hosting the event.

Marketing Events – A Unique Challenge

Marketing is defined as 'the management process responsible for identifying, anticipating and satisfying customer requirements profitably' (CIM, 2009: 2). Is this definition applicable to the marketing of events? The reply is affirmative, but with the stipulation that there are several peculiarities in the application of marketing principles, depending on the nature of the event itself. For example, events can be divided into 'for-profit' and 'non-profit' events. An exhibition for manufactures would likely belong to the former group, whereas an event such as an anti-war rally would belong to the latter. Between the organizer of the latter and its participants there will be relationships and interactions which will not be motivated by profit or typical market forces, such as raising awareness and recruiting supporters. Similarly many events hosted by governmental institutions or a non-governmental organizations (NGOs) would fall into the non-profit category. For these events, very often the government or NGO will host these events to achieve some social objective and usually these organizations will not seek to recover the costs of these events from participants. As such the revenues from the tickets sold usually cover just a fraction of the costs involved in holding such types of events.

The preparation, actualization and marketing of an event is a great challenge indeed. Unlike classical marketing (which focuses on the market success of a given good or service), the marketing of an event has to secure a certain balance between the goals of all stakeholders, so that the objectives of the organizer, for example, could coincide (or at least come close to aligning with) the objectives of participating organizations and also those of the attendees. Like services, events are intangible and cannot be turned into stockpiles to be kept for more favourable times. In other words, there is not much room for any modification of marketing strategy in response to customer demands, as the event is being produced as it is being consumed. Thus, any tickets that remain unsold after the event cannot be resold, so it is vital that the marketing strategy be effective, as mistakes will be very costly to the event organizer. Other important similarities between services and events are listed in the following box.

Events' Similarities to Services

- *Intangibility* – Events cannot be experienced before they have taken place.
- *Inseparability* – Events cannot be separated from the people who produce them.
- *Variability* – People are involved heavily in delivery of events, hence there are numerous opportunities for variation.
- *Perishability* – Tickets that remain unsold for an event cannot be resold at a later date.
- *Lack of ownership* – An attendee will not be able to access an event once it has ended.

To illustrate the range of stakeholders involved in the marketing of events, the marketing strategy involved in the staging of an international exhibition for manufactured goods will be considered. Such a strategy has to combine a range of goals, expectations and outcomes which arise from the organizers, participants and also exhibition attendees. The organizers of such an exhibition will be interested in:

- The occupancy rate of the exhibition areas
- The price at which exhibition space has been rented
- The revenues from the accompanying services at the exhibitions
- Revenues raised from visitor entrance fees
- The attainment of the highest possible return on investment
- The maintenance of competitiveness with respect to the organizers of similar events
- The positioning of the exhibition in the international market for such events.

However, organizers will not necessarily be interested in which specific companies do take part in the exhibition or what their specific goals and interests are. For instance, if there was an increase of Japanese participants at the expense of American or European ones, this will be of no consequence to the organizer. However, such a situation would signal a change in the market positions and/or the need for modifications of the marketing strategies of the participants at the exhibition.

The marketing strategies of exhibition participants directed to attendees, and the possible communication among the participants themselves, will also possess a high degree of autonomy and independence. Each participant will have their own goals, expectations and desired outcomes for the exhibition. These may include displaying their goods and services to potential new customers as well as finding out what competitors or companies in related industries are doing. In this case, the marketing strategies of the exhibition organizer will be less important to the participants as compared with the importance of their marketing strategies to the exhibition organizer. Moreover, the participants are the customers of the exhibition organizer, whereas the attendees are basically customers of the participants and are only indirectly clients of the organizer.

This situation demonstrates the complexity of satisfying the needs and requirements of two sets of customers at the exhibition – participants and attendees – while meeting the exhibition organizer's need for profitability. It signals the need for different marketing strategies to be developed to target the needs of each stakeholder, which raises the question of balance. Which set of needs and requirements should the exhibition organizer prioritize? Ultimately, the market success achieved by the participating companies contributes to the success of the entire event and vice versa. The more successful the event, the more attractive it becomes for future participants, because it offers adequate conditions for the realization of the various market targets and objectives. This creates conditions for a more successful branding of the event and/or the company responsible for its realization, which in turn will attract more attendees. A chain of success will be created when the needs of all stakeholders are satisfied (see Figure 6.1).

This chain can be equally applicable to music festivals which cater to the needs of artists, sponsors and audiences, as well as sporting events which need to appeal to athletes, sponsors and spectators. In both instances, as was the case for the exhibition, the satisfaction of participants (whether artists, athletes or sponsors) will directly impact the satisfaction of the event organizers, which will in turn impact the satisfaction of participants and audiences/spectators. All three will then impact the event's overall marketing success. One event that has been very successful in leveraging the interactions of organizers, participants and attendees is the Dayton International Hamvention. Case Study 6.1 details how the event has succeeded in satisfying the diverse needs of its stakeholders.

Figure 6.1　Chain of event marketing success

Case Study 6.1 – The Dayton International Hamvention, Dayton, Ohio, USA

The Dayton International Hamvention is the most popular and the most prestigious amateur radio convention in the world. It combines trade show, retailing, flea markets, interest group meetings, licence examination sessions and other activities. It is held each May at the Hara Arena near Dayton, Ohio, and not-for-profit Dayton Radio Amateur Association (DRAA) is the main sponsor of the event. The event attracts more than 20,000 radio amateurs (also called 'hams') from all over the world who see it as an opportunity to buy and/or sell new or used equipment, to meet with fellow hams or to take the licence examination sessions. Numerous companies, among them leaders in the field of radio such as ACOM, Ameritron, ICOM, Kenwood, Orion, Palstar and Yaesu, offer electronic components, receivers, transceivers, amplifiers, antenna systems, specialized software programs and books for sale. The event combines a number of commercial, institutional and social activities. The DRAA's expenses for the organization of the event – advertising, rent payments, printing materials and overheads – are covered by two main income sources: entry tickets and re-renting space to commercial companies and organizations.

The multi-dimensional character of the event creates excellent opportunities for mutually supportive marketing activities. These activities are organized by different event stakeholders (for example, radio manufacturers, radio amateur groups and societies, retailers and charity groups). The objectives of the marketing activities of the stakeholders are quite diverse and the hams as well have several distinct reasons for attending the event. For instance, hams who sell used equipment at the flea market often buy new equipment. Some will come to the event to simply upgrade their old equipment, prompted by the renewal of their licences. At the event both groups will find buyers and sellers that satisfy these objectives. Other attendees will bring their families along for a fun day out. There are participating organizations at the event which provide opportunities for shopping in Dayton and visiting museums, exhibitions and theatres.

There are multiple levels of interaction amongst the organizers, radio manufacturers, amateur radio associations, retailers and attendees – creating a dynamic and enjoyable atmosphere.

Steps to Event Marketing Strategy Success

Beunk and Älmeby (2009) propose the following six key steps to building a successful event marketing strategy, which can be adopted by event organizers to ensure the success of their marketing efforts. It outlines a logical, methodical approach to developing, implementing and evaluating event marketing strategies.

1. Know your Market and Target Audience Inside Out

This involves the study of the key parameters of the event market and includes both research secondary (or desk) and primary market research. It is on the basis of this research that answers to the following questions can be found:

- What is the size of the specific market segment(s)?
- What are the key trends?
- Which are the target and reference groups?
- Which are appropriate mechanisms and instruments for communicating with participants and attendees?
- Which are the major direct and indirect competitors?

Other market research that can be undertaken include PEST/STEP/PESTEL analyses and research into the cultural, customs, language and communication styles of those likely to be involved in an event (see also Ferdinand et al., Chapter 2 this volume).

2. Set Clear Objectives

The conclusions made on the basis of marketing research make it possible to define the objectives in more precise terms, including prioritizing which objectives are the most important. The number and type of attendees the event organizer hopes to attract is usually included among the most important objectives. See the box below for other types of event objectives that can be set by event organizers.

Examples of Event Marketing Objectives

- Number of tickets to be sold.
- Number of exhibitors/performers/athletes/businesses to participate.
- Financial value of sponsorship to be raised.

(Continued)

(Continued)

- Percentage increase in market share to be achieved (if the event is competing directly with other similar events).
- Percentage of attendees from different market segments (e.g. local residents, ethnic minorities and disadvantaged groups).

3. Determine a Communication Strategy

This step specifies the content, the attractiveness and convincing power of the main message to be delivered to the potential event attendees. An effective communication strategy should demonstrate to attendees the value-added qualities of an event, how this event differs from other similar events, the distinctive features it has to offer and its unique selling point.

4. Determine the Marketing Mix

The marketing mix can be harnessed effectively by event organizers to market their events, provided their interpretation is adjusted to address the unique characteristics of events. Getz (2007) has proposed adapting Morrison's (1995) 8Ps approach. He also groups the Ps into 'experiential' and 'facilitating' elements. The experiential elements refer to product, place, programming and people – which most directly affect attendees' experiences at an event. The facilitating elements are those that indirectly impact or facilitate attendees' experiences at an event and refer to promotions, partnerships, packaging and price. Regardless of the model that is utilized the marketing mix must be in keeping with the market research findings, objectives set and the communications strategy specified. The marketing strategy of an event can be developed through the services marketing mix of the 7Ps – product, price, place and promotion, process, people, and physical evidence (Booms and Bitner, 1981). However, there needs to be slight variations in how each one is interpreted. While debates might rage over the appropriate mix of Ps, they are just a framework for thinking – event organizers can always adopt other marketing mixes which may cater to the particular characteristics of their events, such as Hoyle's (2002) 5Ps and Getz's (2007) 8Ps of event marketing. Irrespective of the model chosen, the mix can be manipulated to position the event in both the competitive environment and within the consumer's mind.

Product

One of the key product attributes of many events is one of the other 7Ps – promotion. Meetings, music festivals, trade shows, exhibitions, theatrical performances, and cultural and charitable events can all be viewed as channels for promoting the product offered by the participants to the audience attending the event. This makes events unique when compared to other goods and services which typically do not include promotion as part of their benefits. In support of this offering, the event product can also include sponsorship packages (see Kitchin, Chapter 7 this volume), television and broadcast rights and public relations opportunities.

Other key offerings of the event product are the infrastructure constructed at the event venue, services to both participants and visitors (such as food and beverages, entertainment, financial and telecommunication services), and the atmosphere. These offerings highlight both the intangible and tangible nature of the event product. Like many other goods and services, events are a mixture of intangible and tangible qualities. By using Brassington and Pettitt's (2006) anatomy of a product it is also possible to divide the event product into the following attributes.

Anatomy of the Event Product

- *Core attributes* – These provide the main reason for the event. For example, opportunities for event organizers, participants and attendees to interact and distribute and/or receive information, entertainment or key messages.
- *Tangible attributes* – Visible cues that the event organizer uses to communicate the core benefits of the event such as the venue infrastructure, food and beverages.
- *Augmented attributes* – Add-ons or extras that the event organizer provides with the event's core attribute. These include sponsorship packages, broadcast rights and public relations opportunities, entertainment and atmosphere.
- *Potential attributes* – These cater to the evolving nature of events, allowing them to be updated in response to changing trends and situations. For example, many events can be staged virtually in response to emerging concerns about the environment and the economy.

Source: Adapted from Brassington and Pettitt (2006)

Price

Price is a key strategic component of the event marketing mix. Some event marketers base their prices on the fundamental law of demand and supply. Price is also discussed in Kitchin and Wilson (see Chapter 8 this volume) as an important budget decision. However, event pricing will be based on a number of other factors such as the prestige of the event, the quality of services on offer, the expected effectiveness, the purchasing power and number of attendees, the price levels of similar events, the costs of the event, and the organizers' profit expectations. This latter consideration may, in real world settings, take the pricing decisions away from the event marketer.

Promotional pricing can encourage attendance at an experimental event or one that takes place in a remote location. Some events are free to encourage participation. Event organizers staging such events must factor in the opportunity and other costs that attendees will incur to attend the event even though there is no ticket price. It may cost some attendees more to attend a free event as opposed to a ticketed event, depending on their individual circumstances.

Place

For events, place refers to the venue at which the event is held and also to the geographic traits of the location, which include transport accessibility, level of prestige, natural environment and the security and safety of the area. Modern event venues are designed to be 'clean', which offers a space for any event partner to add on signage to their sponsorship activation. This element of the marketing mix is also concerned with the distribution methods for event ticketing, whether via online channels, at cash desks located at the venue, or elsewhere, by direct sales, or a combination of all these methods.

Promotion

Promotion is one of the most important elements of the marketing mix – as it is through promotion that a good's or service's message or attributes are communicated to the consumer. This message initiates engagement with the good/service. Indeed a consumer must first know about an event before attending. The promotional mix can consist of a wider variety of tools; some include publicity and public relations, personal selling/corporate hospitality, price promotions, amongst others. These can also be implemented through traditional and/or social media.

It has already been stated that the event product itself is a channel for promotion, which though typically used by corporate partners to target certain markets, can also be used by event managers to promote their events. These may come in the form of taster or tester events which run prior to an event, or in the form of publicity stunts or additional media events organized to publicize an event.

Process

Events consist of a number of touch-points. Process involves the planning, design, implementation and monitoring of an event's logistics so that these touch-points are well managed. As Ali et al. (Chapter 3) outlined in detail, the importance of these systems in the creation of experiences cannot be understated. Process mapping is stored with the internal event knowledge base (see Williams, Chapter 4 this volume), and it attempts to ensure that the knowledge remains as human resources flow through the event. All manner of processes need to be managed to ensure the right marketing mix is delivered. For example, 28,000 kilograms of strawberries and cream are consumed during the Wimbledon fortnight each year; the strawberries are kept fresh, as they are picked the day before their consumption at the event. The logistics in getting the strawberries from their source in Kent (a county stretching south-east from London) require processes that start many months before the event.

People

With the increased need for security of major events, many attendees experience their initial touch-point when they arrive at the venue. At each touch-point it is essential that the staff a customer comes into contact with, whether paid or a volunteer, treats them with an appropriate welcome. Once the processes are in place it is the event management system that ensures the right people are located in the right location. Due to a significant expansion in the number of security staff required for the London 2012 Olympic and Paralympic Games, combined with internal resource shortages, G4S – the world's largest security company – was unable to honour their contract with the local organizing committee (LOCOG). Twelve-hundred volunteers from the Army, Royal Navy and Royal Air Force were recruited at the last minute to fulfil many roles left by the G4S shortage. Even though the extra resource was required, LOCOG had to run appropriate checks to ensure staff were competent for the security roles in which they were used (Booth and Hopkins, 2012).

Physical evidence

Above we mentioned the importance of process in ensuring the appropriate marketing mix is provided. However, you could ask, why are strawberries and cream so popular at Wimbledon? Strawberries and cream are an excellent example of the final P, physical evidence. Few shoppers would go to purchase a £2.50 punnet of ten strawberries covered in cream – the price is rather high (as a comparison, a 250g or a half-pound packet from Asda Supermarket would cost you about £2). However, during the Wimbledon fortnight, watching the tennis and indulging in strawberries and cream (and a few Pimm's) is part of the event experience. The strawberries and cream are merely a tangible representation of an intangible event. Physical evidence can occur naturally (wading through the mud at Glastonbury), or it can be enhanced by event marketers to provide the physical aspects of the event experience, and as such it is a vital component in making events experiential. Additionally, the development of social media has placed the creation of physical evidence into the realm of the attendees. Event visitors can use their personal digital devices to share rich media from any event. More and more event venues are making wireless internet (wi-fi) freely available to enable sharing to be synonymous with the event.

5. Execution of Marketing Activities

The timeframe and resources needed to accomplish marketing activities depend on the scope and nature of the event. For large-scale, annual, national and international events, the preparation can last for an entire year, commencing immediately after the completion of an event in the previous year, and the resources required can necessitate that funding be acquired from many different sources including donations, sponsors, concession sales and public sources. Other marketing activities may be staged in a single day with minimal resources.

Prior to executing event marketing activities, most event organizers will design an event marketing action plan which includes the key activities, personnel and resources required to deliver the marketing strategy. Event organizers will often make use of project management tools in developing and implementing their event marketing action plans (See Williams, Chapter 4 this volume).

6. Lessons Learnt

Important lessons can be learnt by conducting research of pre-, during- and post-event evaluations. Methods for gathering information can include surveys undertaken pre-, during- and post-event, on-site observation and participant focus groups. Findings from this research will be crucial for the marketing of the event when it is next run, as it will tell event organizers about levels of participation, the promotional tools that were most effective and what participants thought of the event.

Local Versus Global Event Marketing Strategies

Event marketers, like their counterparts in other industries, must be aware of the need to tailor the marketing mix elements of their event marketing strategy for attendees in different countries. Thus event marketers will be required to undertake market research to educate themselves about local conditions before developing market objectives, an overall communication strategy, marketing mix and implementation plan. For example, the poor attendance at the International Cricket Council's 2007 World Cup could be seen as the failure of the event organizers to sufficiently adapt the event's marketing strategy. In particular, the pricing was out of sync with the purchasing power of the local population, and the core product was not sufficiently augmented to encourage West Indian spectators to attend. Music and the ability to enter and leave matches freely proved to be key attributes that were needed to augment the core product of interacting with other spectators at the Cricket World Cup.

However, this is not the case for all events and all countries. In some instances it may be appropriate to pursue a 'global marketing strategy' when promoting events in different countries. When such a strategy is utilized an event's marketing is standardized in all countries where an event is held. In some cases event managers will be staging events in countries quite similar to their own, or due to the requirements of an event franchiser they will be required to follow a standardized marketing strategy. It may also be the case that the event has universal appeal and thus the marketing strategy does not require adaptation. The following event management diary brings to light some of the other local and global considerations of marketing events in different countries.

Diary of an Event Manager – Maria Schuett, Independent Event Marketing Consultant, Germany and the United Kingdom

Maria Schuett offers services to outdoor sporting companies in Germany wishing to enter the market in the United Kingdom and vice versa. She provides clients with press releases, press kits and marketing plans as well as arranging for them to attend major trade shows. She also stages media events to raise awareness of her clients' products and brands. A few years ago she realized that there was an opportunity in the market for a company that was able to provide insider knowledge and understanding of the German and UK markets for outdoor sports, which were becoming increasingly interlinked since the formation of the European Union.

She explains: 'I saw I was in an excellent position to take a hobby and make it into a business. I loved outdoor sports and was born in Germany and educated in the United Kingdom – where I made many contacts in the outdoor sporting community.'

Currently, 60% of her clients are from the UK, where she spends most of her time, and 40% of her clients are from Germany. In working with both sets of clients she has noticed 'working with German clients is more complicated when compared to British clients. German companies are far more formal and hierarchical and their decision-making is a lot slower.'

(Continued)

(Continued)

As she looks towards the future of her business, she says: 'The main thing these days is social media and staying on top of technology, whatever country you are in. The recession and sustainability are also things I need to consider.'

She advises new event marketers to pay close attention to 'creative networking', as this is a valuable source of business opportunities, especially internationally. Maria also suggests that they constantly scan the environment for emerging trends and potential threats.

Global Trends in Event Marketing

In the first chapter of this book, event marketing is described as a method of communicating an organization's message, which echoes the secondary meaning which event marketing is given in this chapter – 'a particular type of marketing that organizations that participate in events undertake to promote their brands, goods and/or services'. Very often organizations' participation in events is achieved through sponsorship, but they can also host their own events in order to achieve the benefits of this promotional tool.

The popularity of event marketing has proven to be an enduring trend over the last two decades. Social media marketing and event marketing have emerged as complementary tools that can be used to enhance the effectiveness of one another. The following section outlines social media marketing and its role in facilitating virtual events.

Social Media and Event Marketing – Complementary Market Tools

Social media marketing tools can often enhance the effectiveness of event marketing and vice versa (see Inversini and Williams, Chapter 11 this volume). Event attendees organize their communication about an event through social media tools. This necessitates the adequate arrangement of an event's social media channels for now and also for the near-future. These channels have to be prioritized and coordinated into the event's marketing goals. While an increasing number of event professionals are digital natives, the capacity and specifics of each of the different social media platforms such as Periscope, Facebook, What'sApp, Snapchat, Twitter, Instagram, Pinterest, Google+ or even LinkedIn require nimble resources and competencies to manage effectively. Social media channels offer excellent opportunities for the two-way delivery of information about the event, its values and themes, its unique features and the expected benefits for the event attendees. These tools provide obvious advantages compared to the traditional channels of communication, such as faster and more secure information delivery and opportunities for receiving preliminary feedback about the impact of the event marketing efficiency. In addition, these tools enable event organizers and event attendees long-lasting interaction with mutual benefits. Social media allows organization of various virtual contests before, during and after the event. A multitude of options can focus on sharing, such as the uploaded photo or video of the day, the best logo proposal, etc. This approach broadens the attendees' base and makes stakeholder interaction more sustainable. Connected, personal digital devices, such as smartphones and tablets, will continue to play an ever-increasing role in this area in the near future.

A recent study by US media consultants BIA/Kelsey found that more than 75% of marketers use Facebook to attract new customers (BIA/Kelsey, 2014). Facebook (at the time of writing) has over 1.5 billion active users (Statista, 2015), and this can be broken down into specific geographic areas, for example, as of 2012, 92% of European festival-goers are on this platform (Jenner et al., 2013). In the United States more than 60% of people between 50 to 60 years of age are active on various social media networks. Social media will play an ever-increasing and more decisive role in event marketing in the future. In 2018 the spending on social media in the United States is predicted to reach US$15b. Back in 2014, companies like BIA/Kelsey were initially sceptical about the social-mobile market but with the growth of mobile advertising many organizations see the platforms as a space where marketing objectives can be realized. For event managers who own and can control these social spaces located around their events this has the potential to increase marketing benefits for all stakeholders.

Social media marketing spending in 17 Western European countries will increase from €2.6b in 2014 to €4.3b by 2019 as the market begins to mature (Merlivat et al., 2014). Despite these impressive figures, a distinction exists between the increasing number of social media users and impact on consumer behaviour. Hypothetically, the efficiency of event marketing is a precondition for greater impact on the behaviour of event attendees. Events combined with social media marketing are proving for some organizations a successful recipe for making their events/goods/services go viral as customers, with the help of social media applications, are becoming effective company spokespersons. Therefore, social media tools are essential elements of a customer-engagement strategy for event marketers.

The Growth of Virtual Event Marketing

With the advance of technology, the further growth of virtual event marketing will be assured because of a number of interrelated factors. First, the costs of reaching and communicating with attendees and other stakeholders have been reduced. Second, virtual marketing events eliminate the need for non-productive meeting time and as such can be marketed as sustainable alternatives to 'real-life' events. Third, these types of events can extend a company's reach into new, more global markets and capture individuals who could not afford to attend the traditional, physical event. For example, the Western financial crisis of 2008–2009 had strong, negative impact on trade-show events, shrinking their number by nearly 30%. Better and more organized event marketing is a way to minimize this negative impact and to strengthen the ground for growth in this post-crisis period. Virtual event marketing is a suitable answer to the above-mentioned post-crisis problems.

Potential Rationales for Launching a Virtual Event

1 Better cost–benefit ratio.
2 Better and long-lasting connection with physical and/or virtual attendees before, during and after the event.
3 Enrichment of the set of applied marketing tools.
4 Lower entry barriers for small marketing companies because of less initial capital requirements.
5 Broader base for collection of attendees' feedback for more precise assessment of the event marketing effectiveness.

The virtual event replaces and/or enhances events in a physical location thus allowing the attendees to 'visit the event' without leaving the office or the house. The widening use of personal digital devices and a range of free apps, such as Periscope, eases the achievement of the event's marketing goals. In many cases physical and virtual events are organized simultaneously and are mutually supportive. In such cases we are dealing with marketing of 'hybrid' events. An increasing number of trade shows, product presentations, job fairs or sales meetings have both physical and virtual presence. This approach substantially improves the cost–benefit ratio and makes the event marketing very powerful and a highly efficient instrument.

Levand (2015) confirms that the potential of virtual events marketing is still underestimated. Her survey reached 340 marketing professionals, and only 50% of them had attended a virtual or even a hybrid event. Another 33% said their institution had hosted a virtual event. Therefore, by exposing more marketing professionals to virtual events there is potential for further development, and tailor-made marketing activities may contribute substantially to that process (the box above outlines some possible rationales for staging a virtual event). Certainly, marketing of 'hybrid' events will further amplify this process because of the possible synergy effect. As an example, the organization of international circus festivals in Russia, Hungary, Spain, Mexico and China has been successful. The first World Festival of Circus Art ('IDOL') was organized in Moscow in 2013 and it has become one of the most attractive cultural events in the circus world and show entertainment (http://idolfest.ru/en/). Artists from more than 15 countries from all over the world took part in the last event in 2015. As it is a niche event, organizers use social media to communicate effectively with their target audiences. Tools such as Facebook, YouTube and Instagram are used for the distribution of rich media highlighting the 'behind the scenes' activity prior to the official opening of the performances. Rich media are constantly uploaded during the event, which usually lasts for three to four days. The international nature of these events allows establishment of well-connected and mutually supportive online platforms for circus activities that take place all over the world. It amplifies the synergy effect and gains additional 'physical' and 'virtual' attendees. As a result of this use and their high perceived efficiency at communicating the vivacity of the event the customer base has been constantly increasing. Further, the overall success of the international and world circus forums attracts additional sponsorships and advertisements and makes the circus events a growing segment of the entertainment industry.

Case Study 6.2 – The 'Made in Bulgaria' National Trade Exhibition of Producers from Bulgaria

The 'Made in Bulgaria' National Trade Exhibition of Producers from Bulgaria is held by a non-profit association called the Made in Bulgaria Union, set up by the National Palace of Culture, the Bulgarian Chamber of Trade and Industry (BCTI), and Business Center-Bulgaria Ltd. The major objective of the association, according to the Chairman, Vassil Droumev, is 'to encourage Bulgarian companies and grant them assistance for their further development'. Since 1995 to date, the trade show has been held on an annual basis. It has been attracting sizeable public interest ever since its inception and, in the week it is held, it is visited by more than 250,000 people.

The marketing activity of the exhibition runs for the entire year, prior to its staging. Direct marketing is targeted to the members of the BCTI through traditional and online communications tools. Interactive marketing is also done through the trade show's online platforms.

The BCTI has set up a special unit which is assigned the task of promotion, organization, and actual hosting of the exhibition. The leader of the unit, Marin Manzelov, says 'the advertising campaign for the next trade show starts on the day the current event is closing'. Yordanka Chavdarova, Manager of the Business Centre-Bulgaria Ltd, has found 'newspaper advertising has proved

(Continued)

(Continued)

to be the most effective for attracting company participants, whereas TV clips mostly contribute to attract the attention of visitors'. She also thinks that newspapers provide the highest rate of return on marketing costs incurred for the exhibition.

The annual advertising budget of 'Made in Bulgaria' is US$100,000 (€90,000) which amounts to just around US$0.4 (€0.36) to attract each visitor. Thus the free publicity that results from hosting press conferences with the media before and after holding every successive trade show is very important. It is also traditional for the Prime Minister and several other ministers to participate at the opening ceremony of each annual event and that their opening speeches are delivered in the presence of members of parliament, ambassadors and representatives of international organizations. This provides another opportunity to attract free media attention. Event coverage is broadcast during prime-time slots of the country's leading television stations.

In November 2010, the sixteenth edition of the exhibition was hosted under the slogan 'Choose Bulgarian' (National Palace of Culture, 2010) in the emblematic National Palace of Culture, which is located in Bulgaria's capital Sofia. It is an impressive structure consisting of 11 floors – eight above ground and three below. The structure also has the unusual distinction of being built with more steel than the Eiffel Tower (National Palace of Culture, 2008). Entry to the exhibition is free and visitors can spend anywhere from half an hour to three hours looking around. In addition to providing the opportunity to learn about and purchase Bulgarian products, the exhibition also provides visitors with the opportunity to learn about Bulgarian culture. For the more than 300 exhibitors that participated in the exhibition, 'Made in Bulgaria' offered several benefits. For first-time exhibitors, it was an opportunity to introduce themselves to the Bulgarian public. For well-established companies, it was an opportunity to enter new markets or to showcase their new product lines. A special poll conducted especially for the exhibition revealed that 27% of the respondents bought goods made in Bulgaria to encourage local industry while 16% preferred them because of their lower prices. The 2010 edition also featured, for the first time, a display of healthy food, beverages and other products under the banner 'Bio & Eco Expo' (Novinite Ltd., 2010).

Over the years the exhibition has continued to be extremely useful, especially for small and medium-sized businesses in Bulgaria, as it serves as a springboard for entry into the national market. Very often visitors to the exhibition are surprised to find that Bulgarian products compare favourably to imported ones in terms of price and quality. Positive feedback like this gives Bulgarian manufacturers encouragement and confidence in the European market.

Case Study Questions

1   Describe the range of stakeholder needs that must be satisfied by the 'Made in Bulgaria' exhibition.
2   How does the product offered to visitors to the exhibition differ from the product offered to exhibitors at 'Made in Bulgaria'?
3   Other than free publicity, what benefits are derived from the public relations activities staged by the exhibition organizers?
4   What features could be included in the potential exhibition product to position 'Made in Bulgaria' for the future?

Chapter Summary

Event marketing can be defined in two ways. First, it can be defined as CIM (2009) suggests, as a process of serving customers profitably (whether these are event participants or attendees) by manipulation of the marketing mix. Second, it can be defined as a particular type of marketing that organizations undertake, which involves the targeting of customers through the hosting of events. When the CIM definition is applied to event marketing there are a few important distinctions. First, an array of stakeholder needs (including for participants, attendees and sponsors) must be addressed by the event product. Second, because events bear many of the same characteristics as services, they are highly perishable, making deficiencies in an event's marketing strategy especially costly – once an event has been held any unsold tickets cannot be offered for sale at a later date. Third, due to events' unique characteristics, the 7Ps of event marketing can be adapted in various ways.

Marketing strategies for events, like those that are designed for other goods or services, should be based on sound research from which clearly defined objectives, communication strategies, marketing mixes and implementation plans are developed. Event marketers can benefit greatly from conducting pre-, during- and post-event marketing research, especially if they are staging an event annually, as they can learn how to adjust their marketing efforts for the next time round. As with other goods and services, it is often necessary to tailor an event's marketing strategy to cater to specific local conditions in different countries.

Event marketing, as it relates to the practice of using events to promote organizations' brands, goods or services, is proving to be an enduring trend. Social media marketing, which facilitates continued audience interaction after an event has ended, has proven to be a strong ally to event marketing, enhancing its effectiveness. Event marketing has proven itself resilient to the increasing prevalence of virtual sales meetings and events and online sales, as many customers continue to value the experience of getting first-hand experiences of the goods and services they buy.

Review Questions

1. How can virtual events extend a company's reach to new global markets?
2. What are the advantages of event marketing over traditional advertising?
3. Why is return-on-investment (ROI) important to event marketers?
4. Explain the role of event marketing in the marketing mix of an event.

Additional Resources

Books / Book Chapters / Journal Articles

Allen, J. (2009). *Event Planning: The Ultimate Guide to Successful Meetings, Corporate Events, Fundraising Galas, Conferences, Conventions, Incentives and Other Special Events*. Ontario: John Wiley & Sons Canada. Provides concrete examples of how different types of events are marketed.

Close, A.G., Finney, R.Z., Lacey, R.Z. and Sneath, J.Z. (2006). Engaging the consumer through event marketing: linking attendees with the sponsor, community, and brand. *Journal of Advertising Research*, 46(4): 420–33. Examines the relationship among event attendees, sponsorship, community involvement, and the title sponsor's brand with respect to purchase intentions.

Kahle, L.R. and Close, A. (2010). *Consumer Behavior Knowledge for Effective Sport and Event Marketing*. New York: Taylor and Francis. This text shows how consumer behaviour research can be applied to sport event marketing.

Masterman, G. and Wood, E. (2011). *Innovative Marketing Communications: Strategies for the Events Industry*. Oxon: Routledge. According to some they 'wrote the book' on this topic. Definitely worth a read.

Raghunathan, R. (2008). Some issues concerning the concept of experiential marketing. In: B. Schmitt and D.L. Rogers (eds), *Handbook on Brand and Experience Management* (pp. 132–43). Gloucestershire: Edward Elgar Publishing. This chapter provides a theoretical discussion on the usefulness of experiential marketing.

Stevens, R.P. (2005). *Tradeshow and Event Marketing: Plan, Promote, Profit*. Toronto: South-Western, Division of Thomson Learning. A comprehensive text which examines how trade-show profits can be maximized.

Useful Websites

www.eventmarketing.com – The Event Marketing Institute provides insights and business intelligence for strategic event management. It highlights the benefits of integrating social media into events.

http://socialmediatoday.com/ – Social Media Today is an independent, online community for professionals in PR, marketing, advertising, or any other discipline where a thorough understanding of social media is mission-critical.

www.worldeventmarketing.com – Highlights creative and innovative strategies to deliver key brand messaging points in the event marketing industry.

References

Beunk, S. and Älmeby, J. (2009). *Marketing Your Event: 6 Steps for a Successful Marketing Strategy*. Congrex [online]. Retrieved from www.congrex.nl/Libraries/Meet_newsletters/Summer_2009_edition.sflb.ashx

BIA/Kelsey, (2014). U.S. Social Media Advertising Revenues to Reach $15B by 2018 [online]. Retrieved from www.biakelsey.com/Company/Press-Releases/140515-U.S.-Social-Media-Advertising-Revenues-to-Reach-$15B-by-2018.asp

Booms, B.H. and Bitner, M. J. (1981). Marketing strategies and organizational structures for service firms. In: J.H. DonSelly and W.R. George (eds), *Marketing of Services* (pp. 47–51). Chicago: American Marketing Association.

Booth, R. and Hopkins, N. (2012). Olympic security chaos: depth of G4S security crisis revealed. *The Guardian* [online]. Retrieved from www.theguardian.com/sport/2012/jul/12/london-2012-g4s-security-crisis

Brassington, F. and Pettitt, S. (2006). *Principles of Marketing* (4th edn.). Harlow: Pearson Education.

CIM (2009). Marketing and the 7Ps: a brief explanation of marketing and how it works. CIM [online]. Retrieved from www.cim.co.uk/marketing_resources

Getz, D. (2007). *Event Studies: Theory, Research and Policy for Planned Events*. Oxford: Butterworth-Heinemann.

Hall, C.M. and Sharples, L. (2008). *Food and Wine Festivals around the World: Development, Management and Markets*. Oxford: Butterworth-Heinemann.

Hoyle, L. (2002). *Event Marketing: How to Successfully Promote Events, Festivals, Conventions, and Expositions*. New York: John Wiley & Sons.

Jenner, S., Barr, U. and Eyre, A. (2013). *The European Festival Market Report 2012*. Stockport: CGA Strategy.

Levand, S. (2015). Webinars and virtual environments in the study: marketers who use virtual events are likely to use them again [online]. Retrieved from www.intercall.com/blog/webinars-virtual-environments/virtual-events-slow-adoption-despite-benefits

Merlivat, S., Elliot, N. and Paderni, L.S. (2014). *Western European Social Media Marketing Forecast, 2014 to 2019*. Cambridge, MA: Forrester Research.

Morrison, A. (1995). *Hospitality and Travel Marketing* (2nd edn). New York: Thomson Delmar Learning.

National Palace of Culture (2008). About NPC. National Palace of Culture [online]. Retrieved from www.ndk.bg/staticpages.php?par=about

National Palace of Culture (2010). Events: The Made in Bulgaria National Trade Fair under the slogan of Choose Bulgarian! National Palace of Culture [online]. Retrieved from www.ndk. bg/eventsdesc.php?eid=2834&langid=2

Novinite Ltd (2010). Made in Bulgaria expo opens in Sofia. Novinite Ltd [online]. Retrieved from www.novinite.com/view_news.php?id=122078

Statista (2015). Leading social networks worldwide as of November 2015, ranked by number of active users (in millions) [online]. Retrieved from www.statista.com/statistics/272014/global-social-networks-ranked-by-number-of-users/

Event Sponsorship 7

Paul J. Kitchin

Learning Objectives

By reading this chapter students should be able to:

- Explain the importance of sponsorship to the staging of international events
- Understand, from an event manager's perspective, how sponsorship works
- Understand a strategic, skills-based approach to developing sponsorship competence
- Outline the key stages of the model of event sponsorship presented in this chapter.

Introduction

This chapter introduces the concept of sponsorship. Sponsorship can provide multiple benefits to many stakeholders but to the event itself it is a key resource. Every resource an event organizer possesses must be managed in an organized and competent manner. This chapter begins by reviewing what constitutes sponsorship and how it works. Next it details a strategic and skills-based approach to sponsorship management to reinforce the importance of sponsorship for international events. Then a model of sponsorship management is presented. Finally, the chapter closes with a case study that explores how sponsorship can assist in transferring the image of an event onto a sponsor and its products.

What is Sponsorship?

International event sponsorship is 'an investment in an individual, event, team or organization with the expectation of achieving certain corporate objectives in multiple countries' (adapted from Amis and Cornwell, 2005: 2). Since the 1980s sponsorship has become one of the key tools in the marketing communications suite. Within a 30-year period sponsorship spending in the USA has risen from US$850 (€760) million to a predicted US$21.4 (€19.2) billion (IEG, 2015a). This 25-fold increase since 1985 has even outstripped the cost of Super Bowl television advertising that has grown nearly 9-fold in the same time period, and this indicates the importance many organizations place on these investments (Kramer, 2015). With global sponsorship revenues rising each year many sponsors are each spending in excess of €92 million per annum (IEG, 2015b). These sponsors come from the beverages, sports equipment, motoring and telecommunications industries; as such Table 7.1 highlights the top ten US Sponsors in 2014. The United States of America is selected as it is still the largest market for sponsorship spend (IEG, 2015a).

Sponsorship is multi-faceted, it is a marketing and communications tool that can be used by both event and sponsor to engage audiences in multiple markets simultaneously. A sponsorship agreement can consist of financial and/or value-in-kind transfer from the sponsor to the event. The motoring and commercial juggernaut that is the Formula 1 racing circuit is held across 19 separate international locations each year. Moving the event and race teams and the basic event infrastructure (the tracks of course stay in situ) is a significant logistical undertaking. For the right to assist in this logistical undertaking Deutsche Post DHL Group is the Official Logistics Partner of

Table 7.1 Top ten US sponsors in 2014

Rank	Company	Estimate Spend US$m	Industry Sector
1	Pepsi Co. Inc.	355–360	Beverage (non-alcohol)
2	Anheuser-Busch InBev	300–305	Beverage (alcohol)
3	The Coca-Cola Co.	290–295	Beverage (non-alcohol)
4	Nike, Inc.	260–265	Sports goods
5	General Motors Co.	190–195	Automotive
6	AT&T, Inc.	185–190	Telecommunications
7	Toyota Motor Sales, USA, Inc.	175–180	Automotive
8	Ford Motor Co.	155–160	Automotive
9	Adidas NH America	135–140	Sports goods
10	Verizon Comms, Inc.	120–125	Telecommunications

Source: IEG (2015b)

Formula 1. For this right, the firm pay the Formula 1 organizers a sponsorship fee, as well as offering their specific value-in-kind services. The benefit for DHL is in the demonstration of these services to a worldwide audience that can lead to a range of image, sales leads and many other benefits (DHL, 2016).

Sponsorship, once acquired, is a resource contributing valuable funds and in-kind services that can boost the capacity of the event. However, the competence in managing sponsorship is distinct at three levels. As outlined below, sponsorship can be divided into five phases: planning; soliciting and pitching; objective setting; activation; and leveraging and evaluation.

How Does Sponsorship Work?

Sponsorship is both a consumer and an industrial product. This means that a company may sponsor an event in order to communicate and engage with the event's consumers, and a sponsor can also use sponsorship as a means to connect with and learn from other organizations.

The way in which sponsorship acts on the behaviour of the consumer receives significant attention in the research literature (Amis and Cornwell, 2005; Cornwell, 2014; Cornwell et al., 2005). It is established that regular fans or recurring attendees of events have favourable associations with the event itself; the event fulfils needs and desires and can also match the values of the individuals with that of the event. When a brand sponsors an event, Gwinner (1997) found that the associations fans held for the event were transferred onto the sponsoring brand. Essentially this transfer of association meant that a sponsor could benefit and build its brand in the minds of the consumer. Event sponsorship can create a space for the creation of brand affinity, that is, the sharing of values between consumer, event and brand. Once these associations are established, the sponsors could benefit from increased positive perceptions, combined with active management of the sponsorship (see below) that could result in benefits such as greater brand awareness, the development of consumer interest and preference with the brand, or even increases in purchase intent, or actual purchase (Bruhn and Holzer, 2015). Importantly for event sponsors, efforts to support corporate social responsibility (CSR) issues, particularly those championed by the event, are an effective way of demonstrating that sponsors are genuine in their associations. This use of CSR through events staves off customers' concern about the lack of authenticity in event sponsorship (Scheinbaum and Lacey, 2015). In addition to these numerous external benefits to event sponsorship there are also internal benefits (Hickman et al., 2005; Meenaghan et al., 2013; Rogan, 2008). Sponsorship has been found to work within organizations that sponsor international events. Edwards (2015) found increases in employee identification and discretionary effort (they went 'above and beyond') in their roles following a sponsorship of the Olympic and Paralympic Games.

The Resource and Competencies of Sponsorship Management

In today's dynamic events industry, event organizers require certain competencies in sponsorship management. Managing any resource in an organization is a matter of strategic capability (Johnson et al., 2008). Financial resources are extremely important in the success, or otherwise, of an event. Yet financial resources on their own cannot make up for the lack of other necessary resources (a well-defined marketing plan, capable staff and volunteers) and competencies (the ability to coordinate event logistics). In a nutshell, it's not what you have but how you use it that is important.

Sponsorship is both a resource and a competence. Once a sponsorship deal is secured and the financial or value-in-kind resources acquired, much work is to be done. However, in a competitive event marketplace, securing sponsorship is not easily done, particularly in light of the attraction of sporting clubs and leagues to sponsors.

Resources are the tangible and intangible assets of an event. For example, Worthy Farm is a functioning asset (land) that provides the setting for the Glastonbury Festival each year. The National Portrait Gallery in London, England, has an intangible resource, the event known as the Portrait Awards. The Portrait Awards has been used by the organization since 1980 to attract commercial sponsorship, first with John Player (a cigarette company) and lately with British Petroleum (BP) (National Portrait Gallery, 2016). Competencies is a term used to describe the process through which resources are used to the benefit of the event, for example, having an appropriate planning system to ensure that the event has cash flow throughout the event operations. Despite the ability to generate significant ticket sales, if the event organizer does not have enough cash in hand at certain times before the event it can fold.

An event organization's resources and competencies exist at two levels. At the first level there are a range of resources and competencies required just for the event to be in existence. These are termed threshold resources and competencies. An example of each could include the necessary financial resources to pay creditors and a competency in securing and managing the artists who are part of the billing. Many events can operate at this threshold level.

The second level is where (sustainable) competitive advantage can be gained. Sustainable competitive advantage is achieved when the mixture of resources and competencies that an event possesses are distinctive or unique (Johnson et al., 2008). There is only one Roskilde Festival. The brand of the event (an intangible resource) is used as a hook to attract the best global artists, and then the experience of the staff (a competence) manage the event including the artists to create a world-class festival. No other event can use the name: it is Roskilde's alone (dictated by geography). As such, there are many types of events that have this unique mixture (FIFA World Cup, Olympic

Games, Glastonbury/Isle of Wight Festivals, amongst others). This does not mean that unique competencies and resources are solely the possession of the highest-profile events. The next section outlines a process that can develop any event's sponsorship management competencies in the move toward sustainable competitive advantage.

A Model of Sponsorship Management

1. Planning

To ensure successful and sustainable sponsorship an initial planning process is required by all event managers. In the previous chapter, Gechev introduced Beunk and Älmeby's (2009) step guide to developing a successful event marketing strategy. These models are fairly common and all aim to do the same thing. They break down the event basics and establish key areas that must be covered. Essentially they are ensuring that event managers know their event inside and out. Before any sponsorship deal can be agreed it is paramount that appropriate planning methods have been used. Sponsorship can engage many areas of the 7Ps but it must be incorporated into the event's marketing communications mix.

Once the event manager and team understand the event, its identity, what is has to offer and also develop an understanding of their target audiences, they can examine where sponsorship could possibly fit into the marketing communications mix. Adding sponsorship to the marketing mix can lead to a range of benefits for the event managers. The right sponsor can use their brand to elevate the event across international borders. This was the case with the Red Bull Flugtag, which started in Vienna in 1991. An air show such as this (also known as birdman events) is where participants launch themselves (and their flying machines) off an elevated platform seeking to travel the furthest. The event rose to international prominence amongst birdman events after 2002 due to the investment from the Red Bull brand. The Red Bull-branded Flugtag event is now staged in many cities across the world, sometimes drawing up to 300,000 visitors (Aaker, 2013). Sponsorship can assist in other elements of the marketing mix. For example, sponsorship can support the place and atmospherics of an event, it can support the promotional tools and processes used, and it provides support for the provision of physical evidence. Sponsorship can also help differentiate event communications in a cluttered communications environment.

2. Soliciting and Pitching to Potential Sponsors

Prepare a targeted list and adapt a proposal for each target. At this stage the scale and scope of the proposed sponsorship is dependent upon the competencies of the event manager. Soliciting sponsorships that are of significant value takes particular skill-sets.

Although a major event might be associated with high-profile and high-value sponsorships, the process is not the same. The higher the value the greater the need for a business case to acquire the sponsorship – hence when brands sign up to The Olympic Partnership (TOP) they are signing a significant deal that commits their company to up to four years or more of investment and obligation.

During the approach to potential sponsors, event managers should be armed with sufficient information to convince them that the opportunity cost of undertaking sponsorship is sufficient. The opportunity cost is the value of any alternative decision not taken if they do choose to sponsor your event; if the sponsorship is unsuccessful and the sponsor does not satisfy their goals they may discontinue the agreement. Hence, the soft skills required for soliciting sponsorships can include effective communication, empathy to understand a client's goals, and the ability to negotiate. These skills can also be seen as competencies, and as managers build experience these competencies will develop; nevertheless they must be present at the outset.

3. Understanding the Sponsors' Objectives

Why would an automotive manufacturer sponsor an art exhibition? Are they not hoping to sell their wares through this association? Each event sponsor is after a multitude of different outcomes. These are expressed as their objectives and they can vary widely. Understanding the objectives of the sponsor can assist event managers with tailoring agreements to satisfy these stakeholder needs. For example, Lexus (the luxury car brand of Toyota) sponsors artistic and performance events in markets they feel are important. An example of this is the brand's sponsorship of the Sydney Film Festival and in particular the Lexus Australia Short Films Fellowship (Lexus, 2016). By linking with these events, Lexus is seeking to achieve a number of objectives, such as increasing awareness of the brand, encouraging employee motivation by offering staff the opportunity to attend and to increase their levels of community involvement in such activities. These are three examples of sponsors' objectives; there are of course many more. Managers need to understand the businesses of the sponsors they are approaching and develop a level of empathy for their business. Table 7.2 outlines a range of objectives, their relevant details and the desired outcome.

The critical success factors (CSFs) should be determined at the objective stage; this will assist in evaluating the sponsorship's outcomes. Value can be added by event managers in tailoring these CSFs to ensure that the event's design can allow them to be captured. An increasing trend in sponsorship is for many larger corporations to demonstrate their commitment to social responsibility. Corporate social responsibility (CSR) is a corporate expression of values, those which an organization cares about. Event sponsorships are sought that allow the corporation to express these values to a range of target groups. Despite the growing trend there is a paucity of evidence to prove that CSR-related sponsorships have any additional evaluation benefits. Uhrich et al. (2014) have shown that the credibility of a brand does moderate consumer evaluations of CSR-related sponsorship impact. As such, a brand with a poor corporate reputation cannot alter it

Table 7.2 Event sponsorship objectives

Objective	Detail	Desired Output/Outcome
Image transfer	To enhance the image of the sponsor by associating with the event.	To reposition brand in the mind of event consumers by associating with a desirable event and its values.
Media awareness	To generate media awareness that positions the brand to various publics.	To increase the levels of awareness via recall by a range of target publics.
Target market perceptions	To increase the favourability of the brand within a specified target market.	To increase the levels of perception and affinity by a range of target publics.
Sales lead increases	To generate sales leads to facilitate increased sales.	To increase sales.
Business and trade relations	Building and developing relationships with partners.	To improve multiple relationships.
Employee motivation	Increasing the motivation of staff and rewarding good performance.	To motivate staff.
Community involvement	To demonstrate the brand's corporate social responsibility.	To generate goodwill with a range of target publics.
'Chairman's Choice'	A selection based on the personal choice of a significant individual/group.	To show support for, and gain access to, an event.

by CSR-related sponsorship in the short term; however, it does suggest that over the long term, event sponsorship can start to create congruence between the consumer and the event they support or attend. This means that CSR-linked sponsorship (Uhrich et al., 2014) is a suitable vehicle to achieve long-term brand objectives.

4. Activation

The next step is to activate the agreement. Once the agreement is signed there is much work to be done as it is during this phase that both the sponsors and the event can maximize the benefits of their partnership. Wakefield defines sponsor activation as a series of 'partnership actions linking the property (the event) with the brand (sponsor) to make the brand distinct in the minds of the audience' (2012: 146). To ensure this distinction takes place, Wakefield recommends that sponsors and events work together to devise creative and memorable activations.

Many established international events have complex sponsorship portfolios, with sponsors allocated to distinct brand channels, such as soft drinks and non-alcoholic beverages. However, when these brands end their sponsorship deal and a new brand takes over, activation is paramount to ensure the event's consumers are aware of the current (and correct) partner. Hence, the focus is on target market and consumer (fan/attendee) engagement around the brand before, during and after the event takes place.

Advances in technology have also created many opportunities for creative activation ideas. Many people in advanced and middle-income countries have access to a mobile phone (GSM Association, 2015). More often than not these are smartphones – 2.6 billion smartphones as of 2014 to be precise (unique subscribers – i.e. not counting those who have more than one phone). The availability of that individual, personal device provides exciting opportunities for event managers to connect with attendees. In addition to smartphones, wearable technology can bring attendees closer to the event; Google glasses, wristbands and other devices can allow live attendees to access information not available to other publics. This ability to get fans close to the action and/or the ability for attendees to connect with each other relates to the experiential motives that have driven the development of international events (see Ferdinand et al., Chapter 1 this volume).

Event managers need to have a sound understanding of these audiences and the experiences they wish to engage in to ensure they can be in a position to assist sponsors in designing creative activations. Research by Wakefield (2012) demonstrated how image transfer was reinforced through these types of creative activations. In addition to these engagement benefits, Wakefield showed how positive returns increased for the event's sponsors. These activations need to be authentic and can be small-scale events at international events. The activation of Renault's CSR-linked sponsorship with Barnado's through the Virgin London Marathon is discussed in the following case study.

Case Study 7.1 – CSR and Event Sponsorship: Activating the Partnership between Renault and Barnardo's

Renault Motor Group opened the Renault Foundation in 2001 to achieve educational and humanistic missions. This Foundation handles the CSR activities for the large motor group. One of the areas they focus upon is social investment to develop diversity and equal opportunity in the markets in which they operate. The Foundation has a series of CSR-related goals but specifically two goals are relevant here:

Create motivating working conditions that respect human rights and well-being so as to attract and develop employees in all our countries; promote diversity and equal opportunity.

Support sustainable economic and social development in our operating territories through actions targeting local communities in the areas of education and access to mobility. (Renault Foundation, 2016)

Renault Motors UK has been a partner of the Virgin London Marathon since the 1990s. In addition to the value-in-kind services and activation devices the company deploys during the event (branded transport and logistics vehicles in addition to the main timing vehicles) the company has a series of runners entered into the marathon itself. In their efforts they raise funds for the children's charity Barnardo's. The charity is one of many who provide services for nearly a quarter of a million children across the United Kingdom. The staff that get involved allows the group to raise funds for the charity to assist with their educational work, reinforce the group's CSR credentials and also develop their staff to become, if not already, more socially aware. These efforts have been on-going since the mid-2000s and will continue into the future for the benefit of the organization and others.

5. Evaluation

Sponsorship can be measured and there is a vast array of measurement techniques that can do so. When evaluating sponsorship we are measuring performance; hence it varies depending on the objectives set and the Key Performance Indicators (KPIs) that are being measured. As seen in Table 7. 1 above, each objective has a different desired outcome, and as such these outcomes (and their outputs and impacts) must be evaluated through different methods.

Before evaluation can take place, the difference between outputs and outcomes must be highlighted. Outputs are a measurement of the results of a sponsorship campaign. For example, they record the percentage of unprompted recall of the brand following the event (see Case Study 7.2). Outcomes are a stronger measure of performance. An outcome measures how an output benefits an organization. This could include a measure that equates an increase in sales that is in some part due to the increased brand affinity that occurred in certain target markets following an event-linked marketing and communications campaign.

Case Study 7.2 –
Stanford 20/20 Cricket Tournament –
Media Exposure as Evaluation of Sponsorship

Allan Stanford is in jail for the development of a Ponzi scheme which defrauded many people out of their life savings. Before his conviction the businessman wanted to use 20/20 cricket to enter the United States sports

(Continued)

(Continued)

market. To do this he organized a one-off match between a team of his own, drawn from the Caribbean cricket-playing nations, and England – the inventors of the sport. On offer was US$20 (€18) million for the winning team, and nothing for the losers. This style of dramatic winner-takes all match would attract a big audience [the competing governing bodies who organize the teams were paid US$3.5 (€3.14) million respectively – hence their acquiescence]. The broadcasting of the event was sold to television stations, and the Stanford organizers also sold the in-ground signage spots to commercial organizations as sponsorship/advertising. To measure how effective these spots were, Comperio Research conducted a media exposure analysis. They found that the event garnered US$10.2 (€9.2) million of sponsorship exposure and US$11.5 (€10.32) million in overall exposure (Comperio Research, 2010). But how did they assess this value? Media exposure evaluation for sponsorships is a tried and trusted method but it measures exposure only. There is little way to determine whether the exposure has had any impact on other determinants of sponsorship effectiveness. Media exposure measures the duration a sponsor's logo appears on screen, and considers how much of the logo is present (for example, it may be blocked by an athlete on the pitch). It then adds these multiple exposures up and compares the total exposure time to the value of purchasing advertising time during the broadcast. Arguably the attention of the viewer may be more attuned during the match play when the sponsor's logo is revealed; however, it is a fairly rudimentary tool for measuring sponsorship exposure and hence value. Comperio found that the Antigua and Barbuda Board of Tourism, the media sponsor and the Caribbean host of the tournament received the greatest exposure outside of Stanford's own company sponsors. Their brand was seen for a total of 205 seconds per hour for the four hours of the broadcast, which had a cumulative audience of 6.7 million people worldwide – giving them a net media value of over US$2 (€1.8) million from a US$1 (€0.90) million investment (Comperio Research, 2010). From an external point of view the success of the sponsorship appears positive, but detailed objectives for the Antigua and Barbuda Board of Tourism are not available. However, it should become clear that the ambition of such a sponsorship is effectively an advertising vehicle and as such it is a fairly blunt evaluation tool.

How Does Evaluation Support the Sponsorship Process?

As illustrated in Case Study 7.2, Antigua and Barbuda's Board of Tourism sponsored the Stanford 20/20 to increase awareness of their country as a place for tourism and potential business. As the objectives were aimed at the cognitive level, the selection of media exposure analysis was appropriate. Table 7.3 outlines a range of traditional

Table 7.3 Traditional and emergent sponsorship evaluation methods

Tool	Purpose	Target on the Hierarchy of Effects
Traditional methods		
Media exposure analysis	A tracking system that measures the exposure of the brand through a broadcast. This can be measured similarly to advertising. These are traditional measurement metrics that include cost per reach, audience reach, media types engaged.	Exposure
Unprompted/ prompted awareness/ association	A field survey methodology that measures live attendees or broadcast audiences' awareness and associations of an event. Unprompted is where a survey respondent recalls an event that sponsors unaided; prompted is when the respondent is given a list of sponsors (including non-sponsors) and asked to recall those associated with the event.	Awareness and knowledge
Consideration set	When making high-involvement decisions, consumers seek a range of options before purchasing. Inclusion within a consumer's consideration set is an important goal for sponsors. Once included it is possible that a consumer may try the brand's wares.	Preference
Image statements	Image statements use field survey methods on event consumers in order to match and measure the extent to which sponsors are associated with the event.	Liking, conviction
Product consumption	This included measures that assess the extent to which consumers either acknowledge purchase intent, or demonstrate consumption.	Conviction, purchase
Emergent methods		
Sponsor buzz	Buzz monitoring involves counting brand mentions during an event. It culminates in a share-of-voice (SOV) over time, indicating 'the scale and content of association' between sponsor and event.	Awareness and knowledge
Sentiment analysis	Brands have a level of public sentiment toward them. As they sponsor events this sentiment can rise or fall. Monitoring of sentiment through online communications can present sponsors with an approximation of the ratio between positive and negative terms.	Liking, preference
Engagement	As Meenaghan et al. (2013) establish, engagement is a higher-order connection between a brand and an event. Likes, follows and shares are indicators on certain platforms of the popularity of a brand, and can be tracked during a sponsorship agreement. A note of caution however: these metrics are useful proxies for engagement but like all quantitative data they do not explain the quality of engagement.	Liking, preference

Sources: IEG (2015b); Meenaghan et al. (2013: 452)

and emergent (in light of social media) sponsorship evaluation tools. Deciding which one to use is dependent on multiple factors, the primary factor being the objective set.

A central factor in determining the successful use of any of these evaluation tools is the competence of the human resource that is conducting the evaluation. It should be noted that only about 40% of sponsorship deals are evaluated, and these are mostly sponsorships over £1,000,000 (Meenaghan, 2005). Two of the issues with evaluation are that it can be costly (and this can be seen as spending good money after bad – particularly if the sponsorship was not deemed successful) and that the original value of the sponsorship was not significant enough to warrant evaluation.

It is possible for brands sponsoring events to appoint external agencies who perform sponsorship evaluation for a lower cost than the brand maintaining a full-time research team. Outsourcing evaluation research means competent staff trained in the specifics of research design and the choice of organizations is extensive. However, to provide greater value, some methods of sponsorship evaluations can be carried out by the event staff. Having staff available to the attendees at the event is an example of the resource required and the competencies involved, including a range of soft skills such as communication and teamwork in addition to the ability to design and evaluate research.

One of the most important considerations from completing an evaluation on the sponsorship deal is not only knowing the outcome, but also having this information to assist in renewing and extending the partnership. Hence, the model outlined above is cyclical.

Case Study 7.3 – Football, Sponsorship and Parking Cars in Consumers' Minds

Nissan are a long-standing incumbent within the European car market. In Britain, many of Nissan's models are manufactured in Sunderland, in the north-east of the country. In the early 'noughties' this factory was threatened with closure as the European car market faced saturation. This meant that all of those buyers who wanted a car had multiple options, and sales stalled. Further innovation across the automotive industry was required. One solution was the introduction of 'cars on stilts', a vehicle more widely known as the 'cross-over'.

The success of Nissan's cross-overs – small sports utility vehicles – has helped revitalize the brand, not just in the UK, but across Europe and around the world. Since entering the top ten best British selling cars in 2010, the Qashqai, and its siblings the Juke and X-trail, have allowed the automotive manufacturer to build its market share year-on-year. This is quite the effort as it bucked the trend during the global financial crisis that negatively affected many other car sales in many markets.

Nissan's market share in the UK has effectively doubled from 2.81% in 2007 to 5.9% in 2014 (*Car Magazine*, 2015). This is no small gain – the British car market sold 2.6 million units in the past 12 months; essentially 140,000 of these were from Nissan. In fact, of all the manufacturers that sold over 100,000 units in 2014, Nissan was the fastest growing, beating the likes of Audi, BMW, Mercedes and even the market's biggest seller, Ford. Nissan's figures are also strong across Europe where they have a 4.5% market share of all vehicles sold.

Despite this success, some at Nissan felt that both market and customer perceptions of their brand did not match what they felt it could be:

> If you're a large brand like us, the most important thing is that you become part of your target customer's world and environment, that you are part of the things that excite them. We spend a lot of marketing dollars like all brands do, but to find the real connections is difficult. So when we communicate with people, when we have a car or a special offer or something to talk about, we refer to our vehicle. But we don't often connect with people when they are more in the relaxed atmosphere, when they're enjoying themselves or when they are doing what they feel like doing, and I feel it's important that as a brand you're also part of their life. (Nissan's Corporate Vice President, Head of Marketing and Brand Strategy, Roel de Vries – cited in Nissan, 2015a)

De Vries' comments reflect a decision that many brand and marketing managers face. What marketing communications tools provide the best ability to engage the target market? Or how do we engage with consumers in their environments, one that they find special, without shouting too loudly about our goods and services? Event sponsorship is an optimal tool for such a problem. Indeed, since 2014 Nissan has invested heavily in sport event sponsorship, particularly in those events that have global appeal: the Rio 2016 Olympic and Paralympic Games, the Africa Cup of Nations, the International Cricket Council and a number of national Olympic teams, including Brazil, Columbia, Mexico and TeamGB/ParalympicsGB (and Northern Ireland). From the 2015-16 season, Nissan have become the Official Automotive Sponsor for the

(Continued)

(Continued)

UEFA (Union of European Football Associations) Champions League around the globe (starting their association across Europe in 2014–15) (Nissan, 2015b).

One question that we could ask is, why have Nissan chosen these sporting events to sponsor? De Vries states:

> We're obviously not doing this just for the fun of it; we're doing it to change perception of our brand ... We therefore decided that in addition to all the communication of vehicles, we need to invest more in becoming part of people's lives and we felt the most engaging activity is watching sports ... If you are visible in those things that engage people then you become part of their world. (Roel de Vries, cited in Nissan, 2015a)

Nissan believe that *Innovation Excites* and much of the sponsorship activity is managed by linking to high-profile, globally recognizable sporting events. Essentially they are able to use their sponsorships to reach multiple local markets simultaneously. With reference to the topics covered in this chapter, it is clear that Nissan's objectives seek to transfer the image of these events to their brand (internationally excellent, exciting, innovative) and as such alter the (mis)perceptions about the brand in their target markets. Event sponsorship is an effective vehicle for these goals.

In addition, a range of activation strategies will be employed during these sponsorships to reinforce the association between the sponsor and event. For the UEFA Champions League, Nissan use four brand ambassadors: elite footballers Max Meyer, Yaya Touré, Andreas Iniesta and Thiago Silva. Each of these athletes have experienced top-level success in their careers playing for leading clubs in the UEFA Champions League, and they also represent their countries – Germany, Ivory Coast, Spain and Brazil respectively. On the match-days when the events take place and throughout the annual schedule of matches, Nissan is rolling out a range of activations to ensure that the general viewer, and in particular their specific target markets, are picking up on the associations between the sponsor and the event. These activations include ticket allocations at tournament matches (some including corporate hospitality); as part of the Centre Circle Carrier activities, special access is provided for some 1,300 young people to join the players on the pitch by carrying the UEFA Champions League emblem; also social media plays a key part in these activations. #ChampionsKey was used across Spain, England

and France to enable fans supporting their teams in the competition to gain two tickets to attend a home match for their team. Each European Nissan Twitter account is active on match nights – engaging with fans and discussing the result. Nissan also host the competition's 'Goal of the Week' where fans can access the website – www.nissan.co.uk/GB/en/experience-nissan/uefa-champions-league/goal-of-the-week-game.html (the British version), review the week's best goals and add their vote for their favourite.

Nissan add their resources and competences to the UEFA deal also. The automotive manufacturer's development of electric vehicles, such as the Nissan Leaf, reflects not only the innovativeness of the organization but also the leading role research plays in developing the company's product lines. Efforts to bring electric cars into the mainstream in Europe also seek to reduce emissions in the largest cities, cleaning up the environment and enhancing their corporate social responsibility objectives. At the final in Berlin in 2015 the organizers and their partners had access to 100 electric vehicles to assist with the event's logistics; Nissan even set up over 120 temporary and permanent charging installations that left a tangible legacy in the city.

As for evaluating the sponsorship deal, de Vries added that:

> we're very happy with the results so far ... We measure the impact that the sponsorship is having and the results in Europe are really encouraging. We are recognised quite strongly for the fact that we sponsor and we also see that the opinion those people have of our brand is strongly improving, which is very encouraging. (Nissan, 2015a)

The specifics of the evaluation method for this sponsorship are not publicly available but general approaches to measuring their aims would require multi-site surveys on a range of publics in key markets, examining target market perceptions and brand associations. The deal is for four years from 2015 and it will be interesting to see how Nissan and UEFA manage the partnership for continued mutual benefit, but it is clear that Nissan are innovating their sponsorship agreement to engage their key publics.

Case Study Questions

1   Consider your own social media usage. Do you engage with brands when they activate their sponsorships through these channels? Why, or why not?

(Continued)

(Continued)

2   What are the risks with using brand ambassadors that currently play the sporting event that is being sponsored?

3   Can you design an activation device that could utilize social media more effectively than the current Nissan and UEFA Champions League deal does? If so, how would it aim to reinforce the partnership?

Chapter Summary

This chapter has introduced the concept of event sponsorship. In particular it has examined the growth in sponsorship and revealed how research has enabled us to better understand how it works in consumers' minds. Sponsorship is both a resource and a competence; once it is acquired it needs to be managed carefully. Nevertheless there are many opportunities where the event manager can add value to sponsorship deals to ensure the best possible partnership and to reduce the expense of having to secure new sponsors each time a contract ends.

A five-stage model was proposed consisting of planning, soliciting and pitching to potential sponsors, objective setting, activation and evaluation. Each of these stages is equally important if sponsorship is to be managed effectively. The contents of this chapter are a mere starting point to a much larger focus on the intricacies of sponsorship and its relationship to the marketing process.

Review Questions

1.   How does sponsorship serve both as a resource and as a competence for event managers?

2.   In what ways can an event manager and staff add value to the sponsorship agreement throughout the model presented above?

3.   How would you design an approach for sponsors to use multiple activation activities to achieve multiple objectives during a live event?

Additional Resources

Books / Book Chapters / Journal Articles

Cornwell, B.T. (2014). *Sponsorship in Marketing: Effective Communication through Sports, Arts and Events*. Oxon.: Routledge. One of the leading scholars on why sponsorship works draws on her significant research experience to craft an excellent textbook on sponsorship.

Silkum-Reid, K. and Grey, A.M. (2014) *The Sponsorship Seeker's Toolkit* (4th edn). USA: McGraw-Hill. A great practical introduction to seeking event sponsorship. Based of the author's significant experience in the industry, this is one of the most accessible titles on sponsorship.

Useful Websites

http://sponsorship.com (IEG) – This website is a great resource for learning more about sponsorship. The blog part of the page is searchable by tag words; try entering 'activation' and reading through some of the free cases.

http://sponsorship.org/ (European Sponsorship Association) – This is a good site for examining sponsorship developments in Europe. They have information about studying for an ESA Diploma which may be of interest to some.

www.nissan.co.uk/GB/en/experience-nissan/uefa-champions-league/goal-of-the-week-game.html (Nissan's 'Goal of the Week') – This site shows one aspect of Nissan's activation of their UEFA Champions' League sponsorship.

References

Aaker, D. (2013). Red Bull: the ultimate brand builder [online]. Retrieved from www.prophet.com/blog/aakeronbrands/140-red-bull

Amis, J.M. and Cornwell, T.B. (2005). Sport sponsorship in a global age. In: Amis, J.M. and Cornwell, T.B. (eds), *Global Sports Sponsorship* (pp. 1–18). Oxford: Berg.

Beunk, S. and Älmeby, J. (2009). *Marketing Your Event: 6 Steps for a Successful Marketing Strategy*. Congrex [online]. Retrieved from www.congrex.nl/Libraries/Meet_newsletters/Summer_2009_edition.sflb.ashx

Bruhn, M. and Holzer, M. (2015). The role of the fit construct and sponsorship portfolio size for event sponsorship success: A field study. *European Journal of Marketing, 49*(5/6): 874–93.

Car Magazine (2015). UK car sales analysis: winners and losers [online]. Retrieved from http://www.carmagazine.co.uk/car-news/industry-news/ford/uk-2014-car-sales-analysis-winners-and-losers/

Comperio Research (2010). *Media Exposure Report: Stanford 20/20 Cricket Tournament*. Toronto: Comperio Research.

Cornwell, B.T. (2014). *Sponsorship in Marketing: Effective Communication through Sports, Arts and Events*. Oxon: Routledge.

Cornwell, B.T., Weeks, C. and Roy, D.P. (2005). Sponsorship-linked marketing: Opening the black box. *Journal of Advertising, 34*(2): 21–42.

DHL (2016). Formula 1 [online]. Retrieved from www.dhl.com/en/about_us/partnerships/motorsports/formula_1.html

Edwards, M.R. (2015). The Olympic effect: employee reactions to their employer's sponsorship of a high-profile global sporting event. *Human Resource Management*, DOI: 10.1002/hrm.21702

GSM Association (2015). The Mobile Economy [online]. Retrieved from www.gsmamobileeconomy.com/GSMA_Global_Mobile_Economy_Report_2015.pdf

Gwinner, K. (1997). A model of image creation and image transfer in event sponsorship. *International Marketing Review, 14*(3): 145–58.

Hickman, T.M., Lawrence, K.E. and Ward, J.C. (2005). A social identities perspective on the effects of corporate sports sponsorship on employees. *Sport Marketing Quarterly, 14*(3): 148–57.

IEG (2015a). Sponsorship spending report: Where the dollars are going and trends for 2015 [online]. Retrieved from www.sponsorship.com/IEG/files/4e/4e525456-b2b1-4049-bd51-03d9c35ac507.pdf

IEG (2015b). The deepest sponsorship pockets of 2014: IEG's Top Spenders List [online]. Retrieved from www.sponsorship.com/IEGSR/2015/08/03/The-Deepest-Sponsorship-Pockets-of-2014—IEG-s-Top.aspx

Johnson, G., Scholes, K. and Whittington, R (2008). *Exploring Corporate Strategy* (8th edn). London: Pearson Education.

Kramer, L. (2015). Super Bowl 2015: How much does a 30-second television commercial cost? [online]. Retrieved from: www.syracuse.com/superbowl/index.ssf/2015/01/super_bowl_2015_how_much_does_commercial_cost_tv_ad_30_second_spot.html

Lexus (2006). Lexus Australia Short Film Fellowship [online]. Retrieved from www.sff.org.au/about/lexus-australia-short-film-fellowship/

Meenaghan, T. (2005). Evaluating sponsorship effects. In: Amis, J.M. and Cornwell, T.B. (eds), *Global Sports Sponsorship* (pp. 243–64). Oxford: Berg.

Meenaghan, T., McLoughlin, D. and McCormack, A. (2013). New challenges in sponsorship evaluation actors, new media, and the context of praxis. *Psychology and Marketing, 30*(5): 444–60.

National Portrait Gallery (2016). Sponsor [online]. Retrieved from www.npg.org.uk/whatson/bp2016/exhibition/sponsor.php

Nissan (2015a). NISSAN UEFA Champions League Sponsorship [online]. Retrieved from http://newsroom.nissan-europe.com/EU/en-gb/Media/Media.aspx?mediaid=133448

Nissan (2015b). Nissan's UEFA Champions League partnership goes global for 2015/16 season [online]. Retrieved from http://newsroom.nissan-europe.com/EU/en-gb/Media/Media.aspx?mediaid=136421

Renault Group (2015). Our corporate social responsibility practices [online]. Retrieved from https://group.renault.com/en/commitments/vision-of-social-responsability/social-responsability-principles/

Rogan, M. (2008). Building the business case for internal sponsorship activation. *Journal of Sponsorship, 1*(3): 267–73.

Scheinbaum, A.C. and Lacey, R. (2015). Event social responsibility: A note to improve outcomes for sponsors and events. *Journal of Business Research, 68*(9): 1982–6.

Uhrich, S., Koenigstorfer, J. and Gröppel-Klein, A. (2014). Leveraging sponsorship with corporate social responsibility. *Journal of Business Research, 67*(9): 2023–9.

Wakefield, K.L. (2012). How sponsorships work: The sponsorship engagement model. *Event Management, 16*: 143–55.

Financing Events

Paul J. Kitchin and Rob Wilson

Learning Objectives

By reading this chapter students should be able to:

- Understand how the organizational context provides the need for sound financial management
- Appreciate why an understanding and application of financial skills are an essential component in the planning and management of events
- Explain the importance of the accurate determination of event costing, pricing and budgets
- Critically evaluate an event's financial performance and achievement of budgeted objectives
- Gain insight into the role of the manager in reporting back to stakeholders who may be interested in the event's financial information.

Introduction

The Importance of Finances for Events

Perhaps more than ever, effective allocation of a festival's limited resources is a critical managerial decision that must be addressed by all organizers. (Smith et al., 2010: 242)

As the statement above indicates, the importance of financial management and res-ource allocation for international events cannot be understated. International events are an important part of cities', regions' and countries' cultural make-up and represent more than simply entertainment for interested consumers. Given this importance it is imperative that their ability to operate on a regular and on-going basis is supported by a strong financial awareness of their management teams. How can we communi-cate our event plan in financial terms? How will we price the event to ensure that our objectives are met? How can we ensure that the management team and staff stay on-time and on-budget? How can we determine if we are generating enough revenue from our event to cover our costs? And how important is our cash-on-hand for our immediate survival? These questions are all related to the understanding and applica-tion of financial skills. They represent skills that all managers need, and your ability to use them will often determine the success or failure of the event.

Depending on the size and scope of the event, managers have different financial processes. The organizational context (Stewart, 2015), or basic business model of the event business, is crucial for determining these reporting needs. These models consist of a number of types. The basic types are that of sole-traders or partnerships where the owners are the legal entities that make up the business. For international oper-ations this is a risky form, as if an event fails to be held the owner or the partners are legally responsible for all the debts that the event incurs. Therefore other legal forms are required. The formation of a company that is a legal entity in the eyes of the law is generally the preferred option for managing large-scale, international events. Andersson and Getz (2008) claim that many event organizations seek these legal, institutional forms in order to establish legitimacy and promote sustainability in the event industry. Stewart (2015) identifies two types in particular: the proprietary, or limited, company and the company limited by guarantee. A limited company is a form of organization that is limited by shares. The company can either be private and owned by a number of shareholders, or it can have its shares publicly traded on a stock exchange. In the UK, Ireland and Australia, a company limited by guarantee is a private legal entity that consists of a company backed by a group of members who make a contribution if the business is wound up. Organizing committees of major events are often established as limited companies. This approach removes the risk from the country/city that is bidding for the event and places the legal responsibility for running the event with the committee. An example of this was the organization of the 2015 Rugby World Cup. England Rugby 2015 was established as the organizing committee by the governing body of the sport in the region – the Rugby Football Union. It was then responsible for the effective delivery of the six-week tournament. Getz's (2005) event types consisted of a variety of these forms of organization with varying company structures; however, even in the case of government organizations the pricing, budgeting and reporting requirements have similarities. Therefore the finance issues discussed in this chapter should be of relevance to all event manage-ment organizations.

This chapter is aimed at students wishing to enter the events management industry. From our experiences a number of students of event management show a keen interest to master the areas of operations, or commercial and public relations aspects of events; however, few talk about finance with the same passion. The saying 'do the math' is absolutely fundamental to successful event management even if it is not many enthusiasts' first choice of career. While this chapter will not make the reader an accountant it will provide a first step in thinking about finance from a managerial perspective. Put very simply, finance is not just about numbers and you do not have to be a skilled mathematician to understand finance or manage money. Instead, you need to understand the guiding rules and principles that help build and structure a set of financial documents. Mastery of these skills will allow you to communicate your plans in financial terms with a confidence and conviction often missing in an event manager's toolbox of skills. A dictionary-based knowledge of finance terms will not save the event from impending financial doom but, possibly, an understanding of the relationships between pricing, budgeting and financial reporting could do so.

This chapter is structured into three main parts. The first part will examine pricing considerations for event management. There are many strategies in determining the price range to charge participants, spectators and other organizations who may use our festivals and events. The key factor in price determination is having a clear understanding of the reasons why we are staging the event. This second part is an introduction to budgeting and how this financial tool is important for both internal stakeholder planning and controlling the finances of the event. The final section will address the three main types of financial reporting. Financial reporting is not simply constructing these statements but actually understanding the relationships between the economic entity of the business, its profitability and its solvency. This chapter also has an extended glossary. It is stressed that readers familiarize themselves with this section, as finance is full of its own jargon that requires defining and it can complicate the process for the novice manager.

Pricing

There are two key considerations that the event manager must address when seeking to establish price. For those managers who are stewards of existing events there is a wealth of historical data that they can use (including last year's price) to establish their pricing levels. Alternatively for managers involved in establishing new events the organization/event objectives and the costs involved in the event's staging are fundamental considerations. Financial management planning can be an extremely accurate consideration of what you aim to achieve and what it costs, but the final key question is: can the customer afford it?

Therefore, knowledge of the event's target market and each segment's willingness and ability to pay is vital. Good marketing research will provide managers with the results required to target, acquire and retain customers for the event while sound financial management should establish accurate budgets that will control costs and allow the correct price to be set. In academic terms, determining price fits within the function of the marketing manager. This is suitable when addressing traditional organizations that have complex product portfolios. These pricing decisions have an important impact on the organization but small errors in the pricing of one product will not bring down a Fast Moving Consumer Goods (FMCG) brand; however, given the importance of pricing for event entry as an all-in product like an entertainment event, it is crucial. Therefore pricing will probably not be left to the marketing manager but rather the senior members of the event management team, if not the director.

Many large-scale events seek to achieve a wide range of objectives for their many stakeholders. Determining the full range of objectives is a difficult task but it can be simplified for finance terms by establishing whether the event company is a for-profit or not-for-profit enterprise (this is a gross simplification but for the purposes of this chapter it should suffice). A for-profit enterprise seeks to maximize its return on the funds invested in the business. This does not mean that every activity is carried out simply to maximize profit (that is, there can be social objectives achieved by for-profit event companies that incur costs) but that a return on investment is a sign of business success and sustainability – important for attracting further patrons, sponsors and other commercial partners.

There are many costs that event organizations must incur in order to manage the event. These costs are broken down into two main categories: variable and fixed. Variable costs are those costs that change with each additional ticket sale that might arise during the event. Fixed costs are those that remain constant over the duration of the event, such as insurance. Fixed costs can be further broken into fixed and semi-fixed costs. Semi-fixed costs remain relatively stable but can increase with a step-change once certain capacity levels are reached (Stewart, 2015; Wilson, 2011). For instance when an indoor venue like a stadium is used for an event it will require cleaning. Unless the event is a sell-out the stadium will have empty banks of seats. If these seats are kept clear then they will not require cleaning and therefore require less cost, not in a variable sense but by a step-change amount. Proper planning will ensure these costs are incorporated into an estimation of the break-even point.

Break-even analysis is a first step in determining the financial management of any project or event. All fixed and variable costs should be calculated to gain an understanding of the relationship between increased sales and increases in costs, giving the manager the total cost. By then ascertaining the contribution sales make, a total revenue figure is made clear. Once this is achieved, the intersect between total cost and total revenue is the break-event point for the event. In a simple situation this would apply for the entire event; however, in a situation where an event has much capacity the step-change of semi-fixed costs incurred would create a number of break-even points. Nevertheless for new events, regardless of their potential size, once the break-even point is achieved the process of pricing strategies and budgeting can begin.

Pricing Strategies

There is a wide range of pricing strategies that management teams may adopt. It is not the purpose of this chapter to review every pricing strategy available to managers; however, the following options are provided to introduce the reader to some basic approaches. The establishment of the break-even point is crucial for these strategies to provide maximum benefit to the event organizers.

Cost-Plus Pricing

Verma (2008) comments that cost-plus pricing is one of the most common approaches for managers. Once all costs are considered and an estimate of total sales is made, a margin can be applied to the figure that provides the profit or surplus for the organization. As each unit is sold, the margin allows the organization to generate profit. For capital intensive events such as the FIFA World Cup of football the fixed costs are high, therefore sales revenue from tickets, broadcasting rights contributions, merchandise sales and commercial sponsorships are vital if a margin is to be achieved.

Prestige Pricing

While events of international significance exist in a competitive field, certain events are positioned at the exclusive end of the quality spectrum. Events such as the European Champions League Final, Cannes Film Festival, and Glastonbury festival are synonymous with certain expectations, and obtaining tickets to these events can be difficult for consumers. This exclusivity allows the creation of ticket packages that cater for this demand. Prestige pricing is also used to reinforce this exclusivity, allowing the event hosts to leverage higher margins on top of the total unit costs of staging the event.

Discriminatory Pricing

International events that are looking to achieve a number of accessibility objectives or those wishing to maximize their ticket sales may use discriminatory pricing in order to attract the widest array of visitors. The range of target groups that may be interested in an event varies considerably and so too does their ability to pay. By offering a discriminatory pricing strategy the event can attract those groups who can afford high prices; for instance the Singapore Grand Prix contains 13 ticketing categories (Henderson et al., 2010). This can be provided through providing seating areas of different proximity to the event itself or by offering a range of tickets to a multi-activity event. The following box highlights the ticketing policy of the Summer and Winter Olympic Games. As the event costs a great amount of money to stage, the policy was established to ensure host cities would make the Games accessible.

Ticket Pricing Policy and the IOC

The Olympic Charter and the *Technical Manual on Ticketing* assist Organizing Committees that host a Summer or Winter Olympic/Paralympic Games to determine the systems governing the allocation of tickets during the event. Discriminatory pricing methods are used to ensure that all of the sporting and cultural events that take place within these two-week periods achieve their maximum ticket sales. Kitchin (2007) highlighted how this can be a minefield for the event managers. The profile of the ticketing systems and the availability and price of tickets to certain events (such as the opening and closing ceremonies and the 100m men's final in athletics) lead to many public relations issues for organizers. However, the discriminatory pricing policies allow the event managers to maximize ticket revenue. In the case of the Olympics this is vital, as all ticket revenues flow to the host city, assisting in the recuperation of the immense costs of the Games. Considering that the bill for the Athens 2004 Summer Olympic Games was estimated at US$11.6 billion, getting the policy right is important (Smith, 2004).

Budgeting

Planning and Controlling Finance

For small-scale events, budgets can be prepared quite quickly and can rely on a manager's experience and judgement. However, the more significant the event the greater the need for the budget to be prepared with precision. To ensure that events are managed effectively, a budget outlining the major financial activities involved in the project must be established from the outset. Budgeting is an important planning and control function for event management. On-going calendar events may have different planning mechanisms to one-off events, but Schneider and Sollenberger (2005: 236) view planning 'as a framework within which managers anticipate future events, develop a plan of action, and estimate future revenues and costs'. Once a budget is created it should then be analysed by the senior management team, as each manager may have expertise in certain areas allowing greater specificity on expected costs and revenues. The control function in financial management seeks to ensure that funds spent during the event project are in line with what is portrayed in the budget. The cost-control process during an event ensures that the amount spent on staging the event is within the planning framework.

**An Event Manager's Budgeting Tips –
Julie Besbrode, Co-founder and Director, Fresh Group**

1   Set up a template structure with all elements that could cost you money; from here you can input costs for in-house resources and supplier costs accordingly.
2   Talk to all suppliers to obtain an understanding of the costs that will be associated with the product or service they are providing.
3   Allocate budget for additional costs that will be incurred on the day.
4   Make sure you cover all crew and associated costs for travel, accommodation and subsistence.
5   Always include a level of contingency and consider the worst-case scenario.

Source: Event Magazine (2008: 73)

Why Budget?

There are a number of reasons to budget. The most important of these is that most major events have a variety of stakeholders that are interested in how funds are spent and earned during the project period before, during and after the event. The downside to budgeting is of course the time it takes for the management team to create the master budget. The use of contingency funds can always be factored in to the budget in order to cater for cost overruns or unexpected items; however, the physical act of getting management to agree on the budget can be tiresome itself. A budget can also create an environment that is not suitable to creativity, as staff will see it as a way of limiting their ideas. Regardless, the benefits of taking the time to budget are listed below:

- *A plan of action*: The budget outlines the relevant cost and revenue centres within the event project. It will allow each section manager within the event to view their financial responsibilities and ensure that the event strategy is followed. If the plan is not working it can be monitored and alterations made if necessary.
- *A communication and integration tool*: The budget acts as a way of communicating management priorities across the project and galvanizing the various elements of the event team towards one set of priorities.
- *To foster control over the event project*: The budget allows managers to keep track of all outgoings and incomings and identify areas of weakness or cost overrun. It allows the manager to implement financial changes that can benefit the event's operations.

Master Budgeting for Event Operations

A feature of many events is their service orientation, relying on extensive human resources that would not be required by a manufacturing organization. Many events rely on the contributions of a volunteer work force. However, research by Smith et al. (2010) and Getz (2007) highlights that in some cases the larger the event the greater the need for professional human resources in lieu of these volunteers. Therefore one of the significant areas of event budgeting is allowing for the human resource; having an appropriate level of staff supporting an event is not only good for customer service but also vital for health and safety requirements. Overstaffing is a must in case incidents occur, such as a medical emergency that occupies staff away from their initial activities. This is why many large-scale events manage their master budget on a project basis. Many projects like outdoor music festivals, international arts festivals and outdoor recreation participation events require flexible organizational event team structures, and therefore budgets featuring sound budgeting principles may remain the same.

Master budgets are prepared up to one year in advance and are linked to the over-all strategic plan. Project budgeting for special events may show that the budget system does not work around an annual calendar. Project budgets can form master budgets but be organized around the timeline leading up to, during and after the event. Once the event is complete, the event management company moves on to other events or in some cases disbands. Therefore project budgets are more flexible in their scope but fulfil all the same advantages of a full master budget.

Managing the Budget

To support the planning, decision-making and control process, it is essential for managers to estimate the costs and expenses involved in implementing plans. They also need to ensure that a range of additional resources are available to support both strategic and operational planning. Understanding and applying conventional budgeting techniques can be the first step in managing finance effectively. The purpose of introducing planning and budgeting is quite simple. Every organization that has designs on being successful, whatever their goals are, will form some sort of plan so that managers and employees work towards the same outcome.

Once these plans have been agreed, managers have to monitor and control activities by comparing what actually occurs with what was planned for. This is the first link between financial and management accounts. If a manager can control the annual costs, then they can manage the organization's cash flow and ultimately help control activities to generate profits, or at least to cover costs. Providing that plans are controlled, any significant deviation can be compensated for, as managers can take action to get the organization back on course to achieve its objectives.

A budget is essentially a plan of action that is expressed in financial terms. Often budgets will be prepared in summary form but they could quite easily be expressed with plenty of detail.

Unlike the income statement, for example, the type of budget and the level of detail contained within it can vary a great deal between organizations, and as such they are not a statutory requirement. Ideally a budget should cover all of the activities of an organization and should involve all of its personnel in its preparation. A common misconception with the preparation of a budget is that it should be done by an accountant and not the full team. If this occurs, the event will not be seen as inclusive by its staff, and budgets will often not be met. Ultimately a budget should be realistic and ensure that goals and aspirations are achieved; it will facilitate other management functions such as planning, coordination, motivation, communication and control.

Management budgets can take a number of iterations to develop. At the most basic of levels, however, they will list the expected income and expenditure for a project, planned activity or general business. If expenditure exceeds income then the budget will need to be re-examined and consideration given to a cheaper alternative, to reduce cost. Budgets are often imperfect in their construction and will require constant monitoring and refinement, as will be explored later.

The Budgeting Process

Budgeting will play a central role in keeping the event's finances on track, and should ensure that debts are paid as they fall due. The budgeting process will include costing, estimating income and allocating financial resources so that the budget can be realistic. Normally a budget will be based on the following information:

- The financial history of the organization
- The general economic climate
- Income and expenditure that are reasonably expected to be generated with the resources available
- Data from competitors.

In advance of the trading year, a good manager will spend time developing their budget, using all of the information outlined above and comparing it to the general organizational objectives. Budgeting effectively forces managers to think ahead and implement any corrective action required or explain any variance to the original projected costs. The budget should cover a defined period of time, and a significant part of the actual budget can be used to provide information for the construction of the income statement. The two primary types of budgeting that will be explored during the remainder of this chapter are continuation budgeting and zero-based budgeting. An illustration of the budgeting process can be seen in Figure 8.1.

Figure 8.1   The budgeting process

Organizational objectives are commonly monitored using performance measurement tools that are principally focused on financial budgeting and financial measurement. Event managers can apply these measurement tools in order to enhance their operational effectiveness and ultimately their financial health.

Budgetary Control and Analysis

For any plan to be achieved, it has to be both monitored and controlled to ensure that the organization is on target to achieve its goals. In event management this can be even more critical; if the event is not on the right course, corrective action can be taken to avoid a budget over-spend or financial loss. If the implementation of the budget is not controlled, then it is likely that the organization will not meet its objectives. By providing a mechanism for translating an event's strategic plan into realistic financial objectives, and staff involved in the delivery and implementation of the event can see where it is going. However, to control the budgets, event managers must allocate responsibility for monitoring actual costs and revenues, to ensure that any problems are identified in a timely manner.

The budgeting process enables event managers to set targets, while the control process allows for performance to be monitored and any necessary corrective action to be taken. Once actions have been taken, the final step should be to undertake some performance analysis, i.e. calculate the achievement of objectives against the budget set. This will assist event managers in making a successful transition into the next financial period or to demonstrate the sustainability of the event.

Without undertaking a performance appraisal of the budget, an event manager cannot review their performance and set budgets for the following year and will not be able to provide sufficient detail to answer their information needs. Providing an analysis of the main financial statements and an organization's budget will help managers prove their worth to their employer, as demonstration of financial management skills will help an organization move forward. Arguably it might be more important to demonstrate these skills if an organization is performing badly, as it will need to steer its way out of trouble.

Continuation Budgets

In the sport and leisure industry the most frequently used method of budgeting is continuation budgeting, especially for voluntary sector clubs and public sector leisure services. Essentially, this type of budgeting refers to the notion that an organization will not change its objectives significantly from one trading period to the next. Such an assumption does not encourage an organization to grow, as it will not challenge organizational goals and aspirations. It is however a very easy method of budgeting to apply – hence it is used frequently in sport and leisure! On the positive side, if the organization is already working efficiently and making a profit or achieving other objectives, then one could argue that continuation budgeting is a sensible and cost-effective way of controlling the financial side of an organization.

Within the continuation budgeting framework there are two types of budgets: incremental and decremental. Incremental budgets will assume that the organization will grow in line with inflation. Consequently, all a manager will have to do is obtain the budget from the previous year and multiply everything by the rate of inflation to generate the new period's figures. Decremental budgeting on the other hand assumes that there will be a standstill within the organization or a reduction in funding, so the budget will either roll over as it is or will provide reductions in specific areas.

Zero-Based Budgets

Zero-based budgeting (ZBB) was developed initially to address some of the criticisms levelled at traditional budgeting techniques such as continuation budgeting, explained above. Continuation budgets do not present a manager with a challenge and do not encourage growth. ZBB takes an altogether different stance by applying a cost–benefit approach to creating a budget for an organization. Ostensibly, ZBB requires a manager to challenge every single item of expenditure based upon the benefits that it is likely to generate.

The typical way of applying this technique is to begin with a blank sheet of paper and start at zero! For example, the expenditure for an entire department commences at zero and the activities that form part of that department's function are clearly evaluated to determine whether they bring an appropriate level of benefit and therefore whether they are really necessary. Given that resources are finite for all organizations, this method of budgeting allows managers to prioritize expenditure according to those inputs which bring about the greatest benefit. In sport and leisure, such budgeting techniques are becoming more popular in the not-for-profit sector, as output is often intangible. ZBB can be applied easily when following these simple questions:

1. What is the purpose of this expenditure?
2. On what exactly will this expenditure be made?
3. What are the quantifiable benefits of this expenditure?
4. What are the alternatives to this proposed expenditure?
5. What would be the outcome of cutting this expenditure completely?

ZBB enables managers to identify and remove operations that are inefficient, and can encourage the avoidance of wasteful expenditure by asking crucial questions. However, it can mean that the emphasis is on short-term returns instead of long-term benefits because the former are more easily measured. Furthermore, it presupposes that commitments for expenditure are made at the time of preparing the budget, so, for example, expenditures that are not supported by the ZBB can be stopped. Moreover, cost–benefit analysis is often problematic, takes time and requires the manager to have a detailed understanding of the organization.

Diary of an Event Manager – Damien Eames, Marketing Chair Volunteer, Sydney Mardi Gras

Working with our business partners, we are starting to leverage the captive audience of several hundred thousand who attend the parade. By far and away the largest revenue source remains ticket sales to the Mardi Gras Party held at the Royal Hall of Industries and Hordern Pavilions at Moore Park, and our annual Sleaze Ball – held at the same venue in the spring of each year. We also derive a significant amount of income from annual membership fees.

Sponsorship is another key revenue source. Last year we signed a three-year AU$1.5 (€0.97) million agreement with gaydar.com.au, which is now the presenting partner of the Sydney Gay and Lesbian Mardi Gras. There are a number of other significant sponsors such as GAL Home Loans, Coca-Cola Amatil, the City of Sydney and Carlton United Breweries, who also support the festival.

The Sydney Gay and Lesbian Mardi Gras has a good track record of attracting mainstream supporters and we continue to do so. A gay and lesbian focus is not a big hindrance with the big brands anymore. The future is about leveraging the broader appeal. Mardi Gras stands for tolerance, diversity, colour and fun, with a dash of edginess. It stands for these things in the eyes of not just a gay audience, but also with the young and well-educated generally. New Mardi Gras will focus on partnerships with brands with similar brand values.

Source: Cited in Goodwin (2006)

Financial Reporting

Financial reporting is going one step further from the budget and feeding back to those who may be interested in the event company's financial performance. If events are to attract a range of financial and commercial partners, due diligence reports should ensure that the business behind the event is sustainable. Financial reporting systems are a feature of a proactive risk management system and a requirement of many nations' company law legislation.

Financial reporting is required to allow managers and other stakeholders to make decisions regarding the use of resources. It allows interested parties to review the profitability, liquidity and solvency (sustainability) of the business as a going concern.

Main Report Types

Balance sheet

The balance sheet is a formal document outlining an event company's accounting equation. The accounting equation represents the relationship between a company's assets, liabilities and capital (see Glossary at the end of this chapter). Assets are in some manner acquired from a funding source – either the company's own funds or from a borrowed funding source. The accounting equation that governs the investment made in a business should always have the following formula:

$$\text{Assets} = \text{Liabilities plus Capital}$$

$$A = L + C$$

Profit and loss (P&L) account (or income statement)

One of the first things to note here is that the profit and loss account is often referred to in a variety of terms ranging from those in the subheading – profit and loss account or income statement – to an income and expenditure account in the not-for-profit sector. Irrespective of its title this statement will detail the event's financial performance historically, i.e. it details what happened. Revenue or income, or turnover as it is alternatively known, will be generated via ticket sales, sponsorships, commercial spend or grants and other funding streams. Expenses are all the costs that are incurred by running an event. For many events the major expenses are derived from the event venue and supporting elements involved in venue preparation such as equipment hire, catering, décor and staging. Other large-expense items include entertainment, wages and insurance (depending on the type of event). These expenses are then deduced to leave an amount of money – hopefully a profit (if you have planned correctly) or a loss. The P&L statement can be calculated through another equation:

$$\text{Revenues - Expenses = Profit (Loss)}$$

$$R - Ex = P \ (L)$$

Cash flow statements

The final statements indicate the ability of an event company to generate the cash required to fulfil business obligations (for instance the repayment of bank loans if and when they fall due). In the balance sheet, cash can be seen changing from year to year, and the profit and loss statement can highlight profitability. Regardless, managers should always be querying how any profits are actually being made. Lee and Wines (2000) indicate that cash flow information is important because it identifies where the money in the business is coming from. You could for example (in the short-term) feasibly sustain the business on borrowed funds, which could demonstrate profitability in the profit and loss statement. But if these backers are lending you the funds based on a rate of return, the business will not survive unless it can generate cash to service those debts. Also having cash allows an organization to trade efficiently with others, and given the just-in-time nature of most event management projects, this is vital.

The cash flow statement examines the solvency (see Glossary) of an event company. International Accounting Standard (IAS) 7 indicates that cash flow information is useful in determining the ability of a company to borrow funds and to indicate how cash flows will be distributed.

Cash reconciliation statements

Determining what cash flows go into which categories is one of the reasons accounting relies on a series of internationally recognized accounting standards. The need for the reconciliation of cash is to provide greater accuracy for determining working capital within the organization; it gives the manager a closer idea of the financial position of knowing how much cash is present. The reconciliation of cash takes another look at the cash flows arising from operating activities as covered in the cash flow statement above. The aim is to ensure that the reader can see that cash generated from operating activities is clearly identified.

The Importance of Financial Reports

Understanding how to construct a balance sheet and a profit and loss statement, and knowing which items go where, is an important part of an event manager's repertoire of knowledge and is linked back to the budget process. However, even more important is understanding the relationship between the two statements. As a business increases its profitability it can either reinvest the funds back into the business as assets or pay out dividends to its investors (if it is a for-profit company). This reinvestment then increases the capital contributions made, subsequently balancing the sheet. A business that fails to make a profit must keep drawing funds from either its own cash reserves or from outside the business through loans. Each of these eventualities impacts on the capital within the business.

Case Study 8.1 – The Financial Performance of Sydney Mardi Gras

Background

A symbol and statement of pride in their community, the Sydney Mardi Gras has been in existence since 1978. From very humble beginnings the Mardi Gras is now one of the top series of events for the Lesbian, Gay, Bi-Sexual, and Transgender (LGBT) community in Australia and around the world. Members of the LGBT community and tourists from inter-state Australia and around the world make their way each year to Sydney for the festivities; the parade itself is preceded by a range of cultural activities. However, soon after the Millennium the management of the Sydney Gay and Lesbian Mardi Gras went into insolvency. There were a number of reasons given for this insolvency – some ranging from increases in public liability insurance to poor financial management. This brief case study will focus on the recent financial reports of the New Mardi Gras Limited

(Continued)

(Continued)

(NMG). This new organization was established to create a not-for-profit sustainable organization and financial platform on which each year's events are built (Goodwin, 2006).

The event has a significant impact on the city and the local economy of Sydney. The organizers themed the activities under the banner of Nations United, which aimed to promote human rights for all members of the LGBT community across the globe. Altman (1997: 420) addressed a wide range of Gay Pride events around the globe and considered the event 'uniquely Australian' due to its flamboyance and irreverence (cited in Markwell and Waitt, 2009). In 2009 there were over 300,000 Mardi Gras party-goers, and 134 floats took part in the main parade.

Although the case highlights the use of financial reports, it makes *no* evaluation of the financial management of NMG Ltd: it is for illustrative purposes only.

An organization such as New Mardi Gras Ltd is a limited company that has to adhere to policies and standards required under Corporations Law in Australia, where the organization is based. While this is an Australian example, most companies registered as a legal entity will be required to publish financial reports. Under this Corporations Law all of these reports must be independently audited. Chapter 15 of NMG Ltd's constitution outlines that the company must prepare and disseminate financial information in the form of a balance sheet, a profit and loss account with statement of cash flows, with a reconciliation of that cash flow. This case example will introduce these reports and highlight how NMG Ltd reported this information over the two accounting periods from 2007/08 and 2008/09.

Balance Sheets NMG

For NMG Ltd the major source of revenue is ticket sales and sponsorship, which many major international events also attract. There are a number of other sources but they are not as significant as these two, interestingly the contra revenues involve business support offered in lieu of cash; one of these deals was the broadcasting of the event. This broadcast is a significant factor in the increase in sponsorship fees a major event can attract – which highlights relationships between various income sources.

Table 8.1   NMG Ltd balance sheet as at 31 March 2009

	31-Mar-09	31-Mar-08	31-Mar-07
	AU$	AU$	AU$
ASSETS			
Current assets			
Cash and cash equivalents	1,469,307	1,538,460	774,687
Trade and other receivables	527,384	96,728	31,278
Other current assets	90,212	94,896	134,284
Total current assets	2,086,903	730,084	940,249
Non-current assets			
Property, plant and equipment	53,178	14,731	12,833
Intangible assets	9,465	25,431	29,096
Total non-current assets	62,643	40,162	41,929
TOTAL ASSETS	2,149,546	1,770,246	982,178
LIABILITIES			
Current liabilities			
Trade and other payables	441,499	410,416	178,544
Other current liabilities	97,038	138,722	39,481
Financial liabilities	0	0	26,695
Total current liabilities	538,537	549,138	244,720
TOTAL LIABILITIES	538,537	549,138	244,720
NET ASSETS	1,611,009	1,221,108	737,458
EQUITY			
Retained earnings	1,611,009	1,221,108	737,458
TOTAL EQUITY	1,611,009	1,221,108	737,458

Some examples of significant expenses in this case are equipment hire, entertainment and venue hire for staging the festival. Other activities such as depreciation charges on non-current assets, equipment and venue hire charges, and insurance payments which occur throughout the reporting period, are also accounted for in the P&L statement.

It is clear from Table 8.2 that companies stating that revenues are increasing year on year are not actually reporting the entire picture. Expenses

(Continued)

(Continued)

Table 8.2   NMG Ltd profit and loss for the year ended 31 March 2009

	2009	2008	2007
	AU$	AU$	AU$
REVENUE			
Ticket sales	2,842,799	3,269,426	2,429,696
Sponsorship	1,050,853	581,855	575,812
Bad debts received	0	0	9,091
Membership income	116,907	74,277	60,887
Stallholder fees for fair day	104,770	91,949	90,133
Sale of goods	106,772	208,929	278,953
Grants	0	0	2,000
Licence fees	48,381	79,856	51,451
Interest income	82,184	35,331	16,969
Other	0	0	10,755
Insurance recoveries	56,838	0	0
Festival entry	63,316	30,842	28,776
Contra revenue	434,689	422,062	170,625
Parade entrance fees and viewing room	38,992	48,545	23,748
Donations	27,782	39,098	15,599
TOTAL REVENUE	4,974,283	4,882,169	3,764,495
EXPENSES			
Occupancy costs	−10,103	−38,591	−28,497
Employee benefits expense	−465,850	−310,241	−274,051
Amounts paid to contractors	−223,984	−293,137	−185,274
Insurance	−125,284	−136,623	−174,237
Venue hire	−445,074	−557,316	−422,188
Amortization of intangible software	−15,965	−13,085	−3,754
Depreciation of property, plant and equipment	−4,307	−9,319	−12,325
Operating lease rental expenses	−57,394	−55,261	−53,206
Marketing and communications	−142,068	−116,999	−192,510
Security	−286,865	−290,048	−231,862
Entertainment	−464,803	−295,587	−271,383
Cost of goods sold	−11,852	−112,598	−181,161
Cost of ticketing	−198,173	−199,029	−153,898

	2009	2008	2007
	AU$	AU$	AU$
Party staging	−188,301	−189,226	−151,018
Equipment hire	−888,653	−757,892	−664,286
Licence expenses	−141,365	−189,421	−55,280
Professional fees	−30,368	−35,983	−64,021
Contra expenses	−434,689	−422,062	−170,625
Donations	−43,322	−142,823	−14,602
Other expenses	−405,963	−231,648	−217,418
TOTAL EXPENSES	−4,584,383	−4,396,888	−3,521,596
PROFIT BEFORE INCOME TAX EXPENSE (INCOME TAX BENEFIT)	389,900	485,280	242,899
FINANCE COSTS	0	−1,630	−2,475
PROFIT FROM CONTINUING OPERATIONS	389,900	483,651	240,424

understandably must be taken into account. It should be noted however that 2008 was the 30th anniversary of the Sydney Gay and Lesbian Mardi Gras and this could have been a cause of the decrease in profitability between 2008 and 2009. Nevertheless as stated throughout this example it is best to use a variety of financial indicators assessed over a series of reporting periods to accurately identify probable causes.

The original company that staged the Sydney Gay and Lesbian Mardi Gras went out of business due to insolvency (Goodwin, 2006). Table 8.3 below shows that there has been a dramatic drop in net cash from operating activities and an increase in funds spent in investing activities (the purchase of property, plant and equipment). As no borrowings have had to be repaid in the last financial year (see balance sheet) there are no outgoings in this area. NMG Ltd has negative cash flows from this period's activities which should raise some questions. However the significant increase in cash holdings at the start and end of the year could put this result in another perspective. A view of over several years should always be undertaken. No single result should indicate overall performance.

From a look at Table 8.4, year-on-year it is clear that the cash situation in NMG Ltd is changing quite dramatically. One negative indicator is not

(Continued)

(Continued)

Table 8.3 NMG Ltd cash flow statement 31 March 2009

	31-Mar-09	31-Mar-08	31-Mar-07
	AU$	AU$	AU$
CASH FLOWS FROM OPERATING ACTIVITIES			
Receipts from customers	5,361,681	4,092,080	3,136,312
Receipts of government grants			2,200
Payments to suppliers and contractors	−5,470,264	−3,314,375	−2,957,789
Interest received	82,164	35,331	16,969
Interest paid	0	−1,631	−2,475
NET CASH PROVIDED BY OPERATING ACTIVITIES	−26,399	811,405	195,217
CASH FLOWS FROM INVESTING ACTIVITIES			
Purchase of property, plant and equipment	−42,754	−11,218	−2,655
Purchase of other non-current assets	0	−9,419	−32,850
NET CASH USED IN INVESTING ACTIVITIES	−42,754	−20,637	−35,505
CASH FLOWS FROM FINANCING ACTIVITIES			
Repayment of borrowings	0	−26,995	−1,885
NET CASH USED IN FINANCING ACTIVITIES	0	−26,995	−1,885
NET INCREASE IN CASH HELD	−69,153	763,773	157,827
CASH AT BEGINNING OF FINANCIAL YEAR	1,538,460	774,687	616,860
CASH AT END OF FINANCIAL YEAR	1,469,307	1,538,460	774,687

Table 8.4 NMG Ltd reconciliation of cash from operations with profit from ordinary activities after income tax

	2009	2008	2007
	AU$	AU$	AU$
Cash at bank	1,469,307	1,583,460	774,687
Profit from ordinary activities after income tax	389,900	483,651	240,424
Non-cash flows in profit from ordinary activities			
Amortization	15,965	13,085	3,754
Depreciation	4,307	9,319	12,325
Bad debts written off	0	0	−80,000
Changes in assets and liabilities			
Increase in receivables	−430,655	−65,450	146,919

	2009	2008	2007
	AU$	AU$	AU$
Decrease in other assets	4,684	39,387	45,776
Increase in payables	31,084	232,172	−148,059
Increase/(decrease) in other current liabilities	−41,684	99,241	−21,667
Increase/(decrease) in provisions	0	0	−4,255
Cash flows from operations	−26,399	811,405	195,217

enough to warrant drastic action in the management of the event. It is best to examine what other event companies are recording for their cash flow levels before appropriate analysis can take place. The key point when using financial reporting is that the various sources of information all work together to paint an accurate picture of the Event company's financial health.

Case Study Questions

1   What key changes do you observe between the 2007/08 and 2008/09 NMG balance sheets?
2   What could the changes between 2007/08 and 2008/09 profit and loss statements reveal about the financial strategy of the NMG?
3   What conclusions would be drawn about the financial viability of the NMG if the cash flow statement for 31 March 2009 alone was looked at?

Chapter Summary

Finance should not be an area that is left to the responsibility of others in event management. All event managers should have some understanding of the basics of financial management to the point where they could converse with specialists and interpret resultant recommendations for managing the future direction of the event. The principles covered in this chapter are a level above a general introduction to the area. This is deliberate as we could fill four chapters with introductory information whereas this chapter demonstrates the key principles in action for events.

This chapter sought to introduce the reader to these event-finance management issues by examining organizational context and the importance of accurate determination of event pricing and budgets, and it examined the relationship between aspects of financial planning and reporting for assessing the financial health of the event company. This chapter was structured into three main parts. The first part examined pricing and the strategies used for determining price. A key factor in price determination is having a clear understanding of event companies' objectives and purpose. The importance of budgeting for service operations such as events was then discussed. The preparation of a master budget is important for controlling the flow of funds throughout the organization. The final section introduced the reader to the importance of financial reporting by examining the balance sheet, P&L statement and the cash flow statement (including reconciliation of cash). The financial reports of New Mardi Gras Ltd were used to examine the relationships between the economic entity of the business and its on-going sustainability.

Glossary

Asset: A resource controlled by the entity as a result of past events and from which future economic benefits are expected to flow to the entity. *

Balance sheet: A statement that represents the financial position of the company at the end of the accounting period.

Break-even point: The sales volume figure where total revenues and total costs intersect.

Capital: The residual interest in the assets of the capital after deducting all its liabilities. *

Capital contributions: Involves the owners of the company contributing additional assets to the firm.

Capital distributions: Involves the distribution of assets to the owner of the company.

Cash flow statement: A statement that highlights how changes in the balance sheet and profit and loss statement impact on the cash and cash equivalents of the company.

Current assets: These are cash; cash equivalents; assets held for collection, sale or consumption within the entity's normal operating cycle; or assets held for trading within the next 12 months. All other assets are non-current. *

Current liabilities: These are those to be settled within the entity's normal operating cycle or due within 12 months; those held for trading; or those for which the entity does not have an unconditional right to defer payment beyond 12 months. Other liabilities are non-current. *

Expenses: Decreases in economic benefits during the accounting period in the form of outflows or depletions of assets or an incurrence of liabilities that result in decreases in capital, other than those relating to distributions to capital participants. *

Financing activities: These are activities that alter the capital and borrowing structure of the entity. *

Fixed costs: The costs incurred to be in the business, for example plant and machinery. These costs remain constant throughout increasing sales.

FMCG: Fast-moving consumer goods (companies) – goods that are sold quickly at low cost where branding plays an important role, for example washing detergent.

For-profit: A business that exists to generate a return on income.

Going concern: The underlying assumption for accounting that the financial statements presume that an entity will continue in operation indefinitely or, if that presumption is not valid, disclosure and a different basis of reporting are required. *

IAS 7: The objective of IAS 7 is to require the presentation of information about the historical changes in cash and cash equivalents of an enterprise by means of a cash flow statement which classifies cash flows during the period according to operating, investing and financing activities. *

Investing activities: These are the acquisition and investing-activities disposal of long-term assets and other investments that are not considered to be cash equivalents. *

Liability: This is a present obligation of the entity arising from past events, the settlement of which is expected to result in an outflow from the entity of resources embodying economic benefits. *

Liquidity: The ability of the company to settle its short-term obligations from its current assets.

Not-for-profit: A business that uses funds generated to reinvest in its business activities.

Operating activities: These are the main revenue operating activities producing activities of the enterprise that are not investing or financing activities, so operating cash flows include cash received from customers and cash paid to suppliers and employees. *

Organizational context: The legal form an organization may adopt (sole-trader, partnership, company limited by guarantee, limited company). These legal forms have implications for the complexity and formality of financial reporting (Stewart, 2015).

Profitability: The ability of the company to generate a profit from its business activities.

Profit and loss (income) statement: A document that represents the revenues (income) and expenses for a financial period resulting in a statement of business profitability.

Reconciliation of cash: A statement to provide greater accuracy for determining working capital within the organization and to ensure that cash and cash equivalents generated from operating activities are clearly identified.

Revenue (income): Increases in economic benefits during the accounting period in the form of inflows, enhancements of assets, or decreases of liabilities that result in increases in capital, other than those relating to contributions from capital participants *

Roll-up reporting: A method of departmental budget reporting where budgeted costs are measured against actual costs from the lowest entity through to the highest.

Solvency: The ability of the company to settle all of its obligations from its assets.

Stakeholders: Parties internal and external to the organization that have a stake or interest in the operations and future directions of a company.

Total cost: A line on a break-even graph representing the cumulative costs incurred by all variable, semi-fixed and fixed costs.

Total revenue (turnover): The total value of sales and revenues generated by a company.

Variable costs: The costs incurred by generating business, for example labour. These costs increase in a relationship with total sales.

[* *Source*: Deloitte (2016)]

Review Questions

1. In determining the break-even point for your event, what is the relationship between variable and fixed costs?
2. How should an event manager respond if a business with a history of profitability reports a loss on the P&L statement?
3. What pricing strategy would you use if you were managing a multi-activity event with a high level of fixed costs? Why would you choose this?
4. What internal considerations would you examine when establishing a sales forecast for an international modern-arts festival?

Additional Resources

Books / Book Chapters / Journal Articles

McLaney, E. and Atrill, P. (2014). *Accounting and Finance for Non-Specialists* (9th edn). Essex: Pearson Education. The industry-leading introductory text for students learning about the subjects of accounting and finance.

Ciconte, B.L. and Jacob, J.G. (2009). *Fundraising Basics: A Complete Guide*. Sudbury: Jones and Bartlett Publishers. A useful guide to raising funds, especially for non-profit event managers.

Kitchin, P.J. (2007). Financing the games. In: J. Gold and M. Gold (eds), *Olympic Cities: Urban Planning, City Agendas and the World's Games, 1896 to the Present* (pp. 103–119). London: Routledge. A general introduction to the major income and expenditure items of the Summer and Winter Olympic Games.

Wilson, R. (2011). *Managing Sport Finance*. Oxon: Routledge. A solid and detailed overview of financing issues in the sports events industry, providing a next step for understanding more about this topic area.

Supovitz, F. and Goldblatt, J.J. (1999). *Dollars and Events: How to Succeed in the Special Events Business*. New York: John Wiley and Sons. An interesting and practical overview of the issues involved in running a special events business.

Useful Websites

www.duncanwil.co.uk/ – An excellent resource that delivers accounting information to the masses. Now with links to a sound introductory e-text.

www.eventscotland.org/assets/178 – A useful and practical guide to budgeting and financial planning for events.

www.iasplus.com/en/standards/other/framework – For an official overview of the International Accounting Framework.

References

Altman, D. (1997). Global gaze, global gays. *GLQ: A Journal of Lesbian and Gay Studies*, 3(4): 417–36.

Andersson, T.D., and Getz, D. (2008). Stakeholder management strategies of festivals. *Journal of Convention and Event Tourism*, 9(3): 199–220.

Besbrode, J. (2008). An event manager's budgeting tips. *Events Magazine*, 73.

Deloitte (2016). Summaries of interpretations [online]. Retrieved from www.iasplus.com/en/standards/other/framework

Getz, D. (2005). *Event Management and Event Tourism* (2nd edn.) Putnam Valley, NY: Cognizant Communication Corporation.

Getz, D. (2007). *Event Studies Theory, Research and Policy for Planned Events*. Oxford: Elsevier.

Goodwin, E. (2006). Queer as folk. *Marketing Magazine Australia*, 16–19 April.

Henderson, J.C., Foo, K., Lim, H. and Yip, S. (2010). Sports events and tourism: The Singapore Formula One Grand Prix. *International Journal of Event and Festival Management, 1*(1): 60–73.

Kitchin, P.J. (2007). Financing the Games. In J.R. Gold and M.M. Gold (eds), *Olympic Cities: City Agendas, Planning, and the World's Games, 1896–2012* (pp. 103–19) Oxon: Routledge.

Lee, T. and Wines, G. (2000). Cash flow reporting and analysis. In G. Carnegie, F. Clark, G. Dean, M. Evans, C. Ikin, C. Ng and G. Wines (eds), *Financial Reporting and Analysis* (pp 3.1–3.31). Geelong: Deakin University.

Markwell, K. and Waitt, G. (2009). Festivals, space and sexuality: Gay pride in Australia. *Tourism Geographies, 11*(2): 143–68.

Schneider, A. and Sollenberger, H.M. (2005). *Managerial Accounting: Manufacturing and Service Applications* (4th edn). USA: Custom Publishing Company.

Smith, D. (2004). Bill for Athens to top $11b. *Sport Business International*, 15 Nov.

Smith, W.W., Litvin, S.W. and Canberg, A. (2010). Setting parameters: Operational budget size and allocation of resources. *International Journal of Event and Festival Management, 1*(3): 238–43.

Stewart, B. (2015). *Sport Funding and Finance* (2nd edn.). Oxford: Elsevier.

Verma, H.A. (2008). *Services Marketing: Text and Cases*. India: Dorling Kindersley/Pearson Education.

Wilson, R. (2011). *Managing Sport Finance*. Oxon: Routledge.

Risk Management

9

Brent W. Ritchie and Sacha Reid

Learning Objectives

By reading this chapter students should be able to:

- Understand the importance of undertaking a systematic approach to risk management
- Understand the influence of event context in identifying and treating relevant risks
- Identify relevant strategies and tools to identify, analyse and treat event-related risks
- Understand the importance of risk communication and monitoring for both internal and external stakeholders.

Introduction

Events have the potential to generate internal and external risks and crises, due to their size, scope, use of equipment, and attraction of large numbers of people to particular site(s) during a defined period. Potential risks can cover all areas of operation, including health and safety of guests and workers, crowding, environmental risks, and compliance with local laws and regulations. Further, risks can be internal and external to the organization and could be created by audience members, suppliers or even event organizers themselves through inaction. Getz (2002) reveals that festival crises and failures are common; he identified the primary reason for event failure as the lack of advanced or strategic planning. This could be attributed to the limited capacity and knowledge of event organizers to plan for and deal with risks in a systematic way. Allen et al. (2008) also note that most event incidents occur as a result of management incompetency, thus making it necessary for all event managers to be familiar with the concept of risk and risk management. This is because event organizers have a duty of care to provide a safe environment for spectators and/or participants, staff, suppliers and even sponsors.

Risk management assists event organizers in devising and conducting events in the safest possible manner, while mitigating losses (Berlonghi, 1994). Therefore, it is essential that event organizations formally plan for and develop strategies to deal with the possible consequences of unplanned events. This chapter provides an overview of risk management for event managers and identifies a range of tools to assist managers in planning and managing risk in the context of hosting an event. The chapter begins by defining risk and risk management from an events perspective, before providing a systematic framework for understanding and managing event risks. The remainder of the chapter addresses the components of the framework, providing examples throughout the text. Finally a case study is provided at the end of the chapter, integrating the chapter content.

Understanding Event Risks

Risk is generally defined as any threat that will negatively impact an organization's ability to achieve its objectives and execute its strategies successfully. The Australian and New Zealand Standard (AS/NZS ISO 31000: 2009) defines risk as the 'effect of uncertainty on objectives'. Glaesser (2006: 38) defines risk as 'the product of magnitude of damage and the probability of occurrence', while Berlonghi (1994: 19) views risk as 'an actual possibility of loss or exposure to loss'. As can be deduced from these definitions, risk involves some form of uncertainty and the potential for this uncertainty to create damage or loss to an organization. Such damage may include physical damage such as injuries, deaths, and property damage, negative public image, lawsuits or financial losses.

Risk, in the event context, is defined as 'the likelihood and consequence of the special event or festival not fulfilling its objectives' (Allen et al., 2008: 588). This could be due to anything that might affect the outcome of an event or event activities, or anything that might expose an event or an event organization to loss. Risk can arise from the dangers which may be linked to environmental characteristics at the site where the activity is conducted, the type and manner in which any equipment is used, or the behaviour of stakeholders involved in the event (such as spectators).

According to Leopkey and Parent (2009a), risk affects not only the organizing committee of an event, but all event stakeholders (including participants, spectators, sponsors, etc.). Risks can be divided into those caused by internal forces and those caused by external influences. Therefore, event managers must understand and manage risks that are not just related to the host organization, but potential external risks from the broader political, economic, environmental, social and technological environment in which the event operates.

Getz (2007: 291) defines risk management as 'the process of anticipating, preventing or minimizing potential costs, losses or problems for the event, organization, partners and guests'. Leopkey and Parent (2009b: 164) consider risk management as 'a process that involves assessing all possible risks to the event and its stakeholders and then strategically avoiding, preventing, reducing, diffusing, reallocating, legalising or using relationship management to mitigate the identified risks'. Effective risk management helps to ensure that the event is conducted in the safest possible manner and that any losses will be mitigated and assets protected (Berlonghi, 1995).

Risk management should be recognized as an integral part of good management practice, consisting of well-defined steps which support better decision-making and contribute greater insights into risks and their possible impacts. The prime objective of risk management is to minimize the potential for physical, social, emotional or financial loss arising from participation in an activity in an unfamiliar environment with unknown outcomes (Ewart and Boone, 1987). Wideman (1992) considers risk management as a process that lasts throughout the life cycle of the event and should begin during the event preparation stage to allow for alternative action plans and strategies to be developed. The process requires a 'thorough and thoughtful procedure that proactively examines and analyses each possibility, then takes the necessary steps and allocates the proper resources to control the risks' (Silvers, 2008: 24). In this way potential risks may be able to be turned into opportunities, perhaps through improving practices and possibly even reducing insurance costs.

Risk Management: A Systematic Framework

Effective risk management requires a systematic approach to control the range and impact of potential losses. Figure 9.1 presents the international standard for risk management (AS/NZS ISO 31000: 2009), which provides a systematic process for managing risks through establishing the context and identifying, analysing, evaluating, treating, monitoring and communicating risks associated with any activity or function. Importantly, it also highlights five parts of a *framework* that assist the risk management process and should occur before risk management begins. The international standard also highlights seven *principles* that should underpin the initial framework and risk management process. Standards help provide a consistent approach to understanding and managing risk across industry sectors and organizations, including the events sector, as they provide principles and generic guidelines on risk management. The remainder of this chapter will discuss the application of the risk management *process* in an events management context providing examples, starting with communication and consultation (see Step 5.2 in Figure 9.1).

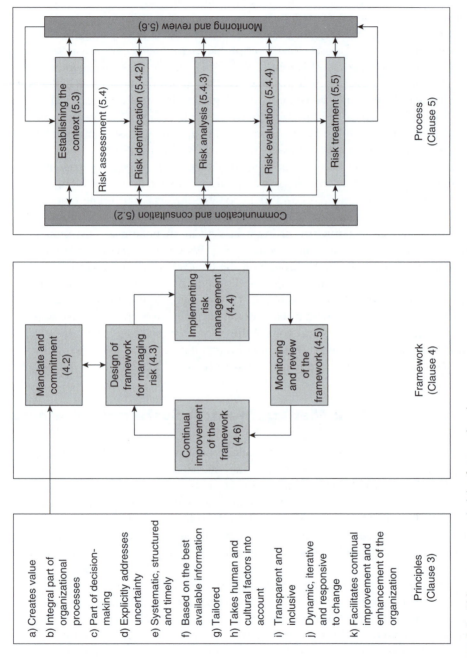

Figure 9.1 Risk management principles, framework and process

Source: AS/NZS ISO 31000 (2009). This is a copy of the relevant standard. Permission to reproduce this illustration has been approved by SAI Global Ltd. The complete standard can be purchased from www.saiglobal.com

Communication and Consultation

Communication and consultation with stakeholders is vital to help with the identification, assessment and treatment of event risks, and is an on-going function of effective event risk management. Internal stakeholders such as paid staff and volunteers have a wealth of experience which can help identify relevant risks and effective risk management actions. External stakeholders can include government authorities such as police, health, meteorological agencies as well as suppliers, sponsors, participants and spectators. These external stakeholders may provide important information which can help assess the likelihood and severity of a risk occurring and its implications. Information may come from secondary data such as that provided by weather or health agencies or from primary research with sponsors and spectators undertaken on behalf of event organizers.

Effective internal and external communication is important to ensure that stakeholders understand the issues relating to the risk and the process to manage it. As noted by Goldblatt (1997), effective communication will ensure that all stakeholders are aware that event risk management is everyone's responsibility. It is only when all the stakeholders become proactively and cooperatively involved in developing a coordinated event that the frequency of risk occurrence can be reduced. Communicating and consulting with internal stakeholders (such as volunteers and staff) is vital not only in implementing risk treatment strategies, but also in the monitoring and feedback stage to help improve future event risk management plans.

Establishing the Context

The risk management process begins with understanding the environment or context in which the event or event host organization operates. The context includes the financial, operational, competitive, political, social, client, cultural and legal aspects of the organization's functions (described as the International Events Environment by Ferdinand and Wang, Chapter 2 this volume) as well as the goals and objectives of the organization hosting the event. From an events management perspective, it includes understanding the type of event, the management structure and resources, organizational culture, stakeholder analysis and a SWOT analysis of the organization in the context of its internal and external operating environment (Allen et al., 2008). The event context is dynamic with frequent changes occurring in the political, economic, environmental, social and technological environment.

Event managers need to understand these changes and their likely impact on their event. For instance, recent terrorist attacks and threats on sporting teams in Pakistan, India and Bangladesh have heightened concerns surrounding potential risks to travelling sporting teams and the need for risk management procedures to be tightened. Further, the western financial crisis in Europe and America have had an impact on the number of business events and exhibitions being held (Allen et al., 2011).

Understanding the type and nature of an event will give an indication of possible risks that the event will be exposed to, while the event purpose, goals and objectives will indicate what risks can be tolerated by the organization. For instance, if the host organization is a private enterprise where individuals live off anticipated profits, then financial risks may be more important than perhaps a community-based event whose purpose is to provide entertainment for the local community.

Risk Assessment

A comprehensive identification of risks using a well-structured systematic process is critical. Berlonghi (1994) purports that identification of risk factors should take place before an event. A number of tools outlined below can help managers to think through the possible causes of the risks, the parties who would be affected and the possible consequences (Berlonghi, 1994). The approaches used to identify risks include using a work breakdown structure, fault diagram, brainstorming, incident report, scenario analysis or environmental scanning (Allen et al., 2008).

Project management techniques, such as the work breakdown structure (described in detail in Williams, Chapter 4 this volume) and fault diagrams, are useful for identifying risks based on operations and help identify possible risk problems and issues. Risk events or actions can be worked backwards to determine the possible causes of the potential risk effects (Allen et al., 2011). Poor ticket sales may be a potential risk for an outdoor festival that does not have many sponsors and is therefore heavily reliant on ticket sales for revenue. Poor weather may reduce ticket sales during the event, so the event managers may decide to sell tickets in advance to reduce possible consequences of poor weather on ticket sales, revenue and ultimately profit.

The convening of a risk assessment meeting to pool together the experience and expertise of event staff and volunteers can be useful to identify risks. Brainstorming and testing a range of scenarios of potential risks and their likely impacts can be useful too (Allen et al., 2008). Scenario planning can also be used to examine the future direction and stakeholder support for the future of events (Moital et al., 2013). Such an approach allows event managers and stakeholders to consider possible risks, possible actions and their consequences in advance. Managerial experience and the event context are crucial in identifying and assessing relevant risks. Previous experience needs to be captured and used to develop even better risk management plans, and highlights the importance of risk monitoring and review both during and after an event. Running test events are also useful to determine possible risks, and are often used for large international events such as the Olympic and Paralympic Games.

This chapter highlights a range of risks for various event types and locations to provide the reader with an overview of the main event risk categories.

Health and Safety Risks

The event organizer is responsible for providing a safe and healthy environment for those attending or involved in running the event. As noted by Sönmez and Graefe (1998) and Hall et al. (2003), the heightened awareness of terrorism following the September 11, 2001 terrorist attacks has caused many travellers to make their destination choices using security as a criterion. This is confirmed by a study conducted by Kim and Chalip (2004) on the 2002 FIFA World Cup, where it was found that attendance at the World Cup was affected by respondents' concerns over safety risks. Sporting events are often potential targets of terrorist threats due to the event's scale and the amount of media attention (Cieslak, 2009; Taylor and Toohey, 2006). The results also demonstrate the importance of sustaining the event with effective safety and security practices.

Avian Flu and Events in the USA

A number of events were changed or cancelled due to the outbreak of Avian Flu in 2014 and 2015. In the United States of America over ten States cancelled their State Fairs and poultry shows in 2015 to limit the spread of the disease. In Ohio the State Fair and the largest poultry exhibition (Ohio National Poultry Show) were cancelled. The State Fair hosts nearly 4,000 poultry entries while the National Poultry Show has 6,000-7,000 entries a year (Gray, 2015). More than 33 million birds were affected in Iowa and more than 1,500 people were expected to lose their jobs, with the Governor calling for a major disaster declaration from President Barack Obama (WhoTV, 2015). Such a declaration would provide funds to help the industry recover from the impact of the outbreak. This case demonstrates the human impact of infectious transmitted by animals.

Health hazards are also a primary concern for event organizers (see, for example, the Avian Flu example in the box above). Communicable diseases can be easily spread in places with large crowds. In Mecca city, for example, the population surges during the Hajj season. Annually, millions of pilgrims congregate within a confined space at this high-profile religious event. This has resulted in outbreaks of a series of infectious diseases, such as meningococcal disease, influenza virus, tuberculosis, etc. (Memish and Ahmed, 2002). Many pilgrims have to struggle against these public health hazards throughout the pilgrimage. The outbreak also has the potential to quickly turn into a global pandemic as overseas pilgrims carry the diseases or viruses back to their home countries. In addition to the above viruses, male pilgrims are also at risk of being infected with blood-borne infections such as hepatitis B and hepatitis C, through sharing or using communal razors during the head-shaving procedure after the pilgrimage.

Both security and health risks can be magnified as the size of the crowd increases. It is therefore important for safety and health management procedures to be established to protect the participants and attendants from health and safety threats (Getz, 2007). In addition to the concerns over the health and safety of the event audience, event managers also have the legal responsibility to provide a safe working environment for their workers, ensuring that they are protected from injury, damage or disease (Silvers, 2008). This is pertinent as events are temporary in nature and may require long working hours in the lead-up to and during the event. This intensive nature can create high levels of stress which require coping strategies for workers (Odio, Walker and Kim, 2013). The authors suggest that, by recognizing stressors, event organizers can monitor employee work patterns and try to prevent burnout and health problems. Hence, workplace health and safety measures must also be set in place to protect employees and volunteers. These measures may differ depending on the country where the event takes place and their respective regulations.

Crowding

Crowding can be defined as a negative assessment of a certain density level in a given area, and may negatively influence the quality of festival participants' experience and their activities (Lee and Graefe, 2003). Over-crowding has also become an inevitable problem at major events. For example, on New Year's Eve in Innsbruck, Austria, between 35,000 and 40,000 visitors gather at 'Bergsilvester' to observe the

Table 9.1   Tragedies at the Hajj

Year	Number of pilgrims
1990	1426 killed by stampede/asphyxiation
1994	270 died in a stampede
1997	343 pilgrims died and 1500 injured in a fire
1998	119 pilgrims died in a stampede
2001	35 pilgrims died in a stampede
2003	14 pilgrims died in a stampede
2004	251 pilgrims died in a stampede
2006	Stampede killed 380, wounded 289
2015	Stampede killed 750, wounded 934 (official, yet-disputed figures)

Source: Ahmed, Arabi and Memish (2006) and Nazer (2015)

fireworks spectacle every year (Peters and Pikkemaat, 2005). The huge crowd posed major transportation and security problems for the event organizer, which needed to be managed.

Stampede as a result of overcrowding had also occurred at other events such as rock concerts and religious events such as the Hajj. Overcrowding is expected in an event of such huge scale, as the population at Mecca city swells to well over two million during the Hajj season (Gatrad and Sheikh, 2005). The most severe stampede at the event took place in 2015 where official sources only reported over 750 people confirmed dead and 934 people injured (see Table 9.1 above), despite the unofficial figures estimating over 1500 fatalities (Nazer, 2015).

Environmental Risks

The effect of climate change on events is becoming an important risk management issue due to the nature of many events (Mair, 2011). In particular, weather has become a universal issue for event organizers. This is because weather can strongly influence the quality of visitor experiences and the success of outdoor events (Jones et al., 2006). Jones et al. (2006: 64) further state that climate marks out the timing and duration of outdoor events as it is the 'principal determinant of the natural resources that define the event's theme and attractions'. For example, climate influences the timing of tulip development, thus affecting the dates of Tulip Festivals (Jones et al., 2006). Natural disasters such as earthquakes and poor weather conditions can also create a crisis situation for any event as they may lead to cancellations, financial losses or legal liability claims against the host organizer.

Studies examining the failure of special events (Carlsen et al., 2010; Getz, 2002) found that weather is the foremost factor that could lead to an event's failure as it can drastically affect turnout and sales. This is further confirmed by Jones et al. (2006) who examined the impact of weather on climate-sensitive special events in Ontario, Canada. Their research demonstrated that the overall success of the events and quality of visitor experience are largely affected by weather and climate. Similarly, Scott et al. (2004) projected that winter tourism will be highly vulnerable to future changes in climate. Due to global warming, the average winter season is shortened and natural snow becomes an increasingly scarce resource. This phenomenon will have a notable threat on the winter recreation sector such as skiing, snowmobile activities and related snow events.

The Hajj provides an excellent example of heat-related risks experienced at an event. The journey to Mecca for Hajj during the summer season is no ordinary undertaking as the temperature can rise to as high as 50 degrees Celsius. According to Gatrad and Sheikh (2005), heat exhaustion and heatstroke during the Hajj are common and can be fatal. The excessive heat in the summer can also cause pilgrims to suffer from deep burns and skin infection to their soles, sustained from standing and walking barefooted along the religious route.

Alcohol and Drug Risks

Events featuring alcohol consumption, dependent on the type of event and their audience, may face various problems such as unruly crowd behaviour, which have also been shown to affect the viability of events (Carlsen et al., 2010; Harris et al., 2014). Getz (2005: 287) lists the following risks associated with alcohol sales at events:

- Personal injuries and criminal acts owing to drunkenness
- Additional insurance costs against the possibility of lawsuits
- Additional security and clean-up costs
- Major financial losses arising from lawsuits
- Vandalism
- Image problems and resultant lost patronage
- Attracting the wrong target segments.

The Gothenburg party event and its vision to create a party atmosphere created alcohol-induced anti-social behaviour by youth, which threatened its future viability. As a publicly-funded event it found itself under intense scrutiny and had to reduce its reliance on government funding and also directly tackle anti-social behaviour at the event (Carlsen et al., 2010). It is therefore important that event organizers carefully consider the distribution, sales and consumption of alcohol at an event (Abbott and Geddie, 2001) and put security measures in place to prevent drug consumption. Getz (2005) suggests that events with the intention to serve alcohol should have an alcohol risk management system in place, including practising responsible service of alcohol (Harris et al., 2014). Local law enforcement and city/council organizations should be involved in this planning process, to mitigate unwanted risks to staff, volunteers, attendees, participants and the local community. However, as Harris et al. (2014) note, the majority of actions undertaken by event organizers flow from licensing or legal conditions imposed upon them by regulatory agencies.

Legal Risks

As mentioned by Silvers (2008), operating an event legally and responsibly is the cornerstone of effective risk management. Hazards faced by persons attending an event can translate into legal risks for event organizers, especially if it is proven that the organizers have been negligent in identifying and preventing those hazards (Getz, 2005). Thus, it is essential that event organizers ensure compliance with the law and exercise duty of care to safeguard all those involved in the event. Duty of care means that if a person suffers injury as a result of negligence of another, they should be compensated for the loss and damage that arises from the negligent act or omission. The key aspect of duty of care is that acts or omissions need to be reasonably foreseen and event organizers need to take reasonable precautions to ensure a safe event. This in turn will reduce their risks and potential consequences such as their legal liability.

In particular, this means complying with local regulations and ensuring that appropriate licences and permits have been secured by event organizations for activities within an event. Furthermore, regulations, such as those concerning noise, regulations may differ between jurisdictions. Allen et al. (2011) provide a list of 10 regulations to be aware of, including:

- Liquor licensing laws
- Health regulations
- Building regulations
- Fire regulations
- Licences governing security personnel
- Police acts
- Local government acts
- Banking acts
- General contract law
- Environmental Protection Authority for noise levels.

Other Event Risks

The types of event risk factors discussed above are certainly non-exhaustive. Silvers (2008) listed several other risks associated with events, including internal risks such as the lack of event planning, finances and organizational structure as well as external risk factors. Different events are exposed to different risk factors and the severity of risks will vary in different contexts. Therefore, it is vital for event organizers to develop a culture of risk awareness and preparedness, so that they are in a better position to anticipate and manage risks, thereby rebounding quickly from any incidents or likely crisis situations. As the diary of an event manager below suggests, risk identification and risk management practices may vary between countries.

Diary of an Event Manager – Anonymous, Event Management Consultant

Risk management is an integral part of every event, though how it is prioritized varies dramatically depending on the professionalism of the event and its location. An event management consultant who works both in Australia and abroad explains how risk management has been incorporated into her roles:

(Continued)

(Continued)

It is very difficult adapting to different standards of risk management throughout the world. In Australia, there are very high standards for major events. Detailed risk matrices are required covering all foreseeable possibilities. It is an ingrained concept that you are responsible for ensuring that your work practices and areas of responsibilities mitigate these risks. For larger events, specific teams are dedicated purely to risk management or, at a minimum, there are health and safety inspections prior to 'gates opening'.

Working overseas challenges these practices at times, particularly in developing countries. Risk management focuses on larger-scale risks, and often is only monitored by overlay personnel, security services and/or venue managers. Risk inspections look at details such as structural safety, security and wet-weather contingencies. Often smaller risks such as trip hazards, safe waste disposal and staff well-being are not considered due to lack of time and budget. International event consultants are often met by resistance when they try to maintain standards of work practice from their home country.

Risk Analysis and Evaluation

The identification of threats and potential hazards should be followed by an assessment of the probability of occurrence and the severity of the consequences on the event goals and strategies. Management will need to rely on foresight and control to reduce either or both of the variables to an acceptable level in order to manage the risk. Priorities and actions will be determined following the risk assessment, with special attention awarded to those with negative and severe consequences.

Allen et al. (2008: 597) recommends that a risk's likelihood of occurrence be rated on a five-point scale from 'rare' to 'almost certain'. The consequence or severity of risks, on the other hand, will be given a rating of insignificant, minor, moderate, major to catastrophic. It is helpful that descriptors are provided and consideration given to tolerance levels and potential impacts if the risk was allowed to be untreated. Table 9.2 provides an example of an event manager's descriptors based on the management of a major cycling event in Australia.

Following the risk analysis, the next step is to evaluate the risks by determining which ones are acceptable and what needs to be treated. These assessments are then combined to evaluate the likely impact and possible risk treatment options (see Figure 9.2). For instance, a risk that was identified to have a likelihood of 5 (almost certain) and a consequence of 5 (catastrophic) would be rated 25 in the matrix and

Table 9.2 Risk likelihood and consequences rating scales and descriptors

Consequences

Level	Descriptor	Financial (AU$)	Safety	Business Activities	Social Impacts	Reputation/ Public Image
1	Insignificant	Less than $10,000	No injuries	No disruption to event activities	No social impacts	No significant adverse impact on organizational reputation
2	Minor	$10,001 – $100,000	First aid treatment	Minimal disruption to event activities	Minimal social impacts	Adverse impacts on organizational reputation
3	Moderate	$100,001 – $1M	Medical treatment	Significant disruption to event activities	Significant social impacts	Direct adverse impact on organizational reputation
4	Major	$1M – $10M	Extensive injuries	Major disruption to event activities	Major social impacts	Direct adverse impact on the CEO / Accountable Officer
5	Catastrophic	Greater than $10M	Death	Severe disruption to event activities	Severe on-going impacts	Extensive damage to organizational reputation

Likelihood

Level	Descriptor	Description
1	Rare	May occur in exceptional circumstances
2	Unlikely	Could occur at some time
3	Possible	Might occur at some time
4	Likely	Will probably occur in most circumstances

rated as a very high risk. The event host organizations should consider avoiding the risk completely, by cancelling/postponing the event or changing the part of the event that creates such a high level of risk. Consequently, an event risk that has a likelihood of 1 (rare) and an impact of 1 (insignificant) would be rated as having a very low level of risk. Event managers may decide to retain the risk and develop contingency plans to deal with it if it does indeed eventuate.

Risk is a subjective concept, and so rating scales are used by managers to try to create a more objective assessment of risk likelihood and consequence. Key questions to help determine the likelihood and consequences are:

- What happens if the risk is not treated?
- Who will it affect?
- Whose responsibility is it to deal with the risk?
- What information do we need to treat it?
- What risks will important event stakeholders accept?

	Consequences				
Likelihood	1	2	3	4	5
5	Medium – 11	High – 16	High – 20	Very High – 23	Very High – 25
4	Medium – 7	Medium – 12	High – 17	High – 21	Very High – 24
3	Low – 4	Medium – 8	High – 14	High – 18	High – 22
2	Low – 2	Low – 5	Medium – 9	Medium – 13	High – 19
1	Low – 1	Low – 3	Medium – 6	Medium – 10	High – 15

Source: Taken from HB 436:2004 'Risk management guidelines companion to AS/NZS 4360'

Figure 9.2   Risk assessment matrix

Weightings can be applied on certain risks if they are less tolerated by event organizers, thus increasing their consequences and overall rating respectively.

Risk Treatment

Risk treatment strategies are considered important to reduce the vulnerability of the event and control any problem that might arise. Risk treatment measures may actually stop a risk incident from occurring (prevention), or they may reduce the severity of the impact of a risk incident on the event (reduction). Other risk treatment options might include risk avoidance or transfer, through the use of third parties such as suppliers or insurance companies. This step in the risk management process involves identifying the range of risk treatment options, assessing the options, preparing risk treatment plans and implementing them by allocating and controlling event resources (financial or human).

Leopkey and Parent (2009a) believe that the use of proper strategies can directly influence the organization's overall performance and the success of the event. Strategies used for controlling risks may require additional documents, such as an emergency evacuation plan, crowd management plan or crisis communication plan. Studies on diffusion, reallocation and avoidance of risks do not seem to be as prevalent compared to material related to prevention, reduction and legal risks. These risk treatment strategies will therefore be the focus of this section of the chapter.

Prevention and Avoidance

Prevention and mitigation are the first line of defence for event organizers. Planning is the phase where the specifications for the event are determined, specifying the activities that will occur and how the resources will be organized (Silvers, 2008). It is also at the planning stage where potential risks are identified so that preventative measures can be devised and their effects considered.

Prior to conceptualizing event goals and strategies, a chain of command should be established to facilitate the orderly operation of the event (Abbott and Geddie, 2001). To improve event operations, the event manager should assemble a team that can assist in identifying the risks and develop the risk management and evacuation plans (Goldblatt, 1997). Operational plans should be developed that clearly specify the responsibilities of the team members and that potential risks and hazards be communicated to all staff and volunteers. This is particularly important if regulations and laws need to be followed.

Planning is a critical component in preparing for the annual Hajj event. The authorities in Saudi Arabia developed a comprehensive plan to ensure that all aspects of the religious rituals are conducted safely (Shafi et al., 2008). Ahmed and Memish (2008) state that preparations for the public health, safety and security of the event are extraordinarily challenging due to the scale of the event and the fact that pilgrims travel from all over the world, and that it occurs annually. Thus, the planning of the event requires close and effective inter-Ministry collaboration. The recent tragic deaths of over 700 pilgrims in 2015 highlight the challenges faced by the event organizers. Prior to this incident, billions of dollars were spent expanding Mecca's Grand Mosque and building bridges and tunnels to manage crowds, and security personnel were deployed and security cameras installed. Organizers, and those that provide tours to Mecca, have also tried to raise awareness of the guidelines to improve safety. Despite these preventive strategies the sheer size and nature of the event shows that it is difficult to prevent injuries, so damage reduction strategies are required.

Damage Reduction

According to Getz (2005), if an event issue is perceived to be too risky or severe, it should be avoided or an attempt made to prevent it. However, not all risks can be easily avoided and hence damage reduction strategies will help to reduce the severity of any potential losses. Leopkey and Parent (2009a) noted that reduction strategies are the most prevalent amongst event managers simply because many risks have to be retained and potential damage reduced. Therefore this risk treatment option involves actions taken to lessen or diminish the potential impact of risks on an event. Risk reduction can be accomplished through better management, training and emergency response procedures to improve response times to incidents, accidents and crises. Resolving a crisis situation also requires the team to carefully analyse the situation, examine the possibilities, selecting the least-damaging option and to properly document every incident (Watt, 1998). Choosing the most appropriate option would also involve a cost–benefit analysis, whereby the cost of implementing each option is measured against the benefits obtained. The event context and tolerance levels are important considerations in conducting a cost–benefit analysis. Some of the reduction strategies implemented in an event context are discussed further in the sections below.

Facility Management

Prior to the commencement of any event, the venue must be inspected to ensure that it is free of explosives, fire hazards or other precarious conditions (Berlonghi, 1994). Inspecting the event site can help too in any last-minute changes to ensure the safety of guests. All fire safety devices such as the emergency broadcast system, smoke detectors, sprinklers and water hydrants and hoses should also be tested (Getz, 2005). A majority of venues require clients to undertake formal induction seminars, to ensure that they are aware of all egress, safety procedures and other health and safety requirements.

Crowd Management

As events grow in popularity, the number of attendees also increases, making crowd management and control an integral part of risk planning management (Abbott and Geddie, 2001). Violent and destructive behaviours of crowds are not only disruptive to the event; they can also lead to fatal incidents in extreme situations. Getz (2007) stresses that crowd management should be integrated throughout the design process and management systems to prevent problems and deliver good experiences. Similarly, Abbott and Geddie (2001) believe that crowd management and control measures will help event organizers to limit their liability, preserve the organization's goodwill, and protect the public, thereby securing the success of the event. If crowds are not managed appropriately they can lead to disasters such as the 1989 Hillsborough disaster, one of the worst stadium related disasters and football accidents in the world, which resulted in the deaths of 96 people after a human crush.

Abbott and Geddie (2001: 259) explain that crowd management includes 'the facilitation, employment and movement of crowds'. It requires event organizers to review the potential crowd's sociological behaviour, ushering, seating arrangements, transportation, parking, public announcements, and size and placement of box office and concession stands for ticket sales (Berlonghi, 1995). Some of the crowd management strategies that can be employed at events include:

- *Flow rate estimation and treatment*: To regulate crowd flow, flow rates for entrances and exits should be estimated for both normal and emergency situations (Getz, 2005). Event organizers should also avoid crowd density in particular areas. Austria's Innsbruck Marketing, for example, organized a variety of activities, stages and attraction points for their annual New Year's Eve event (Peters and Pikkemaat, 2005). This strategy assures that event experience is not diminished by overcrowding at one particular site. However, such a strategy requires good estimates of crowd data, which are difficult to gather in open-air events (Biaett and Hultsman, 2015).

- *Construction of special facilities*: For instance, in the case of the Hajj the Ministry of Hajj built the four-level Jamaraat Bridge to reduce overcrowding (Ahmed et al., 2006) and subsequently increased the number of bridges and tunnels to reduce the impact of any stampedes; however, this did not prevent deaths and injuries in 2015. Furthermore, providing an adequate number of restrooms, advance or group ticketing and electronic ticket scanning can also help to alleviate long queues and avoid bottlenecks (Abbott and Geddie, 2001; Cieslak, 2009).

- *Limiting capacity*: Saudi Arabia, for example, sets an annual quota of 1,000 visas per million population for every country during the Hajj season. Such immigration control helps to avoid excessive congestion at the Holy sites (Ahmed and Memish, 2008). It is necessary to ensure that the maximum capacity at an event venue is not exceeded. Individuals should be turned away once full capacity has been reached. Training should be provided to the ushers and security staff in handling such a situation so as not to exasperate the crowd.

- *Avoid unassigned seating*: Injury can occur as people seek to obtain a good seat. Appointing ushers not only helps to guide guests to their seats; ushers can also help to monitor guests' behaviour and any situations that could cause liability, report accidents and alert security of any potential problems (Abbott and Geddie, 2001).

- *Use signage*: Signage can also help to direct a crowd and advise of potential dangers and risks. For maximum effect, signage must be clear, highly visible and readily recognisable (Abbott and Geddie, 2001). In addition, signs should be placed in highly hazardous areas and on all hazardous equipment or supplies (Silvers, 2008).

Crowd Control

Large crowds can spell disaster if there is any deficiency in crowd management. Crowd control includes decision-making processes to react effectively to a range of potential problems (Getz, 2005). Measures would need to be taken once a crowd has begun to behave in a disorderly or dangerous manner (Abbott and Geddie, 2001). This measure usually involves law enforcement officers or security personnel. Contextual factors such as the mood and age of the crowd may influence crowd control strategies. For instance, Biaett and Hultsman (2015) noted that crowds gathered more at the start and finish points of a parade, suggesting that more attention is needed on how and why spectators group in these locations. Other studies (Hutton et al., 2012) argue that crowd type and mood are essential to understand in order to manage and reduce accidents and injuries. The authors note that mood is dynamic and can change throughout the day depending on the event stimuli (music, alcohol, etc.). There is also a lack of research on crowd panic and behaviour; this lack of research thus limits our understanding of crowd movements and control options (Al-Kodmany, 2013). Some practical crowd control procedures include:

- *Establishing a central control/command centre*: This will enable event organizers to maintain control and coordination throughout the event. Berlonghi (1995) states that the centre has the responsibility to coordinate security efforts, as well as making evacuation announcements when an event is upstaged by an emergency. For example, several Australian sport stadia established a primary command post located inside the stadium and a mobile secondary command post set outside the stadium to better manage emergency situations (Cieslak, 2009). The Notting Hill Carnival in London also uses a command centre to monitor activities via CCTV as well as at the carnival site to deal with unruly behaviour.
- *Implementing effective security measures*: Security relates to the protection of both people and property, through maintaining a safe and secure event environment (Silvers, 2008). This can also enhance the positive experiences of the consumers, taking all necessary measures to satisfy their enjoyment and encourage repeat attendance (Taylor and Toohey, 2006). Security personnel are able to direct crowds during unexpected situations, such as when crowd density exceeds design capacity or when squatters or vendors increase in size. Al-Kodmany (2013) outlines how security guards at Jamarat, Mecca were used to create gaps or crowd bubbles in areas prone to stampedes to reduce crowding during the Hajj.

Berlonghi (1995) stresses the importance of a written security plan that can be tailored to each event. All security personnel should receive appropriate training and thoroughly understand their roles and responsibilities, which include managing disputes and implementing emergency services (Cieslak, 2009). However, there is a need to balance appropriate security while ensuring that spectators' enjoyment of the event is not deterred (Taylor and Toohey, 2006). To prevent offensive individuals from claiming that they were being provoked by security, Abbott and Geddie (2001) suggest that security personnel act with appropriate professionalism or seek assistance from the police when requesting offensive individuals to leave the venue. Another way to control or transfer the risk is to out-source security to a third party under a contract (Cieslak, 2009).

Abbott and Geddie (2001) recommend that event organizers consider the conditions of the event and attempt to predict the behaviour of the guests or spectators so that protective measures can be taken. This view corresponds with Berlonghi (1995) and others (Hutton et al., 2012; Mowen et al., 2003) who believe that crowd conditions such as moods or emotions should be assessed. Event organizers need to be aware of the factors or stimuli that trigger a crowd from being one that is managed to one that needs to be controlled. For example, in the case of football matches, it is noted that more rigorous security will be required as rival groups may potentially turn violent in sporting events (Abbott and Geddie, 2001; Berlonghi, 1995). Berlonghi (1995) cited some catalysts that can affect crowd behaviour, which include operational circumstances, event activities, performers' actions, spectator and social factors, security, weather and natural disasters.

In addition, external stimuli, for example noise level, should also be assessed to avoid affecting the visitors' experience and the neighbouring community. This will reduce the chances for lawsuits and the revoking of permits too (Abbott and Geddie, 2001). The Notting Hill Carnival is one of the world's largest street festivals, attracting one million people and involving 70 floats and 50 sound systems in a residential area in London. Music from floats and audio systems should not cause a nuisance to local residents, and for the first time in 2009 the Carnival's noise levels were monitored to help develop strategies to reduce the noise pollution.

The Notting Hill Carnival has also been associated with criminal activities in the past, including stabbings, shootings, drug distribution and drug taking. According to Abbott and Geddie (2001), policies concerning drug and alcohol consumption and sales should be created to avoid having the event's image tarnished by alcohol-related problems. Trained personnel and on-site law enforcement should be appointed to deal with intoxicated people and to recognize various types of drugs and the symptoms they create. Cieslak (2009) found in his study that the majority of Australian sport stadia had established non-alcohol sections to isolate potential trouble and to better manage the crowd. Surveillance devices can also be used to monitor alcohol and drug consumption and render immediate intervention when needed (Abbott and Geddie, 2001). To manage drug and alcohol-related risks a number of control measures are possible (Harris et al., 2014) including:

- *Entry controls* to the event venues or parts of the venue where alcohol is served. These can include point monitoring, bag searches, ID scanning and capping entry.
- *Alcohol service controls* such as restrictions on alcohol strength, glass serving containers and limits on the number of drinks bought at any one time.
- *Attendee/patron management* including provision of free food and water, CCTV, educational campaigns and progressive shutdown of venues in order to reduce anti-social behaviour.
- *Site/venue layout and design* including adequate number of facilities, chill-out or alcohol-free areas, sufficient space, lighting and heating which can prevent anti-social behaviour.
- *Regulatory and enforcement practices* including defined trading hours, compliance checks by police or licensing authorities, targeted enforcement or venue practices.

Managing Environmental Risks

As climate change increases the vulnerability of the event industry, Abbott and Geddie (2001) highlight the importance for event organizers to be aware of the unpredictability of climate and plan accordingly to reduce control problems. Jones et al. (2006)

believe that successful outdoor or climate-sensitive events should integrate weather data into event planning and develop adaptation plans or have adequate provisions for bad weather. For instance, Canada's National Capital Commission (NCC) implemented a diverse range of adaptation strategies for some of its climate-sensitive events. One such strategy for the Tulip Festival involves employing irrigation and snowmaking to lower soil temperatures so that the tulips will bloom just in time for the festival (Jones et al., 2006).

Furthermore, in preparing for the Canada Day celebrations, contingency plans such as public education through the media, installing cooling systems and positioning medical staff at the event were implemented for heat emergencies (Jones et al., 2006). The Ministry of Hajj also implemented various measures to render heat relief to the Hajj pilgrims. For example, new marble surfaces that do not absorb heat have been installed at the mosque (Ahmed et al., 2006). In addition, cooling units have been fitted along the pilgrimage route (Gatrad and Sheikh, 2005).

Managing Health Risks

Approaches to control and reduce communicable diseases are important as an outbreak has the potential to spread rapidly if not properly contained. Abbott and Geddie (2001) recommend establishing a first aid station at every event so that immediate medical attention can be rendered. As previously mentioned, the Hajj has the potential for widespread infectious disease outbreaks. As such, a multi-pronged health safety approach encompassing immunization, education and awareness programmes, timely treatment and infection control practices was implemented (Shafi et al., 2008). Immigration is also a tool facilitating public health security as the issuance of visas is dependent on evidence of mandatory immunization against influenza and meningococcal disease (Ahmed and Memish, 2008).

Recent outbreaks of SARS, avian flu and swine flu have raised global concerns surrounding the potential for events to spread disease. This has lifted the demand for internationally agreed shared approaches to minimize the risk of a pandemic (Ahmed and Memish, 2008). According to Gatrad et al. (2006), strategies should focus on ways to prevent transmission and treatment for infected individuals. Furthermore, event organizers need to ensure that they adhere to occupational health and safety (OHS) standards, providing a work environment that is safe and free of hazards that may cause injury, damage or disease (Silvers, 2008).

Boo, Ghiselli and Almanza (2000) found that food poisoning is another major concern for visitors at outdoor fairs and festivals. The research indicates that food served at such events is perceived as significantly less healthy and safe than food at other food preparation sites. Therefore, event organizers need to pay more attention to the hygienic practices of food handlers at the event and must ensure that the food vendors obtain insurance to reduce any potential liability.

Managing Legal Risks

Compliance with statutory and regulatory laws not only reduces risk for the event organizer, it also illustrates care and respect to those attending the event (Silvers, 2008). Having written contracts and legal documents for all activities related to the event is essential as it helps to safeguard the event organizer by specifying the responsibilities and risks assumed by each party, thereby limiting legal liability.

Another legal strategy is the use of insurance to protect against financial issues, business interruption due to bad weather, contractual disputes, loss and theft to property, and the risks of being held responsible for damage or injury etc. (Getz, 2005; Leopkey and Parent, 2009a). Many organizations may think that taking out insurance is all they need to do to manage their risk. However, Deloitte et al. (2002, cited in Arcodia and McKinnon, 2004) pointed out that there is increasing evidence to suggest that unless organizations are able to demonstrate that they have adequate risk controls in place, it will be difficult to obtain insurance at an affordable price or perhaps even not at all.

Arcodia and McKinnon (2004) highlighted the impact that the public insurance liability crisis in Australia had on events held particularly in rural areas. The substantial increase in the insurance premium was exacerbated by the collapse of the insurance giant HIH Insurance and the acts of terrorism on September 11, 2001 (Arcodia and McKinnon, 2004). The sudden increase in public liability insurance premium prices led to the cancellation or postponement of not only festivals, but also sporting and recreational facilities, as many of the organizers could not afford to pay the higher insurance premiums. As Arcodia and McKinnon (2004) observed, some of the festivals were found operating without insurance due to the premium increase, thereby putting the festival at risk. Increasingly, more insurance companies are demanding that event organizers demonstrate that they have a risk management strategy in place (Getz, 2005), thus emphasizing the importance of risk planning and management for event managers.

Risk Transfer

Risk transfer (or diffusion) is a process to spread out potential risks. This could include storing equipment at different locations (Berlonghi, 1994), selecting alternative training venues so as to diffuse the use or prevent destruction of the actual competition ground (Leopkey and Parent, 2009a).

Reallocation of risk involves transferring the risk to another company contracted to perform certain tasks and responsibilities. This may involve requesting vendors, suppliers and participants to obtain their own insurance (Getz, 2005). In Australia for example, most performing groups are required to have public liability insurance before they can take part in an event (Allen et al., 2008). Another example is the hiring of private security companies to remove cash from ticket booths or to undertake security on behalf of the event organizers. Although transferring the risk to other parties may reduce the liability of the event organizer, should the other parties fail to manage the risks effectively, the event organizer may still need to find solutions to treat it. If they do not treat potential risks they may be found to be negligent by not providing duty of care.

Monitoring and Review

In light of changing circumstances, risks and the effectiveness of control measures should be constantly monitored. Reviewing strategies is also an integral part of the risk management process to assess the effectiveness and feasibility of the risk management treatment plan. For effective evaluation and feedback, long-term learning from current experience needs to be captured and understood in order to ensure that: (a) the same mistakes/problems do not reoccur; and (b) new strategies are increasingly better informed.

Preskill and Torres (1999) argue that evaluative enquiry is needed for organizations to critically reflect on their strategies and their success. This requires that organization members 'critically consider what they think, say and do in the context of the work environment' (Preskill and Torres, 1999: 92). They use the term because evaluation is used to seek answers and information about an object or outcome, which should include not only the action or object itself, but also the values, standards and assumptions that relate to it. By critically evaluating all the aspects of risk strategy formulation, implementation and outcomes, it should be possible to gain important knowledge for the future and change the currently held collective mental models of organizational members.

Mechanisms, often used to ensure on-going review, include setting up post-review meetings to debrief and assist the event manager to evaluate strategies and avoid future repetition of mistakes. Incident reports that document the causes of incidents and actions taken during the event itself should be assessed at the meeting to help identify areas that need improvement or adjustment (Berlonghi, 1994). A range of stakeholders both internal and external to the event should be consulted, and where appropriate may include sponsors, participants, media, police, emergency services, etc. Workshops and seminars with event managers can also be useful at communicating potential risks through previous experiences. Event associations may be best placed to organize and communicate such seminars or workshops to event organizers.

Case Study 9.1 – Event Managers' Risk Planning Attitudes, Beliefs and Perceived Constraints

There has been a lack of research analysing event risk management planning attitudes, beliefs and factors inhibiting or facilitating adoption levels. The majority of research in the area has focused on mega events, such as the

Olympic Games, a significant yet small subsector of the events industry. Organizational behaviour can be explored at a systems, group or individual level. Although organizations ultimately implement risk planning activities, it is the role of individuals and their psychological factors which may influence the adoption of them. A complex range of factors may influence risk planning including experience, values and beliefs, messages, personal attributes and socio-cultural norms.

A research project was undertaken in Australia to identify event managers' attitudes and beliefs concerning risk management as well as explore social influencers and perceived constraints to implementing risk management planning. The research adopted a qualitative methodology to address the research aim and used Ajzen's (1991, 2005) Theory of Planned Behaviour (TPB) as a framework for exploring event managers' risk, attitudes, beliefs and perceived constraints. To obtain a comprehensive sample, a matrix of events in the region that were diverse across the area by theme, size, organization structure and length of operation was developed, and events chosen. The sample was further refined to ensure representation based on the following criteria: size of event (large, medium, small); theme of event (music, sport, cultural, community); and organizational structure (professional, voluntary organizing committee). Semi-structured interviews with 11 event managers were undertaken, drawn from South East Queensland, Australia.

Respondents' understanding of risk and risk management varied from limited and generalized to a comprehensive in-depth knowledge. Respondents articulated that risk management entailed 'identifying before the event and trying to put measures in place to make sure that you minimize any potential risk or fall out' [I.4]. Safety and physical risks were discussed by most respondents as the key risk factors to consider, however, a respondent went on to note 'also the financial risk and a multitude of other risk factors need to be taken into risk management' [I.10]. There appeared to be a direct connection between the level of professionalism of the event organizational structure (i.e. voluntary or professional) and a respondent's depth of understanding. Nearly all respondents had positive attitudes towards risk management planning. One respondent enthused 'I'm one of these ones that's all for it; let's bring it on; let's be doing it' [I.10].

Respondents were influenced by beliefs related to safety, compliance, decision-making and professionalism. The most common risk identified by

(Continued)

(Continued)

respondents related to safety of employees, volunteers, participants and attendees, particularly as a consequence of activities and planned programming. Compliance considerations, such as legislation and insurance requirements, were also found to influence event managers' attitudes and behaviours.

Internally, respondents identified organizational management, such as directors, section heads or event organizing committees, as well as staff and volunteers as key influencers in undertaking risk planning. One respondent commented: 'The senior management team's actually very supportive of the risk management, they're actually the ones that are pushing it ... he sees it as a priority for the business as a whole. So the senior management team takes it very seriously and they very much are seen as a priority' [I.5]. Externally, event managers were influenced too by the attitudes and beliefs of clients, sponsors, venues, participants and attendees. Significant compliance facilitators such as government organizations, police, security officials and event insurers were also important in influencing the risk management practices of respondents.

However, in addition, seven perceived constraints were identified as important in influencing risk planning in an event context: time, financial costs, human resourcing, knowledge/self-efficacy, adapting to change, restrictions and regulation. As one respondent commented on the time constraint: 'see, I still run a business so I can't give it 100 per cent' [I.2]. Consequently, a number of respondents identified hiring external consultants to assist in this process. Time and consultant costs result in financial costs being incurred by event organizations. However, as one respondent stated: 'I've got private health insurance. I find it the same kind of thing. Like, what's more important? The fact that it costs a lot of money but it's your life. My business is my bread and butter. One incident could put me out of business for the rest of my life too and I wouldn't be employable again' [I.9].

Interestingly, the research identified that event managers were largely concerned about physical and safety risks, followed by financial, weather and organizational risks. These findings are in contrast to the holistic risk planning approach advocated by the Australian and New Zealand International Standards (AS/NZS ISO 31000, 2009). There was some differentiation between respondents based on past experience. 'I think first of all, we are all very much aware of the concept of risk management planning. We are conscious of it, we are developing policies and practices ... that will mean it's a lot easier for us and therefore more enjoyable' [l.4]. The findings indicate that individuals who are active event professionals within larger organizations appear to be driving risk management planning within the sector.

However, event managers were found to have a wider range of reference groups that they considered influential. The social pressure to perform risk-planning practices was exerted internally and externally of the event organization. The findings suggest that event managers may face increased complexity in planning and implementing effective risk management practices in their organizations compared to other sectors. More widely, the industry needs education to enhance the knowledge of practitioners as currently expertise is sought externally for many organizations. The use of external consultants and the time involved in establishing risk management plans, policies and strategies are limiting factors for widespread implementation of risk management practices beyond simply the need for legal compliance and internal risks.

Professional associations, government organizations and tertiary institutions have a significant role to play in educating and assisting the development of event manager competence to understand and plan for a wide range of risks. The use of knowledge management tools to aid in the development of industry manuals, risk assessments and policy guidelines would assist practitioners limited by knowledge, time and available staff – factors uncovered in this research. Creating opportunities to share experiences and knowledge gained would also be beneficial for event managers. Professional event associations could assist through the provision of online portals or discussion groups.

For more detail on this case study please read: Reid, S. and Ritchie, B.W. (2011) Risk management: Event managers' attitudes, beliefs, and perceived constraints, *Event Management*, 15(4): 329–41.

Case Study Questions

1   Why do you think the risk managers in this study are most concerned with physical and safety risks?
2   Why does senior management in an event organization play such an important role in risk management?
3   Suggest ways in which your university can educate current and future event managers about the importance of risk management.
4   How do the events managers' views of risk management in this case study differ from those held by events managers in your own country?

Chapter Summary

As outlined in the introduction of this chapter, the nature of events creates potential for internal and external risks and crises. Potential risks cover all areas in its operation including health and safety of guests and workers, crowding, environmental risks and compliance with local laws and regulations. Risk management assists event organizers in devising and conducting events in the safest possible manner, whilst mitigating losses, and it is essential that event organizations formally plan for and develop strategies to deal with the possible consequences of unplanned events.

This chapter provided an overview of risk management for event managers, and identified a range of tools to assist managers in planning and managing risk in the context of hosting an event. The chapter provided a systematic framework for understanding and managing event risks and used examples throughout the text and a concluding case study to highlight the importance of identifying, assessing and treating risks. It is hoped that this chapter has made the reader aware of the importance of risk management and the process that can be followed to systematically manage risks in an events context.

Glossary

Contingency plan: A set of plans to deal with risks that cannot be reduced or mitigated prior to an event being held.

Monitoring and review: Actions to debrief and review after an event to improve the risk management process.

Risk: Some form of uncertainty and the potential for this uncertainty to create damage or loss to an organization. Risks can be internal or external in nature.

Risk analysis and evaluation: An assessment of the probability of occurrence and the severity of the consequences on the event goals and strategies.

Risk assessment: The identification of a range of internal and external risks using suitable tools.

Risk communication: Communication and consultation with stakeholders is vital to help with the identification, assessment and treatment of event risks.

Risk consequences: The potential impact of the risk on a scale from insignificant to catastrophic. Used in the risk analysis and evaluation stage.

Risk likelihood: The potential occurrence of the risk on a scale from rare to almost certain. Used in the risk analysis and evaluation stage.

Risk management: Process of anticipating, preventing or minimizing potential costs, losses or problems for the event, organization, partners and guests.

Risk prevention and avoidance: Developing plans and preventive actions to reduce or prevent potential risks from occurring.

Risk reduction: Can be accomplished through better management, training and emergency response procedures to improve response times to incidents, accidents and crises.

Risk transfer (or diffusion): A process to spread out potential risks through to suppliers, customers or other organizations.

Risk treatment: Strategies implemented to reduce the vulnerability of the event and control any problem that might arise.

SWOT analysis: An evaluation and analysis of an organization's internal strengths and weaknesses, and external opportunities and threats.

Review Questions

1. Select an outdoor and indoor event. Identify and contrast the likely risks and possible treatment actions for both of these events.
2. Legal liability is becoming a major risk for event managers. What is legal liability and how can event organizations protect themselves from its consequences?
3. What does it mean to transfer risk?
4. How important is communication and consultation in event risk management? Explain and justify your answer with examples.
5. How should event managers ensure that their risk management plans are kept up-to-date?

Additional Resources

Books / Book Chapters / Journal Articles

Allen, J., O'Toole, W., Harris, R. and McDonnell, I. (2011). *Festival and Special Event Management* (5th edn). Queensland: John Wiley & Sons Australia. Chapter 18 provides a good overview of event risk management.

Frosdick, S. and Walley, D. (1999). *Sports and Safety Management*. Oxford: Elsevier Butterworth-Heinemann. A practical guide for event managers and all those involved in staging sporting events.

Kemp, C. and Hill, I. (2004). *Health and Safety Aspects in the Live Music Industry*. Cambridge: Entertainment Technology Press. Outlines the health and safety requirements of concerts, festivals and other musical events.

Reid, S. and Ritchie, B.W. (2011). Risk management: Event managers' attitudes, beliefs and perceived constraints. *Event Management, 15*(4): 329–41. Provides a good research article on risk management from an event manager's perspective.

Silvers, J.R. (2008). *Risk Management for Meetings and Events.* Oxford: Elsevier Butterworth-Heinemann. Provides a comprehensive and detailed analysis of risk management for meetings and events.

Useful Websites

www.hse.gov.uk/ – A useful website which provides general guidance about health and safety at work, as well as free downloadable guides to health and safety at different types of events.

www.oshweb.com/ – OshWeb provides links to, reviews of and comments on websites in the occupational safety and health sector all around the world.

www.safeworkaustralia.gov.au/ – A guide to safe work practices in Australia.

www.theirm.org – The Institute for Risk Management website has a wide range of online resources for risk managers; they are the leading professional body for risk management.

References

AS/NZS ISO 31000 (2009). *Risk Management: Principles and Guidelines.* Sydney: SAI Global.

Abbott, J.L. and Geddie, M.W. (2001). Event and venue management: minimizing liability through effective crowd management techniques. *Event Management, 6*: 259–70.

Ahmed, Q.A., Arabi, Y.M. and Memish, Z.A. (2006). Health risks at the Hajj. *The Lancet, 367*(9515): 1008–15.

Ahmed, Q.A. and Memish, Z.A. (2008). Hajj medicine for the Guests of God: a public health frontier revisited. *Journal of Infection and Public Health, 1*: 57–61.

Al-Kodmany, K. (2013). Crowd management and urban design: New scientific approaches. *Urban Design International, 18*(4): 282–95.

Allen, J., O'Toole, W., Harris, R. and McDonnell, I. (2008). *Festival and Special Event Management* (4th edn). Brisbane: John Wiley & Sons Australia.

Allen, J., O'Toole, W., Harris, R. and McDonnell, I. (2011). *Festival and Special Event Management* (5th edn). Brisbane: John Wiley & Sons Australia.

Ajzen, I. (1991). The theory of planned behavior. *Organizational Behavior and Human Decision Processes, 50*: 179–211.

Ajzen, I. (2005). *Attitudes, Personality and Behavior.* Maidenhead: Open University Press.

Arcodia, C. and McKinnon, S. (2004). Public liability insurance: its impact on Australian rural festivals. *Journal of Convention and Event Tourism, 6*: 101–10.

Berlonghi, A. (1994). *The Special Event Risk Management Manual.* California: Alexander Berlonghi.

Berlonghi, A.E. (1995). Understanding and planning for different spectator crowds. *Safety Science, 18*: 239–47.

Biaett, V. and Hultsman, W. (2015). Everybody loves a parade … but how many is everybody? *Event Management, 19*: 151–7.

Boo, H.C., Ghiselli, R. and Almanza, B.A. (2000). Consumer perceptions and concerns about the healthfulness and safety of food served at fairs and festivals. *Event Management, 2*: 85–92.

Carlsen, J., Andersson, T., Ali-Knight, J., Jaeger, K. and Taylor, R. (2010). Festival management innovation and failure. *International Journal of Event and Festival Management, 1*(2): 120–31.

Cieslak, T.J. (2009). Match day security at Australian sport stadia: A case study of eight venues. *Event Management, 13*: 43–52.

Ewart, A. and Boone, T. (1987). Risk management: Defusing the dragon. *Journal of Experiential Education, 10*: 28–34.

Gatrad, A.R., Shafi, S., Memish, Z.A. and Sheikh, A. (2006). Hajj and the risk of influenza. *BMJ, 333*: 1182–3.

Gatrad, A.R. and Sheikh, A. (2005). Hajj: journey of a lifetime. *BMJ, 330*: 133–7.

Getz, D. (2002). Why festivals fail. *Event Management, 7*: 209–19.

Getz, D. (2005). *Event Management and Event Tourism* (2nd edn). New York: Cognizant Communication Corporation.

Getz, D. (2007). *Event Studies: Theory, Research and Policy for Planned Events*. Burlington: Elsevier.

Glaesser, D. (2006). *Crisis Management in the Tourism Industry*. Oxford: Butterworth-Heinemann.

Goldblatt, J.J. (1997). *Special Events: Best Practices in Modern Event Management* (2nd edn). New Jersey: John Wiley & Sons.

Gray, K.L. (2015). Ohio cancels poultry show to protect state from avian flu. The Columbus Dispatch. 30th September [online]. Retrieved from http://www.dispatch.com/content/stories/local/2015/06/02/ohio-poultry-shows-canceled.html

Hall, C.M., Timothy, D.J. and Duval, D.T. (2003). *Safety and Security in Tourism: Relationships, Management and Marketing*. New York: Haworth Press.

Harris, R., Edwards, D. and Homel, P. (2014). Managing alcohol and drugs in event and venue settings: The Australian case. *Event Management, 18*: 457–70.

Hutton, A., Zeitz, K., Brown, S. and Arbon, P. (2012). Assessing the psychosocial elements of crowds at mass gatherings. *Prehospital and Disaster Medicine, 26*(6): 414–21.

Jones, B., Scott, D. and Khaled, H.A. (2006). Implications of climate change for outdoor event planning: A case study of three special events in Canada's National Capital Region. *Event Management, 10*: 63–76.

Kim, N.S. and Chalip, L. (2004). Why travel to the FIFA World Cup? Effects of motives, background, interest and constraints. *Tourism Management, 25*: 695–707.

Lee, H. and Graefe, A.R. (2003). Crowding at an arts festival: Extending crowding models to the frontcountry. *Tourism Management, 24*: 1–11.

Leopkey, B. and Parent, M.M. (2009a). Risk management in large-scale sporting events: A stakeholder perspective. *European Sport Management Quarterly, 9*: 187–208.

Leopkey, B. and Parent, M.M. (2009b). Risk management strategies by stakeholders in Canadian major sporting events. *Event Management, 13*: 153–70.

Mair, J. (2011). Events and climate change: An Australian perspective. *International Journal of Event and Festival Management, 2*(3): 245–53.

Memish, Z.A. and Ahmed, Q.A. (2002). Mecca bound: The challenges ahead. *Journal of Travel Medicine, 9*(4): 202–10.

Moital, M., Jackson, C. and Le Couillard, J. (2013). Using scenarios to investigate stakeholders' views on the future of a sporting event. *Event Management, 17*(4): 439–52.

Mowen, A.J., Vogelsong, H.G. and Graefe, A.R. (2003). Perceived crowding and its relationship to crowd management practices at park and recreation events. *Event Management, 8*: 63–72.

Nazer, F. (2015). Hajj stampede: Could tragedy have been prevented? [online]. Retrieved from www.bbc.com/news/world-middle-east-34350643.

Odio, M., Walker, M. and Kim, M. (2013). Examining stress and coping process of mega-event employees. *International Journal of Event and Festival Management, 4*(2): 140–55.

Peters, M. and Pikkemaat, B. (2005). The management of city events: The case of 'Bergsilvester' in Innsbruck, Austria. *Event Management, 9*: 147–53.

Preskill, H. and Torres, R.T. (1999). The role of evaluative enquiry in creating learning organizations. In: M. Easterby-Smith, J. Burgoyne and L. Araujo (eds) *Organizational Learning and the Learning Organization* (pp. 92–114). London: Sage.

Reid, S. and Ritchie, B.W. (2011). Risk management: Event managers' attitudes, beliefs, and perceived constraints. *Event Management, 15*(4): 329–41.

Scott, D., McBoyle, G. and Schwartzentruber, M. (2004). Climate change and the distribution of climatic resources for tourism in North America. *Climate Research, 27*: 105–17.

Shafi, S., Booy, R., Haworth, E., Rashid, H. and Memish, Z.A. (2008). Hajj: Health lessons for mass gatherings. *Journal of Infection and Public Health, 1*: 27–32.

Silvers, J.R. (2008). *Risk Management for Meetings and Events*. Oxford: Butterworth-Heinemann.

Sönmez, S.F. and Graefe, A.R. (1998). Influence of terrorism risk on foreign tourism decisions. *Annals of Tourism Research, 25*: 112–44.

Taylor, T. and Toohey, K. (2006). Impacts of terrorism-related safety and security measures at a major sport event. *Event Management, 9*: 199–209.

Watt, C.D. (1998). *Event Management in Leisure and Tourism*. Essex: Addison Wesley Longman.

WhoTV (2015). Bird flu costing Iowa jobs, Recovery unlikely this year. 30th September [online]. Retrieved from http://whotv.com/2015/06/22/bird-flu-costing-iowa-jobs-recovery-unlikely-this-year/

Wideman, M.R. (1992). *Project and Program Risk Management: A Guide to Managing Project Risks and Opportunities*. Newton Square, PA: Project Management Institute.

Event Evaluation

10

Jo-anne Tull and Nigel L. Williams

Learning Objectives

By reading this chapter students should be able to:

- Articulate the nature and importance of evaluation to the events management function
- Describe what event evaluation should focus on
- Explain the purpose of event evaluation, including the needs and expectations of stakeholders
- Describe the cyclical, holistic nature of event evaluation using the three critical Ss of events
- Assess the different forms of evaluation models and methods
- Formulate and prepare an event evaluation report.

Introduction

Events are aimed at generating a range of outcomes, from economic benefits to cultural, social and environmental changes. To ensure that these benefits are delivered, event stakeholders require robust and rigorous examination of processes and impacts. This chapter focuses on the role and function of event evaluation, and offers some insight into the main practices, models and methods that are employed. Event evaluation is now widely accepted as a critical component of the events management function, given the complexities involved in planning and executing events, usually in very dynamic contexts. Event managers cannot simply rely on a single metric such as patron head count or net profits as the main indicator of determining whether the event has fulfilled its objectives.

Experiences of events that operate beyond these early traditions of evaluation demonstrate that events management must give strong consideration to determining, understanding and analysing the nature, relevance, performance and impacts of events to gauge a range of key markers of success. In essence, effective use of event evaluation rests on its integration throughout the entire life of the event, from planning through to execution through to event shutdown. The London 2012 Olympic and Paralympic Games website, for example, offers a detailed account of how evaluation with a focus on sustainability has been incorporated from the planning stages of the Games, and includes targets for evaluation and progress reports (LOCOG, n.d.).

Event evaluation should take a holistic approach that will aid event managers in making prudent decisions at each stage of event development and execution. When executed well, event evaluation offers a solid guide for improvement and allows event managers to give an accurate account of all aspects of the event to its stakeholders. This process may encounter some challenges. The first is that stakeholders are heterogeneous and may each hold differing views of event costs and benefits (Giampiccoli et al., 2015). Therefore one group of stakeholders will be satisfied with event outcomes while another may not. In addition, stakeholders' evaluations may change during pre-, during- and post-event time periods. These time periods are not isolated, as evaluations created in an earlier period may become a reference point for a later one (Tsaur et al., 2015).

Conceptualizing Event Evaluation

Evaluation is a subjective determination that can utilize objective quantitative measures (Getz, 1997). Evaluation is both a monitoring and a control mechanism, and it is a critical component of the overall project management of any event. It offers a means by which decisions made at each stage of the project management cycle can be checked for efficiency and effectiveness. To perform evaluation, event teams engage in continuous processes of measuring and monitoring using numerical data or descriptive data, or a combination of both, as is explained later in this chapter. In this regard, Forrester's definition of event evaluation is instructive. He suggests that event evaluation for sports, recreation and tourism events is:

> the systematic collection and analysis of data in order to make judgments regarding the value or worth of a particular aspect of an event which can then be used to make decisions during the renewal phase of the event planning model regardless of the improvement of the event. (2008: 112–13)

At the practical level, event evaluation is often guided by what is perceived as the main purpose or aim of the event. For example, evaluation of corporate events addresses two distinct areas: 'the content' viz. the speakers, activities and entertainment; and 'the destination' viz. venue, facilities and services. By extension, event evaluation for events ought to focus on determining how well the content matched the purpose of the event and whether the destination fitted the content and purpose of the event (O'Toole and Mikolaitis, 2002).

The use of specialized definitions of events can, however, constrain the event evaluation process and limit the range of variables examined in collecting data. For example, where a festival is deemed primarily a tourism product, focus rests on evaluating the components that relate to tourist activity, usually through a visitor exit survey. Oftentimes, less effort is allocated to evaluating local patron activity or impact on the community, which can also have relevance to evaluation of these event types.

Consequently, as much as possible the event evaluation exercise should be multifaceted to satisfy a range of purposes, while minimizing complexity in its implementation. This requires having a clear understanding of the various purposes of the event, apart from its primary mandate as shown in Figure 10.1. From this, the event manager can identify the broad approach to be taken and the corresponding

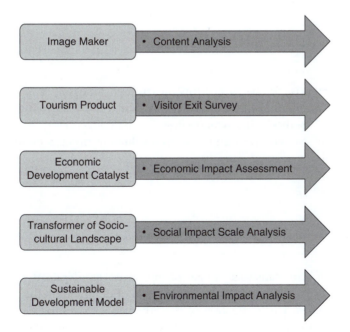

Figure 10.1 Event purposes and tools

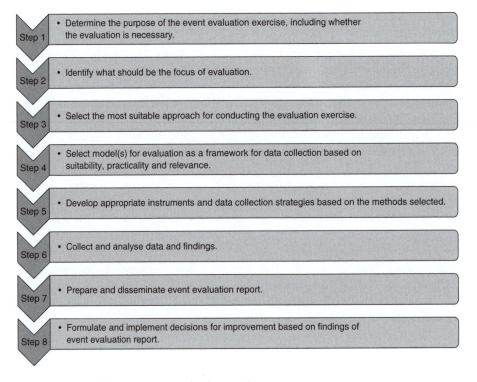

Figure 10.2　Steps for conducting an evaluation exercise

model and methods to be used for measuring, assessment and monitoring. Complexity can be minimized by utilizing a particular evaluation model and a complementary set of methods that would allow for the collection of a diverse range of data on the event, thereby making the event evaluation process more cost effective and time efficient.

Whatever choices are made, the general steps for conducting event evaluation are shown in Figure 10.2.

Why Evaluate?

Event evaluation can satisfy a range of purposes as depicted in Figure 10.3. Fundamentally, event evaluation is a useful means of determining the success of processes and outcomes. This evaluation of performance is driven by the internal needs of the event organization and the external context within which the event operates. For example, many event managers conduct event evaluation not only for the purpose of determining whether functions such as event programming, logistics and revenue

Reasons for All Event Evaluation
- Allows for more informed decisions towards greater efficiency and more positive results to be made
- To measure success or failure

Internally Driven Reasons
- To engender accountability
- To determine whether goals and objectives have been met
- To identify and address problems and challenges
- To determine whether event management functions have achieved expected outcomes
- To understand who attends the event to determine who else can be targeted
- To determine worth of the event to its workers and volunteers
- To determine whether and how the event can remain viable and become sustainable

Externally Driven Reasons
- To satisfy accountability requirements
- To determine level of awareness of sponsors' products/services
- To determine level of media interest and coverage
- To determine event's level of impact on tourist arrivals
- To determine event's level of impact on business and other related industries
- To determine whether event satisfies the expectations of community stakeholders
- To determine worth of the event to its patrons

Figure 10.3 Reasons for conducting event evaluation

generation are meeting their targets – an internally driven concern – but also to satisfy the expectations of stakeholders and provide accountability to investors, funders and sponsors, which are externally driven factors. These insights can contribute to the lessons-learned component of project management as it captures information that can support delivery of future events.

Event managers are accountable to multiple stakeholders. This has made event evaluation particularly critical to building the reputation of the event and its events management team. Stakeholders' needs and expectations can vary according to their level of interest and power with respect to the event. Further, stakeholders may combine their efforts, forming coalitions to increase the strength and salience of their influence. Event managers should therefore be cognizant of the needs and expectations of each stakeholder group and have these adequately addressed through evaluation reporting and documentation. A stakeholder concerns checklist can be developed beforehand and reviewed upon completion of the evaluation exercise to ensure that the key areas of concern for each stakeholder group have been addressed.

The event manager must be very clear as to the reasons for conducting event evaluation given that significant amounts of resources are needed to carry it out. In this regard, it is useful for the event manager to be aware of the following, particularly when the event is not new:

- Does the event organization/event host have – or have access to – the requisite resources to conduct an evaluation exercise?
- Have event evaluations been conducted on the event in the past? And if so, how often, and what kinds of evaluation?
- What use was made of the evaluation report?
- What is the nature of the environment in which the event operates?
- Can it facilitate the execution of an event evaluation?
- Does the event have access to a wide range of information which it can use to conduct the evaluation exercise?

What to Evaluate?

To begin, the event manager should think of the main components of the event, the key event management functions, as well as the context in which the event operates, to decide what should be evaluated. This determination should therefore be made before the evaluation methodology is chosen so as to assure its suitability and practicality. The elements for evaluation range from basic information such as number of patrons to more complex queries such as social impacts and ROI. Some researchers have suggested particular typologies of elements that can guide event managers in making the appropriate choice of elements for evaluation (see Getz, 2005; Henderson and Bialeschki, 2002; McDavid and Hawthorne, 2006). Examples of elements for event evaluation are:

Event Elements: number of patrons; size of group; demographics of patrons; origin of event patron; attendees' address; source of information on the event; number of times attending event; patron satisfaction; quality and impact of event programming; quality of merchandise, food and beverages; the extent to which the event uses 'green' practices; quality of service.

Event Organization Elements: nature and quantum of resources; number of staff; number and percentage share of volunteers; volunteers' perceptions working on the event; income and expenditure; cash flow; level of investment; number of sponsors; sponsorship dollars; extent to which event organization follows 'green' practices; quality of service.

Event Context Elements: nature and amount of local suppliers used; impacts *on* event; impacts *of* event; community perceptions; level of media coverage; media value; internet presence.

How to Approach Event Evaluation

What, then, is an effective way of approaching event evaluation? Some researchers have argued that evaluation is focused on measuring and monitoring the implementation of an event (Getz and Page, 2015). Others still maintain that every aspect of the event must be evaluated (Tum et al., 2006), including factors such as human resource management and volunteerism, facilities and access, and hospitality (Wendroff, 2004). In reality, event evaluation is mostly conducted after the event (Tum et al., 2006) and involves success being measured against predefined objectives (Van der Wagen, 2005).

However, use of post-event evaluation as the sole mechanism for evaluating performance can have its challenges. The event manager can miss opportunities to correct any problems detected from the evaluation exercise, as the event would have ended. There tends to be minimal or no focus on evaluating the planning phase of the event, which is vital to understanding many of the decisions implemented during the executing phase of the event. Evaluation conducted after an event may also result in key elements of the evaluation exercise not being effectively deployed, such as a patron satisfaction survey or crowding assessment. Post-event evaluation as a singular approach may therefore be too narrow in scope, thereby precluding the event manager from obtaining a comprehensive understanding of the event. Roberta Quarless highlights the impact of short timeframes on the decision of how an event is evaluated.

Diary of an Event Manager – Roberta Quarless, Event Manager, The Old Yard, Carnival Masquerade Heritage Fair, Trinidad and Tobago

The Department of Creative and Festival Arts (DCFA), University of the West Indies (UWI), is involved in numerous events every year; one such event is The Old Yard. Roberta explains: 'The Old Yard was an inherited event for the DCFA, and one that I "adopted". The decision to pass the baton of this event onto our department was made a mere five weeks prior to the date carded for the event, and so we had a small window of time to implement the planning and designing phases.'

It was apparent to Roberta from the start that evaluation had to be included, for very little had been documented about the event. She remembers: 'Because of the short timeframe for planning and execution, I focused evaluation on event execution.'

The tools used to evaluate the event were a survey, informal interviewing and observation. Throughout the event, at varying intervals, the event team

(Continued)

(Continued)

walked around, mingling with patrons, questioning them about the event. The team also chatted with the performers and enquired about their experiences at the event as compared to its previous instalment, and also looked out for problems arising such as long queues and crowding at the entrance, and immediately reported them to Roberta.

Interview sheets were distributed to a cross-section of the patrons: tourists, nationals, teachers, children, performers, academics and practitioners in the arts. From the collective responses, the team was able to make recommendations for next year's event. Roberta recalls: 'We discussed how we could improve logistics on the day of the event, as well as how to further improve marketing of the event. We discussed attracting sponsors that would not compromise the theme of the event and how we might expand on opportunities for greater revenue generation.'

The evaluation then served as a starting point for planning the event the following year.

The nature of the evaluation approach is also a key determinant in deciding on the evaluation methodology for a particular event. Evaluation approaches are generally characterized as numerically based or descriptive-oriented and are classified accordingly as:

- Quantitative and qualitative approaches
- Financial and non-financial approaches
- Economic and non-economic approaches.

Quantitative approaches seek to generate insights by examining relationships between variables such as attendance levels, sales and customer satisfaction (Li and Jago, 2013). Quantitative approaches are predominantly used in event evaluation, as stakeholders can view them as more objective and consider the insights to be valid. However, exclusive use of these approaches can have drawbacks. One possible challenge is the limitations of particular data collection methods such as surveys, which may have low response rates among particular populations and settings. Additionally, inconsistencies may arise where terminology used in the survey may be interpreted differently by respondents based on cultural nuance. This may lead to over-calculation or over-estimation, thus affecting the reliability and accuracy of the evaluation exercise.

Financial and economic approaches to event evaluation also focus on the collection of numerical data in their respective areas. Financial approaches are concerned with collecting, assessing and monitoring numerical data on the fiscal elements of the event such as cash flow, gate receipts and other sources of revenue, patron expenditure, profit, loss and debt. Economic approaches predominantly examine numerical data related to employment, tax, visitor expenditure and economic activity triggered by the event in other businesses and related industries, mainly to gauge event impact and context.

On the other hand, qualitative approaches focus on capturing opinion and attitudes on matters such as reasons for attending the event; benefits sought; level of satisfaction; stakeholder attitudes; quality of event; and service offered at the event. Qualitative approaches tend to utilize open-ended questions or observations to capture details about the event. These include assessment of intangible costs and benefits; assessment of net value; assessment of stakeholder perceptions; and assessment of economic and market factors that can influence the event.

While qualitative approaches may be considered more cumbersome to administer and challenging to analyse, they can complement quantitative approaches because useful details emerging out of conversation when conducting surveys cannot be represented numerically and therefore may be lost in the evaluation exercise (see Table 10.1).

Table 10.1 Categories of data – qualitative and quantitative methods

Categories of Data	Qualitative Methods Used	Quantitative Methods Used
Event management and organization	• Interviews • Discussion forums • Staff and partner feedback • Management reports	• Clustering • Surveys • Budgets versus actual spending
Event attendance	• Observation • Focus groups	• Ticket sales • Head counts • Surveys • Police statistics • Box office data
Patron profile		• Visitor surveys • Questionnaire to sponsors/VIPs • Questionnaire (demographic questions)
Role of events in communities/locales	• Focus groups • Interviews • Social media observation	• Clustering • Surveys • Social media content analysis
Economic impacts on the locale	• Feedback from vendors, hoteliers and other service providers on profitability and business gained from the festival	• Visitor surveys • Surveys • Spending at festival
Socio-cultural impacts	• Focus groups • Interviews	• Clustering • Surveys
Market assessments	• Secondary competitor analysis	• Audits • Demographic questionnaire • Cumulative economic impacts

(Continued)

Table 10.1   (Continued)

Categories of Data	Qualitative Methods Used	Quantitative Methods Used
Media impacts	• Content analysis	• Visitor surveys • Advertising equivalents
Festival sustainability	• Interviews • Observation	• Surveys • Repeat attendance data
Environment impacts	• Interviews • Observation	• Surveys
Tourist-related impacts	• Interviews • Discussion boards	• Clustering • Visitor surveys • Surveys • Immigration records
Destination branding	• Interviews	• Surveys
Contribution to development of host communities	• Interviews • Focus groups • Discussion forum	• Surveys

Depending on the focus of the event and the purpose of evaluation, event evaluations can be based solely on numerically based approaches, or solely on descriptive-oriented approaches. Consequently, the event manager must be aware of the uses of the event evaluation in designing and executing the evaluation models. Overall, event evaluation is considered more effective when approached as a cyclical process that is holistically concerned with the event's 'well-being' – from conceptualization and planning through to post-event, utilizing a mixed methodology. The event manager can gain an in-depth understanding of the positive and negative outcomes of the event and have a stronger basis from which to make decisions of improvement at each stage of the event. The event manager can also derive more diverse, substantive analysis on the event that can satisfy a range of reporting needs.

To achieve this, event evaluation ought to engage in assessment and monitoring of key expected outputs, referred to as the *three critical Ss of event evaluation*. These are event significance, event success and event sustainability, which can be paired with the stages of the event's lifecycle, and can also be linked to the three key periods of evaluation identified by Getz (1997) (see Table 10.2).

The three critical Ss of event evaluation fundamentally reflect the three major output factors that any event manager would reference in deeming whether an event has realized its outcomes. The three critical Ss would also involve other events management functions, thereby acting as a check and balance for these other functions. For example, evaluation of event significance is concerned with measuring, assessing and monitoring the nature, purpose and intent of the event and whether the event is able to meet these. This involves the planning function of the event. Evaluation of event

Table 10.2 Critical Ss of event evaluation, the event lifecycle and evaluation process

Critical Ss of Events	Stage of Event Lifecycle	Category of Evaluation Process
● Sustainability of event ● Significance of event	● Concept ● Event planning	● Pre-event assessment
● Significance of event ● Success of event	● Event execution	● Event monitoring
● Success of event ● Sustainability of event	● Post-event	● Post-event evaluation

Source: Adapted from Getz (2007)

success focuses on determining whether execution of the event and the elements contributing to event execution have achieved their outcomes. This involves the events management functions associated with implementation such as programming, marketing, logistics, staging and so on. Evaluation of event sustainability is two-fold: it is concerned with measuring, assessing and monitoring the event in relation to its natural environment and the community in which the event operates; and secondly, it is concerned with determining and understanding the potential of the event to continue and remain viable in the long run. Sustainability evaluation would involve most, if not all, of the event's management functions.

Event Evaluation Methodology: Models and Methods

Holistic event evaluation is conducted through a mix of models and methods, deploying a framework that utilizes particular methods and techniques to carry out the evaluation exercise. An evaluation method is essentially a particular process or practice used to assess and monitor events that encompasses an analytical tool(s) or instrument(s) used to gather and interpret data on the event in keeping with the method. Evaluation models work naturally with certain methods as shown in Table 10.3. Both have their distinctive strengths and can also present some challenges in use. It is therefore important to understand how the main models and methods of evaluation work in order to achieve the most from event evaluation. This is explained in greater detail below.

Models Used in Event Evaluation

There are four models that are generally used when conducting event evaluation: impact assessments; cost–benefit analysis; triple bottom line evaluation; and ethnographic profile. Of the four models, ethnographic profile can easily be used for any type and size of event, although not generally used exclusively, while the other three

Table 10.3   Evaluation methods and models

| | | EVALUATION MODELS | | | | |
		Cost–benefit analysis	Economic impact analysis	Social impact assessment	Socio-cultural impact assessment	Triple bottom line approach (TBL)	Ethnography
EVALUATION METHODS	Questionnaires			✓	✓		
	Surveys	✓	✓	✓	✓	✓	✓
	Interviews			✓	✓		✓
	Secondary data analysis	✓	✓	✓	✓		
	Observation			✓	✓	✓	✓
	Manual content analysis		✓	✓	✓	✓	
	Situational analysis		✓	✓	✓	✓	
	Automated content analysis (text mining)			✓	✓		
	Social network analysis			✓	✓		

tend to be used for evaluations of festivals, expos and rallies and other such events regardless of size. Impact assessments, cost–benefit analysis, and triple bottom line evaluation are also commonly used to evaluate tourism-driven events.

Impact assessments

Impact assessment models focus on measuring economic, social and cultural impacts of events such as festivals. Impact assessments can take several forms – economic impact analysis, environmental impact analysis, social impact analysis and tourism impact analysis. All impact analyses tend to utilize a broad range of indicators (see Table 10.4). This is perhaps the major strength of impact assessments in that it allows for a more in-depth assessment that can provide a high quality of analysis and have great validity. Impact assessments are fairly comprehensive and resource intensive and thus require careful planning to yield data of high and substantive quality. When effectively conducted, impact assessments can identify the costs as well as the benefits. Additionally, impact assessments can track changes as well as monitor trends over time.

Table 10.4 Sample of key variables typically utilized in impact assessment studies

Variables	Impact Assessment Studies			
	EIA	ENIA	SIA	TIA
Number of events in a group	✓	✓	✓	✓
Theme/type of events	✓	✓	✓	✓
Purpose of events	✓	✓	✓	✓
Duration	✓	✓	✓	✓
Structure of events organizing body	✓			
Patron size	✓	✓	✓	
Patron spend	✓			
Number of visitors	✓		✓	✓
Demographics of patrons	✓			✓
Demographics of visitors	✓			
Purpose of visit	✓			✓
Visitor spend	✓			✓
Spending apart from event-related items	✓			✓
Motivation for attending event			✓	✓
Source of information on the event				✓
Medium of transport to event	✓	✓	✓	✓
Employment generated by event	✓		✓	
Tax revenue derived from event	✓			
Increased job opportunities	✓		✓	
Source of funding	✓			
Event income	✓			✓
Event expenditure	✓			✓
Significance of environmental initiatives to event patrons		✓		
Noise pollution		✓		
Use of green energy		✓		

(Continued)

Table 10.4   (Continued)

Variables	Impact Assessment Studies			
	EIA	**ENIA**	**SIA**	**TIA**
Event organizers' awareness of green initiatives and policy				
Practise recycling measures		✓		
Construction of new facilities, new infrastructure	✓	✓	✓	✓
Media value	✓		✓	✓
Level of participation by host community/residents			✓	
Identification with theme			✓	
Community attachment			✓	
Level of traffic congestion			✓	
Level of crowding			✓	
Level of crime		✓	✓	✓

EIA = Economic impact analysis   ENIA = Environmental impact analysis

SIA = Socio-cultural impact analysis   TIA = Tourism impact analysis

A major drawback of impact assessments however is their perceived bias towards the event, since impact assessments are usually commissioned by event hosts and funders seeking to legitimize the event's relevance. This criticism is particularly levelled at economic impact assessments on festivals. There is the view that these studies tend to assess the benefits more so than the costs and thus engage in methods to serve this end. Although the focus of social impact assessments is considered critical to attaining a wider understanding of the changes in the communities and in social relationships resulting from their hosting events, the social dimensions of culture can be difficult to assess. In recent times, a few commonly accepted statistical standards that support the measuring of the social dimensions of culture in events are now being used in event evaluation. These include household and time-use surveys to assess and monitor active and passive cultural participation, and the social impact perception (SIP) scale to assess event attendees' perceptions.

Some researchers argue that impact assessments should be conducted some years after the event, as this could more accurately reflect both the positive and negative impacts. In this regard, the longitudinal approach has been found to be useful, particularly in evaluating expos (Edwards et al., 2004; Lim and Lee, 2006). Overall, while economic impact assessments do raise some concerns, they are useful for clarifying industry and sectoral interaction in the local economies (Hackbert and College, 2009). For large-scale events the concept of legacy, or long-term benefit, has emerged as a critical issue (Karadakis and Kaplanidou, 2012). Impact is viewed as a short-term result from an event while legacy can be achieved if the event transforms its host location (Li and McCabe, 2013). These events require the development of significant purpose-built transport and staging infrastructure that may not be frequently used after the event (Preuss, 2007). While some organizations have identified legacy as physical infrastructure, others include intangible impacts such as increased tourism and business opportunities (Gratton and Preuss, 2008).

Cost–benefit analysis

Cost–benefit analysis identifies and measures the costs and benefits of an event. Although first developed to evaluate alternate uses of public funds from a macro-economic standpoint, cost–benefit analysis has been proven useful in evaluations of special events and corporate events. Cost–benefit analysis can take either a quantitative or qualitative slant – where the quantitative refers to those costs and benefits that can be expressed in economic terms by the assignment of a monetary value, and the qualitative to those that cannot be so valued. This approach also takes into account costs and benefits accruing to the host community, also known as externalities or spill-over costs and benefits (Burgan and Mules, 2000). The contingent valuation method is typically employed in this approach, and it relies on interviews with sample patrons to assess willingness to pay and thus evaluate how patrons perceive the value or worth of the festival.

The major benefit of this model of assessment is that it allows for non-monetary considerations of value and costs to be considered in relative terms. Additionally, it differs from economic impact assessment in that it allows for inclusion of 'intangible' impacts that are traditionally omitted from economic impact analysis. The main weakness is the heavy reliance on the interviewees' honesty on questions pertaining to festival expenditure, which, if not reported accurately, can skew the balance between cost and benefit. Another drawback is that the projected benefits are often intangible whereas costs are tangible, which makes it difficult to engage in comparative analysis.

Triple bottom line approach (TBL)

This model emerged out of calls for business and tourism events to produce valuations of their activity that went beyond economics to include the impact of their events on the environment. As a framework for measuring and reporting the event's performance against economic, social and environmental parameters, the TBL approach evaluates the event's performance in relation to these variables to determine whether they are positively or negatively impacting on their host communities (Fredline et al., 2005).

The TBL approach provides a systematic approach for evaluating environmental or 'green' issues and concerns relating to the event. In this way, the TBL approach is able to draw attention to the 'green' responsibility and the overall environmental footprint of the event. The TBL approach measures the social and natural environmental impact of an activity and correlates this to its financial and economic performance, thereby lending depth to traditional ways of measuring success. Measures can include, for example water and energy use; waste generation; recycling capacity within the event; along with the other usually evaluated elements related to economic impacts and social impacts. Perhaps the main drawback to this approach would be its heavy reliance on qualitative methods which could pose problems for validity. Notwithstanding, the TBL approach offers a systematic model for widening the evaluation net beyond the economic and financial concerns.

Ethnographic profile

An ethnographic profile is considered a useful means of triangulating data derived from the previously mentioned evaluation models. It is developed through the use of ethnography, which utilizes participant observation, interviewing and the use of documentary sources to yield valuable and valid data, particularly within the wider frame of experience-related studies. Ethnography has been used in the analysis of tourism since the 1960s and is often used in the evaluation of cultural festivals and cultural special events.

The drawback to this approach is that the fieldwork would be demanding in terms of time, financial and human resources. The benefit is that the evaluator as the event attendee / event volunteer / local resident (any of the roles that would offer an insider perspective) would capture rich details and nuances of the event (intangibles that have real value) that might otherwise not be accounted for in traditional methods such as visitor surveys, satisfaction surveys and event surveys. This approach would also allow for the understandings of the socio-cultural and environmental impacts of the event from a visitor perspective.

Methods Used in Event Evaluation

Methods are critical to the process of gathering event data, since it is at this stage that misuse or incorrect use of associated instruments can render the results invalid. Table 10.5 outlines the main characteristics of each method, examples of their use in event evaluation, along with their strengths and shortcomings as evaluation techniques for events.

Evaluation Output: Documenting and Reporting

Event evaluation would not be complete without proper recording of the analysis derived from the evaluation exercise. This is the final stage of the event evaluation

Table 10.5 Evaluation methods and strengths and limitations

Evaluation Methods	Examples of uses	Strengths	Limitations
Content Analysis	<ul><li>Nature of the event's documented</li><li>Information (especially historical) that would indicate event type, event content, event duration, event organizers and event sponsors etc.</li><li>Impact of event's documented information</li><li>Compatible with documentation, situational analysis</li><li>Used in media audit and triple bottom line assessments</li></ul>	✓ Inexpensive, comprehensive research tool, user-friendly ✓ Does not require contact with people – unobtrusive ✓ Very useful when combined with other methods such as interviews, observation	✗ Purely descriptive – gives the what but may not give the why and how ✗ Analysis limited by availability of information ✗ Observed trends in media may be inaccurate
Documentation	<ul><li>Trace the history of the event in terms of programming, past evaluation reports and correspondence with stakeholders</li><li>Compatible with stakeholder analysis</li><li>Used in cost–benefit analysis, triple bottom line and all impact assessments</li></ul>	See above	See above
Environmental Audit	<ul><li>Level of green practice being followed by the event</li><li>Nature and level of impact of the event on the physical environment: pollution, impacts on wildlife, waste generated, traffic and crowding</li><li>Used for environmental impact analysis, triple bottom line and cost–benefit analysis</li></ul>	✓ Give a comprehensive picture of event in relation to physical environment	✗ May be limited in scope – focus only on impacts and not on internal approaches to green issues and practice or vice versa
Focus Group	<ul><li>Determine perceptions, opinions, beliefs and attitudes towards the event (e.g. benefits sought, satisfaction) through an interactive group setting</li><li>Analysis of quality management</li><li>Used for ethnography, triple bottom line, cost–benefit evaluation</li><li>Compatible with stakeholder analysis</li></ul>	✓ Allows group members to freely participate in discussion especially ✓ Allows for detailed analysis – can attain specifics on the event ✓ Useful where participants may not like filling out surveys and questionnaires	✗ Does not occur in a naturalistic setting ✗ May not be encouraging to participants ✗ Members may be reluctant to share personal information or feel that they must conform to populist views ✗ Difficult to collate results in a quantifiable manner ✗ Time consuming

(Continued)

Table 10.5 (Continued)

Evaluation Methods	Examples of uses	Strengths	Limitations
Financial Audit	• Cash flow, assets and liabilities, profit and loss, debt and financial worth of event • Used for cost–benefit analysis, economic impact analysis and business impact analysis • Compatible with resource audit and return on event audit	✓ Useful in determining financial performance and status of the event	✕ Does not explain context behind numerical analysis presented
Interviews Structured Unstructured	• Perceptions, opinions, beliefs and attitudes towards the event through a one-on-one face-to-face interaction • Compatible with volunteer value analysis, stakeholder analysis, content analysis and situational analysis • Can be used with all the evaluation models	✓ Attain insights and specifics on aspects of the event ✓ Useful where participants may not like filling out surveys and questionnaires ✓ Allows for honest discussion ✓ Complementary with other methods	✕ Time consuming ✕ Requires use of other methods such as content analysis ✕ Difficult to collate results in a quantifiable manner ✕ Lack of flexibility in structured interviews makes it difficult to probe further
Media Audit	• Nature of media coverage • Extent of media exposure (quantity and quality) • Worth of media coverage • Worth of event for sponsors and funders • Compatible with interviews, questionnaires and surveys • Can be used in all evaluation models	✓ Can be executed in-house by marketing/PR team members ✓ Give comprehensive picture of event through the lens of the media	✕ Can be expensive ✕ May require outside expert assistance ✕ Can be time consuming
Website Audit	• Nature of internet coverage • Extent of website exposure (quantity and quality) • Worth of internet coverage	See above	See above
Social Media Audit	• Frequency of shares • Duration of shares • Geographic reach of posts • Demographic reach of posts • Sentiment of posts • Value of social media coverage	See above	See above

Evaluation Methods	Examples of uses	Strengths	Limitations
Observation	• Quality of management • Level of guest satisfaction • Profile of visitors attending the event • Profile of patrons • Trip type • Impact on physical environment and community • Compatible with all methods • Used in all evaluation • Models	✓ Best method for studying natural behaviour ✓ Allows for specifics to be incorporated in the evaluation	✗ May not be the most reliable method ✗ Can sometimes be too subjective ✗ Time consuming to collate information gleaned
Participant Observation	• Quality of management • Level of guest satisfaction • Profile of visitors attending the event • Profile of patrons • Quality of event programming • Compatible with all methods • Used principally in ethnographic sketch • Can also be used in triple bottom line and impact assessments	✓ Considered to yield rich description because evaluator is directly involved in the event while observing	✗ May be biased given the closeness of the evaluator to the event
Questionnaire Closed-ended Open-ended	• Analysis of market and marketing issues • Visitor profile: activities and spending, attendance, reason for attendance, reasons for trip • Patron profile: patron origin, patron demographics and information sources on the event • Return on investment for sponsors and funders • Compatible with all methods with the exception of ethnographic sketch	✓ Can reach numbers larger than focus group, although not generally used for the volume as would a survey (see Survey) ✓ Easy to fill out ✓ Results easily quantifiable (for closed-ended questions) ✓ Easy to administer; can be done face to face or via email/post ✓ Not expensive to administer ✓ Allows for anonymity	✗ Does not give context behind results ✗ Response rate tends to be low ✗ Difficult to extract adequate sample sometimes

(Continued)

Table 10.5 (Continued)

Evaluation Methods	Examples of uses	Strengths	Limitations
Resource Audit	<ul><li>Nature and level of capacity of event organization</li><li>Internal workings of the event organization</li><li>Volunteer value</li><li>Compatible with stakeholder analysis, content analysis, documentation, situational analysis, questionnaire, survey and interviews</li><li>Can be used for most evaluation models</li></ul>	✓ Contributes to SWOT analysis	
Situational Analysis	<ul><li>Context in which event operates</li><li>Internalities of event organization</li><li>Compatible with stakeholder analysis, content analysis, documentation, resource audit, questionnaire, survey and interviews</li><li>Can be used for most evaluation models</li></ul>	✓ Contributes to SWOT analysis ✓ Feeds into impact analyses	× Can be limited by availability of information
Stakeholder Analysis	<ul><li>Level of power and interest of stakeholders in event</li><li>Impact of event on stakeholders</li><li>Stakeholder interests and expectations fulfilled</li><li>Compatible with most methods</li><li>Used in triple bottom line, impact assessments and cost–benefit analysis</li></ul>		× May be sympathetic to stakeholders' views of the event in deference to the event
Survey Accommodation Business Exit Market Visitor	Same as for Questionnaire	× More appropriate for larger numbers of respondents, particularly in the case of polling visitors (See Questionnaire for more)	Same as for Questionnaire

process before the further decision-making. It is generally referred to as documentation and reporting. Documentation and reporting is critical to triggering the feedback loop that characterizes evaluation as a continuous process. After the evaluation report is disseminated and reviewed, decisions must be made about improvements to the event arising out of the report, which are in turn fed back into the event planning and preparation stage, thus restarting the project management cycle and lifecycle of the event.

Since the evaluation exercise is conducted in a systematic manner, documentation and reporting should similarly follow a structured systematic layout, which could also be used when making presentations to major stakeholders. Evaluation reporting should essentially address: what the evaluation exercise entailed; why the particular choices of methodology were employed; how the evaluation was executed; findings and analysis; and finally recommendations. The findings and analysis derived from the evaluation models and methods selected and the ensuing recommendations should essentially answer the following questions:

- What went right?
- What went wrong?
- How can the positive outcomes be further capitalized upon?
- How can the negative outcomes be improved upon?

An example of an outline of an event evaluation report is shown in the box below.

Framework for an Event Evaluation Report

- Executive Summary
- Introduction
- Rationale
- Aims
- Evaluation Methodology
  - Justifications and limitations
- Outline of the Evaluation Report
- Profile of the Event
  - Nature, purpose location, history, main products/services, profiles, and facts and figures
- Profile of the Event Organizer
  - Background, number and type of employees/events management team and their areas of responsibility

(Continued)

(Continued)

- Brief Background on Event Partners
  - o   Major funders and/or sponsors
- Strategic Analysis of the Event
  - o   Situational analysis (SWOT)
- Assessment of Event Planning
  - o   Methods used
  - o   Findings and analysis

  Event sustainability and event significance

- Assessment of Event Execution
  - o   Methods used
  - o   Findings and analysis
  - o   Event sustainability and event significance
- Post-Event Evaluation
  - o   Methods used
  - o   Findings and analysis
  - o   Event sustainability and event significance
- Evaluation of Stakeholder Needs
  - o   Methods used
  - o   Findings and analysis
  - o   Event sustainability and event significance
- Financial Reporting and Analysis
- Recommendations and Conclusion

Case Study 10.1 – In Search of a Host Country for CARIFESTA

Introduction

Following the recommendations of the most recent strategic plan for the Caribbean Festival of Arts (CARIFESTA), the search began again for another country host for this regional mega-festival. CARIFESTA now had a renewed vision and needed a country host capable of redefining and reorganizing this Caribbean celebration to make it a vibrant and sustainable cultural enterprise (Nurse, 2004).

Given that the core strengths of CARIFESTA lie in its mobility, Caribbean appeal and multi-disciplinary approach to the arts, steps needed to be taken to ensure that these were maintained, and where possible expanded. The strategic plan has called for a systemic in-depth evaluation; and so any Caribbean country seeking to win the bid to host the next instalment of CARIFESTA needed to demonstrate a commitment to this new requirement.

Background

Over its 30-year existence, CARIFESTA has made a significant impact on Caribbean development, in terms of the arts, artists and arts infrastructure of its various host countries. CARIFESTA has also aided in deepening Caribbean integration by making Caribbean arts accessible and fostering a vision of Caribbean unity and a pan-Caribbean outlook. It is, however, acknowledged that these positive impacts are derivatives more so of earlier CARIFESTAs, and have seldom been spin-offs of CARIFESTAs in the post-1990 era.

There were a number of external forces that challenged the success of CARIFESTA. In particular, CARIFESTA has been staged within an increasingly competitive market where consumer tastes and trends constantly shift at a rapid rate, particularly within the Caribbean – its primary market. It is therefore clear that part of the success of the next CARIFESTA would rest on the ability of the host to understand and respond to this dynamic environment.

Broad Strategy

It has been recommended that the next host country should be open to staging CARIFESTA while another mega event is being held in the Caribbean, such as a sporting championship event. This is considered a strategic choice given that there are many synergies to be gained from combining sport and cultural events. Additionally, many successful mega events have followed the approach of hosting cultural fringe events that celebrate the multiculturalism of the destination, alongside the main event. The 2002 Manchester Commonwealth Games is one such notable example, where apart from hosting a superb sporting event, the host country was also able to promote

(Continued)

(Continued)

cultural excellence 'to secure a lasting legacy' for the destination region (Bowdin et al., 2006: 23). It was felt that the Caribbean could similarly benefit from hosting CARIFESTA around the time of the ICC Cricket World Cup as a sporting event of this nature would give the Caribbean the opportunity to present a cultural/entertainment extravaganza to the world and give nearby destinations an opportunity to share in promoting the Caribbean's cultural and artistic excellence. To achieve these goals particular attention was to be paid to attaining operational excellence and market leadership, and building and maintaining stakeholder partnerships.

Festival Format, Programming and Marketing

CARIFESTA comprises ten days of arts and cultural celebrations spanning two weekends. The Festival usually encompasses a number of events that serve both the commercial/trade and artistic interests of artists and entrepreneurs. These include:

- The Grand Market
- Cultural Industries Trade Fair
- Book Fair
- Film Festival
- Visual Arts Festival and Exhibition
- Symposia
- Community festivals
- Super concerts.

The Festival also strives to incorporate a number of innovative elements that will aid in transforming CARIFESTA into a 'hallmark' event. Consequently, the marketing strategy must be primarily aimed at rebranding CARIFESTA. The intention is to create a hallmark mega event that draws people from the Caribbean and the Caribbean diaspora. The goal is also to create a festival that further enhances the image of the host country and that of the Caribbean in general. Thus, the marketing strategy was to be based on building partnerships, packaging and programming, alongside the standard marketing principles of place, product, price and promotion. Not to be forgotten is the role that public relations can play in rejuvenating the interest and enthusiasm of the Festival's primary market of Caribbean citizens.

Finances

It was decided that CARIFESTA will continue to receive support from Caribbean governments but must seek ways to attract other sources of income. Bearing in mind that expenditure includes artist fees, venue rental and website development and maintenance, there must be a clear financial strategy developed and implemented to assure that the return on investment by all key stakeholders is realized.

Evaluating CARIFESTA

The host country must be fully committed to engaging in event evaluation and be able to clearly articulate the nature of that evaluation process, the approach to be taken, and the methodology to be used. The host country must also be able to justify choices made in conducting the evaluation.

Case Study Questions

1   Based on the case study, list the possible elements of focus for evaluation of CARIFESTA.
2   Why would the successful country host need to conduct evaluation of CARIFESTA?
3   What would be the long-term benefits of a festival such as CARIFESTA?
4   Write a brief outlining how CARIFESTA might be evaluated, incorporating details from the case study where possible.

Chapter Summary

Event evaluation is an important function that spans the entire lifecycle of an event – from planning and design, to execution and event shutdown and post-event. It is important that event managers determine and understand the reasons for conducting event evaluation given the quantum of resources that go into such an exercise. Knowing what to evaluate can be guided by the event manager taking into consideration the main components of the event; the key functions of the event organization; and the contexts in which the event operates. Although event evaluations can exclusively employ quantitatively based approaches or qualitatively based approaches, a holistic approach to event evaluation, which includes a mixture of the two approaches, can offer a more in-depth and comprehensive analysis. Event evaluation is executed using an evaluation methodology, which comprises evaluation models and evaluation methods. Evaluation models and methods can have their strengths and limitations and should therefore be carefully reviewed for suitability and practicality in relation to the event to be evaluated. Reporting and documentation is the final stage of the event evaluation process. It is critical in triggering the feedback loop that characterizes evaluation as a continuous process and is essential for communicating with key stakeholders on the performance of the event.

Review Questions

1. Explain the event evaluation function. What are the main benefits of conducting event evaluation?
2. What is holistic event evaluation? How might such an evaluation be conducted?
3. Design a stakeholders' concerns checklist for a community-based special event.
4. Describe the main models and methods used in event evaluation, and discuss their respective strengths and limitations in use, with reference to an event with which you are familiar.
5. Obtain three examples of event evaluation reports, and compare and contrast them.

Additional Resources

Books / Book Chapters / Journal Articles

Andersson, T.D., Persson, C., Sahlberg, B. and Strom, L. (eds) (1999). *The Impact of Mega Events*. Ostersund: European Tourism Research Institute. This edited book provides a useful resource for those examining the impact of mega events.

Hede, A. (2008). Managing special events in the new era of the Triple Bottom Line. *Event Management, 11*(1–2): 13–22. This article proposes a framework for applying the TBL to the planning stage of special event management.

Phillips, J.J., Breining, M.T. and Phillips, P.P. (2008). *Return on Investment in Meetings and Events: Tools and Techniques to Measure the Success of All Types of Meetings and Events*. Oxford: Butterworth-Heinemann. Introduces and demonstrates Jack J. Phillips' well-established ROI measurement methodology to address the growing demands from stakeholders to prove the value of meetings through data analysis.

Preuss, H. (2006). *The Economics of Staging the Olympics: A Comparison of the Games 1972–2008*. Cheltenham: Edward Elgar. Especially useful to those interested in economic impacts of mega events. Also covers tourism, urban regeneration and social impacts to some extent.

Sinclair-Maragh, G. (2011). A critical socio-economic assessment of the ICC Cricket World Cup on the hosting Caribbean. In: L. Jordan, B. Tyson, C. Hayle and D. Truly (eds), *Sports Event Management: The Caribbean Experience*. Surrey: Ashgate. This chapter assesses the socio-economic impacts of the ICC Cricket World Cup.

Useful Websites

www.juliasilvers.com/embok.htm – This website hosts the EMBOK project and includes information on all areas of the event management process including evaluation.

https://www.olympic.org/london-2012 – The official archived site from the International Olympic Committee that contains a gateway to Olympic and Paralympic evaluation documents.

www.wrap.org.uk/ – WRAP's website provides a host of free evaluation tools for businesses, individuals and communities wishing to evaluate their efficiency in consuming and recycling resources.

References

Bowdin, G. A. J., McDonnell, I., Allen, J. and O'Toole, W. (2006). *Events Management* (2nd edn). Oxford: Butterworth-Heinemann.

Burgan, B. and Mules, T. (2000). Reconciling cost–benefit and economic impact assessment. In: L. K. Jago, A. J. Veal, J. Allen and R. Harris (eds), *Events Beyond 2000: Setting the Agenda: Proceedings of Conference on Event Evaluation, Research and Education, Sydney (July 2000)* (pp. 46–51). Lindfield: Australian Centre for Event Management.

Edwards, J., Moital, M. and Vaughan, R. (2004). The impacts of mega-events: The case of EXPO 98 – Lisbon. In: P. Long and M. Robinson (eds), *Festival Tourism: Marketing, Management and Evaluation* (pp. 196–215). Sunderland: Business Education Publishers.

Forrester, S. (2008). The event planning model: the evaluation and renewal phase, Part I. In: C. Mallen and L. J. Adams (eds), *Sport Recreation and Tourism Event Management* (pp. 25–52). Oxford: Butterworth-Heinemann.

Fredline, L., Raybould, M., Jago, L. and Deery, M. (2005). Triple bottom line event evaluation: a proposed framework for holistic event evaluation. Third International Event Conference, the Impacts of Events: Triple Bottom Line Evaluation and Event Legacies, Sydney.

Getz, D. (1997). *Event Management and Event Tourism*. New York: Cognizant Communications Corporation.

Getz, D. (1997). *Event Management and Event Tourism* (2nd edn). New York: Cognizant Communication Corporation.

Getz, D. and Page, S. J. (2015). Progress in tourism management: progress and prospects for event tourism. *Tourism Management*, *52*(1): 593–631.

Giampiccoli, A., Lee, S. S. and Nauright, J. (2015). Destination South Africa: comparing global sports mega-events and recurring localised sports events in South Africa for tourism and economic development. *Current Issues in Tourism*, *18*(3): 229–48.

Gratton, C. and Preuss, H. (2008). Maximizing Olympic impacts by building up legacies. *International Journal of the History of Sport*, *25*(14): 1922–38.

Hackbert, P. H. and College, B. (2009). Economic impacts of Appalachian festivals. In: *Proceedings of ASBBS*, *16* (1). Retrieved from http://asbbs.org/files/2009/PDF/H/HackbertP.pdf

Henderson, K. A. and Bialeschki, M. D. (2002). *Evaluating Leisure Services: Making Enlightened Decisions*. State College, PA: Venture Publishing.

Karadakis, K. and Kaplanidou, K. (2012). Legacy perceptions among host and non-host Olympic Games residents: a longitudinal study of the 2010 Vancouver Olympic Games. *European Sport Management Quarterly*, *12*(3): 243–64.

Li, S. and Jago, L. (2013). Evaluating economic impacts of major sports events – a meta analysis of the key trends. *Current Issues in Tourism, 16*(6): 591–611.

Li, S. and McCabe, S. (2013). Measuring the socio-economic legacies of mega-events: concepts, propositions and indicators. *International Journal of Tourism Research, 15*(4): 388–402.

Lim, S. T. and Lee, J. S. (2006). Host population perceptions of the impact of mega-events. *Asia Pacific Journal of Tourism Research, 11*(4): 407–21.

LOCOG (n.d.). Sustainability. LOCOG [online]. Retrieved from www.london2012.com/making-it-happen/sustainability/index.php

McDavid, J. C. and Hawthorne, L. (2006). *Program Evaluation and Performance Measurement: An Introduction to Practice*. Thousand Oaks: McGraw-Hill.

Nurse, K. (2004). *Reinventing CARIFESTA: A Strategic Plan Prepared for CARICOM Taskforce on CARIFESTA*. CARICOM [online]. Retrieved from www.caricom.org/jsp/community_organs/carifesta-strategicplan.pdf

O'Toole, W. and Mikolaitis, P. (2002). *Corporate Event Project Management*. New York: John Wiley & Sons.

Preuss, H. (2007). The conceptualisation and measurement of mega sport event legacies. *Journal of Sport & Tourism, 12*(3–4): 207–28.

Tsaur, S. H., Yen, C. H., Tu, J. H., Wang, C. H. and Liang, Y. W. (2015). Evaluation of the 2010 Taipei International Flora Exposition from the perceptions of host-city residents: a new framework for mega-event legacies measurement. *Leisure Studies*, 1–24.

Tum, J., Norton, P. and Wright, J. N. (2006). *Management of Event Operations*. Oxford: Butterworth-Heinemann.

Van der Wagen, L. (2005). *Event Management for Tourism, Cultural, Business and Sporting Events*. Frenchs Forest: Pearson Education Australia.

Wendroff, A. (2004). *Special Events: Proven Strategies for Non-Profit Fundraising*. Hoboken: John Wiley & Sons.

Part 3

Contemporary Issues in International Events Management

The first two Parts of this text established the need for an international perspective and reviewed the main principles of effective event management practice at an international level. The convergence of socio-cultural, economic, political and technological forces on current event management practice requires staff to be immersed in a process of continual learning. Events are not simply a vocation for event managers; to many stakeholders they are a reason to save their hard-earned cash, or a reason to discipline their bodies through training, and events provide the rationale for the allocation of public monies at the expense of other community initiatives. The personal, social and cultural importance should be at the forefront of management thought. To this end, this final section of *Events Management: An International Approach* (2nd edn) builds upon these initial, functional contributions and examines certain emerging issues in events management practice. Each of the chapters in the following section applies event management principles to particular areas of concern. Contemporary event managers must be aware that these principles encapsulate the issues discussed above.

In Chapter 11, Inversini and Williams provide an overview of the ways in which social media is changing the event landscape. They first examine the development of the use of ICT in events, in order to demonstrate the fundamental way in which attendees' engagement with technology has changed, from a passive one-to-many relationship, driven primarily by the event organizer, to an active many-to-many relationship, in which the event consumer has great power and influence over the content about an event that is communicated and shared. The authors also highlight the need for event organizations to engage with their attendees throughout their entire experience journey with an event. Additionally, the cases in Chapter 11 provide specific strategies of how event professionals can deploy effective strategies to harness the great potential offered by social media to enhance the reach and also the quality of their events.

The nexus of corporate social responsibility (CSR) and sustainable development is the focus of Chapter 12 by Cavagnaro, Postma and de Brito. These authors provide an analysis of the established need for sustainable guidelines to assist in the management of events so that events can contribute to social, cultural, economic and environmental goals. Through a series of case studies and an examination of international standards, the principles of sustainability are introduced and applied. The authors, however, question the importance of sustainability in event management paying particular attention as to whether the green credentials of an event are an antecedent for attendance, that is – do consumers really care?

In the penultimate chapter, Devine and Devine examine the strategic importance of international events as a driver of tourism. The authors examine the short- and long-term impacts of event-led tourism as the justification for why governmental and non-governmental agencies should adopt a strategic approach to event bidding and staging. Event strategies are part of the event policy process, but as most national policies are inherently domestic, Devine and Devine's model is well suited for addressing the involvement of policy-makers in event planning in a range of international contexts. A six-stage model is outlined and then applied through the main case study focusing on the region of Northern Ireland and its use of event-led tourism generation.

Ferdinand, Postma and White bring our collection to a close in Chapter 14, but not before charting the future directions for international events. In addition to their analysis of this industry they provide the thinking tools to allow event managers to plan for the future, particularly by learning to recognize the key drivers of change. This is demonstrated through the use of a case study highlighting how managers at the Notting Hill Carnival are future-proofing their event. The chapter concludes with some advice for those seeking to enter into or develop their careers further within the international events industry. The authors suggest that students not only prepare for what is needed now, but also think carefully about where international events are heading and how they can take personal advantage of future opportunities.

Social Media and Events

11

Alessandro Inversini and Nigel L. Williams

Learning Objectives

By reading this chapter students should be able to:

- Define the role of social media in event marketing and management
- Classify the digital information needs of event attendees
- Synthesize the roles played by technology and social media in the event experience
- Recognize communities of interest in social media
- Identify the opportunities to enhance attendees' experiences offered with the effective use of social media in events

Introduction

The rise of digital technology has had an unprecedented impact on the services sector, modifying existing business models and enabling new ones (Dubosson-Torbay et al., 2002). Lately, the competitive landscape of sectors such as tourism, hospitality and events has been profoundly affected and dramatically changed by the rise of the internet, social media and mobile technologies (Inversini et al., 2015). Service providers need to keep up with the ever-changing technological scenery because customers are increasingly exploiting digital advances to choose, book, manage and even customize their service experiences.

In comparison to other industries, the event sector received scant attention in the literature when it comes to the impact of digital technology on event organizations, marketing and management. Event attendees may have different information needs before, during and after their experience (Gretzel et al., 2006). Depending on the size and nature of the event, technology can have a significant impact on promotion, management, customer service and experience recall (Inversini and Cantoni, 2014).

Before the event it is necessary, for example, to manage online communications on different digital channels, such as the event website, the event's social media channels and the third-party websites contributing to the promotion of the event (for example, online newspapers and ticketing websites). These activities aim to promote the event, sell tickets and create expectations of the event in the minds of potential attendees. During the event, it is necessary to provide participants with detailed and updated information, such as notifications of any changes in the event programme. It is becoming increasingly important to also provide event-goers on the move with good mobile communications, via mobile applications, to a number of devices (for example, smartphones or tablets) and with other technologies, such as digital signage (for example, via TV screens used to deliver information and advertising). After the event it is imperative to establish a relationship with both event attendees and interested individuals who were unable to attend the event. Post-event communications give people who attended the event the opportunity to re-experience the event from a different point of view, with photos, videos and interviews, and they can provide people who could not attend the event the opportunity to get a better idea of what happened.

This is just the starting point for discussing the importance of ICTs in the event sector. This chapter will highlight the increasing importance of ICTs in general and social media in particular to event organizers. It will first provide an overview of the changing role of ICTs within events and then demonstrate the increasing pervasiveness and the ubiquity of new technologies which promote social media usage. The opening case study describes how an international film festival uses a number of digital solutions to serve attendees' information needs. The case provides the basis for an in-depth theoretical discussion about social media and their use in the event sector. The chapter closes by providing event organizers, marketing managers and other industry professionals with guidance for leveraging event attendees' increasing social media usage.

Information Needs in the Event Experience

Customer experience can be generally understood as the sum of interactions customers have with the experience provider over the duration of their relationship with that supplier. In the experience consumption journey, which can be described as a sequence of three successive stages (pre-, during and post-event), event attendees have different types of information needs to be met. Gretzel et al. (2006) identified a series of information needs in each stage of the consumers' experiential journey. These information needs include, for example: 'planning and transaction' before the experience; 'connection, navigation, short-term decision-making' during the experience;

and 'sharing, documenting and re-experiencing' after the actual experience. This is in line with the complex and the multifaceted nature of the customer experience during an event, as highlighted by Palmer (2010).

It is clear that the emergence of new communication technologies has changed the relational landscape between experience providers and consumers (Christodoulides, 2009). On the one hand, technology is nowadays ubiquitous (Fesenmaier and Xiang, 2013) and users do rely massively on their mobile phones and on social media to get relevant information. On the other hand, events marketers and events managers need to recognize this shifts towards a more digitalized way of interacting with customers (for marketing, selling and management purposes) in each and every phase of the experience consumption.

Events attendees are looking for a unique experience each and every time. They are much more exigent and want to participate in the experience creation. In other words they want to co-create the experience (Binkhorst and Den Dekker, 2009) with event organizers. Therefore, event organizers need to be able to understand customer experience and experience touchpoints (Hogan et al., 2005) in order to be able to deliver outstanding experiences, which can be collaboratively created with the event attendee.

It is with the advent of the internet (and especially with the advent of social media) and mobile communication that experience touchpoints are becoming more digitalized. Customers can access official and social network-mediated information at their fingerprints at any time and everywhere. This poses challenges to event organizers but also provides a range of opportunities that can be exploited to optimize marketing and management tasks.

To better understand the role played by the internet and by digital technologies in event customer experiences, it is important to first understand how the online world has evolved in the recent years towards a pervasive and ubiquitous system that is influencing on the one hand, customers' ways of perceiving and living an event, and on the other hand, managers' ways of marketing and managing an event.

The Rise of the Internet

The internet has been described as the last technological evolution in the field of ICT. It allows customers to access reliable and accurate information about a given event as well as undertake actions, such as booking tickets, within seconds. The internet provides access to transparent and easy-to-compare information as well as to real-time prices and booking technologies (Buhalis and Inversini, 2014). Initially the information available on the internet was chaotic and loosely structured, mainly due to the immaturity of ICTs and the lack of any type of standardization. The service industry was also not prepared to embrace the changes required by the management of a 24/7 worldwide contact point, provided by a company website, and a 24/7 worldwide sales centre, facilitated by a reservations or booking page (Card et al., 2003).

Managers needed to ask themselves what level of involvement they wanted to have with the internet based on intrinsic factors (for example, the importance of online communication and online promotion for the company) and extrinsic factors (for example, the competitors' engagement with the internet) (Inversini and Cantoni, 2014). These factors will differ from organization to organization. However, researchers have identified three main reasons (see Figure 11.1) that event organizations engage with the internet (Cantoni and Blas, 2002):

- *To 'be there'* – In this case the event organization wants to be present on the web by having a virtual reference that points to the real world. Some events managers prefer to manage a simple web page with contact information. This practice, widespread in the early 2000s, is still relevant for small local events which rely mainly on non-digital communication and promotion channels (for example, word of mouth). For most contemporary event organizers, their website is more than a technological instrument. It is an integrated communications tool to execute business strategy. In other words, the event website is considered a strategic and tactical tool for marketing and management and where possible event operations.
- *To 'operate'* – In this case the event organization wants to delegate one or more tasks to the event website. For example, a music event organizing the line-up for its main stage will use its website to collect emails from interested customers to inform them about the progress of the line-up and the overall programme. In this case, the website collects the email addresses of possible event-goers and stores them in a database for the purpose of sending out updates. The website in this instance has an active role within event promotion and management.
- *To 'integrate'* – In this case, some tasks performed by the website are of vital importance for the event organization. These tasks bring added value to the entire event value chain, and the website is the cornerstone of these activities. These activities can range from customer relationship management (CRM) to upselling of ancillary products and services.

For most event organizations, the event website is no longer just a nice-to-have tool but a fundamentally important channel for promotion, distribution and management of products and services. Additionally, the rise of Web 2.0 (O'Reilly, 2007) and of social media have facilitated the creation of consumer-generated content. Consumers are not passive receivers of communication anymore but active contributors. Consumer communication happens mainly through review portals, multimedia sharing, blogs and micro blogging sites. Social media has facilitated the creation of widespread online accessible content and has simultaneously led to an increase in the level of information available on a global basis (Gretzel and Yoo, 2008). Social media applications, or apps as they are more widely known, are described as those which employ internet-based technologies, and also mobile technologies, to create interactive communication platforms via which individuals, groups and organizations create, generate, discuss and modify user-generated content (Keitzman et al., 2011). User-generated content, as

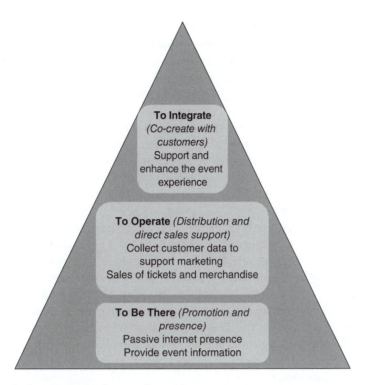

Figure 11.1 Service organizations' reasons for a web presence

opposed to content created by an event organization or its advertising agency, is content created by members of the public rather than paid professionals. Its main mode of distribution is via social media channels rather than traditional communications media such as print newspapers, television or radio (Daugherty et al., 2008).

CRITICAL THINKING EXERCISE

List some of the ways the Internet and Social Media has changed your experience at events.

Pervasiveness and Ubiquity

A recent study by Fesenmaier and Xiang (2013) considered the evolution of the internet in the field of travel and tourism and identified two eras (the first decade and the second decade), which have distinct characteristics.

In the first decade (roughly from 1991 to 2002) the internet assumed a critical role in communications. Service organizations rapidly established a web presence and the discussion both at research and practical level focused on development and usability. In other words, managers were interested in having an easy-to-use website which was strategically and tactically aligned with business goals and stakeholders' needs and wants.

It is only in the second decade (roughly from 2002–present) that it is possible to observe a radical shift in the use of this medium. The start of the second decade brought a greater change in marketing, communication and management practices over the internet. The focus of the discussion shifted from website development and usability to persuasion and customer empowerment to reach and more recently to the topic of customer mobility.

More recent technology developments such as the expansion of high-speed connections and the rise of mobile social media have led to consumers moving towards a ubiquitous internet experience in which they communicate their impressions of experiences whenever these experiences occur and wherever they happen. The presence of mobile communication devices in people's lives is mediating their event experiences and it is potentially intensifying the participation in social networking sites (Inversini et al., 2015). The internet, together with the new interactive way of communication provided by social media and location-based mobile browsing, have fundamentally changed the nature of event experiences (Gretzel et al., 2006) and their marketing and management.

These new realities mean that event organizers need to embrace a holistic technological presence before, during and after the event and utilize relevant technological channels in order to satisfy attendees' needs and wants. Having a holistic technological presence is now considered a necessity but current research suggests not enough event organizers are making the most of opportunities to engage with audiences through the internet and other digital channels (Robertson et al., 2015).

A rounded digital strategy and presence can extend the lifetime of the event significantly, adding value both before and after the event. It is important, for example, to have a post-event website to re-engage attendees before the buzz of the event wears off and to gauge responses, which can assist in the design and improvement of subsequent events. Social media can dramatically increase the impact of an event, both geographically and in terms of time, by allowing people to share content before, during and after the event (Mair, 2014).

Case Study 11.1 presents the experience of an international film festival. The 65th Annual Locarno Film Festival heavily invested in its technological presence and in its digital strategy by: further developing its website to be the main digital presence of the film festival; developing a mobile app in order to meet the needs of festival attendees on the move; and launching a series of social media channels to engage with customers on different levels.

Case Study 11.1 – The 65th Annual Locarno Film Festival, Switzerland

The Locarno Film Festival began in 1946 and is the third-oldest film festival in the world after Venice (started in 1932) and Moscow (started in 1935). It was also founded in the same year as the Cannes Film Festival. The Locarno Film Festival is the most important film event in Switzerland and it is classified as a competitive festival. The Locarno Film Festival winner is awarded the Golden Leopard. The event takes place in the first two weeks of August in Locarno, a small city in the heart of the Italian canton of Switzerland. A distinctive feature of the festival is the use of the Piazza Grande in Locarno, the main square of the city, as a screening room. Piazza Grande is recognized as one of the largest open-air cinema screening venues in the world, with one of the world's largest cinema screens (26m long and 14m high), which allows a viewing audience of 8,000 spectators.

This case study examines the 65th edition of the Film Festival, or 'Loc65'. Loc65 was a turning point for the use of new technology during the film festival. Festival organizers spent a lot of time and effort understanding the potential of new media in order to exploit these platforms to give festival-goers a more rounded and relevant experience.

Loc65's digital landscape was composed of the event website a mobile app and social media channels. See Figure 11.2.

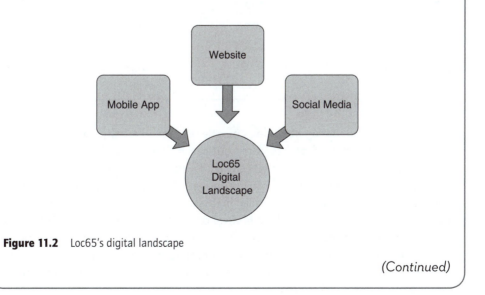

Figure 11.2 Loc65's digital landscape

(Continued)

(Continued)

The website (pardolive.ch) was designed as the central point of the digital ecosystem. It was designed to publish all the relevant information about the event and the programme (for example, all programme updates and changes). It also hosted the daily fanzine and the comments of the artists. The mobile app was created to assist the festival attendees on the go and had information about the different projection rooms, located around the city of Locarno. It was not directly updated with new information because it was designed to work both online and offline (an external link pointed to the relevant page at pardolive.ch). Social media channels (Facebook and Twitter) were – for the first time at this edition of the festival – designed to engage with festival attendees with three main hashtags or conversations: #Locarno65 – the official hashtag of the festival used by journalists and film critics; #PardoLive – which was used to discuss the website contents and the daily fanzine contents; and #iPardo – used to share Loc65 moments with social network users.

After the festival the event organizers published a survey on the website to assess the use of the digital tools by event attendees. See Table 11.1.

Table 11.1 Loc65's digital communication channel usage

Digital Communication Channel	Before	During	After
Loc65 website	67.3%	48.5%	57.4%
Loc65 mobile app	19.8%	41.6%	12.8%
Loc65 social media	42.6%	53.5%	54.5%
Other	4%	6%	3.9%

Before the festival, Loc65 attendees mostly used the website to find out what to expect at the festival and to carry out tasks related to planning their visit and decision-making. During the festival the website was still important, but the app – which was supposed to be more relevant at that point in time – seemed not to be so important. Social media applications were the main digital communication channels used by festival-goers for connections (with friends and family) and short-term decision-making. After the festival the website assumed paramount importance in documenting the event experience. Social media applications were also critical because they are powerful tools to share event experiences and re-experience what happened during an event.

Social Media and their Impact on Events

The emergence of Web 2.0 (O'Reilly, 2009) and social media has generated important impacts in the event industry. Event organizers need to engage with social media, as Flinn and Frew (2014) argue – they no longer have a choice whether to or not. However, even though Holtzblatt et al. (2013) argue that social media marketing is being embraced throughout the event industry, the true potential of these communication channels has not yet been effectively exploited by the sector.

Social media can be generally understood as internet-based applications that encompass media impressions created by consumers, typically informed by relevant experiences, and archived or shared online for easy access by other impressionable consumers (Blackshaw, 2006). These impressions are referred to as user-generated content and are hosted on social media websites which support consumers in posting and sharing their comments, opinions and personal experiences, which can then serve as potentially valuable information for others, including event managers. Social media differs from traditional websites, as they are populated by user-generated content created by consumers (Dickey and Lewis, 2010). Social media applications have made real-time, many-to-many (peer-to-peer) communications between consumers possible (Mangold and Faulds, 2009), replacing the earlier model of providing information on a one-to-many basis. In this way, social media stimulates participation, openness, conversation, connections and a sense of community (Saravanakumar and SuganthaLakshmi, 2012).

Social media has also stimulated the rise of electronic word of mouth or eWOM (Litvin et al., 2008), which has emerged as one of the most powerful tools for online marketing (Inversini and Masiero, 2014). Adoption of social media as a marketing tool has been widespread among service-oriented organizations, which have used it for public relations as well as predicting market trends (Hudson and Thal, 2013). Schmallegger and Carson (2008) suggest that these tools can also be used for promotion, product distribution, management and market research.

Additionally, social networking sites offer innovative ways to develop customer relationship management strategies and engagement that can have a direct influence on a company's credibility, influence, reputation and word-of-mouth advertising. It has emerged as a significant force that drives the online conversations in a wide variety of travel, tourism and leisure experiences. However, the loss of control over online communications has raised a challenge for organizations (Fotis et al., 2011). Negative comments or reviews along with misinformation can be widely shared with potential customers and can have a devastating impact on businesses (Dellarocas, 2001).

Furthermore, the rise of social media has reshaped the consumer behaviour making it more interactive. Consumers are much more exigent than before (Buhalis and Law, 2008) and to some extent more impressionable (Blackshaw, 2006) as they tend to trust internet-mediated peers' recommendations and impressions, which most of the time contain a mixture of fact and opinion, impression and sentiment, experiences, and

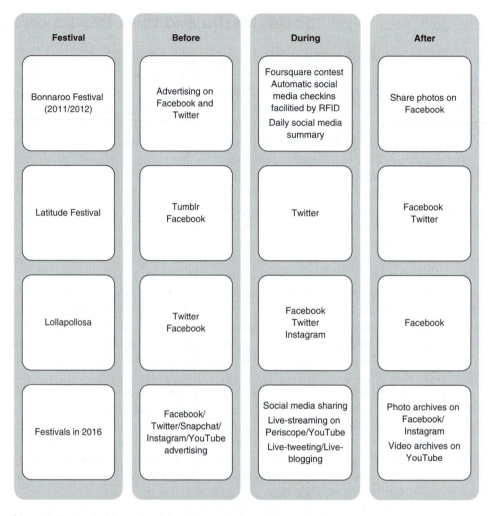

Festival	Before	During	After
Bonnaroo Festival (2011/2012)	Advertising on Facebook and Twitter	Foursquare contest Automatic social media checkins facilitied by RFID Daily social media summary	Share photos on Facebook
Latitude Festival	Tumblr Facebook	Twitter	Facebook Twitter
Lollapollosa	Twitter Facebook	Facebook Twitter Instagram	Facebook
Festivals in 2016	Facebook/ Twitter/Snapchat/ Instagram/YouTube advertising	Social media sharing Live-streaming on Periscope/YouTube Live-tweeting/Live-blogging	Photo archives on Facebook/ Instagram Video archives on YouTube

Figure 11.3   Festivals' use of social media apps before, during and after events

even rumours (Blackshaw and Nazzaro, 2006). Qualman (2010) adds that social media has caused a shift in how consumers communicate, as social media touches nearly every facet of personal and business lives. Innovative event organizations will need to rapidly identify consumer needs and to interact with prospective clients by using comprehensive, personalised and up-to-date communication media for the design of products that satisfy their demands.

Some event managers have embraced social media as marketing channels (Holtzblatt et al., 2013; Lee et al., 2011) to reach organizational and marketing goals. For example, meeting and conference organizers have been quick to recognize the value of social media beyond promotion. However, the rest of the industry has generally not adopted social media as a measurement and a management tool (Inversini and Sykes, 2014). As highlighted earlier in the chapter, in the event industry, social media can not only be used for marketing, but to extend experiences by creating interactive communication between attendees/participants before, during and after the event (Brown and Hutton, 2013). Before the event, interactions on social media can influence the motivation to attend a given event. Pre-event communications can set expectations or heighten anticipation for the experience to be delivered. During the event, mobile social media such as Facebook, Twitter, Instagram and Snapchat can be used to share user-generated content. The emergence of live-streaming platforms hosted on mobile phones also enables the sharing of live video from an event, extending the experience geographically to participants who may not actually be physically present at the event. See Figure 11.3.

Currently, meeting planners are adopting social networks to enhance their events and to create interactive communities between attendees before and after events. For instance social networks such as Facebook, LinkedIn and some blogs are useful for peer ratings of sessions, speakers and exhibits before the event. Also if a web search or web browsing is not able to provide sufficient information about local attractions that meeting attendees could visit outside of the conference or exhibition they have chosen to attend, social media content, which may include photos, videos and/or texts about these attractions, can be used to help make decisions in planning their trip (Huertas and Marine-Roig, 2016).

Leveraging Social Media in the Event Industry

It is now imperative for events to have a holistic digital presence to support attendees' experiential journey in addition to their information needs. Technologies are ubiquitous and pervasive (Xiang et al., 2014) and influence not only the consumers' experience, but also the way attendees experience the event.

Social media requires event organizers, but also events marketers, to change their strategies, by adopting new ways of thinking (Kaplan and Haenlein, 2010). The shift towards a more dialogic and social approach to marketing and management can be seen as the first step towards a technology-based experience co-creation (Neuhofer et al., 2013). In other words if event organizers and events marketers are ready to engage before, during and after the actual experience with attendees there is an opportunity to really empower social media users to personalize their event experiences.

In order to engage social media users effectively, an important first step is to identify the community of interest around a particular event on social media (Williams et al., 2015). A community of interest (COI) can be understood as an informal cluster of people who virtually show an interest or a passion for something. Identifying, understanding and leveraging the social media users with these communities (particularly the hubs – a small number of users who are likely to attract a large number of followers, mentions and replies – can help in getting meaningful marketing and/or management messages across to the wider event community.

Case Study 11.2 – Bournemouth Air Festival, eWOM and Community of Interest on Twitter

Social media postings on Twitter can appear to be a confusing stream of information that is difficult to decipher. However, approaches and techniques are available to make sense of this information. One such approach is viewing social media updates as online communities of interest (COIs). These are defined as online domains in which members share content and communication about specific topics (Obst et al., 2002). Events can create temporary COIs hosted on social media before, during and after staging that can be analysed to understand the structure and content of discussions. This information can be very valuable to event managers when planning future events.

This case presents an example based on the study of Twitter conversations of the Bournemouth Air Festival 2013. Figure 11.4 provides an overview of the research process.

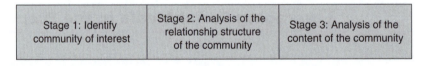

Stage 1: Identify community of interest	Stage 2: Analysis of the relationship structure of the community	Stage 3: Analysis of the content of the community

Figure 11.4   The research process for the Bournemouth Air Festival 2013

Stage 1: Identification of COI

Twitter postings related to the festival and the destination were archived over a two-week period of time. Tweets were then filtered to identify the underlying information relationships.

Stage 2: Analysis of the relationship structure of the community

The overall network was analysed using social network analysis to understand its structure and to identify segments or subgroups with particular interests.

Stage 3: Analysis of the content of the community

The content of Twitter discussions was identified by an analysis of frequently used words within the subgroups identified in stage 2. This information was used to classify the groups by content and user characteristics. See Table 11.2.

Table 11.2   Top five Bournemouth Air Festival Twitter user-group classifications compared

Group Number	Bournemouth Air Festival	
	Characteristics of Users in Hub	**Location of Users in Hubs**
1	Official Bournemouth media accounts and personal Twitter accounts of media personnel	Bournemouth region (Dorset) terms mentioned most often. Little evidence of users from outside UK.
2	Music fans	Bournemouth region (Dorset) terms mentioned most often. Little evidence of users from outside UK.
3	Bournemouth media	Bournemouth region (Dorset) terms mentioned most often. Little evidence of users from outside UK.
4	Fans of bands	Bournemouth region (Dorset) terms mentioned most often. Little evidence of users from outside UK.
5	Accounts of support services, charities	Bournemouth region (Dorset) terms mentioned most often. Little evidence of users from outside UK.

From this analysis, it is clear that the Bournemouth Air Show attracted a primarily local audience on Twitter. This indicates that, despite its billing as an international event, the key social media audience was drawn from the nearby region. For event managers, this is a useful insight. If the organization is seeking to reach potential international visitors, it suggests that it may need to adopt specific strategies to target these individuals. These may include social-media-based contests or promotions aimed at an international audience and the inclusion of international features for the event such as performers from international target markets.

Case Study Questions

1   What are the limitations of using a single social media application, such as Twitter, exclusively as an event evaluation tool?
2   Why do you think the Bournemouth Air Festival attracted a Twitter audience primarily made of local users?
3   Is it a good idea for event managers to focus their marketing efforts on hubs (accounts with a large number of connections)? Why or why not?

Chapter Summary

Despite the scant attention paid to the impact of digital technologies and social media, in particular, in the events management literature, they are playing an increasingly crucial role in event communications. This reality has placed new demands on event organizers to embrace a holistic technological presence so that they can engage with event attendees before, during and after an event. Many event organizations are yet to fully embrace the shift towards a more dialogic and social approach to marketing and management which is needed to facilitate technology-based experience/co-creation of events. Engaging with communities of interest and social hubs can provide event organizers with the opportunity to communicate meaningful marketing and/or management messages across a wider event community.

Review Questions

1. How can event managers use social media to support event operations?
2. If the Locarno Film Festival was staged today, what social media tools would you use and why?
3. Why do you think the dedicated apps like the one created for the Locarno Film Festival may receive little usage during events?
4. What would you suggest as an alternative to creating a mobile app for an event to engage event attendees on the move?

Additional Resources

Books / Book Chapters / Journal Articles

Hudson, S., Roth, M. S., Madden, T. J. and Hudson, R. (2015). The effects of social media on emotions, brand relationship quality, and word of mouth: an empirical study of music festival attendees. *Tourism Management*, 47: 68–76. This journal article examines the influence of social media on customer relationships at a music festival.

Sigala, M., Christou, E. and Gretzel, U. (2012). *Social Media in Travel, Tourism and Hospitality: Theory, Practice and Cases*. Farnham: Ashgate. This text presents cutting-edge theory, practice and cases highlighting the use of Web 2.0 applications in a range of leisure experiences, including events.

Strickland, P., Williams, K. M., Laing, J. and Frost, W. (2015). The use of social media in the wine event industry: a case study of the high country harvest in Australia. In: G. Szolnoki, T. Thac and D. Kolb (eds), *Successful Social Media and Ecommerce Strategies in the Wine Industry* (pp. 74–92). Basingstoke: Palgrave Macmillan. This book chapter explores the use of social media as a platform to increase customer involvement and patronage at wine events.

Useful Websites

discovertext.com – This website hosts a social media collection, analysis and reporting tool.

http://sifter.texifter.com/ – A website which allows users to purchase archived tweets.

netlytic.org – This website offers a Facebook, Instagram and Twitter data collection and analysis tool.

www.tagsleuth.com/ – A website which hosts an Instagram, Twitter, Vine and Tumblr data collection tool.

www.tweetarchivist.com/ – This website allows users to archive current tweets.

References

Binkhorst, E. and Den Dekker, T. (2009). Agenda for co-creation tourism experience research. *Journal of Hospitality Marketing & Management*, *18*(2–3): 311–27.

Blackshaw, P. (2006). The consumer-generated surveillance culture [online]. Retrieved from www.clickz.com/showPage.html?page=3576076.

Blackshaw, P. and Nazzaro, M. (2006). *Consumer-Generated Media (CGM) 101: Word-Of-Mouth in the Age of the Web-Fortified Consumer*. New York: Nielsen BuzzMetrics.

Brown, S. and Hutton, A. (2013). Developments in the real-time evaluation of audience behaviour at planned events. *International Journal of Event and Festival Management*, *4*(1): 43–55.

Buhalis, D. and Inversini, A. (2014). Tourism branding and reputation in the age of social media. In: R. Mariani, R. Baggio, D. Bhualis and C. Longhi (eds) *Tourism Management, Marketing and Development: the Importance of Networks and ICTs* (pp. 15–40). New York: Palgrave, Macmillan.

Buhalis, D. and Law, R. (2008). Progress in information technology and tourism management: 20 years on and 10 years after the Internet – The state of eTourism research. *Tourism Management*, *29*(4): 609–23.

Cantoni, L. and Blas, N. D. (2002). *Teoria e Pratiche Della Comunicazione*. Milano: Apogeo.

Card, J. A., Chen, C.-Y. and Cole, S. T. (2003). Online travel products shopping: differences between shoppers and non-shoppers. *Journal of Travel Research*, *42*(2): 133–9.

Christodoulides, G. (2009). Branding in the post-internet era. *Marketing Theory*, *9*(1): 141–4.

Daugherty, T., Eastin, M. S. and Bright, L. (2008). Exploring consumer motivations for creating user-generated content. *Journal of Interactive Advertising*, *8*(2): 16–25.

Dellarocas, C. (2001). Analyzing the economic efficiency of eBay-like online reputation reporting mechanisms. In: *Proceedings of the 3rd ACM conference on Electronic Commerce* (pp. 171–9). New York, NY: ACM.

Dickey, I. J. and Lewis, W. F. (2010). Social media perceptions and usage by Generation Y and relevant marketing implications. In: W. Kehoe and L. Whitten (eds), *Advances in Marketing: Going Green – Best Marketing Practices for a Global World*. Mobile: Society for Marketing Advances.

Dubosson-Torbay, M., Osterwalder, A. and Pigneur, Y. (2002). E-business model design, classification, and measurements. *Thunderbird International Business Review*, *44*(1): 5–23.

Fesenmaier, D. R. and Xiang, Z. (2013). Tourism marketing from 1990–2010: two decades and a new paradigm. In: *The Handbook of Tourism Marketing*. London: Routledge.

Flinn, J. and Frew, M. (2014). Glastonbury: managing the mystification of festivity. *Leisure Studies*, *33*(4): 418–33.

Fotis, J., Buhalis, D. and Rossides, N. (2011). Social media impact on holiday travel planning. *International Journal of Online Marketing, 1*(4): 1–19.

Gretzel, U., Fesenmaier, D. and O'Leary, J. T. (2006). The transformation of consumer behaviour. In: D. Buhalis and C. Costa (eds), *Tourism Business Frontiers: Consumers, Products and Industry* (pp. 9–18). Burlington, MA: Elsevier.

Gretzel, U. and Yoo, K. H. (2008). Use and impact of online travel reviews. In: D. P. O'Connor, D. W. Höpken and D. U. Gretzel (eds), *Information and Communication Technologies in Tourism* 2008 (pp. 35–46). Springer Vienna [online] Retrieved from http://link.springer.com/chapter/10.1007/978-3-211-77280-5_4

Hogan, S., Almquist, E. and Glynn, S. E. (2005). Brand-building: finding the touchpoints that count. *Journal of Business Strategy, 26*(2): 11–18.

Holtzblatt, L., Drury, J. L., Weiss, D., Damianos, L. E. and Cuomo, D. (2013). Evaluating the uses and benefits of an enterprise social media platform. *Journal of Social Media for Organizations, 1*(1): 1–21.

Hudson, S. and Hudson, R. (2013). Engaging with consumers using social media: a case study of music festivals. *International Journal of Event and Festival Management, 4*(3): 206–23.

Hudson, S. and Thal, K. (2013). The impact of social media on the consumer decision process: implications for tourism marketing. *Journal of Travel & Tourism Marketing, 30*(1–2): 156–60.

Huertas, A. and Marine-Roig, E. (2016). Differential destination content communication strategies through multiple social media. In: *Information and Communication Technologies in Tourism* 2016 (pp. 239–52). Springer International Publishing.

Inversini, A. and Cantoni, L. (2014). *Nuovi Media Nella Comunicazione Turistica*. Roma: Societá Editrice Dante Alighieri.

Inversini, A. and Masiero, L. (2014). Selling rooms online: the use of social media and online travel agents. *International Journal of Contemporary Hospitality Management, 26*(2): 272–92.

Inversini, A., Sage, R., Williams, N. and Buhalis, D. (2015). The social impact of events in social media conversation. In: *Information and Communication Technologies in Tourism* 2015 (pp. 283–94). Springer International Publishing.

Inversini, A. and Sykes, E. (2014). An investigation into the use of social media marketing and measuring its effectiveness in the events industry. In: Z. Xiang and I. Tussyadiah (eds), *Information and Communication Technologies in Tourism* 2014 (pp. 131–44). Springer International Publishing [online]. Retrieved from http://link.springer.com/chapter/10.1007/978-3-319-03973-2_10

Kaplan, A. M. and Haenlein, M. (2010). Users of the world, unite! The challenges and opportunities of social media. *Business Horizons, 53*(1), 59–68.

Kietzmann, J. H., Hermkens, K., McCarthy, I. P. and Silvestre, B. S. (2011). Social media? Get serious! Understanding the functional building blocks of social media. *Business Horizons, 54*(3): 241–51.

Litvin, S. W., Goldsmith, R. E. and Pan, B. (2008). Electronic word-of-mouth in hospitality and tourism management. *Tourism Management, 29*(3): 458–68.

Mair, J. (2014). *Conferences and Conventions: A Research Perspective*. Routledge [online]. Retrieved from http://espace.library.uq.edu.au/view/UQ:341475

Mangold, W. G. and Faulds, D. J. (2009). Social media: the new hybrid element of the promotion mix. *Business Horizons, 52*(4): 357–65.

Neuhofer, B., Buhalis, D. and Ladkin, A. (2013). A typology of technology-enhanced tourism experiences. *International Journal of Tourism Research, 16*(4): 340–50.

O'Reilly, T. (2007). *What is Web 2.0? Design Patterns and Business Models for the Next Generation of Software* (SSRN Scholarly Paper No. ID 1008839). Rochester, NY: Social Science Research Network.

O'Reilly, T. (2009). *What is Web 2.0?* O'Reilly Media.

Obst, P., Zinkiewicz, L. and Smith, S. G. (2002). Sense of community in science fiction fandom, Part 1: Understanding sense of community in an international community of interest. *Journal of Community Psychology*, *30*(1): 87–103.

Palmer, A. (2010). Customer experience management: a critical review of an emerging idea. *Journal of Services Marketing*, *24*(3): 196–208.

Qualman, E. (2010). *Socialnomics: How Social Media Transforms the Way We Live and Do Business*. Hoboken: John Wiley & Sons.

Robertson, M., Yeoman, I., Smith, K. A. and McMahon-Beattie, U. (2015). Technology, society, and visioning the future of music festivals. *Event Management*, *19*(4): 567–87.

Saravanakumar, M. and SuganthaLakshmi, T. (2012). Social media marketing. *Life Science Journal*, *9*(4): 4444–51.

Schmallegger, D. and Carson, D. (2008). Blogs in tourism: changing approaches to information exchange. *Journal of Vacation Marketing*, *14*(2): 99–110.

Williams, N. L., Inversini, A., Buhalis, D. and Ferdinand, N. (2015). Community crosstalk: an exploratory analysis of destination and festival eWOM on Twitter. *Journal of Marketing Management*, *31*(9–10): 1–28.

Xiang, Z., Dan, W., O'Leary, J. T. and Fesenmaier, D. R. (2014) Adapting to the Internet: trends in travelers' use of the web for trip planning. *Journal of Travel Research*, *54*(4): 511–27.

The Sustainability Agenda and Events 12

Elena Cavagnaro, Albert Postma
and Marisa P. de Brito[1]

Learning Objectives

By reading this chapter students should be able to:

- Define the concepts of corporate social responsibility (CSR) and sustainable development
- Understand and explain the relevance of CSR and sustainable development for the events industry
- Identify the main approaches towards sustainable events
- List the key indicators for sustainable events
- Identify, analyse and evaluate existing events on the basis of sustainable events indicators.

Introduction

Celebrations, contests and gatherings have been part of all cultures ever since the beginnings of human history, and in today's world, even though updated in appearance, they still have a vital role in our daily lives. In the last three decades or so, the event sector has experienced an unprecedented boom in popularity. For example, in

[1] With thanks to Thomas Neese, former master's student at Stenden University.

the United Kingdom (UK) alone, in 2011, 1.3 million meetings were held in more than 10,000 venues. Attendees' expenditures during these meetings were just under £40 billion, while the contribution of meetings to the UK's 2011 gross domestic product was estimated at 2.9%. Moreover, the meeting industry is a major employer in the UK. It generates 423,500 jobs directly, and indirectly the employment of over one million people can be traced to this industry (MPI Foundation, 2013).

Events, though, not only have an impact on the economy of the hosting country or city; they also have a positive or negative impact on the people of the hosting community, their culture and the natural environment. As has been the case in other industries, the growth in the number and size of events has made their impact more visible and raised the question of responsibility for both their positive and negative consequences on communities and the natural environment. It is not surprising therefore that a pool of experts has identified the impacts and outcomes of events as the most important topic for events research in the future (Mair and Whitford, 2013). In short, the quest for a more sustainable event has begun.

This chapter explores the challenges posed and opportunities offered by sustainability to events. It defines the concepts of sustainability and corporate social responsibility (CSR), and the relationship between the two is highlighted. It also refutes the idea that events by their very nature are incompatible with sustainability, and shows how events and sustainability are related. Examples are used to illustrate how events can embrace sustainability and at the same time raise the quality of the experience to their audiences. Additionally, the chapter provides guidelines for sustainable events. It closes by highlighting research on customer awareness of the social and environmental impacts of the events they visit and their perceptions of sustainable events.

On Corporate Social Responsibility and Sustainable Development

After a difficult start in the 1980s, sustainable development and corporate social responsibility (CSR) have earned a stable position on political and business agendas (Jamali, 2006). Even though both concepts are perceived as vague and imprecise by some scholars (Sutton, 2007), there is a growing consensus that CSR is rooted in the acknowledgement that businesses have obligations towards society that go beyond their economic responsibility (Carroll, 1991; Elkington, 1997; and more recently Idowu and Towler, 2004; Jones et al., 2005). John Elkington's proposal of a triple bottom line, which means businesses measure and report on their economic, environmental and social impact (or people, planet and profit), has been embraced by both for-profit and not-for-profit organizations. From 2006 to 2011 the yearly increase in organizations that have published their 'triple-p' reports using the global Reporting Initiative (GRI) guidelines, increased from 22% to 58%.

Sustainable development was set at the centre of academic and political debate by the UN World Commission on Environment and Development, also known as the Brundtland commission because of the name of its Chair, former Norwegian Prime Minister Gro Harlem Brundtland. The Brundtland commission recognized that the current path of development not only has a negative impact on the natural environment but also fails to successfully address social inequalities both among nations and between nations. Therefore it cannot and should not be sustained indefinitely.

Change is needed towards a sustainable form of development that 'seeks to meet the needs and aspirations of the present without compromising the ability to meet those of the future' (1987: 40). The purpose of sustainable development is thus a better quality of life for present and future generations. The main point made by the Brundtland commission is that a better quality of life cannot be achieved by relying only on economic growth alone. A healthy natural environment and equitable social development are also essential dimensions of a sustainable pattern of development.

Sustainable development was quickly embraced by multilateral organizations such as the UN, and several NGOs. By now, however, it informs not only UN programmes, but also local, national and regional policy. For example, the Maastricht Treaty, signed on 7 February 1992, states that the goal of the European Union is to achieve sustainable development (EU, 1992, article B). Also, thanks to the on-going work of the World Business Council for Sustainable Development, more and more companies have answered the call to become agents of change towards sustainability by redesigning their operations to achieve a positive impact on people, planet and profit – the triple bottom line proposed by John Elkington (Schmidheiny, 1992; WBCSD, 2000).

Based on the above, the following definition of CSR will be used in this chapter:

CSR is the voluntary dedication of business towards sustainable development resulting in benefits for society (people), environment (planet) and the economy (profit). At the consumer level, sustainability entails consideration of not only the prices of goods and services but also their impacts on people and the natural environment. (Cavagnaro and Curiel, 2012; Jackson 2005; UN 1992)

Corporate Social Responsibility and Sustainable Development

- Sustainable development aims at a better quality of life for present and future generations, all over the globe.
- To achieve sustainable development, value should be created on an environmental, social and economic dimension.
- CSR translates sustainable development to the level of organizations.
- CSR is defined as the voluntary dedication of business towards sustainable development, resulting in benefits for society (people), environment (planet) and the economy (profit).

Sustainability and Events

It may be clear from the above that sustainability is not a new issue on academic, political and business agendas. However, the initial reaction of the events industry to appeals to engage in sustainable practices has been one of reluctance. Currently, an increasing number of events are embracing sustainability while enhancing the experience of their visitors. Before diving into these examples, it is appropriate to consider where this initial hesitancy came from.

The hesitancy to consider sustainable development and CSR relevant as applicable to the event industry may be explained by the tendency to understand both as referring to something that should go on indefinitely, and then contrasting this definition with the unique and ephemeral nature of events. It is true that one of the meanings of the verb 'to sustain' is to endure and be long-lasting. Yet, though sustainability aims at a form of development that can be sustained indefinitely, the message of sustainable development and CSR is that activities are unsustainable if they do not benefit the people involved, the community in which they take place and the natural environment. The stress is on the impacts of a specific activity, not on how long that activity lasts.

It is undeniable that events have impact on the people involved, the hosting community and the natural environment. Consider the Sziget Festival in Budapest, Hungary. This festival was born as a student music festival with 43,000 visitors in 1993. In 2006 it attracted 385,000 visitors and generated 2,200 cubic metres of waste, an amount similar to the waste accumulated by residents of a ten-storey building in about 9–10 years (Dávid, 2009). In face of these numbers it is difficult to deny that sustainable development and CSR are relevant concepts for the events industry.

As Getz has argued, 'sustainable events are not just those that can endure indefinitely, they are also events that fulfil important social, cultural, economic and environmental roles that people value' (2007: 70). Similarly Smith-Christensen argues that responsible events are 'sensitive to the economic, socio-cultural and environmental needs within the local host community, and organized in such a way to maximize the net holistic (positive) output' (2009: 25). Moreover, following a long tradition connecting CSR with stakeholders' thinking (Carroll, 1991; Elkington, 1997), Getz argues that to achieve sustainability 'accountability has to extend beyond internal shareholders to encompass all stakeholders interested in and affected by planned events, including visitors and especially the affected communities' (2007: 71).

Sustainable events can therefore be defined as: events that impact positively on people, planet and profit and thus contribute to the economic, socio-cultural and environmental needs of the involved stakeholders, including the hosting community.[2]

---

[2] Impact is chosen above output or outcome following the recent debate on the relative strengths of these concepts in the context of sustainability (Maas, 2009). In brief, while output and outcome highlight the results of a business activity, e.g. a well-attended event, impact focuses on the positive or negative change and legacy that it leaves behind, e.g. disruption in a community that had to be relocated to make space to host a mega event such as the Olympic Games.

As John Elkington (1997) observed in his landmark book, while organizations have learnt to address environmental issues rather quickly, the socio-cultural aspects of sustainability and CSR are still difficult to address. The efforts at greening the Olympic Games offers an excellent illustration of this point (see Case Study 12.5 below).

The social impacts of events are effectively illustrated by events that are developed by destinations to prolong their tourist seasons – for example those staged by three West Frisian islands in the Netherlands: Terschelling, Ameland and Vlieland. On these islands several events are organized before and after the high season (the so-called shoulder season) to trigger tourists to visit the island in the months of April to June, and September to December. Examples of events are: on Vlieland 'Into the Great Wide Open' (pop festival in September); on Ameland 'November Kunstmaand' (arts festival in November), 'Tri-Ambla' (triathlon in September), 'Adventure Run' (in December); on Terschelling 'Fjoertoer' (walking on an April night in the lights of fires), 'Oerol' (location theatre festival early in June), 'Bereloop' (marathon in November), 'Terschellinger Filmdagen' (film festival in November) and 'Follek' (hospitality event in November).

Figure 12.1   Photo by Jonathan Sipkema and Brian Esselbrugge during 'Into the Great Wide Open' 2015

The 'Weltevree's Strandtuin' project. The 'Strandtuin' (Beach garden) was developed by the innovative brand Weltevree (http://www. weltevree.nl/ENG) in co-operation with LAB Vlieland (http://labvlieland.nl/about-lab-vlieland). Here sustainability projects were presented in a cozy, comfortable and well-designed setting.

Sources: http://www.intothegreatwideopen.nl/bericht/welcome-to-tomorrow-weltevree-s-strandtuin and http://www.weltevree.nl/ENG/ nieuws/into-the-great-wide-open

Figure 12.2   An upside-down house built by artist Ina Smits at the 'Into the Great Wide Open' 2015 pop festival

Photo by Sander Heezen. This upside-down house was built for the project Starfishing.

Sources: www.intothegreatwideopen.nl/bericht/into-the-great-wide-open-2015-in-foto-s-1 and www.inasmits.nl

There is no doubt that such events bring economic benefits to the islands. They offer employment and raise the incomes of many families. These events have positive social implications as well. The visitors bring liveliness to the islands in a period that would otherwise be rather quiet. Moreover shops, public transport, leisure facilities and the like stay open for a longer period thanks to the visitors. This surely improves the quality of life for inhabitants on the islands.

However, off-season events also have downsides: the crowds occupy the roads, cycling tracks, shops, and ferries used by the residents, hampering locals' use of these and other amenities. The Oerol festival on Terschelling, in early June, offers a good example of an off-season event. Research by Postma (2013) shows that around 55,000 people visit the destination and the residents (less than 5,000 in total) in response adjust their behaviour to escape the crowds. They change their shopping times, the time they take the ferry to the mainland and the time they take their children to school. They lock their houses and bikes – something that normally they would not do – and secure the furniture in their gardens. Although the locals usually like the type of visitors attracted by the events, there are situations in which the behaviour of tourists causes annoyance as well (for example, increases in crime, noise and litter). Nevertheless, as long as the positive effects of such events outweigh the negative, the attitude of residents will remain positive.

To achieve positive impacts on the triple bottom line and thus contribute to sustainable development, an organization should set sustainability principles at the centre of its vision and mission (Cavagnaro and Curiel, 2012; Edwards, 2005). An early attempt to engender sustainability within the event industry was the development of the Hannover Principles, a set of nine maxims proposed as guidelines in designing competitions and projects for the World Exposition held in 2000 in Hannover, Germany (McDonough and Partners, 1992; Musgrave and Raj, 2009). Sustainable design principles were set in relation to the elements *earth* (e.g. lifecycle analysis of all materials, recycling), *air* (e.g. minimize air and noise pollution and artificial indoor climate control), *fire* (e.g. on-site energy production and heating), *water* (e.g. minimize water use and impermeable ground cover) and *spirit* (e.g. embrace people's feeling of belonging to the earth).

The Hannover Principles demonstrate that although a mission based on sustainability principles is essential, sustainable impacts are primarily the result of sustainable processes and operations (Cavagnaro and Curiel, 2012). The degree of sustainability of an activity depends primarily on its impacts on people, planet and profit, even when sustainability is the theme of that activity. An example of such an event is held yearly in the Netherlands. It is called the Frisian Solar Challenge and is described in Case Study 12.1.

Case Study 12.1 – The Frisian Solar Challenge, the World Cup in Solar Boat Racing

Fryslân, a northern province of the Netherlands, is renowned for its many lakes, rivers and canals, and can be regarded as a unique water sport region. The Frisian provincial government has set sustainable development as a policy goal since 2007. In this context, Frisian economic policy is geared towards supporting innovative entrepreneurs and the development of sustainable technology. In the Frisian Solar Challenge these two elements are combined successfully.

The Frisian Solar Challenge is an international racing event for boats driven by solar energy. The participating boats race over six days on a route that passes through all 11 cities of the province of Fryslân, starting and finishing in the capital of Leeuwarden. Almost 50 international teams participate every year. They compete in three classes: one sailor, two sailors and a top class, which can include a crew composed of any number of people. The event offers a stage on which innovative technology can be presented to a large audience in a safe, pleasant and naturally beautiful environment. In this way the Frisian Solar Challenge hopes to support the development of solar energy and to stimulate its use. A second aim of this event is to promote the province of Fryslân not only as a tourism destination for water sport lovers, but also as an innovative and entrepreneurial region.

CRITICAL THINKING EXERCISE 1

How does the Frisian Solar Challenge exemplify the principles of sustainable development?

From the example above, it is clear that isolated events have been making efforts to become more sustainable for many years. However within the last five years or so, the industry as a whole has come together and shown an eagerness in addressing the issue like never before. This goes hand-in-hand with the rise in consumer awareness of sustainability issues. As the Eurobarometer (2014) shows, 95% of Europeans (EU-28) believe that protecting the environment is important.

A clear sign that a turning point has been reached by the whole industry was given at the end of 2010 during the first Green Events Conference. During the conference several experts related to the industry created the Go Group, 'an independent pan-European think-tank to inspire people in the music festival and events industry to run their operations greener and smarter'. This think-tank has been active and growing since then, pushing the sustainability agenda at festivals and involving their stakeholders. In 2014, 16 festivals from ten different European countries made it to the final nominees of the Go Group 'Green Operations Award', highlighting that more festivals are going green.

It is no longer possible for event organizations to bid on large sports or cultural events without a sustainability chapter in the bid book explaining concretely how they intend to tackle sustainability. Consider the European Capitals of Culture bids described in Case Study 12.2.

Case Study 12.2 – European Capitals of Culture

Each year two cities in Europe receive the title of 'European Capital of Culture' (ECOC). The Member States getting the award are known well in advance and cities in these Member States can make a bid for it by developing a plan with a cultural programme and highlighting its impacts. After the event, there is an evaluation report on the outcomes, submitted to the European Commission.

In particular, 'sustainable cultural, economic and social impact' is sought. Regarding the social dimension, the event should generate opportunities '*for a wide range of citizens to attend or participate*', including young people and the elderly, marginalized groups, ethnic minorities, and people with disabilities.

(Continued)

(Continued)

The bidding guidance documents state: 'Successful ECOCs have used it as a catalyst for a step change in the city's cultural and general development producing sustainable cultural, social and economic impact' (European Commission, 2014: 9).

Leeuwarden (the Netherlands) and Valetta (Malta) were awarded the title for 2018. Both cities paid special attention to sustainability when submitting their bids. The titles and highlights of their winning bids are described below.

Leeuwarden, the Netherlands – Bid Title: Iepen Mienskip (Criss-crossing Communities)

The bid book clearly identifies how Leeuwarden will work towards sustainability challenges, such as matters of cultural diversity, the preservation of

Figure 12.3   The project DORP at the Welcome to the Village 2015 festival illustrates the Frisian concept of 'mienskip'. In the DORP (Dutch for village) the festival collaborates with numerous inquisitive partners, including event guests, to investigate ways to build future editions of Welcome to the Village on fair and sustainable principles.

Photo by Hans Jellema.

Source: http://welcometothevillage.nl/project-en/dorp

nature and natural heritage, isolation and desertion of peripheral areas, loss of bio-diversity, and poverty. Leeuwarden proposes to design events which encompass these focus areas and pay specific attention to the relationship between nature and culture, the relationship between countryside and city, and social differences. The bid also shows how existing festivals in the region will address the challenges, such as the 'Welcome to the Village' Festival. This community-based festival is renowned for its 'global village' feeling, where visitors and artists from all over Europe meet and co-create the festival. The food eaten at the festival is grown on an on-site garden and harvested by the attendees (Stichting Kulturele Haadstêd 2018, 2013).

Valetta, Malta – Bid Title: Imagine, 18

Valetta's bid book identifies key priorities related to urban infrastructure and quality of life, such as motor vehicles (transportation), public spaces, urban design, urban biodiversity, deterioration of buildings, and impacts of construction activity. These issues were derived from the National Environmental Policy set by the Ministry of Tourism, Culture and the Environment of Malta, and its targets for 2020. The rationale is to transform urban areas into attractive places where people can 'live, work, play and interact'. In addition, the bid book proposes a governance structure which includes the creation of an agency that will, in collaboration with already-existing bodies, coordinate the delivery of an 'Integrated Public Space and Mobility Plan' (Valletta 2018 Foundation, 2015).

Sustainability Guidelines for Events

From the examples briefly described above, it is clear that the word 'event' covers very different activities. Indeed, events differ greatly. Common classifications distinguish events by size and content. In size, events range from weddings, involving only the families of the bride and groom, to mega events, such as the Olympics, which affect whole economies and command global coverage. Content-wise, scholars mostly distinguish cultural, business and sport events (Bowdin et al., 2006: 15–23). This diversity is reflected in the impacts that specific events have on people, planet and profit. It therefore follows that different events will require specific sustainability indicators and guidelines. However, there are some general issues that apply to the majority of events and should therefore be of concern to every event organizer. These include transport, energy and water use, water and sewage, food consumption and accommodation, and communication with the attendees.

Before going into more detail, it is important to remember that, as Getz points out:

> Placing a value on festivals and other planned events has been obscured by an over-emphasis on event tourism and other economic benefits. The social and cultural values of events have been given inadequate attention, so that until recently we have had trouble identifying let alone measuring them. And the environmental impacts of event tourism have until very recently been ignored, so that the carbon footprint and energy costs of event tourism have for the most part not been included in impact assessments. (Getz, 2009: 70)

The challenge is to integrate the well-known economic measures with indicators on environmental quality and social development. In this respect the event industry is in the same predicament as other businesses that embraced sustainability before being able to effectively evaluate their efforts.

The early engagement of the tourism industry with sustainability might be explained with a reference to the rapid growth of mass tourism in the 1970s and 1980s. Since then it has dawned on many destinations, especially in those third world countries where tourism was considered as the panacea for all development issues, that tourism is a double-edged sword. While tourism often boosts short-term socio-economic development, provides employment, enriches the lives of hosts, encourages conservation and enhances the image of destinations that were previously unknown, it is also true that tourism contributes to environmental degradation, socio-cultural erosion, drug trafficking and prostitution. Moreover, revenue leakages are estimated to be between 50% and 70% of total tourism revenues. It has been observed that 'Tourism contains the seeds of its own destruction: tourism can kill tourism, destroying the very attraction visitors have come to experience' (Plog, 1974: 58).

Since the 1970s, the negative environmental and social impacts of tourism have fuelled the call for a more sustainable development of tourism (Butler, 1990). The World Tourism Organization, for example, has reflected on the role of tourism in social and environmental sustainability since 1980. The International Eco-tourism Society (founded in 1990), the World Heritage Alliance for Sustainable Tourism (created in 2005 by the UN Foundation and Expedia, the online travel company), and the Tourism Sustainability Council (created in 2009 when the Partnership for Global Sustainable Tourism Criteria merged with the Sustainable Tourism Stewardship Council), alongside international tour operators such as Transeat and several other players in the tourism industry, developed guidelines and codes to support a more sustainable stance both by the tourism industry and by individual tourists. This multiplicity of actors has resulted in tens of different guidelines, with different scopes and criteria. See Table 12.1.

Recently, though, the Tourism Sustainability Council has unified 60 existing guidelines, principles and sets of standards into the Global Sustainable Tourism Criteria (Global Sustainable Tourism Council, 2015). The four main criteria are also broadly applicable to the event industry. They are: demonstrate effective sustainable management; maximize social and economic benefits to the local community and minimize negative impacts; maximize benefits to cultural heritage and minimize negative impacts; and maximize benefits to the environment and minimize negative impacts.

Table 12.1 Overview of sustainability guidelines applicable to events

Guidelines	Highlights (in brief)
Tourism Sustainability Council (Visit www.sustainabletourismcriteria.org for more details)	<ul><li>Sustainable management</li><li>Socio-economic community impact</li><li>Cultural heritage impact</li><li>Environmental impact</li></ul>
Sustainable Exhibition Industry Project [SEXI] promoted by Midlands Environmental Business Company (www.aeo.org.uk)	<ul><li>Eco-efficiency (e.g. reducing consumption of water/energy)</li><li>Reducing waste</li></ul>
Environmentally Sustainable Meeting Standards of the Convention Industry Council (APEX/ASTM)	<ul><li>Gives strategies and an implementation guide (the 'how to')</li><li>Forms to track and report progress</li></ul>
SSE Toolkit developed by AISTS and VANOC for sporting events (www.aists.org)	<ul><li>Integrates guidelines on sustainability recommended by various international organizations into a pragmatic tool</li></ul>
UNEP (Sustainable Events Guide) (www.unep.org)	Includes checklists for: <ul><li>Selecting the venue</li><li>Accommodation</li><li>Catering</li><li>Transport</li></ul>
BS 8901 by the British Standards Institution (BSI) (www.bsigroup.com)	<ul><li>Sustainability policy</li><li>Stakeholder identification and engagement</li><li>Performance against principles of sustainable development</li></ul>
ISO 20121 on Event Management by the International Standards Organization	<ul><li>The management of improved sustainability throughout the entire event management cycle</li></ul>
Event Organizers Sector Supplement (EOSS) by the Global Reporting Initiative (www.globalreporting.org)	<ul><li>Site selection</li><li>Transport of attendees</li><li>Recruiting and training of the event workforce, participants and volunteers</li><li>Sourcing of materials, supplies and services</li><li>Managing impacts on communities, natural environments, and local and global economies</li><li>Planning and managing potential legacies</li><li>Accessibility of an event</li></ul>

Similar to the tourism industry, several checklists have been published for fostering sustainability in events, such as the 'Greening your event checklist' developed by the New Zealand Government which, despite the name, not only focuses on the natural environment but also considers the need to involve and educate the public (New Zealand Government, 2003).

Guidelines for specific events have also been developed, such as the Hannover Principles briefly described above. The Sustainable Exhibition Industry Project (SEXI) promoted by Midlands Environmental Business Company in 2002 is an initiative which is quite similar. The project addresses primarily the waste issue, a most pressing problem for an industry that, due to 'time pressures, contractual relationships, extremely tight margins and the need for the "WOW" factor results in some difficult, possibly unique, waste management problem issues' (Laybourn, 2002: 2). Estimated waste from UK exhibitions alone is 60,000 tons per annum (Laybourn, 2002: 12), making reducing waste indeed a good stepping stone to confront the event industry with sustainability issues. Moreover, reducing waste, like reducing consumption of energy and water, makes perfect business sense because businesses do not pay for what they do not use or dispose of (Schmidheiny, 1992). As highlighted by Laybourn (2002), although the cost of waste for the exhibition industry is significant, its true cost, which includes the cost of products which were purchased and subsequently thrown away unused, is more than 20 times more.

Eco-efficiency is thus a smart thing to do in all events, not only for exhibitions. However, as has been observed, environmental quality is only one of the aims of sustainability: social and economic impacts should be considered, too.

Another well-known sustainable standard for the meeting and convention industry is the Standards of Convention Industry Council (APEX/ASTM). In addition to strategic guidelines for sustainability, this standard includes an implementation guide as well as forms to track progress and report to stakeholders. The United Nations Environment Programme (UNEP) also provides extensive guidelines on how to green meetings, covering specific indicators on climate neutrality (emissions reduction, calculation and offsetting), with checklists on venue, accommodation, catering and transport.

For sporting events, in particular, AISTS was established by the International Olympic Committee and other respected organizations and academic institutions to respond directly to the need felt by various international organizations for a pragmatic tool.

Efforts at setting guidelines to manage sustainability in events in its entirety have also been made. In November 2007, the British Standards Institution (BSI) published BS 8901, a general standard for sustainable event management that addresses all dimensions of sustainability, and not only the environmental one. The London 2012 Olympics was a major driver in the development of BS 8901. Following the Denim cycle common to similar standards, such as ISO 14000 on environmental management, BS 8901 insists on the need to start from the planning phase, so that sustainability principles are embedded in the policy and relevant impacts are specified from the beginning. BS 8901 was revised and reissued in September 2009 (BSI, 2010) and became the starting point for the draft of international standards for Sustainability in Event Management released by ISO (ISO 20121).

The G4 guidelines ('G4' indicates the version Guideline No. 4) by the Global Reporting Initiative (GRI) also offer standards for sustainability reporting on an international level. The guide encompasses 58 general and 92 key performance indicators addressing the economic, environmental and social performance of organizations (GRI, 2007, 2012, 2013; Sherman, 2009). For event organizers a separate supplement has been published in 2012 based on the third version of the GRI Guidelines (G3). This supplement addresses the demands of event stakeholders such as industry associations, journalists, local authorities, investors and visitors for the sustainability credentials of the events they attend. It covers key-sector specific issues such as the selection of a site; the transport of attendees; recruitment and training of the event workforce, including volunteers and performers; and the sourcing of materials, supplies and services (GRI, 2012). The GRI events supplement makes a provision for the time-bound nature of events by stating that in looking forward to the main future challenges, the organization's lifecycle and span of activities should be considered.

The supplement also specifies disclosure on business practices such as revenues and expenditures on grants or penalties as one of the major challenges of events organizers 'because of the perception by some stakeholders that organizations are not transparent about all practices' (GRI, 2012: 40). Alongside the impact on the involved communities, communication with stakeholders, and especially towards dissenting stakeholders, is also considered a specific core area of attention for events organizers (GRI, 2012: 53). Dissenting stakeholders will include performers that have not be selected to participate in events and representatives of the local communities near the event site that may have suffered inconvenience due to the event. Inclusivity and accessibility of the event are the last core indicators specific to the industry that will be considered here. Inclusivity and accessibility have been highlighted by the UN report on a disability-inclusive agenda issued in 2013, where inclusiveness is framed as a necessary prerequisite for sustainable development (UN, 2013). As defined by GRI, 'an accessible event environment is one with no barriers (including non-physical barriers) preventing it from being used equally, safely, confidently, independently and with dignity by everyone' (GRI, 2012, Supplement: 19). Inclusivity even goes a step further and considers, alongside physical, also economic or social barriers to participation.

Members of the GRI Working Group that developed the events' supplement were, among others, the Austrian and the Swiss governments (who hosted the European Football Championships 2008), Live Earth, WWF, the Organizing Committee of the Vancouver 2010 Olympics and the Organizing Committee of the London 2012 Olympics. Undoubtedly, the latter has played an important role within the UK in regards to implementing sustainability into the event industry.

GRI is not the only organization offering reporting guidelines specifically for events organizers. The Dutch branch of GreenKey, an international NGO recognized by the World Travel Organization, also offers (alongside guidelines) the opportunity to certify an event as sustainable.

In 2012, the International Standardization Organisation (ISO) launched a new standard to support event organizers in setting up a sustainable event – the ISO 20121: Sustainable Events. The ISO 20121 Sustainable Events standard offers practical guidelines on managing events and controlling their social, economic and environmental impacts. It can be used for all kinds of events, such as music festivals, school outings and conventions, and by different kinds of organizations, such as convention centres, events and sport venues, suppliers and contractors (International Organization for Standardization, 2012a, 2012b).

The ISO 20121 Sustainable Events has been successfully used immediately after its inception in 2012 (Lambert, 2013). It was used by the organizers of the Olympic and

Paralympic Games in London in 2012 and by Coca-Cola as one of its main sponsors. Coca-Cola developed a dedicated sustainability policy for the Games which improved its procurement, training and progress meetings regarding its sustainability targets. Coca-cola invested in a recycling infrastructure and used it intensely in its marketing campaign (SGS United Kingdom Ltd, 2012). Research shows that these recycling messages had a positive impact on the intention and motivation of, potentially, millions of spectators of the Games (WRAP, 2012).

Other early adopters of ISO 21121 were the Danish Presidency of the European Union in 2012, which hosted hundreds of political meetings with participants numbering from dozens to hundreds, and Manchester United Ltd, whose stadium is a venue which hosts not only football matches but also conferences, ceremonies and other events (Lambert, 2013). The city of Malmö in Sweden too saw the ISO 20121 as an opportunity 'to enhance its profile as a green destination' by applying the standard to the Eurovision Song Contest in 2013. It trained more than 500 volunteers, enabling them to become good examples and ambassadors of the sustainability of the event.

Case Study 12.3 – Leeuwarden and Valetta European Capitals of Culture 2018

Both Leeuwarden and Valetta highlighted the importance of sustainability in their bid book to become European Capitals of Culture in 2018. This case briefly examines the preparations of both cities as of the year 2015, three years away for the award date.

The major events organizers in Leeuwarden have committed to sustainability and have agreed to show their commitment through certification. Their chosen certification in 2014 was GreenKey, a well-known organization in the Netherlands. Yet, while working towards the thus-set certification goal, two major issues become evident. The first is that certification schemes in general and the GreenKey in particular are perceived to be rather inflexible, and thus not easily applied to the changing nature of events. Representatives from major Frisian events highlighted this point by explaining that changing locations of the same events in different years are not accounted for in the GreenKey certification system. Transport for example is influenced by the location of an event, so the fact that in year 2 more kilometres were travelled than in year 1 by attendees does not necessarily signify a decrease in sustainability. It may only be due to the fact that the festival locations in year 2 are further away from the main area or a road than in year 1.

The second issue is that certification schemes have been set up to cover national or even international events, and therefore have little provisions for sustainability goals that may be specific to one region. In other words, they are not customizable by event, organization or destination. Frisian event organizers developing events in the run-up to Leeuwarden, European Capital of Culture 2018, noted that the typical Frisian sustainability goals of 'water', 'energy' and 'mienskip' – bottom-up community involvement – were poorly represented in the existing certification's systems.

Leeuwarden 2018 event organizations, with the support of local universities of applied sciences, are currently researching which certification schemes are most appropriate for them. In addition, they are investigating additional indicators to do justice to the specific, distinctive character of the Frisian events.

Valetta is also preparing to be European Capital of Culture 2018 and looking to its long-term impact on both the community and the environment. An article from the *Times of Malta*, for example, highlighted that the benefits of Valetta 2018 will be measured by the success of the programme throughout 2018 but more importantly by its lasting effects, i.e. its legacy (Bonnici, 2015). To strengthen the city's cultural capital is the ambition, and investments are being made both in the physical infrastructure (historical buildings) and in its social fibre (cultural and creative hubs).

In the meantime Valetta too is devoting time and resources to small-scale eco-projects in preparation for 2018. These include: the Grey to Green project, which brings together horticulturists, researchers and the residents to foster social capital, and the Recycled Percussion Workshop, a project featuring children and adults working together to make drums (out of recycled materials) and create music. In 2014, the Valetta 2018 Foundation also launched the Valetta Green Festival. The festival is meant to involve residents in improving the local environment, in their own towns and villages, by creating more open and green spaces (Valetta Green Festival, 2014). These initiatives are meant to raise the environmental consciousness of local communities.

Unfortunately the guidelines from the European Commission for the evaluation of the impact of the European Capitals of Culture do not take a triple-p approach (European Commission, 2014). The main objective of European Capitals of Culture is to promote the diversity of cultures in Europe, with sub-objectives including collaboration across borders, reinforcing the capacity of the cultural sector, and boosting the international profile of cities. One sub-objective does have a strong social component: to broaden the accessibility and participation in culture. However, environment or sustainability in its broader sense is not featured. In light of these realities, the efforts both by Leeuwarden and Valetta to assess the impacts of the 2018 events in the long term and to the triple bottom line are even more admirable.

In concluding this discussion on sustainability guidelines for events, it is important to stress that event impacts are both negative and positive in nature. It is also essential to consider that these impacts will occur directly and/or indirectly, willingly and/or

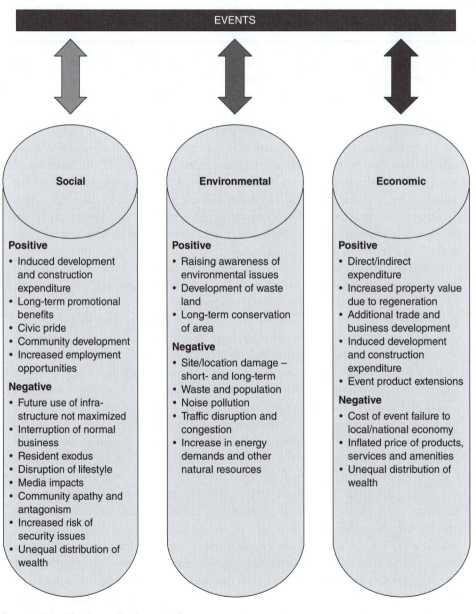

Figure 12.4   The three-pillar impacts of events

Source: Musgrave and Raj (2009: 5)

unwillingly, to all stakeholders, including the host community and natural environment (Maas, 2009). In this respect, a good summary of the main issues to be considered by event organizers is offered by Musgrave and Raj (2009). See Figure 12.4.

Case Study 12.4 – Oerol Festival

Each year in June, the West Frisian Island of Terschelling in the Netherlands is the setting for the summer festival Oerol. The festival lasts for ten days and is focused on live public location theatre, music, visual arts and installations. As its name says (oerol means 'everywhere') the festival uses the entire island as its stage and source of inspiration, including for instance the beaches, the woods, the dunes and fields. A close relationship between Oerol and Staadsbosbeheer – a governmental organization in charge of natural parks and reserves in the Netherlands – assures a respectful use of the natural environment. Yet, it is not only the landscape that acts as a performance space. Man-made artefacts like farm sheds, boat-houses and army bunkers are used for the acts and shows as well. Culture, nature and experiment go hand-in-hand.

Since its birth in 1982, the festival has grown into a leading, internationally renowned multidisciplinary festival. Each year the festival is visited by more than 55,000 culture lovers. They are brought to the island by ferries and travel inland by bike or buses. No visitor vehicles are allowed on the island.

The festival is famous for its unique and innovative programming every year, which is focused around a specific theme inspired by the natural conditions and the special atmosphere on an island. For the residents and entrepreneurs the festival means hard work, day and night. However, a large part of the summer turnover on the island is earned in these ten days. As the festival is important for the island economically, involves large parts of the community and operates in harmony with nature, it can be regarded as a good illustration of an event that is sustainable. However, the balance between the economic, social and environmental values needs to be maintained. In the past few years complaints about the enormous crowds the festival brings to the island have been increasing.

CRITICAL THINKING EXERCISE 2

How can the organizers of Oerol festival maintain a good balance between economic, social and environmental values?

Sustainability and Events

- Even though events are transitory happenings, they definitely leave a footprint on the people involved (from employees to guests; from suppliers to the adjoining community) and on the surrounding natural environment (think, for example, of transport-related pollution). Therefore sustainability is relevant to events.
- Sustainable events impact positively on people, planet and profit and thus contribute to fulfil the economic, socio-cultural and environmental needs of the involved stakeholders, including the hosting community.

Sustainability Guidelines for Events

- Sustainability guidelines integrate the well-known economic measures with indicators on environmental quality and social development.
- The first efforts to develop sustainability guidelines for tourism date from the 1980s.
- Since 2002 several guidelines, checklists and certification systems have been developed that are specifically dedicated to events.
- Most guidelines feature a holistic approach and include environmental, social and economic dimensions of sustainability integrated into the vision and mission of the event organization as well as its strategy and processes.
- Amongst the most recent events guidelines are:
  - o G4 GRI guidelines featuring a specific supplement for Events (2012)
  - o The Dutch-based GreenKey certification for sustainable public events (2012)
  - o ISO 201121 for sustainable events.

Is There a Market Out There for Sustainable Events?

The 2012 Co-operative Bank's Ethical Consumerism Report revealed that since the onset of the recession in 2008 the total value of the ethical markets increased from 35.5 to 47.2 billion pounds (roughly 53.7 – 71.3 billion US dollars). The report, which has been compiled since 1999, comprises expenditure figures on goods and services in the areas of ethical food and drinks, green homes, eco-travel and transport, ethical personal products, community and finances. While some areas show more increases than others, overall the sales figures showed a continuing positive trend when it comes to ethical or sustainable consumption – even in difficult economical times.

So far, consumer behaviour analyses related to ethical consumption have not included event-related consumerism. The question therefore arises as to whether people consider 'greener' or more environmentally friendly options when it comes to attending an event. In other words: is there a market out there for sustainable events?

In research conducted in 2010, the authors explored answers to this question, focusing on the UK market. The first step in the research was to measure the general environmental attitudes of events' customers and their awareness of the environmental and social impacts of events. This has been done by adapting one of the most commonly used scales to evaluate environmental orientation, attitudes and behaviour – the revised New Environmental Paradigm or NEP (Dunlap, 2008; Dunlap and van Liere, 1978; Dunlap et al., 2000). Results show that while the vast majority of respondents (88.1%) scored relatively moderately on general pro-environmental orientation, about the same number of respondents (87.9%) scored relatively highly in terms of awareness of event-related sustainability issues. These figures show that, even without being environmentalists themselves, people are aware that events do cause environmental and social impacts. More specifically they are quite sensitive to issues regarding waste, water and energy consumption, transportation and food consumption.

The big surprise? People want to know what is going on behind the scenes. To the question whether they were willing to be informed about the environmental impact of the events they are visiting, the majority of respondents answered positively. Respondents also preferred information on what was being done to reduce the impact (e.g. how much energy is saved) instead of information on how high the impact was (e.g. how much energy is consumed). The positive attitude by the majority of respondents about receiving information is important. Information is the first step in a chain leading to the involvement of visitors and clients in enhancing the sustainability of events.

Additionally, about 70% of respondents confirmed their willingness to actively contribute to reduce the impacts caused by the events they are visiting. Only 13% did not want to get personally involved, while 16% were unsure. Sharing information on achieved impact reductions strongly enhanced respondents' willingness to contribute to sustainability efforts, while only giving information on how high (or low) the impact was did not seem to have any influence on the willingness of the event visitor to join the effort towards sustainability. In this sense, visitors seem to be led by the example set by the organizer.

Several options on how to contribute to reducing impacts were offered to the respondents. Among the most popular were paperless promotion, correspondence and ticketing; changing from individual to shared and public transportation; as well as travelling by train instead of plane whenever possible. Of course, the choice to use public transport instead of a personal vehicle might also be influenced by other motives than contributing to a more sustainable event. It may, for example, be the cheapest option. However, it is important to note that the attendees' willingness to participate in sustainability initiatives is essential to achieving sustainable events, alongside the efforts and contributions made by the organizer. In this sense, it is encouraging that a large majority of respondents – when properly solicited – were willingly to cooperate.

A further encouraging fact for everyone involved in planning, organizing and hosting sustainable events is that results show that efforts made towards a more sustainable approach will pay off in a higher level of satisfaction among visitors. In the research described here satisfaction was measured by describing two scenarios for a congress event, where five aspects were examined in terms of sustainability. These five aspects were chosen from the event visitor's perspective and therefore included only areas that are visible and easily understandable for an event visitor. These areas were: promotion, invitation and ticketing procedures, transportation options, food and beverages provided at the event, and the way additional information was distributed. Even though using scenarios as a research method has its limitations, the responses were so clearly skewed in favour of more sustainable events that the conclusion seems unavoidable. Attendees' satisfaction is indeed positively affected by sustainable choices (53% vs. 81% satisfied customers). In particular, respondents' satisfaction was increased by good connections to public transport and the offer of organic, fair-trade and locally produced food. The online distribution of event-related information packs rather than paper brochures also contributed to a higher average level of satisfaction.

The research conducted showed that the vast majority of event visitors do have a high level of awareness about event (environmental) impacts. It also demonstrated that the majority of them are willing to be informed about these impacts and that two out of three visitors do not exclude themselves from the responsibility of reducing impacts when they know that action has already been taken by the organizers. Moreover, respondents' satisfaction is significantly higher when they are asked to imagine themselves visiting an event that has clear sustainability policies as compared to one that does not.

Indeed, event sustainability is not just the obligation of event organizers and their subcontractors throughout the supply chain – it also involves the consumer. Additionally, rather than trying to shield attendees from their responsibility in making events sustainable, event organizers should ask for their cooperation, as such action enhances the satisfaction of the attendee with an event. In short, there is definitely a market out there for sustainable events.

Since 2010, the year of the research summarized above, awareness for environmental and social issues in general and specifically at events has been increasing. As Yeoman (2013) observes, one of the consumer trends shaping the future of festivals and events is the rise of the ethical consumer. Calvo-Soraluze et al. (2015) concur that there is a new consumer with new demands calling for new business models in the events sector. In line with these observations, events known for their sustainable values such as Boom in Portugal, the Paleo festival in Switzerland and Roskilde in Denmark continue to grow and attract a loyal audience (De Brito and Terzieva, 2016).

The value system of consumers is shifting with more weight being given to 'caring and sharing' and participation. Consumers expect brands to care and take a position regarding civic issues (Trendwatching.com, 2015). At the same time consumers do not want to just be spectators. They want to be involved. Sometimes they go as far as taking the initiative and compel brands to follow their lead. For instance, the summer of 2015 was marked by the 'biggest refugee crisis since the Second World War' (Kingsley, 2015), and after visiting a refugee camp in Calais, a group of young people in the Netherlands approached several summer festivals so they could collect the camping materials left behind by festival visitors. In less than one week the group had managed to get commitments from two well-established festivals in the Netherlands (Lowlands and Mysteryland) and set up a website and a Facebook page to get further support for their project (Stichting Doneer je Deken, n.d.). In their first collection they managed to arrange the logistics and manpower to inspect, separate and collect 250 air mattresses, 60 tents and 50 sleeping bags (van Doorn, 2015).

Research has revealed that 95% of the population of the 28 European member states believes protecting the environment to be important (Eurobarometer, 2014). In the US, researchers have found about 70% of Americans consider the environment when they shop, but at the same time 50% feel overwhelmed with the environmental messages (Dailey, 2013). Research done specifically on event consumers has also shown that there is now a significant segment of European festival-goers (28%) that like to eat vegetarian food (EFA, 2014).

These findings illustrate that there is ample room for events to involve the audience and the general consumer in sustainability issues. In fact, embracing causes in an authentic way can also be a path to targeting new customer segments. In the current digital era, all kinds of data can be analysed to learn more about the wishes and wants of the consumer. It can start with simply asking feedback from consumers, initiating the dialogue on what are the sustainability/humanitarian causes/issues they most care about, and how they would like to be involved. There are still very few companies that add a feedback form or use social media feedback to either solicit suggestions or inform customers about sustainability initiatives (Yeldar and the Global Reporting Initiative, 2011). Thus, there is a significantly active and large latent group of caring consumers (for the environment and for others) that needs to be better understood, listened to and properly addressed by events (Cavagnaro and Curiel, 2012).

The Sustainable Events Market

- Consumers are more and more aware of the environmental and social impacts of the modern economy.
- Consumers' willingness to act in order to reduce negative environmental impacts is increasing, too.
- In general, the market for ethical, organic, local products and services is growing rapidly.

Case Study 12. 5 – Greening the Olympic Games

Though sustainability requires that positive impacts are achieved both on the people (through social impacts) and planet (through environmental impacts), the main focus of many sustainability initiatives is on lessening the impact on the natural environment. The event industry makes no exception. Lesjø (2000) analysed the first 'green' Winter Games in Lillehammer 1994. Even though the concept of 'Green Games' was not included in the original bidding requirements, disputes with environmental groups emerged in the planning process about the future of the Lillehammer region. Plans were changed and new policies introduced to develop an environment-friendly agenda based on four pillars of action: minimizing the use of natural material; conserving energy in heating and cooling systems; developing a recycling scheme for the Winter Games region; and avoiding 'visual pollution' by appropriately embedding all facilities in the surrounding landscape.

Since Lillehammer, major steps have been taken to maintain a 'green' image for both the summer and winter Olympic Games. Beijing 2008 and Vancouver 2010 have strengthened the focus on the environment, while the Olympic 2012 Games in London were designed to be the most sustainable games to date. Non-governmental organizations (NGOs) were involved from the beginning; as *Towards a One Planet 2012*, the sustainability master plan for London 2012, states, it is based on the initiative *One Planet Living* by the World Wildlife Fund (WWF) and BioRegional (LOCOG, 2009a). The plan addresses five key themes: minimizing negative impacts such as greenhouse gas emissions; reducing waste throughout the entire project; reducing negative impact on wildlife and their habitats; enhancing positive impacts, such as promotion of diversity, creation of new employment and business opportunities; and inspiring residents of the United Kingdom to take up physical activity and maintain a healthy lifestyle. It includes one economic aim (employment opportunities) and one social aim (healthy lifestyle) within its environmental goals.

This attempt at integration of the three dimensions of CSR (people, planet and profit) is also visible in other guidelines that have been published to support the organizer's aims. *The Sustainability Sourcing Code*, for example, explains strategies in procurement and unites 'internationally acceptable environmental, social and ethical guidelines and standards' for LOCOG's internal buyers as well as for their suppliers and licensees (LOCOG, 2009b). As monitoring, evaluating and reporting is paramount in the process of sustainable event management, the Commission for a Sustainable London 2012 has been set up as an independent body to fulfil this role.

Case Study Questions

1   Do you consider the London 2012 Olympic Games 'sustainable'? Justify your answer.
2   Which environmental, social and economic issues should be considered in planning the 2020 Olympic Games?
3   Look at the lists of issues from question 2 above. How do you suggest measuring the impact of the Olympic Games on these issues?
4   Look again at the lists of issues from question 2 above. How could positive impacts be maximized and negative impacts minimized?

Chapter Summary

Though the event industry has joined the sustainability challenge only in the last few years, progress has been swift and is still accelerating. In this sense the coming years are going to be crucial. Consider, for example, that in 2012, event-related guidelines for sustainability have been published by the Global Reporting Initiative while the 2012 London Olympics have set a worldwide example of a successful sustainable event. The sensibility of the market, already present even in economically difficult times, will in all probability only be enhanced by these developments. Sustainability therefore offers not only a challenge to the event industry but also an opportunity to be seized with both hands.

Review Questions

1.   What is the relevance of CSR and sustainable development for the event industry?
2.   Which are the main indicators for sustainable events?
3.   Which arguments could you put forward to convince the government officials in your city or the manager of the event company you are working for to organize sustainable events?
4.   Imagine you are involved in a heated debate with someone who is very sceptical about sustainability and sustainable events. Develop three arguments you could use to convince this person.
5.   Using an event that has been recently organized in your home country as an example, critically evaluate whether it was a sustainable event or not.

Additional resources

Books / Book Chapters / Journal Articles

Dredge, D. and Whitford, M. (2010). Policy for sustainable and responsible festivals and events: institutionalisation of a new paradigm – a response. *Journal of Policy Research in Tourism, Leisure and Events*, *2*(1): 1–13. This article takes a broad agenda on events policy research that embraces a wider range of epistemologies, ontologies and methodologies.

Freeman, R.E. (2008). Managing for stakeholders. In: T.L. Beauchamp, N. Bowie and D. Arnold (eds), *Ethical Theory and Business* (8th edn) (pp. 56–68). New Jersey: Prentice Hall. A useful guide to involving stakeholders in ethical business operations.

Getz, D. (2009). Policy for sustainable and responsible festivals and events: institutionalization of a new paradigm. *Journal of Policy Research in Tourism, Leisure and Events*, *1*(1): 61–78. Provides specific advice on what is needed to embed the new sustainable and responsible events paradigm in public policy.

Laing, J. and Frost, W. (2010). How green was my festival: exploring challenges and opportunities associated with staging green events. *International Journal of Hospitality Management*, *29*(2): 261–7. This paper considers some of the challenges involved in incorporating green messages into an event theme.

McDonough, W. and Braungart, M. (2002). *Cradle to Cradle: Remaking the Way We Make Things*. New York: North Point Press. A manifesto for a radically different philosophy and practice of manufacture and environmentalism.

Useful Websites

www.co-operative.coop/PageFiles/416561607/Ethical-Consumer-Markets-Report-2012.pdf – A site featuring the 2012 edition of the Ethical Consumers Market Report for the UK market.

www.eventsustainability.co.uk/pages/index.php – The objective of the eventsustainability.com website is to share resources, tools and ideas with the aim of increasing the positive impact events have on our economy, society and environment.

www.sustainable.org/ – A website originally developed in the 1990s in the US by the Sustainable Communities Network. It hosts information on sustainability, including advice and further resources on how to plan a sustainable event.

References

Bonnici, O. (2015). Exciting times ahead for culture, *The Times of Malta*, Sunday, January 18, 2015 [online]. Retrieved from www.timesofmalta.com/articles/view/20150118/opinion/Exciting-times-ahead-for-culture.552303

Bowdin, G.A.J., Allen, J., O'Toole, W., Harris, R. and McDonnell, I. (2006). *Events Management* (2nd edn). Oxford: Butterworth-Heinemann Elsevier.

BSI British Standards Institution (2007). *BSI British Standards launches new standard for managing a more sustainable event*. British Standards Institute [online]. Retrieved from www.

bsigroup.com/en/About-BSI/News-Room/BSI-News – Content/Disciplines/Sustainability/BS8901-Launch

BSI British Standards Institution (2010). *BSI 8901 – Sustainable Event Management Systems for Events* [online]. Retrieved from www.bsigroup.com/en/BSI – UK/Assessment-and-Certification-services/Management-systems/Standards - and-Schemes/BS-8901/?sb=1

Butler, R.W. (1989). Alternative tourism: pious hope or Trojan horse? *World Leisure & Recreation, 31*(4): 9–17.

Butler, R.W. (1990). Tourism, heritage and sustainable development. In J.G. Nelson and S. Woodley (eds), *Heritage, Conservation and Sustainable Development* (pp. 49–66). Waterloo: Heritage Resources Centre, University of Waterloo.

Calvo-Soraluze, J., de Brito, M.P. and San Salvador Del Valle, R. (2015). Making waves in events: from trends to future competences. In Making Waves in Events, International Conference on Events, Sept 7–9, Macao, China.

Carroll, A.B. (1991). The pyramid of corporate social responsibility: toward the moral management of organizational stakeholders. *Business Horizons, 34*(4): 39–48.

Cavagnaro, E. and Curiel, G.H. (2012). *The Three Levels of Sustainability*. Sheffield: Greenleaf Publishing.

Dailey, W. (2013). *Green Gap Trend Tracker*, Cone Releases, Cone Communications [online]. Retrieved from www.conecomm.com/2013-green-gap-trend-tracker-1>

Dávid, L. (2009). Environmental impacts of events. In: R. Raj and J. Musgrave (eds), *Event Management and Sustainabilty* (pp. 67–75). Oxfordshire: CAB International.

De Brito, M.P. and Terzieva, L. (2016). Critical factors to generate social and environmental value: a comparative study of festivals. *Research in Hospitality Management* (under revision).

Dunlap, R.E. (2008). The new environmental paradigm scale: from marginality to worldwide use. *Journal of Environmental Education, 40*(1): 3–18.

Dunlap, R.E. and van Liere, K. (1978). The New Environmental Paradigm – a proposed measuring instrument and preliminary results. *Journal of Environmental Education, 9*(1): 10–19.

Dunlap, R.E., van Liere, K., Mertig, A.G. and Jones, R.E. (2000). Measuring endorsement of the new ecological paradigm: a revised NEP scale. *Journal of Social Issues, 56*(3): 425–42.

Edwards, A.R. (2005). *The Sustainability Revolution, Portrait of a Paradigm Shift*. Gabriola Island (Canada): New Society Publishers.

EFA (2014). *Showguide* [online]. Retrieved from http://issuu.com/mondiale/docs/efa2014_showguide

Elkington, J. (1997). *Cannibals with Forks: The Triple Bottom Line of 21st Century Business*. Oxford: Capstone.

Eurobarometer (2014). *Attitudes of European Citizens Towards the Environment* [online]. Retrieved from http://ec.europa.eu/public_opinion/archives/ebs/ebs_416_sum_en.pdf

European Capitals of Culture (n.d.). [online]. Retrieved from http://ec.europa.eu/programmes/creative-europe/actions/capitals-culture_en.htm

European Commission (2014). *European Capitals of Culture (ECoC) 2020–2033 Guidelines for the cities' own evaluations of the results of each ECoC* [online]. Retrieved from http://ec.europa.eu/programmes/creative-europe/actions/documents/ecoc/city-own-guide_en.pdf

EU (1992). *Treaty on European Union*. Official Journal C 191 [online]. Retrieved from http://eur-lex.europa.eu/en/treaties/dat/11992M/htm/11992M.html

Getz, D. (2007). *Event Studies: Theory, Research and Policy for Planned Events*. Oxford: Butterworth-Heinemann/Elsevier.

Getz, D. (2009). Policy for sustainable and responsible festivals and events: institutionalization of a new paradigm. *Journal of Policy Research in Tourism, Leisure and Events*, *1*(1): 61–78.

Global Sustainable Tourism Council (2015). What are the GSTC Criteria? [online]. Retrieved from www.gstcouncil.org/en/gstc-criteria/sustainable-tourism-gstc- criteria.html

GRI (Global Reporting Initiative) (2007). Making the switch [online]. Retrieved from www.global reporting.org/NR/rdonlyres/D8AD5DDE-546A-4D5D-9617-20C75B242AAC/450/Makingthe Switch.pdf

GRI (2012). Sustainability reporting guidelines & event organizers sector supplement [online]. Retrieved from www.globalreporting.org/resourcelibrary/G3-1-English-Event-Organizers-Sector-Supplement.pdf

GRI (2013). *Sustainability reporting G4 guidelines* [online]. Retrieved from www.globalreport-ing.org/resourcelibrary/GRIG4-Part1-Reporting-Principles-and-Standard-Disclosures.pdf

Idowu, S.O. and Towler, B.A. (2004). A comparative study of the contents of Corporate Social Responsibility reports of UK companies. *Management of Environmental Quality*, *15*(4): 420–37.

ISO (International Organization for Standardization) (2012a). ISO 20121 – Sustainable events [online]. Retrieved from www.iso.org/iso/iso20121, 17 April 2015.

ISO (2012b). Sustainable events with ISO 20121 [online]. Retrieved from www.iso.org/iso/sustainable_events_iso_2012.pdf, 17 April 2015.

Jackson, T. (2005). *Motivating Sustainable Consumption: A Review of Evidence on Consumer Behaviour and Behavioural Change*. London: Policy Studies Institute.

Jamali, D. (2006). Insights into triple bottom line integration from a learning organization per-spective. *Business Process Management Journal*, *12*(6): 809–21.

Jones, P., Comfort, D. and Hillier, D. (2005). Corporate Social Responsibility and the UK top ten retailers. *International Journal of Retail and Distribution Management*, *33*(12): 882–92.

Kingsley, P. (2015). Ten truths about Europe's migrant crisis, *The Guardian* [online]. Retrieved from www.theguardian.com/uk-news/2015/aug/10/10-truths-about-europes-refugee-crisis

Lambert, G. (2013). Event sustainability management – ISO 20121 passes 2012 Olympic Games test [online]. Retrieved from www.iso.org/iso/home/news_index/news_archive/news.htm?Refid=Ref1690, 17 April 2015.

Laybourn, P. (2002). *Sustainable Exhibition Industry Project: A Waste-Focused First Step Towards Sustainable Development by the UK's Exhibition Industry*. Birmingham: Midlands Envi-ronmental Business Club Ltd [online]. Retrieved from www.mebconline.com/Portals/0/PDF/Sexi.pdf

Lesjø, J.H. (2000). Lillehammer 1994: planning, figurations and the 'green' winter games. *International Review for the Sociology of Sport*, *35*(3): 281–93.

LOCOG (London Organising Committee of the Olympic Games and Paralympic Games) (2009a). *Towards a One Planet 2010, London 2012 Sustainability Plan* (2nd edn). London: LOCOG. [Online] retrieved from: www.london2012.com/documents/locog-publications/lon-don-2012-sustainability-plan.pdf

LOCOG (2009b). *LOCOG Sustainable Sourcing Code* (2nd edn). London: LOCOG. [Online] retrieved from www.london2012.com/documents/locog-publications/sustainable-sourcing-code.pdf

Maas, K. (2009). *Corporate Social Performance: From Output Measurement to Impact Mea-surement* (doctoral thesis). Rotterdam: Erasmus University Rotterdam [online]. Retrieved from http://repub.eur.nl/res/pub/17627/EPS2009182STR9058922250Maas.pdf

Mair, J. and Whitford, M. (2013). An exploration of events research: event topics, themes and emerging trends. *International Journal of Event and Festival Management*, *4*(1): 6–30.

McDonough, W. and Partners (1992). *The Hannover Principles – Design for Sustainability.* Charlottesville: William McDonough Architect [online]. Retrieved from www.mcdonough.com/principles.pdf

MPI Foundation (2013). *The Economic Impact of the UK Meeting and Event Industry* [online] Retrieved from: www.mpiweb.it/documents/MPI_UKEIS_Final_Report.pdf

Musgrave, J. and Raj, R. (2009). Introduction to a conceptual framework for sustainable events. In: R. Raj and J. Musgrave (eds), *Event Management and Sustainability* (pp. 1–12). Oxford: CAB International.

NewZealand.govt.nz (n.d.). About us. Retrieved from http://sustainability.govt.nz/more/about-us

Plog, S.C. (1974). Why destination areas rise and fall in popularity. *Cornell Hotel and Restaurant Quarterly, 14*(4): 55–8.

Postma, A. (2013). *When the Tourists Flew in: Critical Encounters in the Development of Tourism.* PhD thesis. Groningen: Rijksuniversiteit Groningen, Faculty of Spatial Sciences.

Schmidheiny, S. (1992). *Changing Course.* Cambridge: MIT Press.

SGS United Kingdom Ltd (2012). Case Study: Coca-Cola GB Gains ISO 20121 for London 2012 [online]. Retrieved from www.sgs.com/~/media/Global/Documents/Brochures/SGS-SSC-Coca-Cola%20GB%20gains%20ISO%2020121-A4-EN-12-09.pdf, accessed 17 April 2015.

Sherman, W.R. (2009). *Making Triple Bottom Line Reporting Comparable: Adoption of the GRI G3 Framework.* Conference paper for 2009 Oxford Business & Economics Conference (OBEC) [online]. Retrieved from www.gcbe.us/2009_OBEC/data/W.%20Richard%20Sherman.doc, accessed 20 August 2010.

Smith-Christensen, C. (2009). Sustainability as a concept within events. In: R. Raj and J. Musgrave (eds), *Event Management and Sustainability* (pp. 22–31). Oxford: CAB International.

Stichting Doneer je Deken (n.d.). Over Doner je Deken [online]. Retrieved from http://doneerjedeken.org/over-doneer-je-deken/

Stichting Kulturele Haadstêd 2018 (2013). *Leeuwarden-Ljouwert's application for European Capital of Culture 2018* [online]. Retrieved from www.2018.nl

Sustainability New Zealand (2003). Sustainable development for New Zealand: programme of action. [online]. Retrieved from https://www.msd.govt.nz/documents/about-msd-and-our-work/publications-resources/archive/2003-sustainable-development.pdf

Sutton, P.W. (2007). *The Environment: A Sociological Introduction.* Cambridge: Polity Press.

Trendwatching.com (2015). *Consumer Trends and Insights* [online]. Retrieved from Trend watching.com

UN (1992). *Agenda 21* [online]. Retrieved from www.un.org/esa/sustdev/documents/agenda21/english/agenda21toc.htm

UN United nations (2013). *The Way Forward: A Disability Inclusive Development Agenda Towards 2015 and Beyond, Report to the Secretary-General, A/68/95* [online]. Retrieved from www.un.org/disabilities/default.asp?id=1590

Valletta Foundation (2012). Imagine 18: Final Application for the Title of European Capital of Culture 2018 in Malta, Valletta 2018 Foundation, September 2012 [online]. Retrieved from http://valletta2018.org/the-bid-book-story/

Valetta 2018 Foundation (2015). *Valetta 2018 European Capital of Culture: Highlights of 2014* [online]. Retrieved from http://valletta2018.org/wp-content/uploads/2015/01/Highlights-of-2014.pdf

Valetta Green Festival (2014). [online]. Retrieved from www.visitmalta.com/nl/event-details/2014-5/valletta-green-festival-7609

Van Doorn (2015, August, 26). Vrienden sturen tenten Lowlands naar vluchtelingen. *Metro* [online]. Retrieved from http://www.metronieuws.nl/binnenland/2015/08/vrienden-sturen-tenten-lowlands-naar-vluchtelingen

WBCSD (World Business Council for Sustainable Development) (2000). *Eco-Efficiency: More Value with Less Impact*. Geneva: WBCSD.

WRAP (2012). Final Report. London 2012 legacy transfer report: recycling communications [online]. Retrieved from www.wrap.org.uk/sites/files/wrap/WRAP%20London%202012%20 Legacy%20Transfer%20Report%20-%20Recycling%20Communications%20Coca%20Cola.pdf, accessed 17 April 2015.

Yeldar, R. and the Global Reporting Initiative (2011). *Trends in Online Sustainability Reporting 2009–10* [online]. Retrieved from www.globalreporting.org/resourcelibrary/Trends-in-online-sustainability-reporting.pdf

Yeoman, I. (2013). A futurist's thoughts on consumer trends shaping future festivals and events. *International Journal of Event and Festival Management*, 4(3): 249–60.

A Strategic Approach to International Event Tourism

13

Adrian Devine and Frances Devine

Learning Objectives

By reading this chapter students should be able to:

- Understand what is meant by event tourism
- Discuss the short-term and long-term tourism impacts of events
- Appreciate why countries must adopt a strategic approach to event tourism
- Understand what is involved in developing a strategic approach to event tourism.

Introduction

Whitford (2009), in her analysis of event policy, discusses how the popularity of events and the positive association attached to them means they are coveted by governments around the world. The tourism potential of events is one of the main economic reasons why governments are so keen to support them. This is summed up by Roberts (2004), who discusses how towns, cities and countries bid for and host events primarily because they attract visitors and their money. In fact, Roberts (2004) goes as far as to state that the economy of most cities and holiday resorts would stutter without a stream of major and minor events. However, it would be naive for a destination to simply jump on the 'event tourism bandwagon' and assume that an event will generate tourism benefits. To maximize the tourism potential of an event it is essential that tourism impacts are planned properly. In this chapter the authors will discuss why the host destination must adopt a strategic approach to event tourism, and the tenets of this approach, before applying its use to the region of Northern Ireland in the case study.

Short-Term Tourism Impacts

Getz (2008: 406) defined event tourism as 'the development and marketing of events for tourism and economic development purposes'. Building on this definition Smith (2012) discusses how events can assist a destination both in the short term and long term. The most obvious short-term impact would be increased visitor numbers to the host destination. Duffy and Mair (2015) discuss how festivals and events have strong tourism potential because they can create a 'product', enliven a destination, animate static attractions and promise a glimpse into the authentic culture of a place. Events can also entice people to extend their stay or spend more money at the destination (Chalip, 2004). To illustrate this, the authors will use a number of examples from Northern Ireland, the country featured in the case study later in the chapter.

In 2011 Northern Ireland's capital city, Belfast, hosted the MTV European Music Awards (EMAs), which placed Northern Ireland firmly on the world music stage. To maximize tourism spend and lengthen visitor stay, Belfast leveraged this event by organizing Belfast Music Week alongside the MTV EMAs. Combined, they created 8,000 bed nights in Belfast hotels and the total economic impact for the city was £22 million. The following year the coastal town of Portrush hosted the Irish Open Golf Tournament, which provided another boost for Northern Ireland's tourism industry. Over 130,000 tickets were sold for this three-day event, generating £9.5 million. The National Tourism Organisation helped fund this event and their return on investment was £1:£4.29, which meant that for every £1 they invested in this event the Northern Ireland economy made £4.29 profit. Building on the success of the Irish Open, Northern Ireland secured the rights to host the first three stages of another prestigious international sports event, the Giro d'Italia 2014. This 'Grand Depart' attracted 227,000 national and international spectators. The tourism impact was £12.7m, which equated to a return of investment of £1:£2.45.

Long-Term Tourism Impacts

The longer-term tourism effects which Smith (2012) referred to relate primarily to post-event demand, as events can provide a marketing opportunity which some destinations use to rebrand and reimage the area (Dredge and Whitford, 2010). This point is highlighted by Quinn (2013: 149) when she states that 'even the most cursory analysis of any number of national tourism strategies shows how strongly festival and events have come to feature in destination marketing initiatives'. Raj et al. (2013) argue that events have become part of an image-making process playing a critical role in positioning destinations against their competitors. They go on to discuss how events can be marketed to reach niche as well as mass audiences, not simply through increasing visitor numbers at events, but by creating powerful associations of the destination in the minds of visitors. This links into Hall (1992) and Ritchie's (1984) argument that events are an effective enhancer of destination image.

The idea that a major event can showcase a state or city was first empirically measured by Richie and Smith (1991), who identified an international increase in awareness of Calgary as a result of hosting the 1998 Winter Olympic Games. They found that Europeans' awareness of Calgary increased significantly in the build-up to the Games and during the event. However, there was a slight drop-off in the year following the Games, suggesting decay is a legitimate concern and challenge to sustaining an event's image-related benefits. But this was not the case in Webb and Magnussen's (2002) study of the Welsh hosting of the 1999 Rugby World Cup. Their initial research phase estimated that the short-term impact of the Rugby World Cup was £82.3 million. A follow-up survey of non-Welsh respondents conducted in 2002 indicated that 44% of the sample had subsequently returned to Wales and 77% had recommended Wales as a place to visit. However, it is just not those who attend that can be influenced by an event. For instance, Hede (2005) studied the effects of Australian media telecasts during the Athens 2004 Summer Olympic Games. The results indicated that 39% of the sample had improved their overall impression of Greece as a tourist destination and a place to visit. This would support Avraham and Ketter's (2008) argument that the media can play an important role in shaping the image of both the event and the host destination.

In recent years an increasing number of emerging economies have used events to raise their tourism profile. Grix (2012) for instance discusses how India's staging of the Commonwealth Games in 2010 and Brazil's hosting of both the 2014 FIFA Football World Cup and 2016 Summer Olympic and Paralympic Games are examples of emerging economies ready to announce they have finally arrived on the international stage. More recently, small Gulf states, such as Qatar and Bahrain, have become interested in staging mega events, with Qatar scheduled to host the 2022 FIFA Football World Cup. It is not just emerging countries that use events for reimaging purposes. Foley et al. (2012), for instance, discuss how Germany used the 2006 FIFA World Cup to alter perceptions of their nation by developing an outward-facing strategy that had at its heart the slogan 'A Time to Make Friends'. The campaign had the full backing of the German Chancellor, Angela Merkel, who described the 2006 World Cup as 'a unique opportunity for Germany to present herself as a hospitable, joyful and modern nation, bursting with ideas' (Florek et al., 2008: 203). The findings from Florek et al.'s (2008) study would suggest that this campaign was a success, with the respondents describing Germany as a friendly multicultural place.

According to Grix (2012) the systematic and purposeful leveraging of a mega event to alter a nation's image is easier for countries which suffer or have suffered from a poor national image. Lepp and Gibson's (2011) study of South Africa lends support to this argument. They discuss how during the apartheid period (1948–94) the state was increasingly characterized as a rogue nation and was the subject of international boy-cotts, embargos and sanctions. Clearly, at the end of the apartheid period, a significant challenge to the 'new' South Africa and its iconic President Mandela was reimaging the nation. As a response South Africa placed major sporting events at the centre of its reimaging strategy. According to Lepp and Gibson (2011) this strategy has been a success and the image of South Africa has improved on the world stage.

CRITICAL THINKING EXERCISE

During 2015–16 major event organizers such as FIFA and the International Association of Athletics Federations (IAAF) were engulfed in scandals con-cerning corruption and the abuse of power. What are the likely risks to the hosting of mega events if these issues persist?

A Strategic Approach to Event Tourism

Following on from this discussion on the short-term and long-term tourism impacts of events, it is no surprise that the competition to host events has intensified in recent years. According to Foley et al. (2012), however, the tourism potential of events are often exaggerated, and tourism figures are inflated in bid documents. Building on this argument, Smith (2012) discusses how too many destinations simply assume that events will guarantee them increased tourism receipts and positive exposure. This point was reiterated by Getz (2012: 339), who states that 'staging an event will not automatically make the host destination more attractive to tourists'. For instance, the anticipated rise in tourism demand did not materialize after the 2004 Olympic Games in Athens (Kissoudi, 2010). If not properly managed an event can, in fact, have a nega-tive impact on the image of the host destination. For example, the protests in Sao Paulo, Brazil, against the hosting of the 2014 FIFA World Cup dominated the news in the weeks leading up to this mega event. Such images coupled with stories of inequal-ity projected Brazil and its tourism product in a negative light.

In order to maximize their return on investment, the host destination must adopt a strategic approach to event tourism. The World Tourism Organization emphasized this in their *Practical Guide to Tourism Destinations* (2007, cited by Quinn, 2013) in which it discusses the tourism potential of events under a number of headings including: brand builders, generators of business growth, tactical levers and the need for vehicles for local pride and community building. However, too many countries still take event tourism for granted and, according to Smith (2012), tourism is sometimes lazily used to justify events. This was highlighted by Bramwell (1993) when he analysed how the English city of Sheffield promoted the 1991 World Student Games (WSG). Before, during and after the 1991 WSG, Sheffield City Council stated its desire to use the Games to generate and promote tourism. However, despite this commitment, Bramwell (1993: 17) suggests that 'there was no clear view of how the World Student Games facilities could help the city's tourism industry'. According to Bramwell (1993: 18) during the planning of the WSG and in the immediate aftermath of the Games there was no strategic plan at local or national level that outlined 'specific objectives and precise mechanisms that would ensure long tourism benefits'.

This is in contrast to how the UK strategically leveraged the 2012 Summer Olympic Games in London. In total 685,000 people attended officially ticketed events. According to VisitBritain (2013) these visitors generated a spend of £925 million, with the average spend per visit amounting to £1,350. During the Games, London hotels saw an average occupancy of 88.5% and total revenue per available room increased by 3.8%. Local visitor attractions also benefited, with the Victoria and Albert Museum for example recording a 15% increase in visitors. With Britain's image and reputation around the world riding high after the Games, VisitBritain seized the moment to turn viewers into visitors and rolled out a post-Games marketing campaign the day after the Games ended called 'GREAT Britain'. The campaign showcased the very best of Britain, promoting culture, heritage, countryside and sport. According to Sandie Dawe, Chief Executive at VisitBritain, the London 2012 Games presented a great opportunity which they had planned to strategically exploit: 'The long-term benefits of an event do simply not fall into the lap of the host nation – we started work on our tourism strategy as soon as London was announced as the host city seven years prior to the event and have ramped up our marketing and PR around the world to capitalise on it' (VisitBritain, 2013).

According to Getz (2013) London's approach to event tourism was not unique and merely built on what some countries have been doing since the early 1990s to facilitate the development of event tourism. For instance, Barcelona is one city that has pursued strategic tourism initiatives in association with a major event. Alongside using the 1992 Olympic Games to regenerate urban infrastructure and derelict land, Barcelona used the event to 'launch its tourism strategy for the next century' (Glyptis, 1991: 179). Australia also used the 2000 Olympic Games to enhance its overall market position, to encourage repeat visits and to build new relationships amongst a fragmented tourism sector (Faulkner et al., 2001). Malaysia too has tied major events to the development of its tourism industry (Van der Westhuizen, 2004: 1284). The successful 'Visit Malaysia Year' was timed to coincide with the staging of the 1998 Commonwealth Games in Kuala Lumpur, and it increased tourism revenue by 190% (Van der Westhuizen, 2004, cited by Smith, 2012).

The common thread that links these four international examples is strategic planning. Event tourism is highly competitive and if a country wants to target event tourism then it must plan accordingly. A strategic approach would involve analysing the unique geographical, economic, political and social characteristics of a country which would help identify the type of events it should and could target. However, the authors have identified five generic issues that a country should also consider when planning for event tourism: seasonality, strategic fit, industry development, funding and collaboration.

Seasonality

According to Fletcher (2012) seasonality is a major problem for tourism destinations, creating labour force and capacity utilization issues. A strategic approach to event tourism should address the issue of seasonality by targeting events that attract visitors during off-peak periods (Chalip, 2004). This links into Getz's (2007) and Jago et al.'s (2003) argument that a country should aim for a balanced portfolio of events – bidding for and organizing events of different types and scale at different times of the year. According to Higham (2005) a 'balanced portfolio approach' is also more likely to appeal to wider market segments and encourage regional spread. This view is shared by Zammit (2015), who discussed how the National Tourism Authority in Malta used local events such as the Hal Kirkop Food Festival to spread the benefits of tourism to parts of the island not traditionally affected by mass tourism.

Strategic Fit

In terms of marketing and branding there must be a strategic fit between the host destination and the type of event to be organized (Masterman, 2009). For instance, if a country is blessed with beautiful beaches it must prioritize events that would promote these natural assets to potential visitors. According to Harrison-Hill and Chalip (2006) it is simply not enough, however, to match an event with the destination. The attributes and benefits that marketers seek to transfer from the event to the destination brand need to be explicitly articulated in marketing communications, and this too requires skilful negotiation and strategic planning. For instance, when the Republic of Ireland hosted the Ryder Cup in 2006 they used the opening ceremony to showcase the best of Irish culture to an international audience by including Irish dancing and traditional music.

Industry Development

A strategic approach to event tourism should also consider industry development. Event tourism is after all a by-product of an event and, in the long term, event tourism will only be sustained if the destination develops a reputation for hosting quality events. The event industry is very competitive and to attract an international audience a country must invest in developing the expertise, competence and professionalism of local event organizers. This links into what Getz (2013) refers to as the facilitation role, which includes key areas such as training, education and the sharing of good practice.

Funding

Bidding for and hosting events costs money, and a strategic approach to event tourism would be meaningless unless consideration is given to how events will be funded. In an open economy the private sector will often take the lead but in some instances the return on investment for a particular event may not be enough to attract sufficient private sector interest, and public sector intervention is required. This can take many forms, for example grants, subsidies and sponsorship. To administer event funding some countries and regions have gone as far as to establish an events development unit either within an existing government agency or as a stand-alone entity, an example of the latter being the Victorian Major Events Corporation, which brings in events for the Australian state of Victoria. Whatever approach is taken, the funding criteria must align with the objectives set for event tourism. Spending must also be monitored as this is public money and those spending the money must be held accountable for their actions and performance.

Collaboration

A strategic approach to event tourism will require collaboration, communication and coordination between key stakeholders. For instance, at national level a joined-up approach is required to ensure that towns and cities within the country are able to bid for international events without unnecessarily damaging and competing against each other. This requires mechanics to be in place to encourage cross-government support. Local government and public agencies must also be consulted and committed to event tourism. The trade and professional organizations which represent tourism and events must recognize the mutual benefits to be gained from event tourism and communicate these to their respective members. Additionally, it is important to involve and inform the community so they too are aware of the benefits of event tourism.

Case Study 13.1 – A Strategic Approach to International Event Tourism in Northern Ireland

Northern Ireland is an example of a country that has adopted a strategic approach to event tourism. In 2010 the National Tourism Authority, Northern Ireland Tourism, was given national responsibility for events. In 2014 it published Northern Ireland's first National Events Strategy, and event tourism was at the core of this strategy. However, before discussing the content of this strategy the authors will first provide a brief insight into Northern

(Continued)

(Continued)

Ireland's political history, which will help to explain why Northern Ireland has targeted events and event tourism as a policy tool.

During 1968–98 Northern Ireland was a war zone with an on-going cycle of protest and violence fuelled by sectarian division and hatred. During this period, which is often referred to as 'the Troubles', over 3,600 people were killed and over 30,000 injured. Understandably this had an adverse impact on both tourism and events. The following quote from Kerr (2003: 105) sums up how difficult it was to market Northern Ireland as a tourist destination during the Troubles: 'Belfast became more famous for conflict than tourism; indeed it was once renowned as the Beirut of Western Europe.' In 1998 the Good Friday Agreement was signed and this provided a historic opportunity for the people of Northern Ireland to put aside the divisions and violence of the past and to move forward and build a stable future together. For those involved in tourism and events, the Good Friday Agreement generated a sense of relief and optimism, but they were also well aware of the challenges they faced. Northern Ireland has been forced to play 'catch-up' and to recover from what Baum (1995) described as the 'lost years'.

The National Tourism Strategy 2010–

In the 'post-Troubles' era, events have emerged as a major tourism policy instrument in Northern Ireland. According to Arlene Foster, the former government minister responsible for tourism, 'events are now part of Northern Ireland's tourism fabric'. This was reflected in the National Tourism Strategy 2010–20 which identified events as a key driver of tourism:

> The aim is to create the new Northern Ireland experience and get it on everyone's destination wish list ... Events have a key role to play in driving this ambition. Event-led short breaks is one of the key market segments. Events, whether home grown or major one-off international events, have the capability of showcasing the people and place on a global stage.

> Major global events in particular are able to fulfil the objective of showcasing Northern Ireland as a unique destination to live, work, study and visit. Events can provide a specific reason for visitors to come to Northern Ireland or extend their stay to attend a particular event. They can also

drive visitor numbers, generate increased spend and provide platforms for the visitor to interact with the local culture, local people and explore our scenic landscapes and cities. Events also have the capacity to enhance a visitor's experience of Northern Ireland and therefore positively change perceptions. (Tourism Strategy for Northern Ireland, 2010–20)

'Northern Ireland Home of Great Events – Events Strategic Vision 2014–2020'

In 2014 the Events Unit within Tourism Northern Ireland published Northern Ireland's first National Events Strategy entitled 'Northern Ireland Home of Great Events – Events Strategic Vision 2014–2020'. The vision was to make Northern Ireland known as the 'home of great events' and in doing so attract international visitors and media coverage. To this end the specific objectives of this strategic vision were to:

1   Create a sustainable visitor-inspired events future for Northern Ireland
2   Develop a progressive, diverse and cohesive events industry, attracting significant additional visitors and revenue into the economy of Northern Ireland
3   Bid for and attract high-profile, international-scale events to Northern Ireland that have the potential to showcase its landscapes, cities and characters in a positive light to audiences around the world
4   Develop events with international appeal/profile 'hosted' in Northern Ireland and drive the Northern Ireland brand by being built around key/major themes and demonstrating quality and authenticity
5   Create a culture of attending events within the domestic market.

Funding

Tourism Northern Ireland has two funding schemes in place to support its National Events Strategy:

1   The International Tourism Events Fund is a grant scheme which extends to three years. Under this scheme the Events Unit within Tourism Northern Ireland will also work with event organizers to develop their event to make it more sustainable.
2   The National Tourism Events Fund is administered as a sponsorship scheme.

(Continued)

(Continued)

Event tourism is at the core of both of these schemes. To be considered for either scheme an event must:

- be visitor-focused
- increase visitor numbers
- generate tourism spend e.g. accommodation and eating out and
- drive the Northern Ireland brand.

Structure

To help implement its National Events Strategy, Tourism Northern Ireland has also created an events structure (see Figure 13.1). This four-tier structure was introduced to help Tourism Northern Ireland categorize events applying for funding. However, it envisaged that the structure will also help ensure geographical coverage and calendar spread and encourage partnership across industry and stakeholders to deliver the overall vision for events in Northern Ireland. The following section will discuss each of the four tiers and what an event in each tier is expected to achieve.

Figure 13.1   Events structure 2014–20

1. Bidding for Global Events

The strategic vision was for Tourism Northern Ireland, in conjunction with key partners, to bid for/host at least one major, global-scale event each year. Bidding structures, including a Northern Ireland bidding group, have been set up to ensure this vision is realized. Tourism Northern Ireland's primary role will be to bring key partners together who have the strategic expertise and knowledge to identify major events which could showcase Northern Ireland on a world stage and drive visitor numbers and spend. Events identified for bidding should deliver key objectives including:

1   Showcase Northern Ireland's iconic landscapes and stand-out features
2   Highlight Northern Ireland's unique character and culture
3   Change perceptions of Northern Ireland as a place to live, work, study and visit
4   Have capacity to attract out-of-state visitors specifically for the event.
5   Generate significant visitor spend
6   Act as a focal point for marketing campaigns and activity in Northern Ireland, Republic of Ireland and Great Britain in particular
7   Act as a catalyst for wider industry to develop related products and embrace the opportunities presented
8   Act as a catalyst for bidding for other major events.

A global event which Northern Ireland is currently bidding to co-host with the Republic of Ireland is the 2023 Rugby World Cup. An event of this magnitude has huge tourism potential. In addition to the thousands of international visitors who would travel to watch the games, the Rugby World Cup is now broadcast in over 200 countries, providing Northern Ireland with a global platform to promote its tourism product.

2. International Tourism Events

Tourism Northern Ireland has defined an International Tourism Event as an event that attracts out-of-state visitors (not participants) to Northern Ireland, where the event has played a key role in attracting them to visit. An event of this nature also showcases Northern Ireland on a global stage as a unique destination. This would include generating significant out-of-state media coverage (such as TV and print) both pre-event and during the event. The

(Continued)

(Continued)

coverage would showcase Northern Ireland's authentic people and places, highlighting iconic landscapes and attractions.

At their very core these events have the capacity to attract visitors to Northern Ireland and attract significant out-of-state media attention while helping to change perceptions of the area. International Tourism Events should cover several streams of Tourism Northern Ireland's product portfolio including culture, arts and heritage. International Tourism Events should:

1   Generate substantial economic benefits for Northern Ireland through increased visitation including tourists, spectators and participants
2   Highlight Northern Ireland as an event and tourism destination through high-profile, international media coverage
3   Enhance Northern Ireland's opportunities to host further major events
4   Additionally, demonstrate sustainability and creativity
5   Create a lasting legacy for Northern Ireland leaving a footprint of benefits for years to come
6   Fit with the visitor segments and 'experience pillars' outlined in the National Tourism Strategy
7   Attract total visitor numbers greater than 4,000 (not participants)
8   Provide an aimed return on investment of 5:1.

It should be noted that this tier includes already-established high-profile events such as the North West 200. This annual international motorbike race takes place in the month of May and attracts over 200,000 visitors. The fact that this event is held outside the peak tourism season means it is a life-line for many small tourism businesses in the region.

3. National Tourism Events

National Tourism Events will showcase Northern Ireland's regions and destinations, allowing visitors to get closer to an authentic experience of Northern Ireland. These events will cover a wide range of themes such as music, culture, food, art, theatre and sport, and appeal to niche markets. National Tourism Events will also allow for geographical spread and enhance off-peak times where there is surplus capacity in the tourism industry. National Tourism Events highlight the best that the regions of Northern Ireland have to offer and should:

1   Encourage attendance of out-of-state visitors and/or visitors who are already in Northern Ireland
2   Generate economic benefits for Northern Ireland through increased visitor numbers and spend
3   Enhance the profile and appeal of the area
4   Focus on building legacy and sustainability
5   Ensure year-round motivators
6   Enhance the visitor experience
7   Provide an aimed return of investment of 3:1.

'The Ould Lammas Fair' would be an example of a National Tourism Event. This annual event draws thousands of visitors to Ballycastle, a small seaside town on the North Coast, to celebrate the end of summer and beginning of harvest. It appeals to both domestic and international tourists who come to enjoy the carnival atmosphere and sample the local farm produce in the 400+ stalls.

4. Local Events

Responsibility for local events in Northern Ireland rests with the local government. There are 11 Local Authorities in Northern Ireland and each one has a remit for tourism and events. Under the current Event Tourism Structure local events are not eligible for funding from Tourism Northern Ireland. To ensure quality events and improve the visitor experience, local event organizers can, however, avail of the support and advice provided by the Events Unit within Tourism Northern Ireland. Local events that have benefited from this service include the Danny Boy Jazz and Blues Festival and the Castlewellan and District Agriculture Show.

Northern Ireland Industry Development

To help achieve the objectives outlined in its National Events Strategy, Tourism Northern Ireland will support and work with the industry and other key partners including 'In Any Event' (professional trade organization) to encourage up-skilling and bench-marking. Strategic partnerships and networking groups will also be developed to ensure the key stakeholders bring together their expertise, knowledge and work collectively towards a clear

(Continued)

(Continued)

strategic vision for the industry. The key aims of these strategic partnerships and groups will be as follows:

1   To advise on strategic direction and priorities
2   To coordinate and develop an annual events calendar for Northern Ireland
3   To promote sharing of best practice with regard to all elements of events
4   To ensure effective communication between funders and organizers
5   To support the development of the Northern Ireland events industry
6   To share insights and research into the events industry
7   To support development of International Events
8   To deliver the vision that Northern Ireland will become known as the 'Home of Great Events'.

Case Study Summary

Event tourism is not guaranteed and must be planned and managed. This case study illustrated how Tourism Northern Ireland realized this and, having identified event tourism as a key market in the National Tourism Strategy, placed event tourism at the heart of its National Events Strategy. This strategy recognized the unique challenges and opportunities Northern Ireland faced in the post-'Troubles' era plus it considered the five generic issues the authors identified earlier in this chapter: seasonality, strategic fit, industry development, funding and collaboration. Moving this strategic approach forward will ensure a more effective and efficient approach to event tourism as it will help Northern Ireland prioritize events, events that align with its strategic vision.

Case Study Questions

1   Discuss why Northern Ireland has targeted events as a policy tool.
2   Use the 'hierarchy of events' to catalogue the events a nation or region of your choice hosts.

Chapter Summary

This chapter has discussed event tourism and why countries must adopt a strategic approach to its development. Event tourism is a by-product of an event, but it would be a mistake for a country to simply assume that their events will attract visitors and promote the host destination in a positive light. Event tourism must be planned around the unique features of a country and take into consideration generic factors such as seasonality, strategic fit, industry development, funding and collaboration. This was illustrated through the case study of Northern Ireland, a country which has identified event tourism as a key driver in both its National Tourism Strategy and the National Events Strategy. However, a strategy is only the beginning of a 'programme of work'. Implementing what has been proposed in a strategy will not be without its challenges. Event tourism is a very competitive market and a strategy will only have positive outcomes if it is properly funded and has the support of key stakeholders.

Review Questions

1. What is meant by the long-term tourism impacts of events?
2. Discuss the five generic issues that a country or region must include in an event tourism strategy?
3. Discuss why one country cannot simply use another country's event tourism strategy.

Additional Resources

Books / Book Chapters / Journal Articles

Getz, D. (2013). *Event Tourism: Concepts, International Case Studies and Research*. New York: Cognizant Communication Corporation. A key resource for students seeking further detail on the importance of event-led tourism.

Foley, M., McGillivary, D. and McPherson, G. (2012). *Event Policy: From Theory to Strategy*. London: Routledge. A timely and well-crafted examination of the event policy process, which is touched upon in the present chapter.

Devine, A., Bolan P. and Devine, F. (2010). Online destination marketing: maximising the tourism potential of a sports event. *International Journal of Sport Management and Marketing*, 7(1/2): 58–75. An interesting examination of the entrepreneurial skills of event marketers, suggesting continued innovation as way of managing best practice.

Mintel Report (2014). *Event Tourism: November 2010*. UK: Mintel. An up-to-date review of the current state of event tourism across Great Britain and Northern Ireland.

Useful Websites

www.ceo-uab.net/ – A multilingual repository of Olympic knowledge online curated by the Centre d'Estudis Olimpics.

www.meetinireland.com/Event-Ireland – A website for the Irish Events Industry, arguably seen as a competitor in Northern Ireland's attempt to achieve its strategic vision.

www.tourismni.com/Portals/2/SharePointDocs/2715/NITB%20Events%20Strategic%20Vision%20to%202020.pdf – The Events Strategic Vision to 2020 that is referred to in Case Study 13.1.

References

Avraham, E. and Ketter, E. (2008). *Media Strategies for Marketing Places in Crisis: Improving the Image of Cities, Countries and Tourist Destinations*. London: Butterworth-Heinemann.

Baum, T. (1995). Ireland – the peace dividend. *Insights, July* (9–14): 2–4.

Bramwell, B. (1993). Planning for tourism in an industrial city. *Town and Country Planning*, 62(1/2): 17–19.

Chalip, L. (2004). Beyond impact: a general model for event leverage. In B. Ritchie and D. Adair (eds), *Sport Tourism: Interrelationships, Impacts and Issues* (pp. 54–69). Great Britain: Channel View.

Dredge, D. and Whitford, M. (2010). Policy for sustainable and responsible festivals and events: institutionalisation of a new paradigm – a response. *Journal of Policy Research in Tourism, Leisure and Events*, 2(1): 1–13.

Duffy, M. and Mair, J. (2015). Festivals and sense of community in places of transition: the Yakkerboo Festival, an Australian case study. In: A. Jepson and A. Clarke (eds), *Exploring Community Festivals and Events* (pp. 54–65). London: Routledge.

Faulkner, B., Chalip, L., Brown, G., Jago, L., March, R. and Woodside, A. (2001). Monitoring the tourism impacts of the Sydney 2000 Olympics. *Event Management*, 6: 231–46.

Fletcher, J. (2012). Economics of international tourism. In: T. Jamal and M. Robinson (eds), *The SAGE Handbook of Tourism Studies* (pp. 166–87). London: SAGE.

Florek, M., Breithbarth, T. and Conejo, F. (2008). Mega event = mega impact? Travelling fans' experience and perceptions of the 2006 FIFA World Cup host nation. *Journal of Sport & Tourism*, 13(3): 199–219.

Foley, M., McGillivary, D. and McPherson, G. (2012). *Event Policy: From Theory to Strategy*. London: Routledge.

Getz, D. (2007). *Event Studies: Theory, Research and Policy for Planned Events*. Oxford: Elsevier.

Getz, D. (2008). Event tourism: definition, evolution and research. *Tourism Management*, 29(3): 403–28.

Getz, D. (2012). *Event Studies – Theory, Research and Policy for Planned Events*. London: Routledge.

Getz, D. (2013). *Event Tourism: Concepts, International Case Studies and Research*. New York: Cognizant Communication Corporation.

Glyptis, S. (1991). Sport and tourism. In: C. Cooper (ed.), *Progress in Tourism, Recreation and Hospitality Management 3*. London: Bellhaven.

Grix, J. (2012). Image leveraging and sports mega events: Germany and the 2006 FIFA World Cup. *Journal of Sport & Tourism*, 17(4): 289–312.

Hall, M. (1992). *Hallmark Tourist Events: Impacts, Management and Planning*. London: Belhaven Press.

Harrison-Hill, T. and Chalip, L. (2006). Marketing sport tourism: creating synergy between sport and destination. In: H. Gibson (ed.), *Sport Tourism*. New York: Routledge.

Hede, A. (2005). Sport-events, tourism and destination marketing strategies: an Australian case study of Athens and its media telecast. *Journal of Sport Tourism*, 10(3): 187–200.

Higham, J. (2005). *Sport Tourism Destinations – Issues, Opportunities and Analysis*. London: Butterworth and Heineman.

Jago, L., Chalip, L., Brown, G., Mules, T. and Shameem, A. (2003). Building events into destination branding: insights from experts. *Event Management*, 8(1): 3–14.

Kerr, W. (2003). *Tourism Public Policy and the Strategic Management of Failure*. Oxford: Pergamon.

Kissoudi, P. (2010). Athens' post-Olympic aspirations and the extent of their realisation. *International Journal of the History of Sport*, *27*(16–18): 2780–97.

Lepp, A. and Gibson, H. (2011). Reimaging a nation: South Africa and the 2010 FIFA World Cup. *Journal of Sport and Tourism*, *16*(3): 211–30.

Masterman, G. (2009). *Strategic Sports Event Management: An International Approach* (2nd edn). Oxford: Elsevier.

Quinn, B. (2013). *Key Concepts in Event Management*. London: Sage.

Raj, R., Walters, P. and Rashid, T. (2013). *Events Management: Principles and Practice* (2nd edn). London: Sage.

Ritchie, J. (1984). Assessing the impact of hallmark events: conceptual and research issues. *Journal of Travel Research*, *23*(1): 2–11.

Ritchie, J. and Smith, B. (1991). The impact of mega-events on host region awareness: a longitudinal study. *Journal of Travel Research*, *30*(1): 3–10.

Roberts, K. (2004). *The Leisure Industries*. China: Palgrave Macmillian.

Smith, A. (2012). *Events and Urban Regeneration. The Strategic Use of Events to Revitalise Cities*. London: Routledge.

Van der Westhuizen, J. (2004). Marketing Malaysia as a model modern Muslim state: the significance of the 16th Commonwealth Games. *Third World Quarterly*, *25*(7): 1277–91.

VisitBritain (2013). *The Olympic Wrap*. VisitBritain Shifting the Dial, October.

Webb, S. and Magnussen, B. (2002). Evaluating major sporting events as cultural icons and economic drivers: a case study of Rugby World Cup 1999. Paper presented at the Tourism Research Conference, Cardiff.

Whitford, M. (2009). A framework for the development of event public policy: facilitating regional development. *Tourism Management* 30: 674–82.

Zammit, V. (2015). Pride, identity and authenticity in community festivals and events in Malta. In: A. Jepson and A. Clarke (eds), *Exploring Community Festivals and Events* (pp. 118–29). London: Routledge.

The Future of International Events

14

Nicole Ferdinand, Albert Postma and Christian White

Learning Objectives

By reading this chapter students should be able to:

- Describe the different approaches that can be used in planning for future international events
- Identify current key drivers that are shaping the future of international events
- Discuss possible directions for the future of international events research
- Develop strategies for charting a career in events management that is future-proof.

Introduction

The events industry has witnessed unprecedented levels of growth in the last three decades and, even in the face of economically difficult times, it is showing little sign of slowing down. However, this is not to say that event organizers are not facing challenging times ahead. The terrorist attacks in Paris in 2015 raised new concerns about public safety at events, and international events hosted in major cities especially. Terrorists coordinated seven attacks which killed 130 people, and two of these attacks place in the vicinity of events – an international friendly football match between France and Germany held at the Stade de France and a music concert at the Bataclan concert venue, where music fans were fired upon by attackers (Steafel et al., 2015).

At the same time advances in the development of virtual reality and the emergence of 'Big Data' are creating new opportunities to enhance and also reimagine the ways in which events are delivered and experienced. As with other aspects of life, it is impossible to state with certainty what international events will be like in the future, but surely there are some exciting times ahead. As Getz (2015) has noted, a world without events is not one that can be envisioned. They have been and continue to be central to human existence: by facilitating 'social and economic exchanges'; providing 'highly desired experiences'; embodying 'cultural differences'; communicating 'symbolic meaning'; and nourishing 'individual and group identity' (p. 20). So whilst there is little doubt that events will continue to persist in the future, given the dynamic environment in which they take place there are many questions to be answered about the changing forms and functions that events, and in particular international events, will serve in our lives.

The purpose of this chapter is to provide students with approaches that they can use to conceptualize the future of international events and also strategies for facing it. The chapter begins with outlining contrasting methods that have been used in planning for the future of international events. It then discusses some of the key drivers of change within the events industry which are shaping the future of international events. The chapter goes on to explore future directions for international event research, given some of the recent developments which have taken place within the event industry. It closes by putting forward suggestions for students and young professionals seeking to chart a career within this fast-changing, challenging and exciting sector.

Planning for the Future

Why plan for the future? It is impossible to predict and some of the changes we have witnessed in the last two decades have highlighted how quickly the future can change. For example '9/11' – the terrorist attacks in New York on 11 September 2001 – completely transformed the airline industry, and the increased costs of security, coupled with the initial sharp reductions in air travel, caused unforeseen shocks that made weaker airline carriers bankrupt within months (IATA, n.d.). A 'Kodak moment', once part of a tagline that referred to the fourth most valuable brand in the United States, is now used to describe the demise of the Kodak company following the increasing affordability of digital cameras. The company went from declaring US$2.5 billion in profits in 1999 (*The Economist*, 2012) to declaring bankruptcy in 2012 (Usborne, 2012). Following the financial crisis many festivals had their own 'moment', when they had to be cancelled due to financial pressures causing analysts to wonder if, after a period of seemingly unbridled growth, the good times were finally at an end (Bignel, 2012; Johnston, 2013). For international event organizers that wish to remain in business for the long term, planning for the future is about understanding future possibilities, crafting strategies take advantage of opportunities that may arise and to defending against impending threats. Whereas it is not possible to predict when the next unforeseen shock or Kodak moment will occur, by applying different methodologies or approaches to conceptualizing the future, event organizers can manage some of the uncertainty they face. They can clarify what they currently know, understand what they can find out and, using this information, try to chart future possibilities and prepare for them. Three of the more common approaches to planning for the future are described in this section.

Trend Extrapolation

Trend extrapolation involves using information from the past to predict the future. It is best suited to shorter time horizons as it can only incorporate a limited amount of information or variables. The underlying assumption of the approach is that relationships between variables that held in the past will continue to hold in the future (Meek and Meek, 2003). Most event organizers will have used this type of information and many of the reports done on the events industry will include a section which seeks to forecast future trends using this type of approach. Mintel's (2015) report on the United Kingdom's live music industry provides an example of trend extrapolation in its forecast of the UK's music concert and festival market size up until 2020. Mintel has produced this forecast based on historical market size data taken from its own database in addition to macro and socio-economic data sourced from other organizations, such as the UK's Office for National Statistics. For the music concerts and festivals

Table 14.1   Mintel's forecast of the UK's music concert and festival market size during 2010–20

YEAR	Total Expenditure	% Annual Change
	£m	
2010	1,473	n/a
2011	1,634	10.9
2012	1,517	−7.2
2013	1,908	25.8
2014	2,012	5.5
2015 (forecasted)	2,140	6.4
2016 (forecasted)	2,287	6.9
2017 (forecasted)	2,449	7.1
2018 (forecasted)	2,640	7.8
2019 (forecasted)	2,868	8.6
2020 (forecasted)	3,047	6.2

Source: Adapted from Mintel (2015)

market, the UK's gross domestic product (GDP) was identified as having the most influence on market value. See Table 14.1 for Mintel's forecast of the UK's music concert and festival market size from 2010 to 2020.

However, it is important to understand that, in real life, data is far more variable and cannot neatly fit into the statistical techniques that are applied when undertaking trend extrapolation. Thus, data that come out of such extrapolations should be used with caution. A key limitation of the approach is that it ignores wider changes or shocks that may occur in the environment in which event organizers operate. It is a quick and relatively inexpensive approach, though, and can be effective if, for the planning horizon under consideration, consumer demand and the market environment remain relatively stable (Boon and Kurtz, 2015).

Environmental Scanning and Analysis

Environmental scanning is a process of collecting information about an organization's business environment (Beamish and Ashford, 2007). This information can generally be divided into two types:

1. Macro-environmental factors, such as those affecting the political and/or legal environment, economic indicators and socio-cultural issues
2. Micro-environmental factors, such as those affecting the competitive environment in which an organization operates and the supply and demand of the factors of production used by the firm.

In Chapter 2 of this text this combination of factors is described as the international events environment. In an environmental analysis, these factors are assessed and an organization evaluates its objectives and performance to ensure that they are consistent with the changing market environment (Pride and Ferrell, 2016). In event organizations, environmental scanning and analysis can be carried out by functional managers, strategic planner(s), consultants who have been retained for that purpose, or a combination of functional and senior management. Undertaking environmental scanning and analysis has a number of benefits for event organizations which devote the significant time and energy required to engage in these processes, including: better awareness of and responsiveness to environmental changes; improved resource allocation and diversification decisions; and more effective strategic planning and decision-making (Diffenbach, 1983, cited by Moutinho and Chien, 2008). However, these processes can also cause problems within organizations. Functional managers who are assigned environmental scanning and analysis tasks can become resentful if time, resources and training are not given for them to carry out tasks. There may be unrealistic expectations of environmental scanning and analysis processes, and contributors may come away demotivated if strategic planners do not make full use of their analyses or apply their recommendations.

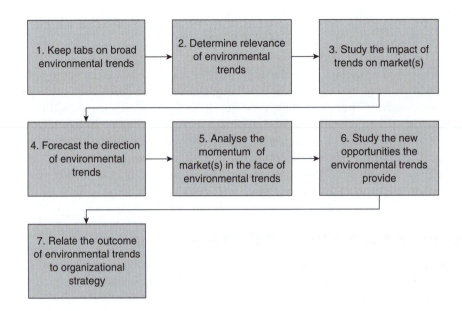

Figure 14.1 Steps in environmental scanning

The domination of the processes by individuals can also have a debilitating effect (Thomas, 1995). Applying a formal series of steps in environmental scanning and analysis may assist in avoiding some of the difficulties associated with these processes (see Figure 14.1).

Scenario Planning

Scenario planning is a method of planning for the future which involves creating multiple stories about what the future will be like. It may be undertaken in conjunction with environmental scanning and analysis. The time horizon that is under consideration is generally quite long because the process of scenario planning is a very expensive one. It is generally done in groups – which can range from 9 or 10 to up to 30 people (Wade, 2012) – and it is time-consuming. The purpose of scenario planning is not to predict the future but to get individuals in organizations to practise out-of-the-box thinking so that they can more effectively adapt to future changes (Bryson, 2011). There are no hard-and-fast rules for the process of scenario planning but it broadly involves the eight steps described in Figure 14.2.

Scenario planning offers a number of advantages over other methods which event organizations can use to plan for the future. These include: the legitimization of divergent ways of thinking, which are essential for success in a dynamic business environment; the fostering of strategic conversations about critical uncertainties; the building of a common vocabulary; and the development of plans for many future

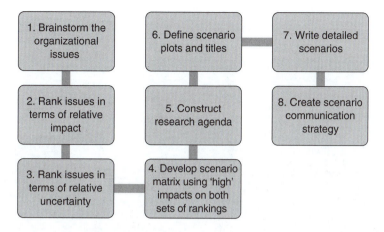

Figure 14.2 Steps in the scenario planning process

Source: Adapted from Chermack (2011)

scenarios. However, in addition to being more costly, complex and time-consuming than other methods, such as trend extrapolation, scenario planning has been criticized for leading to wishful thinking because there is often a desire for those involved to focus on one particular future outcome (Garvin and Schoemaker, 2006, cited by Chang, 2010). A worked example of a scenario planning process is given in Case Study 14.1.

Case Study 14.1 – Future Scenarios for Notting Hill Carnival 2020 and Beyond

What is the Notting Hill Carnival?

The Notting Hill Carnival began when British social worker Rhuane Laslett decided to add a steel band procession (which was a traditional musical instrument of the Trinidad Carnival) to another event, the Notting Hill Fayre, in 1964. This addition led to the spontaneous jumping and dancing in the streets from some of the Trinidadian and other Caribbean immigrants who had settled in the Notting Hill area in London in the United Kingdom and the eventual birth of the Notting Hill Carnival. The roots of the Notting Hill Carnival, like many community-based, cultural festivals, is linked to the celebration and expression of the historical, social or cultural aspects of a host

(Continued)

(Continued)

Figure 14.3   The Notting Hill Carnival, London

community (Getz, 2005) – in this instance, the Caribbean community of migrants which lived in the Notting Hill area when the festival began. However, since that historic day in 1964, the Notting Hill Carnival has gone on to become an international multicultural event attracting millions of visitors and also raising millions of pounds of revenue for the city of London.

Rationale for the Scenario Planning Exercise

In 2013, as the Notting Hill Carnival prepared to celebrate its 50th year, it was perhaps an opportune time for the organizers and other stakeholders involved in the staging to take stock and revisit their strategies for the festival. Consultants from the King's Cultural Institute and the European Tourism Futures Institute (ETFI) were contacted by stakeholders within the Notting Hill Carnival community to assist them in the process of planning for the future. This was a collaborative undertaking in which consultants acted as facilitators rather than experts in the research process. Scenario planning was chosen as of the method for planning for the future. One of the key benefits of the approach that was highlighted was that it minimized stakeholders' tendencies to rehash past mistakes. The expected outcome of this future-oriented, collaborative methodology was that organizations involved in the staging of the

Notting Hill Carnival would be better able to anticipate future changes and would develop a proactive attitude.

The Scenario Planning Approach

In assisting the Notting Hill Carnival's stakeholders plan for the future, the critical uncertainties were used as a starting point. Combinations of the possible directions to which such uncertainties could develop were used to frame a number of scenarios of possible yet plausible futures. None of the scenarios were more likely than the others; the scenarios were just possible future alternative realities. The lively projections offered inspiration for stakeholders to develop new concepts, business models, strategies and courses of action. It took a bottom-up approach to planning for the future. Rather than acting as experts, the consultants worked with stakeholders as facilitators, allowing the stakeholders to lead the research process.

The scenarios were crafted using a combination of environmental factors and internal characteristics which were detailed by the organizers and other key stakeholders. The key environmental factors or uncertainties identified for the Notting Hill Carnival were the changing funding environment and the new crop of emerging carnival artists coming out of the diverse cultural community in London. The internal characteristics, also described as core values and unique selling points, were music, transformation, tradition and the sense of freedom from the street atmosphere (Postma et al., 2014).

The Future Scenarios for the Notting Hill Carnival

From the environmental factors and internal characteristics put forward by individuals engaged in the scenario planning process, four scenarios were put forward. They were described using the present tense in order to make them more real to stakeholders and to encourage them to use the scenarios as a starting point for future planning.

1   *Notting Hill Carnival as Caribbean cultural celebration* – The Carnival is a celebration of Caribbean cultural traditions. It features Caribbean culture exclusively. The battles of steel bands and of the bands of costumed revellers are its highlights. The music is reggae, calypso and soca. The Carnival stays true to its roots and remains in the streets of Notting Hill.

(Continued)

(Continued)

Figure 14.4   Notting Hill Carnival scenarios
Source: Postma et al., 2014: 28

2   *Notting Hill Carnival as tourist spectacle* – This event is one which strives to bring Caribbean culture to as wide an audience as possible. While retaining some authentic aspects, it includes other more commercial features to broaden its appeal. Alongside calypso and reggae artists, there will be well-known dance hall, grime and garage artists and top DJs. This event caters to the audience's needs and provides an enclosed comfortable venue where people can feel secure whilst enjoying the Carnival.

3   *Notting Hill Carnival as international arts festival* – The Carnival builds on its fame of being Europe's biggest street party to become a world mecca for carnival arts and artists. This event will attract global media attention and will showcase the world's leading carnival artists in London's world-famous iconic venues, such as the Royal Albert Hall, ExCel and the Olympic Park.

4   *Notting Hill Carnival as cultural fusion* – Rhuane Laslett's dream of a multicultural festival bringing together London's diverse cultural and ethnic communities is realized. However, it goes beyond her 1964 vision by taking into account the new hybridized cultures that London has now produced. This event provides a platform for fusion art forms to be displayed and created. It will draw heavily on the host of grassroots organizations that are creating art in London. It will take place in a green, open space allowing for freedom of both movement and creativity.

Future Strategies and Courses of Action

The key areas highlighted by the scenarios for reconfiguration were the Notting Hill Carnival's cultural aspects, its size, its human resources, funding models, promotion and/or branding and the location. Even though the Carnival's organizers may wish to work towards a particular scenario, to make the Notting Hill Carnival future-proof they should be prepared for all of the four scenarios and not choose only one that seems most preferable. So, ideally, the courses of action they should take for the future should transcend the individual scenarios. It was therefore recommended that the organizers and other key stakeholders should focus on three key priorities:

1   Developing human resource capacity by engaging younger people and embarking on a deliberate strategy to transfer knowledge, skills and leadership
2   Diversifying funding sources and in particular paying more attention to the international network that the Notting Hill Carnival belongs to as the UK's funding environment is so competitive
3   Developing a distinctive brand identity which is in line with both attendees' and funding bodies' requirements.

CRITICAL THINKING EXERCISE 1

What trends or driving forces would be included in an environmental analysis for the Notting Hill Carnival? What types of data would be useful for the short-term planning of the organizers?

Key Drivers Shaping the Future of International Events

In Case Study 14.1, the changing funding environment which festivals face in the United Kingdom and the changing demographics and psychographics of carnival artists beginning to participate in the Notting Hill Carnival were identified as the key drivers of uncertainty. Like other international events, the future Notting Hill Carnival is being shaped by a particular set of drivers. However, there are some key drivers that have been identified by researchers as pertinent for the events industry as a whole because their effects are apparent across a broad spectrum of events. Yeoman, Robertson and Wheatley (2015) group these drivers into three key areas:

- Evolving consumer values and identities
- The changing politics of events
- The increasing role of technology within events.

Each of these areas highlights a number of drivers which are shaping the future of international events. It is not possible to discuss all the drivers highlighted by the authors in their entirety. The following sections seek to provide a summary of those which have significant relevance over a wide range of events.

Evolving Consumer Values and Identities

This area encompasses the growing popularity of the green agenda, highlighted in Chapter 12 of this text; the pervasiveness of social media consumption, also discussed earlier in Chapter 11; the ageing of populations in the Western world and also in countries such as China and Japan; and the persistence of creative consumption, which describes the closely related practices of co-creation (Prahalad and Ramaswamy, 2004) and prosumption (Ritzer and Jurgenson, 2010). Each of these drivers has implications for the design, promotion and staging of events.

In Chapter 12, Cavagnaro et al. observed that currently event organizers are yet to effectively capitalize on the significant opportunities to actively involve consumers in the greening of events; they suggest a first step towards doing this could be simply asking for feedback from consumers about how they would like to get involved. A similar observation is made in Chapter 11 by Inversini and Williams concerning the tremendous potential of social media to enhance event experiences. Most event organizers have not effectively aggregated and analysed data generated about their events to improve customer experiences in real time. These two as-yet-under-exploited opportunities may be better harnessed by event organizers in the future.

The ageing of populations, particularly in Western countries, presents event organizers with the opportunity to target a growing and very attractive market segment of consumers with ample leisure time, disposable incomes as well as the health and vitality required to access an array of leisure options. However, there will be some challenges as well. Events such as music festivals and concerts – traditionally thought of as events for young people – must be adjusted to address the needs of older consumers. These adjustments will undoubtedly create new requirements for accessibility, as older consumers, even those in good health, will be less able to stand for long periods and will likely have difficulties in accessing event websites or online ticketing applications due to the impaired eyesight and loss of manual dexterity which accompanies the ageing process.

As the line between production and consumption continues to blur, there will be even more new and exciting prospects for event organizers who wish to involve attendees in co-creating or 'prosuming' experiences. Co-creation has the potential to result in not only new and exciting attendee-organizer-created events but also new methods of market segmentation, communication and feedback (Rihova et al., 2014). However, the implications of the shifting power dynamics between producer and consumer needs are yet to be fully understood, and without analyses of the changing power relations at work within events, event organizers will be limited in their ability to collaboratively manage the processes that shape production and consumption (Jepson and Clarke, 2015).

CRITICAL THINKING EXERCISE 2

Give some examples of changes you have seen at events you have recently attended that have come about because of evolving consumer values and/ or identities. Have the resulting changes improved the events or made the events worse?

The Changing Politics of Events

Events, especially international ones, have always been political in nature. Among the political reasons that destinations choose to host international events are: to improve a city's or country's prestige or international standing; to convey key political messages of the political regimes responsible for their hosting; and/or for individual politicians or political parties to capitalize on the goodwill international events generate to garner political support (Roberts, 2011). Events are also increasingly being used by groups either directly or indirectly involved to deliver political messages. As part of the 2012 Olympics, for example, Fair Play used its campaign for the rights of workers making Olympic merchandise as a platform to draw public attention to wider issues such as global inequality, poverty and the structural problems that exist in trans-national labour markets (Timms, 2012). Political activism can also be subversive or occur accidently, as seen in the public's reaction to Germany's colourful Winter Olympic uniforms, which were speculated to be a protest against Russia's anti-gay propaganda laws. These speculations were denied by the German Olympic Sports Confederation, but nonetheless the uniforms did contribute to raising awareness of gay rights issues (Nichols, 2013).

There are also, unfortunately, many examples throughout history of well-known international events that were targeted for far more sinister reasons by terrorists seeking to capitalize on the global media attention that mega sporting events in particular attract. With the advent of social media, international events have become all the more appealing to terror groups as news of terrorist attacks can be spread to millions within minutes through social media networks such as Twitter and Facebook.

Considering the persistence that both developed and developing countries have shown in using international events as part of their urban development strategies, it is very likely that this trend is likely to continue in the future. However, both governments and city planners will continue to be faced with the considerable challenge of balancing the positive political and other impacts that international events are intended to achieve with their negative consequences. Recent terrorist attacks such as the Boston Marathon bombings in 2013, which killed three people, and the 2015 Paris bombings near the Stade de France will very likely result in new security requirements for international sporting events. Thanks in large part to social media, official as well as unofficial and unsanctioned use of international events to communicate political messages is also likely to be another trend that will have to be managed and monitored by event organizers in the future.

The Increasing Role of Technology Within Events

Technology promises some very exciting opportunities for the international event managers of the future. Throughout this text there have been a number of examples which highlighted how new technologies are improving how events are planned (see Chapter 4), designed (see Chapters 3 and 7) and evaluated (see Chapter 10). However, recent developments such as the 'internet of things', a phenomenon which describes the embedding of everyday objects with electronics so that can they interact with internet technologies and thereby 'communicate, dialogue, compute and coordinate' (Miorandi et al., 2012: 1497) has understandably raised concerns about threats to data security and identity and also potential manipulation (Sarma and Girao, 2009, cited by Yeoman et al., 2015).

Additionally the unbridled enthusiasm event attendees have shown for recording and sharing the experiences as they happen on social media have caused music artists in particular to issue bans on photography, videos and cell phones at their events. Attendees can get so caught up in capturing and sharing their experiences, they fail to actually enjoy them while they happen. Consideration should also be given to the annoyance caused to other patrons when their views are blocked by recording devices.

As a counter to the pervasiveness of technology in our lives, recently there has been the launch of festivals which have a 'no phones and no laptops' policy on entry. Their goal is that patrons disconnect from the outside world and immerse themselves in the festival environment. Innocent Unplugged, for example, promotes its event as a 'weekend off the grid' for people who want recharge. It takes place in a secluded wooded area and one of its features is a 'spa under the sky' which includes wood-fire hot tubs, saunas and showers (Innocent Unplugged, n.d.).

Thus even as technology continues to totally re-make events in the most fantastic of ways through virtual and augmented reality, automation from event applications and also the blending of virtual and live event formats, at same time a niche audience for low-tech events is developing.

Future Directions for International Events Management Research

In Chapter 1 of this text, Ferdinand et al. noted that much of the research on international events is published within the domain of event/festival tourism. It is thus fitting to look to researchers within this field to get a sense of the likely future directions for international events management research. Getz and Page's (2015) article on the progress and also prospects for event/festival tourism provides a useful road map which can be applied to the future of international events management. Four key areas are:

- Event meanings and experiences
- The antecedents or drivers of event tourism
- The planning and management of events
- The patterns and processes which facilitate events.

Event Meanings and Experiences

Although this is a well-researched area within event/festival tourism, there are number of gaps still to be addressed. One overlooked area of the event experience is the period just preceding the event. Getz and Page (2015) specifically highlight the travel to events by tourists as a component of the international event experience which needs to be better understood because the journey often incorporates aspects which can further enhance attendees' enjoyment of an event, such as socializing and identity building. Negative travel experiences such as delays and lost luggage can also detract from attendees' overall event experiences. Post-event experiences and the role of nostalgia in the overall event experience is another area that has been overlooked. Other aspects of the event experience highlighted for deeper exploration in future by the authors are events' emotional components and the application of under-utilized/alternative methodologies such as experiential sampling (e.g. analyses of written, audio or video diaries) and using biometrics (e.g. body temperature and pulse readings) to understand attendees' reactions to event design and other behaviours (Getz and Page, 2015).

The Antecedents or Drivers of Event Experience

This is another well-established area of research on international events. A great deal of attention has been devoted within the literature on festival/event tourism to understanding why visitors attend international events. However, technological improvements in augmented reality, video-conferencing and home entertainment systems are increasingly challenging the traditional mode of participating in events. It thus raises interesting questions about attendees continuing motivations to attend events in person. Getz and Page's (2015: 612) question about whether attendees will continue to believe that they 'need' to travel to events seems prescient, especially when we consider the speed at which some of these technologies are developing. The widespread use of social media is another way in which technology has changed and will continue to change attendees' motivations to go to events. Social media applications make it possible to have knowledge about a wider range of activities than ever before, far more than could be pursued given the limited time individuals have. This situation has driven popular interest in the phenomenon known as the 'fear of missing out' or 'FoMO', which is defined as a pervasive anxiety of being left out of rewarding experiences in which others are participating (Przybylski et al., 2013). Researchers have yet to explore how FoMO is affecting attendees' event motivations, and as social media continues to play an increasingly important role in our lives, this will also be a significant gap in the literature to be addressed in the future.

The Planning and Management of Events

A great deal of the literature on international events which seeks to improve their planning and management is focused on understanding consumer behaviours and motivations. For example, researchers have explored differing purchasing patterns among first-time and repeat visitors (Kruger et al., 2010) and links between motivations, satisfaction and intended future behaviour (Lee and Hsu, 2013), with a view to assisting international event organizers to better design and promote their events to attendees. There has also been considerable research on how international events are used as part of branding and image-building strategies for destinations. However, as Getz and Page (2015) have observed, international event management strategy is still a fairly new area of research. The continuing importance of events in urban planning agendas and organizational marketing strategies suggests a need to examine international events at a more strategic level than has traditionally been the case. Ferdinand and Williams (2013) suggest that event organizers must move to a macro level when coordinating and configuring the resources required for staging international events, and view them as an 'experience production system'. Additionally, the experience production system in most cases will extend across national borders, so that mapping the linkages of an event or group of events across a number of countries will result in event organizers being able to maximize the benefits of an international experience production network. As an increasing number of staged events are now international, thanks in large part to the effects of globalization, in the future there will be a greater need for research which explores the international strategic dimensions of international events.

The Patterns and Processes which Facilitate Events

In Chapter 2 of this text, Ferdinand et al. highlighted that international events do not exist in a vacuum. There are a number of global and local forces which influence their outcomes which must be carefully studied so that these outcomes are not comprised unduly by unforeseen or overlooked factors. Likewise, Getz and Page (2015) propose that there is a critical need to understand the patterns and processes which facilitate events. Among these patterns and processes are: migration and the general movement of people; time of year or seasonality within destinations; the policy environment; and also the event lifecycle. As international events grow in number, size and complexity there will be an even greater need to understand the context in which these events take place, especially if event organizers wish to adopt a more strategic approach to international event management in the future. Additionally, as the environment within which international events are hosted is changing at an increasingly rapid pace, it will be of even greater importance to continuously monitor the forces which are shaping this environment. Research on the patterns and processes which facilitate events therefore is a much needed addition to literature on international events.

Planning for a Career in International Events Management

It is a very exciting time to pursue a career in international events management. However, the current business climate is also one of great uncertainty. Professor Cathy Davidson, a distinguished scholar of the history of technology at Duke University, in her recently published book, *Now You See It: How Technology and Brain Science Will Transform Schools and Business for the 21st Century*, predicted that 65% of elementary school students in the United States would grow up to do jobs not currently in existence (Davidson, 2011). This widely publicized statistic sparked a great deal of debate in the United States and also internationally on how education should be re-engineered and reimagined to address the needs of students who will be doing these future occupations. There was widespread consensus that a significant overhaul of the teaching and learning methods used in current education institutions was needed if students were to be adequately prepared for the jobs of tomorrow. Indeed many jobs that graduates are doing today in events management companies did not exist when they first started university. So how do today's students prepare themselves for future careers in international event management? The following sections highlight some useful suggestions put forward by educators, human resource experts and consultants in a range of disciplines that are applicable to international events management.

Focus on Transferable Skills

To thrive in the economies of the future in which the specific skill-sets required are still unknown, students seeking employment need to focus on developing transferable skills which can apply to a range of career paths. These include skills such as innovation and creativity, because in the future they will be required to invent new products, services and business models. They will also be working in economies defined by serious and escalating global challenges including global warming, unchecked population growth and financial systems prone to unforeseen disasters (Duncan, 2010). In Chapter 12 of this text Cavagnaro et al. highlighted that we all have a responsibility to address these challenges to ensure a sustainable world for future generations. Thus students pursuing careers in international event management, like other students, will be required to do their part. To do so, they must acquire 'a sophisticated set of skills: an ability to think critically; problem-solving skills that can be applied to a wide variety of contexts; and an ability to form transnational coalitions' (Duncan, 2010: 306).

Adjust Attitudes and Expectations

Students must also adjust their mindsets regarding the nature of work. It is no longer realistic to expect a stable job and income indefinitely from a single employer. This has perhaps always been the case in the field of events management. However, jobs of the future will be even less location-specific, and be based around business networks rather than a single organization. They will be increasingly technology intensive too (Störmer et al., 2014). To forge a career in such a climate requires a proactive approach to education and training and a flexible approach to career management, as highlighted in Table 14.2.

Table 14.2　Career management skills for 2030 and beyond

Adopt a flexible mindset	• Be prepared to travel • Be open to working for more than one employer • Get used to jobs being temporary or project-based
Take greater personal responsibility for your own training and development	• Continuously update and acquire training and skills for success • Ask for personal development opportunities from employers as part of compensation • Keep abreast of latest labour market developments and skill requirements
Be open to new types of learning	• Look for opportunities for bite-sized learning • Make the most of peer-to-peer learning opportunities at work • Take advantage of technology-enabled training opportunities that allow you to learn at your own pace
Focus on those transferable skills that will be at a premium in the future	• Develop your ability to work both in teams and autonomously to prepare for project-based work • Focus on creativity and problem-solving skills which can apply across a range of sectors • Build resilience, adaptability and resourcefulness in order to cope with the challenges of the future job market

Don't be Afraid to Opt Out

'Opting out' is a phrase that has been used in the last decade or so to describe the phenomenon of highly educated women choosing to opt out of high pressure, full-time employment when they have children, in order to have less stressful lifestyles by avoiding the challenges of juggling careers with childcare responsibilities. Although numerous research studies have debunked the recent popular media assertion that large numbers of women were voluntarily, permanently leaving the workforce, for the purpose of raising children and returning to the traditional roles of wife and mother (Boushey, 2005; Cabrera, 2007; Stone, 2007), women as well as men are increasingly seeking more balanced working lives and to live more authentically. As a result, there is a growing segment of the workforce that are choosing alternatives to the traditionally desired career path that seeks a continuous upward trajectory of work, responsibility and financial reward. Opting out can take many forms. For some, it involves making lateral career moves instead of upward ones so that they have varied careers without the additional pressures that come with promotion. For others it may involve working part-time, freelance or on a project basis so that they have time to pursue other activities, such as caring for children, travelling or volunteering. Others still may leave the workforce entirely to become homesteaders and live off the land or choose to live on their partners' income. It is important to understand that each form of opting out carries risk. In some workplaces employees who are not actively seeking advancement are considered undesirable, whereas individuals without permanent employment do not have the protection of paid sick-leave should they be incapacitated for a time and unable to work. However, choosing to opt out also carries significant rewards as well and is becoming an increasingly attractive choice for millions of people around the world (Lee, 2012).

Create Your Own Job

Another way students can prepare for a future career in international events management is to develop their own career paths by creating their own jobs. This can be done in a variety of ways. For example, students can consider pursuing a multi-tasking career (Lee, 2012) in which, in addition to a main source of employment, they develop other income streams, ideally from activities that are enjoyable and require little investment; Slim (2010) suggests businesses such as web design, personal training or coaching, photography and tax preparation. Pursuing such a strategy provides them with backup income in the event of job loss. Conversely, as is often the case in the creative industries, they could choose to pursue an entirely self-managed career by developing a professional portfolio and building career networks to continuously create opportunities for self-employment. They could also choose to take advantage of market opportunities that arise in the dynamic, technology-driven markets of the future and launch their own businesses. To do so they must be able to manage (and have) skills across global business networks and adapt to open business models and more fluid ways of working.

Case Study 14.2 – Is #Glasto Losing its Social Conscience?

Introduction

This case study highlights the findings of social-media-based research conducted into contemporary meaning and values ascribed to the Glastonbury Festival in 2013 by Twitter users. Since the first festival back in 1970, Glastonbury has grown to become the UK's biggest live music festival, attracting over 180,000 music fans each year (UK Music, 2013). The study sought to discover whether posts on Twitter reveal music fans' connections with the events' social and political agendas or confirm the often-quoted assertion made by Paul Weller, a well-known British song writer and musician, that the festival has 'abandoned its hippy roots and become a perfect cultural barometer for British culture' (Michaels, 2002). His statement summarizes the remarkable evolution the festival has undergone in its more than 40 years of existence – transforming from a 'counter-cultural retreat' for hippies, ecological awareness and great bands to a heavily corporate-sponsored music festival which is able to include the world's top music acts in its line-up (Michaels, 2002). Recent headline acts have included Jay-Z, Kanye West and Beyoncé.

Figure 14.5 Glastonbury Festival, UK

The festival remains dedicated to raising awareness for charitable causes and ecological issues, in particular. For nearly 25 years Glastonbury tickets have displayed the logos of Oxfam, Greenpeace and WaterAid. The festival makes a sizeable donation to these organizations each year and provides them with stalls at the event so that they can display the work that they do to festival attendees and to the wider viewing audience watching elsewhere (Glastonbury, 2016). However, Twitter posts about the event reveal that attendees are mainly focused on the music and a great deal of online conversation is focused on corporate sponsors – not on the charities the festival seeks to promote.

Glastonbury Economics

It has been estimated that Glastonbury Festival contributes over £100 million annually to the UK economy, with a substantial portion of expenditure benefiting the community in which the event is staged and its environs – £52 million is spent in Somerset and the south-west. Glastonbury Festival is part of the UK's vibrant, major music concert and festivals industry, which attracts more than 7.7 million visitors (including locals and an increasing number of visitors from overseas). A number of businesses also credit the event with providing their organizations with a major boost in revenues (UK Music, 2013).

Glastonbury on Social Media

Glastonbury Festival uses social media extensively to promote the event, to provide updates and even to release event secrets. The festival has been described as a 'king of user-generated content' (Ofei, 2015) and a 'digital giant' (Digital Annexe, 2016) thanks in large part to the effectiveness of its social media strategy and particularly how it manages its Twitter presence. To keep attendees up to speed during the festival, it uses three different Twitter accounts to handle different types of content:

@GlastoFest: The official year-round Glastonbury Twitter account

@GlastoLive: The live festival account, which provides updates

@GlastoInfo: The information account, to answer attendee queries

(Continued)

(Continued)

Table 14.3   Examples of the most common tweet types at Glastonbury Festival 2013

Artist promotion	*@TDCinemaClub: You can catch our set from #glastonbury live on the bbc red button at 7.30pm TONIGHT! We're playing the other stage!*
Corporate marketing	*@guardianmusic: Public Enemy at Glastonbury - review: http://t.co/bwSLQOeiVS*
Fan nostalgia	*@coldplay: Two years ago today, on the Pyramid Stage at Glastonbury. Incredible night. http://t.co/HBsjBdyFyL A*
Fan opinions	*@nilerodgers not only was it a brilliant gig, but you completely got the #glastonbury vibe. Just fab. Good times x*
Individuals 'missing out'	*We are watching the BBC Glastonbury live stream in the office, wishing we were there! @laurenlaverne #glastojealousy*

Dividing the content among different Twitter accounts means users will find it much easier to find information they need and they will be more likely to receive a response, especially from the @GlastoInfo Twitter account, which was set up specifically to communicate with attendees (Digital Annexe, 2016). In 2013, the year in which this study was undertaken, Mumford and Sons' closing set at the festival, which featured The Vaccines and Vampire Weekend, was ranked in the UK's Twitter top ten trending topics (Telegraph Sport, 2013). Thus the event's tweets provide a rich source of data which can reveal a number of insights into its contemporary meaning and values.

Findings from the Study

From the tweets it was apparent that most of the conversation was dominated by bands publicizing their appearance at the event and their new releases; companies directing web traffic to their sites; fans or attendees engaging in nostalgia (for example reminiscing about festivals they attended in previous years) and expressing their opinions about the current year's performances; and individuals expressing regret that they were unable to attend the festival that year and were missing out. See Table 14.3.

These findings confirm previous research which suggests that modern festivals are really now entertainment productions (Getz, 2012) and that the more media attention a festival attracts, the more commercialization will be apparent (Getz, 2007). In the case of Glastonbury, festival tweets showed organizations exploiting the social media traffic it generated on Twitter in a variety of ways. One method was to try to use Twitter to generate product sales as seen in this tweet from HMV (2013):

The @ArcticMonkeys nailed it last night at #Glastonbury. New tracks from #AM were amazing, out 9/9/2013 & you can pre-order ...

Other organizations, such as newspaper *The Guardian*, chose to provide links to their free online content (*The Guardian*, 2013). Although this type of promotion does not lead to immediate commercial benefits, it increases brand awareness, which can have a positive impact on sales in the longer term. By attracting additional viewers to the newspaper's online content, *The Guardian* will enhance its appeal to online advertisers and it might be able to convert some of these online viewers of its free content into paying customers.

Despite the festival's apparent commercialization, it seems to have remained at its core an important vehicle for musicians and fans to connect with one another. For example, Ora (2013) tweets this thank-you message:

We did it!!!!!!!! Glastonbury my life has changed forever!!!!!! Thank you!!! Pyramid stage! Main Stage!!! Thank you!!

Fans also tweet their appreciation directly to the artists performing, as is seen in this congratulatory message to Nile Rogers from Twitter user GarethW2610 (Williams, 2013):

@nilerodgers Best part of Glastonbury so far was Chic and yours truly!! Boss..

The Twitter exchanges between music artists and fans highlight that the Glastonbury Festival continues to provide important social benefits such as providing a shared experience and broadening attendees' cultural horizons (Bowdin et al., 2006).

The numerous tweets by those who were not able to attend seem to be reflective of the current social trend – 'fear of missing out'. Twitter users' feelings of missing out seemed amplified by their ability to view images and video of the festival via a variety of media platforms (see Table 14.4).

Conclusion

It is clear that Glastonbury Festival, like many modern-day festivals, is one that will constantly change. As highlighted by Ferdinand et al. in Chapter 2 of this text, international events do not occur in a vacuum; they will be

(Continued)

(Continued)

Table 14.4 'Missing-out' tweets

User	Tweet
pop_vixen	The moment I wished I was at Glastonbury 2013 via @nilerodgers #GoodTimes #GetLucky https://t.co/vp7NNQ2P6o
Musobox	We are watching the BBC Glastonbury live stream in the office, wishing we were there! @laurenlaverne #glastojealousy
iam_melsome	i wish i could go to glastonbury just to see @cleanbandit
BeccaJohnson_	So jealous of people @GlastoFest. Great weather, great music #wishiwasthere #glastonbury
greg_kit	.@bbcthree I so wish I was at Glastonbury. I said 2 years ago I'd be there the next time. Definitely next year! #bbcglasto
JoJoWeav	@RollingStones you were incredible at the Isle of Wight festival! So want to be at Glastonbury!
LucyRu89	Watching @foalsfoalsfoals highlights from #glastonbury #missedout #needtobethere
92_stanny	Wish I was at Glastonbury to see @example tonight :(
miarosemolloy	I SHOULD be at GLASTONBURY now getting ready to watch my favourite @JakeBugg #gutted #whyarntithere #notfair

affected by the political, economic, social and technological contexts in which they are staged. If Glastonbury Festival persists for the next 40 years, it will continue to reflect aspects of the wider society as it evolves.

Case Study Questions

1 What drivers of change for the UK music industry are highlighted by this case study?
2 What sources of information should be used to undertake an environmental scan that will be used to inform Glastonbury Festival's strategic planning for the next five years?
3 What recommendations for future research would you propose to academics investigating the changing nature of the event experience at music festivals?

Chapter Summary

International events are staged in a dynamic environment which is changing at a faster rate than ever before. In such an environment it is becoming increasingly difficult to make accurate predictions about the future. Nevertheless, businesses wishing to be part of the international events industry in the long term need to plan and be prepared. Rather than trying to predict the future, businesses can seek to conceptualize the future using a variety of techniques and use the information they uncover to try to manage some of the uncertainty they face. A critical part of trying to conceptualize the future of any industry is to understand what the current drivers of change are. Among the key drivers of change in the international event management industry are: the increasing importance of the green agenda; the ageing of populations; terrorism threats; and technological developments such as the growing popularity of social media and the recent phenomenon described as the internet of things. Researchers within the domain of event and festival tourism have provided a useful road map into future additions to the literature on international events management. New areas for exploration include the travel phase of the event experience, how technology and related phenomena such as the fear of missing out affect event motivation, and the strategic dimensions of international events. Event management students preparing for a future career in international events must recognize that the industry is one that is changing quickly and that they may be doing jobs in the future which do not exist today. To prepare, students can focus on developing transferable skills which apply to a range of job roles, or consider creating their own jobs by launching new businesses. They must also be willing to take a proactive approach to their own education and training and be flexible in their approach to career management.

Review Questions

1. Given that the events industry is changing at an ever-increasing pace, what benefits are there to be gained for individuals and organizations from planning for the future?
2. If you were asked to do a scenario plan for your events organization to predict demand in the sector for the next five years, how would you respond to the request?
3. What steps would you take to ensure that staff at your events organization were able to contribute positively to environmental scanning and analysis exercises?
4. What advice would you give a university student seeking stable employment in the events industry when they graduate from university?

Acknowledgement

The authors wish to thank King's Cultural Institute and the European Tourism Futures Institute for granting us permission to publish the findings of *Carnival Futures: Notting Hill Carnival 2020* for Case Study 14.1. For the full report, please go to: www.kcl.ac.uk/cultural/-/Past-Projects/CarnivalFutures.aspx

Additional Resources

Books / Book Chapters / Journal Articles

Yeoman, I., Robertson, M., McMahon-Beattie, U., Smith, K.A. and Backer, E. (eds) (2014). *The Future of Events & Festivals*. Oxon: Routledge. This text allows readers to reflect on the legacies that a wide range of events will have for future generations.

Robertson, M., Yeoman, I., Smith, K.A. and McMahon-Beattie, U. (2015). Technology, society, and visioning the future of music festivals. *Event Management, 19*(4): 567–87. This paper employs trend analysis, scenarios and science fiction to develop options for event experiences for future music festivals.

Yeoman, I. (2013). A futurist's thoughts on consumer trends shaping future festivals and events. *International Journal of Event and Festival Management, 4*(3): 249–60. This paper identifies ten key consumer trends that are likely to affect the behaviour of festival-goers in the future.

Useful Websites

www.etfi.eu/ – Provides free online access to reports, videos and journal articles which consider the future of leisure, tourism, hospitality and events.

www.jisc.ac.uk/full-guide/scenario-planning – JISC (2013): 'Scenario planning: A guide to using this strategic planning tool for making flexible long-term plans'. An online guide which shows practical examples and exercises for organizations wishing to undertake scenario planning.

www.wfs.org/ – The website for the first membership organization in the world for people who research, envision and create potential futures.

References

Beamish, K. and Ashford, R. (2007). *Marketing Planning 2006–2007*. Oxford: Butterworth-Heinemann.

Bignel, P. (2012, February 26). Music festivals face a lean 2012. *The Independent* [online]. Retrieved from www.independent.co.uk/arts-entertainment/music/news/music festivals-face-a-lean-2012-7440940.html

Boon, L.E. and Kurtz, D.L. (2015). *Contemporary Marketing* (17th edn). Boston: Cengage Learning.

Boushey, H. (2005). Are women opting out? Debunking the myth. Center for Economic and Policy Research, briefing paper.

Bowdin, G., McDonnell, I., Allen, J. and O'Toole, W. (2006). *Events Management* (2nd edn). Oxford: Butterworth-Heinemann.

Bryson, J. (2011). *Strategic Planning for Public and Non-Profit Sector Organizations: A Guide to Strengthening and Sustaining Organizational Achievement* (4th edn). New Jersey: John Wiley and Sons.

Cabrera, E.F. (2007). Opting out and opting in: understanding the complexities of women's career transitions. *Career Development International, 12*(3): 218–37.

Chang, C.M. (2010). *Service Systems Management and Engineering: Creating Strategic Differentiation and Operational Excellence*. New Jersey: John Wiley and Sons.

Chermack, T.J. (2011). *Scenario Planning in Organizations: How to Create, Use, and Assess Scenarios*. Berrett-Koehler Publishers.

Davidson, C. (2011). *Now You See It: How Technology and Brain Science Will Transform Schools and Business for the 21st Century*. New York: Penguin Books.

Digital Annexe (2016). Glastonbury: digital giants in the festival world. Digital Annex [online]. Retrieved from www.digitalannexe.com/glastonbury-2014/

Duncan, A. (2010). Through the schoolhouse gate: the changing role of education in the 21st century. *Notre Dame Journal of Law, Ethics and Public Policy*, *24*(2): 293–307.

The Economist (2012, January 14). The last Kodak moment? *The Economist* [online]. Retrieved from www.economist.com/node/21542796

Ferdinand, N. and Williams, N.L. (2013). International festivals as experience production systems. *Tourism Management*, *34*(1): 202–10.

Getz, D. (2005). *Event Management and Event Tourism* (2nd edn). New York: Cognizant.

Getz, D. (2007). *Event Studies: Theory, Research and Policy for Planned Events*. Oxford: Butterworth Heinemann.

Getz, D. (2012). *Event Studies: Theory, Research and Policy for Planned Events* (2nd edn). Oxon: Routledge.

Getz, D. (2015). The forms and functions of planned events. In: I. Yeoman, M. Robertson, U. McMahon-Beattie, E. Bakar and K.A. Smith (eds), *The Future of Events and Festivals* (pp. 20–35). Oxon: Routledge.

Getz, D. and Page, S.J. (2015). Progress in tourism management: progress and prospects for event tourism. *Tourism Management*, *52*(1): 593–631.

Glastonbury (2016). Worthy causes. Retrieved from www.glastonburyfestivals.co.uk/worthy-causes/

The Guardian [guardian] (2013, June 30). Another Glastonbury first: the baby crowd-surfer: http://gu.com/p/3hx8c/tf. Retrieved from https://twitter.com/guardian/status/351311293082374145

HMV [hmvtweets] (2013, June 29). The @ArcticMonkeys nailed it last night at #Glastonbury. Retrieved from https://twitter.com/hmvtweets/status/350927860841713664

IATA (n.d.). The impact of September 11 2001 on aviation. IATA [online]. Retrieved from www.iata.org/pressroom/Documents/impact-9-11-aviation.pdf

Innocent Unplugged (n.d.). Innocent Unplugged: A weekend off the grid 23rd/24th May 2015 [online]. Retrieved from www.innocentunplugged.com/

Jepson, A. and Clarke, A. (2015). The future power of decision making in community festivals. In: I. Yeoman, M. Robertson, U. McMahon-Beattie, E. Bakar and K.A. Smith (eds), *The Future of Events and Festivals* (pp. 67–83). Oxon: Routledge.

Johnston, C. (2013, October 20). The crisis rocking Australia's music festival. *The Sydney Morning Herald* [online]. Retrieved from www.smh.com.au/entertainment/music/the-crisis-rocking-australias-music-festivals-20131019-2vtbx.html

Kruger, M., Saayman, M. and Ellis, S. (2010). Determinants of visitor expenditure at the Aardklop National Arts Festival. *Event Management*, *14*(2): 137–48.

Lee, J.H. (2012). Hard at work in the jobless future. *The Futurist*, *46*(2): 32–5.

Lee, T.H. and Hsu, F.Y. (2013). Examining how attending motivation and satisfaction affects the loyalty for attendees at Aboriginal festivals. *International Journal of Tourism Research*, *15*(1): 18–34.

Meek, H. and Meek, R. (2003). *Strategic Marketing Management: Planning and Control 2003–2004*. Oxford: Butterworth Heinemann.

Michaels, L. (2002). Has Glastonbury sold out? Corporate Watch [online]. Retrieved from www.headheritage.co.uk/uknow/features/?id=36

Mintel (2015). Music concerts and festivals – UK. Mintel [online]. Retrieved from http://store.mintel.com/music-concerts-and-festivals-uk-august-2015

Miorandi, D., Sicari, S., De Pellegrini, F. and Chlamtac, I. (2012). Internet of things: vision, applications and research challenges. *Ad Hoc Networks*, *10*(7): 1497–516.

Moutinho, L. and Chien, C.S. (2008). *Problems in Marketing: Applying Key Concepts and Techniques* (2nd edn). London: Sage Publications.

Nichols, J. (2013, October 3). Germany Sochi Olympic team insists 'rainbow' uniforms aren't a gay rights protest. *The Huffington Post* [online]. Retrieved from www.huffingtonpost.com/2013/10/02/germany-olympics-rainbow-uniform_n_4030737.html

Ofei, A. (2015). How Glastonbury Festival is king of user-generated content. Just Add Social [online]. Retrieved from www.justaddsocial.net/glastonbury-festival-on-social-media/

Ora, R. [RitaOra] (2013, June 28). We did it!!!!!!! Glastonbury my life has changedhforever!!!!!! … Retrieved from https://twitter.com/RitaOra/status/350646624437010433

Postma, A., Ferdinand, N. and Gouthro, M.B. (2013). *Carnival Futures: Notting Hill Carnival 2020*. Leeuwarden, The Netherlands: European Tourism Futures Institute / London, United Kingdom: King's College London.

Prahalad, C.K. and Ramaswamy, V. (2004). Co-creation experiences: the next practice in value creation. *Journal of Interactive Marketing*, *18*(3): 5–14.

Pride, W. and Ferrell, O.C. (2016). *Foundations of Marketing* (17th edn). Boston: Cengage Learning.

Przybylski, A.K., Murayama, K., DeHaan, C.R. and Gladwell, V. (2013). Motivational, emotional and behavioral correlates of fear of missing out. *Computers in Human Behavior*, *29*(4): 1841–8.

Rihova, I., Buhalis, D., Moital, M. and Gouthro, M. (2014). Social constructions of value: marketing considerations for the context of events and festival participation. In: O. Moufakkir and T. Pernecky (eds), *Ideological, Social and Cultural Aspects of Events* (pp. 74–85). CABI.

Ritzer, G. and Jurgenson, N. (2010). Production, consumption, presumption: the nature of capitalism in the age of the digital 'prosumer'. *Journal of Consumer Culture*, *10*(1): 13–36.

Roberts, L. (2011). Regeneration, mobility and contested space: cultural reflections on a city in transition. In: J. Harris and R. Williams (eds), *Regenerating Culture and Society: Art Architecture and Urban Style within the Global Politics of City Branding* (pp. 314–40). Liverpool: Liverpool University Press.

Slim, P. (2010). *Escape From Cubicle Nation: From Corporate Prisoner to Thriving Entrepreneur*. New York: Penguin Group.

Steafel, E., Nulholland, R., Sabur, R., Malnick, E., Trotman, A. and Harley, N. (2015, November 21). Paris terror attack: everything we know on Saturday afternoon. *The Telegraph* [online]. Retrieved from www.telegraph.co.uk/news/worldnews/europe/france/11995246/Paris-shootingWhat-we-know-so-far.html

Stone, P. (2007). *Opting Out? Why Women Really Quit Careers and Head Home*. Berkley and Los Angeles: University of California Press.

Störmer, E., Patscha, C., Prendergast, J., Daheim, C., Rhisiart, M., Glover, P. and Beck, H. (2014). The future of work: jobs and skills in 2030. UK Commission for Employment and Skills [online]. Retrieved from http://dera.ioe.ac.uk/19601/2/the-future-of-work-key-findings.pdf

Telegraph Sport (2013, December 12). Sport dominates top 10 UK moments on Twitter. *The Telegraph* [online]. Retrieved from www.telegraph.co.uk/sport/10511151/Sport-dominates-top-10-UK-moments-on-Twitter.html

Thomas, J.C. (1995). *Public Participation in Public Decisions*. San Francisco: Jossey-Bass

Timms, J. (2012). The Olympics as a platform for protest: a case study of the London 2012 'ethical' Games and the Fair Play campaign for workers' rights. *Leisure Studies, 31*(3): 355–72.

UK Music (2013). *Wish You Were Here: Music Tourism's Contribution to the UK Economy October 2013*. UK Music [online]. Retrieved from www.ukmusic.org/assets/general/LOWRESFORHOME PRINTING.pdf

Usborne, D. (2012, January 20). The moment it all went wrong for Kodak. *Independent* [online]. Retrieved from www.independent.co.uk/news/business/analysis-and-features/the-moment-it-all-went-wrong-for-kodak-6292212.html

Wade, W. (2012). *Scenario Planning: A Field Guide to the Future*. New Jersey: John Wiley and Sons.

Williams, G. [GarethW2610] (2013, June, 29). @nilerodgers Best part of Glastonbury so far was Chic and yours truly!! Boss. Retrieved from https://twitter.com/GarethW2610/status/3511342 65897009152

Yeoman, I., Robertson, M. and Wheatley, C. (2015). Cognitive map(s) of event and festival futures. In: I. Yeoman, M. Robertson, U. McMahon-Beattie, E. Bakar and K.A. Smith (eds), *The Future of Events and Festivals* (pp. 271–314). Oxon: Routledge.

Index

Page references to definitions will be in **bold**
Page references to Boxes, Figures or Tables will be in *italics*